CHILDREN'S POCKET DICTIONARY

CHILDREN'S POCKET DICTIONARY

Harold E. Priestley M.A., M.Ed., Ph.D.

DEAN

This edition first published 1993 by
Dean, an imprint of Reed Children's Books,
Michelin House, 81 Fulham Road, London SW3 6RB
and Auckland, Melbourne, Singapore and Toronto

Reprinted 1994, 1996

ISBN 0 603 55137 8

A CIP catalogue record for this book is available in the British Library.

Produced by Mandarin Offset
Printed and bound in China

Many of the illustrations in this book appeared originally in *The
Hamlyn All-Colour Dictionary.*

About this Dictionary

In this book the main words, or headwords as they are called, are printed in **bold** type and are followed by the same word in brackets divided into parts or syllables. Sometimes two words may look alike, whereas in fact they are not pronounced in the same way, and have different meanings. In such cases, stress marks are shown to help you; for example, **conduct** (cón-duct) and **conduct** (con-dúct) are two separate words with two separate meanings. Instructions are also given as to how to pronounce certain difficult words.

Abbreviations used

a. = adjective	n. = noun
adv. = adverb	prep. = preposition
conj. = conjunction	pron. = pronoun
e.g. = for example	v. = verb
etc. = and other things	

A

abandon (a-ban-don) *v.* leave for ever, give up.

ability (a-bil-i-ty) *n.* the physical or mental power to do something.

aboard (a-board) *adv. & prep.* on or on to a ship, aeroplane, bus etc.

aborigine (ab-o-rig-i-ne) *n.* one of a race of people living in a country from the earliest times (e.g. Australia).

about (a-bout) *adv. & prep.* around, everywhere, here and there, almost, a little more or a little less, around the other way. .

above (a-bove) *adv. & prep.* overhead, higher than; greater in number, price or quality than.

abroad (a-broad) *adv.* near and far; to or in another country.

abrupt (a-brupt) *a.* sudden. **abruptly** in haste or without good manners (of speech); quickly (of stopping).

absence (ab-sence) *n.* time spent away, being without something or somebody. **absent** *a.* away, not present.

absorb (ab-sorb) *v.* soak up, take up. **absorbent** *a.* able to soak up.

absurd (ab-surd) *a.* foolish.

accept (ac-cept) *v.* agree to receive; answer 'yes' to. **acceptable** *a.* welcome, would be gratefully received.

accident (ac-ci-dent) *n.* something which happens and has not been expected. **accidental** *a.* by accident.

accompany (ac-com-pa-ny) *v.* go with; play music with.

accordion (ac-cor-dion) *n.* a portable musical instrument which has bellows and keys that look like piano keys.

account (ac-count) *n.* a statement of money paid, received or owing; an explanation, report or description. *v.* explain or tell what has happened; give reasons.

accurate (ac-cu-rate) *a.* correct, free from mistakes. **accuracy** *n.* being correct, having no mistakes.

accuse (ac-cuse) *v.* say that somebody has done wrong.

accustom (ac-cus-tom) *v.* become or make used to.

ace *n.* a card showing only one heart, diamond, spade or club; a person who shows great skill, a champion.

ache *v.* be in lasting pain. *n.* pain that lasts.

achieve (a-chieve) *v.* get something done; do something successfully; obtain by trying.

acid (ac-id) *n.* a substance which burns or tastes sour. *a.* sour.

acorn (a-corn) *n.* the seed of an oak tree.

acquaint (ac-quaint) *v.* make known to. **acquaintance** *n.* a friend, friendship.

acquire (ac-quire) *v.* get, obtain for oneself.

acre (a-cre) *n.* 4,840 square yards of land.

acrobat (ac-ro-bat) *n.* a person who can do clever tricks with his body.

across (a-cross) *adv. & prep.* from side to side; on or to the other side of.

act *n.* anything you do; the main division of a play. *v.* take part in some kind of entertainment; do, behave. **actor, actress** *n.* a person who takes part in a play or plays. **active** *a.* always doing things. **activity** *n.* a hobby or occupation.

acute (a-cute) *a.* sharp, pointed; keen.

add *v.* join or put one thing or number with another. **addition** *n.* adding; something added.

address (ad-dress) *v.* say something to others; direct something to the attention of. *n.* a speech or talk to an audience; the place to which one's letters should be sent, or where one lives.

adenoids (ad-e-noids) *n.* growths at the back of the nose and in the throat which sometimes prevent breathing through the nose.

adhesive (ad-hes-ive) *a.* sticky. **adhesive tape** *n.* tape which is sticky on one side and is used for fastening parcels and bandages.

adjust (ad-just) *v.* change something to make it right.

admiral (ad-mi-ral) *n.* a high-ranking naval officer.

admire (ad-mire) *v.* think of a person with respect and wonder; like and enjoy (of views etc.). **admiration** *n.* respect, wonder, pleasure.

admit (ad-mit) *v.* let in; confess (to a deed). **admission** *n.* being let in; the price paid for being let in; a confession.

adopt (a-dopt) *v.* take the child from another family as a member of one's own family; take an idea or custom.

adore (a-dore) *v.* love and respect. **adorable** *a.* worthy of being adored.

adult (a-dult) *n.* a grown-up person. *a.* grown-up (person or manners).

advance (ad-vance) *v.* move forward, go ahead; raise or rise. *n.* money paid before it need be paid.

advantage (ad-van-tage) *n.* something which helps; gain; opportunity (take advantage of).

adventure (ad-ven-ture) *n.* an exciting experience.

advertise (ad-ver-tise) *v.* make something known to people by means of newspapers, posters, handbills, television, radio etc. **advertisement** *n.* a means of telling people something.

advice (ad-vice) *n.* (rhymes with *ice*) opinions given by one person as to what another person should do.

advise (ad-vise) *v.* (rhymes with *size*) offer or state an opinion; inform the public of something.

aero (ae-ro) a prefix denoting that the word has to do with air, aircraft, gas or atmosphere.

affair (af-fair) *n.* something which happens; business of any kind.

affect (af-fect) *v.* change, make a difference to.

affection (af-fec-tion) *n.* fondness between person and person or person and thing. **affectionate** *a.* loving (of a relative, friend, pet etc.).

afford (af-ford) *v.* have enough money or time for something.

afraid (a-fraid) *a.* feeling fear, frightened.

after (af-ter) *prep. & adv.* following behind. **afternoon** *n.* the time between noon and evening. **afterwards** *adv.* at a later time.

again (a-gain) *adv.* one more time; another time.

against (a-gainst) *prep.* touching; not agreeing with; in an opposite direction to.

age *n.* the number of years a person has lived; a time or period in history; a time in one's life. *v.* grow old.

agent (a-gent) *n.* a person who manages the business of other persons for them; a spy. **agency** *n.* a firm which works as an agent.

agitate (a-gi-tate) *v.* make trouble, cause anxiety. **agitator** *n.* someone who stirs up others to cause trouble.

ago (a-go) *a. & adv.* in the past, in time which has gone by.

agony (ag-o-ny) *n.* great pain.

agree (a-gree) *v.* say 'yes' to; have similar opinions to; be equal to the same. **agreeable** *a.* giving pleasure. **agreement** *n.* a promise or arrangement.

agriculture (ag-ri-cul-ture) *n.* growing crops for food and rearing animals on farms. **agricultural** *a.* having to do with agriculture.

ah *int.* an expression of happiness, sudden surprise, pity, sorrow or gladness.

ahead (a-head) *a. & adv.* forwards, in front, before (of time).

aid *n.* help; something which helps. **first aid** *n.* treatment given to the sick and injured before the doctor comes.

ail *v.* be in trouble in body or mind. **ailment** *n.* an illness.

aim *v.* point (a weapon etc.). *n.* the act of pointing; a purpose.

air *n.* a mixture of gases that surrounds the earth. *v.* expose to the fresh air.

aisle *n.* (rhymes with *mile*) a passageway between rows of seats, in a hall, church etc.

ajar (a-jar) *adv.* slightly open.

alarm (a-larm) *n.* a signal to warn of danger; something which gives an alarm. *v.* frighten.

alas (a-las) *int.* a word used mostly in stories as a cry of sadness or pity.

album (al-bum) *n.* a book with blank pages on which one can write or stick pictures and stamps.

alcohol (al-co-hol) *n.* a colourless, intoxicating liquid found in drinks such as brandy, whisky, wine and beer. **alcoholic** *a.* containing alcohol. *n.* a person who cannot stop taking alcohol.

alderman (al-der-man) *n.* a member of a town council who is elected by the other members.

ale *n.* a light-coloured beer.

alert (a-lert) *a.* quick to notice or understand things; on the lookout.

algebra (al-ge-bra) *n.* a form of mathematics in which letters are used for numbers.

alias (a-li-as) *n.* a name taken by a person in addition to his own.

alibi (a-li-bi) *n.* (rhymes with *sky*) evidence that one was in another place when a crime was committed.

alien (a-li-en) *n.* a person who lives in a foreign country without the rights of its own citizens.

alike (a-like) *a.* very much the same, similar.

alive (a-live) *a.* living, not dead.

all *a.* every bit of, the whole of. *n.* every one.

alley (al-ley) *n.* a narrow roadway, usually between buildings; a smooth, enclosed pathway for bowling, a bowling alley.

alligator (al-li-ga-tor) *n.* a large, broad-snouted reptile related to the crocodile which lives in lakes and rivers in America and China.

allow (al-low) *v.* permit; agree to give. **allowance** *n.* a fixed amount of money granted.

ally (al-ly) *v.* join with another in making an agreement or treaty. *n.* a person or country which has done this **alliance** *n.* an agreement made between two countries to help each other against a common enemy.

almighty (al-might-y) *a.* having all power, powerful. *n.* a name given to God – the Almighty.

almond (al-mond) *n.* (pronounced *ah-mond*) the stone of the fruit of the almond tree, used in the making of cakes and sweets.

almost (al-most) *adv.* nearly.

alone (a-lone) *adv.* by oneself, without others being present, only, by itself.

along (a-long) *adv.* from one end to the other, or part of the way; onwards; with (a person).

aloud (a-loud) *adv.* loud enough to be heard easily.

alphabet (al-pha-bet) *n.* all the letters used in any language arranged in a certain order. **alphabetical** *a.* in the order of the alphabet.

already (al-read-y) *adv.* on or before this time.

alsatian (al-sa-tian) *n.* a large dog which looks like a wolf, whose ancestors came from Alsace in France.

also (al-so) *adv.* too, in addition.

altar (al-tar) *n.* a table in a church where a priest performs the ceremony of Holy Communion.

alter (al-ter) *v.* change, make different.

although (al-though) *conj.* even if, though.

altitude (al-ti-tude) *n.* height, distance above the earth or above sea level.

altogether (al-to-geth-er) *adv.* fully, entirely, completely.

aluminium (a-lu-min-i-um) *n.* a dull, silver-coloured metal that is very light in weight, used for making parts of aircraft and cooking utensils.

always (al-ways) *adv.* at all times.

amateur (am-a-teur) *a.* making or studying anything for pleasure and not for profit. *n.* a person who does this.

amaze (a-maze) *v.* surprise. **amazement** *n.* being surprised.

ambassador (am-bas-sa-dor) *n.* an official of the highest rank sent by the government of one country to live in another country so as to keep contact with its government.

ambulance (am-bu-lance) *n.* a car or van specially built for carrying sick and injured people.

ambush (am-bush) *n.* a surprise attack from an enemy who has been in hiding.

amen (a-men) *int.* a word said at the end of a prayer meaning 'so be it'.

ammonia (am-mo-ni-a) *n.* a colourless gas with a sharp, strong smell.

ammunition (am-mu-ni-tion) *n.* gunpowder, shells, bullets and all other explosives used for shooting from guns and cannon.

among (a-mong) *prep.* with many other things or people; between all persons. **amongst** *prep.* surrounded by.

amount (a-mount) *v.* add up to or become. *n.* total or whole quantity.

ample (am-ple) *a.* more than enough. **amply** *adv.* sufficiently.

amputate (am-pu-tate) *v.* cut off (part of the body). **amputation** *n.* a cutting off.

amuse (a-muse) *v.* entertain, make laugh or smile. **amusement** n. something which entertains.

analyze (an-a-lyze) *v.* separate something into its parts to find out what it is made of. **analysis** *n.* an examination made by separating into parts.

ancestor (an-ces-tor) *n.* a person who came before others in a family.

anchor (an-chor) *n.* a heavy metal hook on an iron chain used to hold a ship in place. *v.* fasten in place with an anchor; fix or fasten.

ancient (an-cient) *adj.* of times long ago.

and *conj.* a word used to join words and groups; added to (of numbers).

angel (an-gel) *n.* a messenger of God who comes from heaven; a charming person or child.

anger (an-ger) *n.* bad temper, fury, displeasure. **angry** *a.* showing resentment, feeling anger. **angrily** *adv.* in an angry manner.

angle (an-gle) *n.* a point where two lines meet, or the space between two lines meeting at a point.

animal (an-i-mal) *n.* a living thing that can feel and move about, including all birds, fishes and insects.

ankle (an-kle) *n.* the joint between the leg and the foot.

anniversary (an-ni-ver-sa-ry) *n.* a date of the year on which something important happened in an earlier year.

annoy (an-noy) *v.* irritate, cause trouble to. **annoyance** *n.* something which irritates, being irritated.

annual (an-nu-al) *a.* coming once a year. *n.* a plant that lives for one year or less. **annually** *a.* once a year.

anorak (an-o-rak) *n.* a warm, waterproof jacket with a hood.

another (an-o-ther) *a. & pron.* one more; a different one.

answer (an-swer) *n.* a reply. *v.* go to see what is wanted or who is calling; be suitable for a purpose.

antarctic (ant-arc-tic) *a. & n.* near the South Pole.

antelope (an-te-lope) *n.* an animal very much like a deer.

anthem (an-them) *n.* a song, usually a sacred one sung by a choir.

anti (an-ti) a prefix meaning against, used before nouns, verbs and adjectives.

antique (an-tique) *a. & n.* something made long ago which is valuable because of its age.

anxious (anx-ious) *a.* troubled, in some fear as to what may happen. **anxiety** *n.* fear as to what may happen.

any (an-y) *a. & pron.* not even one or a little; no special or particular one, some. **anybody** *n.* any person. **anyone** *n. & pron.* any person. **anything** *n. & pron.* something, one thing. **anyway** *adv.* anyhow. **anywhere** *adv.* in any place.

apart (a-part) *adv.* away, off, to one side; one from the other; to pieces; distant.

apartment (a-part-ment) *n.* a room or group of rooms in a larger building forming a separate home.

ape *n.* an animal that belongs to the monkey family. *v.* imitate, copy.

apologize (a-pol-o-gize) *v.* admit making a mistake or doing wrong and say that one is sorry. **apology** *n.* words saying that one is sorry.

apostle (a-pos-tle) *n.* a messenger, especially one of the twelve men chosen by Jesus Christ to spread his teaching.

apparel (ap-par-el) *n.* clothes, dresses, suits.

appeal (ap-peal) *v.* ask, plead; take a case to a higher court; attract, seem pleasant. *n.* the act of pleading; attraction.

appear (ap-pear) *v.* be seen, show itself; seem or look. **appearance** *n.* the way a person or thing looks.

appetite (ap-pe-tite) *n.* a desire for food or drink. **appetizing** *a.* good to eat, good looking or smelling delicious.

applaud (ap-plaud) *v.* clap one's hands to show pleasure at the end of a speech, song, piece of music etc. **applause** *n.* clapping and demonstration of approval after a performance.

apple (ap-ple) *n.* a round fruit that grows on a tree and is red, yellow or green.

apply (ap-ply) *v.* put on; have to do with; ask to be given. **appliance** *n.* a tool or instrument. **application** *n.* request for a thing or post.

appoint (ap-point) *v.* select, choose. **appointment** *n.* an agreement to meet; a position or post.

apprentice (ap-pren-tice) *n.* a person who has agreed to serve a master for a number of years in return for learning a trade.

approach (ap-proach) *v.* come near. *n.*

the act of coming nearer; a way or road to a place.

approve (ap-prove) *v.* give consent. **approval** *n.* satisfaction, agreement.

apricot (ap-ri-cot) *n.* a pinkish-yellow fruit resembling a peach.

apron (a-pron) *n.* the article of clothing worn over a dress to keep it clean.

aqua, aque a prefix denoting that a word has to do with water.

arc *n.* part of the line which makes a circle.

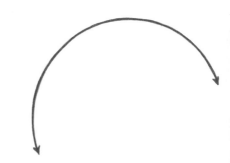

arcade (ar-cade) *n.* a number of arches on columns making a covered way with shops.

arch *n.* part of a building or wall curved like the arc of a circle. *v.* shape like an arch, curve upwards.

archbishop (arch-bish-op) *n.* a bishop of the highest rank.

archer (arch-er) *n.* a person who shoots with a bow and arrows. **archery** *n.* a pastime or sport in which one shoots with the bow.

architect (ar-chi-tect) *n.* someone who

designs buildings and makes sure that the builders carry out his plans.

arctic (arc-tic) *n.* the most northerly part of the world nearest the North Pole. *a.* belonging to this region; very cold.

area (a-re-a) *n.* the size in any kind of measurement (square feet, square metres etc.) of a flat or curved space.

arena (a-re-na) *n.* a space, usually a circle, with seats all round, in which the Romans held games and fights, and where today games or contests are sometimes held.

argue (ar-gue) *v.* present reasons for or against a thing. **argument** *n.* a discussion or debate.

arise (a-rise) *v.* get up; result from some former state or action.

arithmetic (a-rith-me-tic) *n.* the study of using numbers.

ark *n.* the large boat which Noah built to save his family and the world's animals from the Great Flood; a chest containing tables of the Jewish law.

arm *v.* take up weapons or arms to make war. *n.* one of the two upper limbs of a person; a part at the side or end of a seat to support a person's arm.

around (a-round) *adv. & prep.* along all sides; to another side of; about or near; in a circle; about a certain time; in all directions.

arrange (ar-range) *v.* put into some order; make plans. **arrangement** *n.* order in which objects etc. are put.

arrears (ar-rears) *n.* money owing which has not been paid, or work which has not been done.

arrest (ar-rest) *v.* seize by authority of the law; stop.

arrive (ar-rive) *v.* come, get to a place. **arrival** *n.* the act of arriving.

arrow (ar-row) *n.* a pointed stick shot from a bow; a sign pointing in a certain direction.

arsenic (ar-sen-ic) *n.* a substance used for making glass and in dyeing; a white substance which is a deadly poison.

art *n.* drawing, painting, sculpture, music etc.

artery (ar-te-ry) *n.* one of the tubes which carry blood from the heart to other parts of the body. **arterial** *a.* (of a road) specially made to carry traffic between large towns.

article (ar-ti-cle) *n.* a thing, a separate part; a piece of writing in a newspaper, magazine or book.

articulated (ar-tic-u-la-ted) *a.* having separate parts joined together as in lorries and tractors.

artificial (ar-ti-fi-cial) *a.* not found in nature but made by man.

artist (ar-tist) *n.* a person who draws, paints pictures, makes models or statues; a person who is very good at some art such as music and the writing of poems, novels and plays.

asbestos (as-bes-tos) *n.* a grey substance which does not catch fire and can be made into fireproof garments and other articles.

ascend (as-cend) *v.* go or come up. **ascent** *n.* going or coming up.

ash *n.* the powdery remains of a thing that has been burnt; a tree with silver-grey bark and hard wood. 'The Ashes' a trophy gained by the cricket team winning a series of Test Matches between England and Australia.

ashamed (a-shamed) *a.* feeling unhappy because of having done something wrong or having failed in some way.

ashore (a-shore) *adv.* to the shore; on land.

aside (a-side) *adv.* to one side; apart.

ask *v.* call for something; call for an answer; invite.

asleep (a-sleep) *adv.* sleeping; numb (of a limb).

asphalt (as-phalt) *n.* a dark, sticky substance like tar, mixed with stone to make roads.

aspirin (as-pi-rin) *n.* a medicine that helps to relieve pain.

ass *n.* a long-eared animal resembling a horse but smaller, a donkey; a silly, stupid person.

assassin (as-sas-sin) *n.* a person who is paid to murder another person.

assemble (as-sem-ble) *v.* come together; collect, put together. **assembly** *n.* meeting (of people;) putting together (of things).

assign (as-sign) *v.* give work to be done. **assignment** *n.* a piece of work given.

assist (as-sist) *v.* give assistance or help. **assistance** *n.* help. **assistant** *n.* a helper; one who serves customers.

associate (as-so-ci-ate) *v.* be in the company of somebody; think of two or more things or persons in connection with each other. *n.* a person who joins with another in some activity. **association football** a football game in which nobody but the goalkeeper may touch the ball with his hands.

asthma *n.* an illness affecting the chest which makes breathing very difficult.

astonish (as-ton-ish) *v.* amaze, fill with surprise. **astonishment** *n.* surprise, amazement.

astro (as-tro) a prefix used in words having to do with the stars. **astronomy** *n.* the study of the stars. **astrology** *n.* the telling of fortunes by the stars. **astronaut** *n.* a traveller in space.

asylum (a-sy-lum) *n.* a place to which people go who are unable to look after themselves; protection given by a country to a foreigner who has fled from his own country.

at *prep.* a place where or a time when things are done; in the direction of.

athlete (ath-lete) *n.* a person who is good at some sport. **athletic** *a.* having to do with athletics, concerned with sports. **athletics** *n.* games and sports requiring physical fitness.

atlas (at-las) *n.* a book of maps.

atmosphere (at-mo-sphere) *n.* the air and gases which surround the earth.

atom (a-tom) *n.* the smallest particle of which anything is made up. **atom bomb** one of the most powerful bombs ever made. **atomic pile** a great power station used for the making of electricity.

attach (at-tach) *v.* fasten or join. **attachment** *n.* something fastened or used with; affection for a person.

attack (at-tack) *v.* make a violent attempt to hurt a person or capture a place. *n.* an attempt made against a person or place.

attempt (at-tempt) *v.* try to do something. *n.* a try, an effort.

attend (at-tend) *v.* go to, be present at. **attend to** keep one's mind on; look after; serve. **attendance** *n.* being present; the number present. **attention** *n.* notice, thought given to something. **at attention** standing straight and still.

attic (at-tic) *n.* the room just under the roof of a house.

attitude (at-ti-tude) *n.* what one thinks or feels about somebody or something.

attract (at-tract) *v.* draw or pull towards; get the attention of. **attractive** *a.* pleasant, noticed by all.

auction (auc-tion) *n.* a public sale at which goods are sold to the person who offers the highest price. **auctioneer** *n.* a person who sells goods by auction.

audible (au-di-ble) *a.* loud enough to be heard.

aunt *n.* the sister of one's father or mother. Aunts by marriage are the wives of the brothers of a father or mother.

author (au-thor) *n.* the writer of a book,

story, play or essay; the person who started some action or movement.
authority *n.* the power and right to give orders and make others obey; a book or person who can give information; the person or persons in charge.
autobiography (au-to-bi-og-ra-phy) *n.* the story of a person's life written by himself or herself.
autograph (au-to-graph) *n.* a person's signature. *v.* write one's own signature on a document or in a book.
automatic (au-to-ma-tic) *a.* working by itself, mechanical; done without thought. *n.* a small pistol.
automobile (au-to-mo-bile) *n.* a car, bus or van that moves under its own power.
autumn (au-tumn) *n.* the third season of the year coming between summer and winter.
avalanche (av-a-lanche) *n.* a great mass of snow, ice or earth which slides down the side of a mountain; a large amount (of praise, protest etc.).
avenue (av-e-nue) *n.* a roadway with trees on both sides; a way, direction.
average (av-e-rage) *n.* the result when several quantities are added and the total is divided by the number of quantities; usual, normal (of ability, intelligence etc.).
avoid (a-void) *v.* keep or get away from.
await (a-wait) *v.* wait for.
awake (a-wake) *a.* not asleep. **awaken** *v.* wake up a person, rouse from sleep.
award (a-ward) *v.* give as a prize. *n.* something such as a medal, given as a prize.
aware (a-ware) *a.* conscious, able to notice things.
away (a-way) *adv.* to or at another place; on and on, all the time; having gone, melted or vanished.
awe *n.* respect and wonder, sometimes with fear. **awful** *a.* very bad. **awfully** *adv.* very or very much.
awhile (a-while) *adv.* for a short time.
awkward (awk-ward) *a.* clumsy, not having much skill in movement; not very safe or convenient (of weather, roads etc.).
axe *n.* a tool with a sharp edge and a long handle.
axle (ax-le) *n.* a bar on which the wheels of a vehicle are fastened and on which they turn.

B

babble (bab-ble) *v.* talk like a baby in words not easy to understand; murmur as of a stream or a brook.
baboon (ba-boon) *n.* a large monkey which has a face like that of a dog.
baby (ba-by) *n.* a very young child.
bachelor (bach-e-lor) *n.* a man who has not been married; a man or woman who has taken the first degree in a university.
back *n.* the rear side of the body, house etc.; a football player who helps to keep the ball away from his side's goal. *a.* on the rear side. *v.* move or make move backwards; support with money or help. *adv.* (with give, take etc.) again to a person or thing. **background** *n.* that part of a picture, scene or design which is behind all the rest, in the distance. **backwards** *adv.* towards the back or rear. **backward** *a.* slow to learn.
bacon (ba-con) *n.* meat from the back and sides of a pig, preserved with salt.
bacteria (bac-te-ri-a) *n.* the simplest living things, too small to be seen without a microscope, some of which cause diseases.
bad *a.* no good, evil, wicked; unlucky; severe (of weather etc.); not of good quality, rotten.
badge *n.* something worn to show that a person belongs to a certain class or group of people (scouts, guides etc.).
badger (badg-er) *n.* a small four-legged animal which lives in holes in the ground and only comes out at night.
badminton (bad-min-ton) *n.* a game played with rackets and shuttlecocks.

baffle (baf-fle) *v.* puzzle; stop, prevent.
bag *n.* a sack or container made of paper, cloth, string, plastic or leather. **baggage** *n.* suit-cases. **bagpipe** *n.* a musical instrument played by blowing air into a bag and pressing it out through pipes.

bagatelle (bag-a-telle) *n.* a game like billiards played by striking a ball into holes at the far end of a table.

bail (sometimes spelt **bale**) *v.* scoop (of water out of a boat); pay money to free a prisoner until the day he is to be tried. *n.* the money paid for this purpose; two small pieces of wood laid across the stumps in cricket.

bait *n.* food or something looking like food to tempt fish or animals so that they can be caught. *v.* use bait.

bake *v.* cook in an oven; harden, become hard through heat. **baker** *n.* a person who makes bread and cakes in a bakery.

balance (bal-ance) *n.* an instrument for weighing; the power to keep steady or upright. *v.* keep the amount or weight equal on both sides.

balcony (bal-co-ny) *n.* a raised platform standing high up on the wall of a building.

bald *a.* having no hair or very little hair; without trees or bushes.

bale (see **bail**) *n.* a large bundle of material packed for sending to another place. **bale out** *v.* jump with a parachute out of an aircraft which can no longer fly.

ball *n.* a round object which may be solid or hollow; a game played with a ball; a party where there is dancing.

ballast (bal-last) *n.* something heavy which is carried in a ship to keep it steady and to stop it turning over.

ballet (bal-let) *n.* (pronounced *bal-lay*) an entertainment which consists of dancing and music and which usually tells a story.

balloon (bal-loon) *n.* a bag filled with hot air or gas lighter than air, which makes it rise when set free; a small coloured bag of rubber which expands when filled with air and is used in children's games.

ballot (bal-lot) *n.* a piece of paper given out in elections on which to mark the names of the people one wants to elect. *v.* the act of marking the paper. **ballot-box** *n.* the box in which ballot papers are put after voting.

balm *n.* a sweet-smelling ointment used to ease pain. **balmy** *a.* soft, gentle and warm (of the weather).

balustrade (bal-us-trade) *n.* a row of short upright posts which support a railing.

bamboo (bam-boo) *n.* a tall, tropical or semi-tropical plant with hollow stalks; the stick of the plant used to support other plants in a garden.

banana (ba-na-na) *n.* a fruit which is slightly curved, with creamy flesh and a yellow skin.

band *n.* a strip of cloth or other material; a long narrow stripe different in colour from the background; several musicians who play together; a group of pirates etc. *v.* come together in a group. **bandage** *n.* a narrow strip of cloth for binding a wound.

bandit (ban-dit) *n.* a robber, often one of an armed band which attacks travellers.

bang *n.* a loud, sudden noise; a hard knock or blow. *v.* make a loud, sudden noise.

bangle (bang-le) *n.* a band of metal or other material worn as an ornament round the wrist or ankle.

banish (ban-ish) *v.* punish by sending away.

banister (ban-is-ter) *n.* a handrail running down the open side of a staircase to prevent people falling off.

banjo (ban-jo) *n.* a musical instrument with strings which are plucked with the fingers.

bank *n.* a long pile or heap of earth; the land along the sides of a river, stream, lake or canal; a company which keeps money for others; the building in which those employed by such a company work; a box in which money is kept. *v.* put money into a bank for safe keeping. **banker** *n.* a man who manages a bank. **banknote** *n.* a piece of paper issued by a bank and used as money. **bankrupt** *a.* unable to pay one's debts so that one's goods have to be sold.

banner (ban-ner) *n.* a flag or large sheet bearing words and carried on long poles.

banquet (ban-quet) *n.* a meal, usually costly, provided for some special event.

banter (ban-ter) *v.* joke with or tease a person. *n.* playful talk, merry teasing.

baptize (bap-tize) *v.* dip a person in water or pour water over him to make him a member of a Christian church; give a name to a person in church. **baptism** *n.* the act of baptizing.

bar *n.* a solid piece of metal; a piece (of soap, chocolate etc.); a bank of sand across the mouth of a river; anything standing in a person's way; a line running up and down on written music dividing it into beats; a counter where drinks and meals are served; the railing in a court behind which the prisoner stands. *v.* keep out of a place or a society.

barb *n.* a short, sharp point curving backwards from the main shaft. **barbed wire** wire with points sticking out, used in fences.

barbarian (bar-ba-ri-an) *n.* a person who is savage, uncivilized. **barbarous** *a.* cruel and savage.

barbecue (bar-be-cue) *n.* a meal in the open air for which meat is roasted over a fire. *v.* roast meat in the open air.

barber (bar-ber) *n.* a person, usually a man, who shaves and cuts his customers' hair.

bare *a.* without covering, without clothing; empty. *v.* show, uncover. **barely** *adv.* hardly, scarcely. **barefoot, bareheaded** *a.* with feet or head uncovered.

bargain (bar-gain) *n.* an agreement to buy, sell or exchange; something bought cheaply. *v.* try to agree about a price.

barge *n.* a large, flat-bottomed boat for carrying goods on rivers or canals and round coasts.

bark *n.* a loud, harsh cry made by a dog; the rough outside covering of the trunk and branches of a tree.

barley (bar-ley) *n.* a plant which looks like grass and is grown for its seed, also called barley. It is used for drinks such as barley water, and the manufacture of beer and whisky.

barn *n.* a large building in which hay and corn are stored and in which animals may be kept. **barnyard** *n.* the enclosed space round a barn.

barometer (ba-rom-e-ter) *n.* an instrument which measures the pressure of the atmosphere and can tell us what kind of weather we may expect.

barracks (bar-racks) *n.* large buildings built for soldiers to live in.

barrel (bar-rel) *n.* a large wooden vessel with curved sides used to store liquids such as beer, vinegar and oil; the tube of a gun or pistol out of which the bullet is fired.

barricade (bar-ri-cade) *n.* a number of objects such as tree trunks, cars, carts and buses placed across a street or in front of a building to defend it. *v.* put up a barricade.

barrier (bar-ri-er) *n.* something which stands in the way or stops progress — such as a fence, a desert, a range of mountains.

barrow (bar-row) *n.* a small cart pushed or pulled by hand.

barter (bar-ter) *v.* exchange goods without using money.

base *n.* the bottom part of anything, the part on which all other parts stand; a protected area where an army is stationed and where the army keeps its stores. *v.*

build, found something on. **baseball** *n.* an American game played with a bat and ball by two teams on a field with four bases. **base camp** a camp climbers use as a headquarters. **basement** *n.* the lowest part of a building which is often below ground level.

bashful (bash-ful) *a.* shy, easily frightened.

basin (ba-sin) *n.* a dish, wide at the top, of metal or pottery; the area drained by one river. **wash-basin** *n.* a bowl fixed to a wall or floor and fitted with taps and a pipe so that water can drain away.

basket (bas-ket) *n.* a container made of twigs, grasses or thin strips of wool woven together. **basketball** *n.* a game played by two teams with a large round ball, each team trying to throw it through a basket on a pole.

bass *n.* (rhymes with *case*) the lowest part in music; the man who sings that part; the large violin on which it is played.

bat *n.* a wooden stick used in games for hitting a ball. *v.* use such a stick. *n.* an animal like a mouse which has wings and flies at night.

batch *n.* a quantity or number of things or persons coming at one time.

bath *v.* wash the body. *n.* a washing of the whole body; water for a bath; a container for water and other liquids; the building where baths may be taken. **bathroom** *n.* a room with a bath, also sometimes with a washbasin and lavatory.

bathe *v.* enter water; take a bath in the sea or a river; put water on (a wound etc.). **bathing hut** a small building where clothes can be changed for bathing. **bathing suit** a short, light garment worn for bathing.

baton (bat-on) *n.* a short, thin stick used by the conductor of a band, choir or orchestra to beat time; a short thick stick carried by a policeman; a short stick carried by a field-marshal.

battalion (bat-tal-ion) *n.* part of an army made up of several companies, three or more battalions making a regiment.

batter (bat-ter) *n.* a mixture of flour, eggs, milk, sugar and butter beaten together and used for cooking. *v.* strike hard and often; beat out of shape.

battery (bat-ter-y) *n.* a device for making electricity; a group of guns in an army or on a ship; a large number of cages in

which hens are kept for the production of eggs.

battle (bat-tle) *n.* a fight between two armies. *v.* struggle. **battlefield** *n.* a place where a battle takes place or has taken place. **battleship** *n.* one of the largest ships of war carrying thousands of men.

bawl *v.* cry out loudly.

bay *n.* a broad expanse of water partly surrounded by land. *a.* reddish brown (of horses). *v.* bark or howl (of a hound). **bay window** a window built out from a room with glass on three sides.

bayonet (bay-o-net) *n.* a dagger used for slashing, thrusting and stabbing, which can be fixed on to the barrel of a rifle.

bazaar (ba-zaar) *n.* the sale of goods to raise money for charity given to a church or some other organization; a marketplace or street of shops in an eastern country.

be *v.* exist. With other words parts of be show how things and persons are and what they do. (I am sorry etc.).

beach *n.* the seashore, covered with sand or pebbles. *v.* push or pull a boat on to the shore.

beacon (bea-con) *n.* a fire lit on top of a hill as a signal; a high post carrying a flashing lamp where there is a street crossing.

bead *n.* a small ball of wood, glass or metal with a hole through it for thread or string; a drop (sweat, dew etc.).

beagle (bea-gle) *n.* a small hound with short legs, used for hunting.

beak *n.* the strong, hard part of a bird's mouth.

beaker (bea-ker) *n.* a large cup without a handle, for drinking; a glass vessel used for experiments in chemistry.

beam *n.* a strong, heavy piece of wood; a ray of light or electricity; a smile. *v.* give a broad smile, send out rays.

bean *n.* a plant which bears seeds in long pods. The seeds, and sometimes the pods are eaten.

bear *n.* a large, heavy animal with thick fur and large claws. *v.* produce (of fruit trees etc.); carry; endure; support. **bearer** *n.* one who carries.

beard *n.* hair on the cheeks and chin.

bearings *n.* direction in which a place lies.

beast *n.* an animal with four feet; a person who behaves badly. **beastly** *a.* bad, nasty.

beat *v.* hit again and again; mix well with a fork or other utensil; defeat. *n.* a repeated throbbing sound; a regular stroke; the route which a sentry or policeman walks regularly. **beater** *n.* a person or tool that beats. **beating** *n.* a thrashing with the hand or a stick.

beauty (beau-ty) *n.* everything which gives pleasure to those who see or hear; a lovely person or thing. **beautiful** *a.* lovely, pretty. **beautify** *v.* make beautiful.

beaver (bea-ver) *n.* an animal with fur that lives in ponds and streams, and makes dams across rivers using its sharp teeth.

because (be-cause) *conj.* for the reason that.

beckon (beck-on) *v.* signal by a movement of the hand, arm or head.

become (be-come) *v.* come or grow to be. **become of** *v.* happen to.

bed *n.* a piece of furniture on which to sleep; a small piece of ground on which there are plants; the bottom of a body of water. **bedroom** *n.* the room in which the beds stand.

bee *n.* a small insect which makes honey.

beehive *n.* a box of wood or straw specially made for bees to live in.

beech *n.* a tree with smooth bark and hard wood which bears small nuts.

beef *n.* the flesh of a cow, ox or bull, used as meat.

beer *n.* an alcoholic drink made with malt and hops.

beet *n.* a plant with a large red or white root. Red beetroot may be boiled and eaten in salad; white beet is used to make sugar.

beetle (bee-tle) *n.* an insect which has hard, shiny forewings.

before (be-fore) *adv., prep. & conj.* earlier than; in front of; in the presence of; at some time past. **beforehand** *adv.* at some time before a certain thing happened.

beg *v.* ask for something — food, money, help. **beggar** *n.* a person who begs or belongs to a group of people who beg.

begin *v.* start. **beginner** *n.* a person who is beginning to learn something **beginning** *n.* the start

behave (be-have) *v.* act correctly with good manners, be polite. **behaviour** *n.* the way one behaves or acts.

behind (be-hind) *prep.* at or at the back of; late.

behold (be-hold) *v.* look at or see (used by poets and in the Bible).

being (be-ing) *n.* existence; a living thing.

belch *v.* throw out flame or smoke; bring gas up from the stomach through the mouth.

belfry (bel-fry) *n.* a room in which bells are placed, usually high up in a church tower.

belief (be-lief) *n.* anything we feel sure is true. **believe** *v.* be sure that something is true.

bell *n.* a vessel like a cup, made of metal. Most bells have a tongue inside which strikes the metal and makes a ringing sound; any device used for making a ringing sound.

bellow (bel-low) *v.* make a loud noise like a bull; *n.* a loud roar or cry like that of a large animal.

belly (bel-ly) *n.* the lower front part of the body. *v.* swell out (of the sails of a boat).

belong (be-long) *v.* be owned by; have as a right or proper place; be a member of. **belongings** *n.* the things one owns.

beloved (be-loved or be-lov-ed) *a.* loved. *n.* a dearly loved person.

below (be-low) *prep.* under, lower than; at the bottom of a page or farther on in the book.

belt *n.* a flexible band or strip of cloth, leather etc., worn round the waist; an endless strap connecting the wheels of machinery; any wide strip of land.

bench *n.* a long wooden or stone seat; the table on which a carpenter, shoe-maker, factory worker etc. does his work.

bend *v.* curve or make something curve; stoop. *n.* a curve in a thing (road etc.).

beneath (be-neath) *prep.* under, below.

benefit (ben-e-fit) *v.* help, do good to. *n.* gain, profit; kindness; a performance to raise money for a charity or for a person. **benefit by** *v.* be helped by.

beret (be-ret) *n.* (pronounced *be-ray*) a soft round cap of cloth or other material worn by schoolchildren, soldiers etc.

berry (ber-ry) *n.* a small fruit with seeds which usually grows on a bush.

berth *n.* a bed usually fixed to a wall or the floor. On a ship there are usually two berths, one above the other.

beside (be-side) *prep.* at the side of, close to.

besides (be-sides) *prep.* in addition to, as well as.

bet *v.* risk money on one's own forecast of the result of a race, a match or an election; *n.* an agreement to pay something if one is wrong. **betting shop** a shop into which people go to make (or lay) bets.

betray (be-tray) *v.* act with deceit towards, give away the secrets of others; show something that one wants to hide. **betrayal** *n.* the act of betraying.

better (bet-ter) *adj. & adv.* one form of the word good.

between (be-tween) *adv.* from one place or time to another. *prep.* keeping apart; a word to show sharing, etc. among two people or things.

bevel (be-vel) *n.* a surface which slopes, such as a picture frame.

beverage (bev-er-age) *n.* any kind of drink: tea, lemonade, coffee etc.

beware (be-ware) *v.* be watchful, take care.

beyond (be-yond) *prep. & adv.* at or to the other side of; farther than.

bib *n.* a piece of cloth fastened under a child's chin to stop food from spoiling its clothes; the part of an apron which covers the chest.

Bible (Bi-ble) *n.* the sacred writings of the Christian and Jewish religions.

biceps (bi-ceps) *n.* a large muscle on the front of the upper arm.

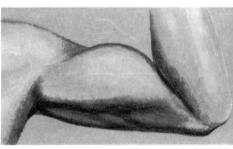

bicycle (bi-cy-cle) *n.* a two-wheeled vehicle for riding on, made to go by pressing one's feet on the pedals.

bid *v.* offer money; order or command; invite (to a meal, wedding etc.); say or tell (welcome or farewell) *n.* an order or command; the amount of money offered in an auction.

big *a.* large; very important.

bikini (bi-ki-ni) *n.* a very brief two-piece garment worn by girls and women for bathing.

bill *n.* the beak of a bird; a statement in writing saying how much money one owes; a proposal for a law, to be discussed in Parliament.

billet (bil-let) *v.* lodge soldiers, sailors or other people in private houses by order of the government; *n.* a temporary home.

billiards (bill-iards) *n.* a game for two people played with long sticks called cues and ivory balls, on an oblong table covered with cloth.

billow (bil-low) *n.* a large wave. *v.* rise and move like a wave (of smoke etc.).

billygoat (bil-ly-goat) *n.* a male goat.

bin *n.* a large container for storing coal, corn, flour or bread, usually having a lid.

bind *v.* tie or fasten; fasten a strip of tape or cloth along and over the edge of; fasten sheets of paper into a cover or book; tie round or put a bandage on; be forced to agree to do something, be bound to do a thing.

binding *n.* the cover of a book.

biography (bi-og-ra-phy) *n.* the story of one person's life written by another (see autobiography).

biplane (bi-plane) *n.* an aeroplane with two pairs of wings, one pair above the other.

birch *n.* a tree with smooth bark; a bundle of birch rods tied together to make a whip, once used for punishing boys.

bird *n.* a creature with wings and covered with feathers.

birth *n.* being born; the beginning of life; descent. **birthday** *n.* the day of one's birth or the anniversary of that day.

biscuit (bis-cuit) *n.* a small, dry piece of bread made from dough rolled flat and baked. Biscuits may be either sweet or savoury.

bisect (bi-sect) *v.* divide into two parts, usually equal.

bishop (bish-op) *n.* a clergyman who is head of a number of churches in a diocese or district.

bison (bi-son) *n.* a wild ox, the American buffalo.

bit *n.* a small piece; a small metal bar which forms part of a horse's bridle; a tool which fits into another tool called a brace and is used for boring holes.

bite *v.* cut into something with the teeth, sting (of insects). *n.* a piece bitten off or broken off; a small piece; the act of biting; an injury caused by being bitten or stung.

bitter (bit-ter) *a.* having a harsh, disagreeable taste; very cold and fierce (of the wind etc.); angry, disappointed, sorrowful.

black *n.* the opposite of white, without colour. *a.* dark. **blackguard** *n.* an evil, dishonest person. **blackleg** *n.* a name given by workpeople on strike to those who refuse to join them. **blackmail** *n.* taking money from people by threatening to reveal things they wish to keep secret. **black sheep** a lazy, wasteful person; a disgrace to friends or family.

blacksmith *n.* a man who repairs and makes things out of iron.

bladder (blad-der) *n.* a bag inside the body in which urine or waste liquid collects; the rubber or plastic bag inside a football which is blown up through a tube.

blade *n.* the flat part of a knife, axe or chisel which cuts; the flat part of a cricket bat or propeller; a long, narrow leaf.

blame *v.* believe or say that someone is in the wrong; accuse. *n.* responsibility for having failed or done wrong. **to blame** in the wrong, responsible for.

blank *n.* an empty space on paper; a cartridge with no bullet. *a.* unmarked, not written on or printed on; without interest or expression (a stare); having forgotten.

blanket (blan-ket) *n.* a thick cover used on a bed. *v.* to cover as with a blanket (of fog etc.).

blast *n.* a strong, sudden rush of wind; a gust or rush spreading outwards from an explosion; the sound made by the blowing of a trumpet or horn. *v.* blow up, destroy.

blaze *n.* a bright flame or fire. *v.* burst into flame, burn brightly; shine brightly. **blazer** *n.* an informal jacket worn for sporting activities, sometimes in the colours or carrying the badge of a school or club.

bleach *v.* make or become white. *n.* a preparation to make hair, clothes, baths etc. white.

bleak *a.* cold, bare; swept by winds; cheerless.

bleary *a.* faint or dim to the sight. **blear** *v.* make faint or dim.

bleat *n.* the cry of a sheep, lamb, goat or calf. *v.* make a cry like that of a sheep.

bleed *v.* lose blood from wounds, draw blood from wounds.

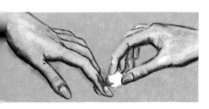

bleep *n.* a high-pitched sound sent out by radio, earth satellites or spacecraft.

blend *v.* mix together; go well together. *n.* a mixture.

bless *v.* ask or hope that God may protect; make holy; call God holy; praise God. **blessed** *a.* fortunate, gifted with. **blessing** *n.* a favour given by God, a happy result.

blind *a.* unable to see. *v.* make blind. *n.* a cover for a window which can be raised or lowered. **blind alley** an alley that has no way out, a job in which there is no chance of promotion. **blindfold** *v.* cover the eyes. *a.* with the eyes covered by a bandage. **blind to** unable or not willing to understand. **blind turning** a turning in the road, dangerous because one cannot see what is coming.

blink *v.* open and shut the eyes quickly; shine unsteadily, often in the dark.

bliss *n.* perfect happiness. **blissful** *a.* full of happiness, delightful.

blister (blis-ter) *n.* a small swelling under the skin, filled with liquid; a similar swelling on metal or painted wood. *v.* make or get blisters on.

blitz *n.* a word from the German language meaning a sudden attack, as by a large force of aircraft.

blizzard (bliz-zard) *n.* a severe storm, with snow driven by a fierce wind.

block *n.* a piece of wood or stone used for building; a large piece of wood on which a person rests his neck for execution; a building or large group of buildings joined together. *v.* stand in the way of; stop; (in cricket) stop a ball with the bat

to prevent it hitting the wicket. **blockage** *n.* something stopping the flow or movement, usually in a pipe or drain.

blood *n.* the red liquid flowing through the veins and arteries of the body. **blood donor** a person who allows his blood to be taken for transfusion into the veins of other people. **bloodhound** *n.* a large dog which can trace people or game by following their scent. **bloodthirsty** *a.* eager to kill and taking pleasure in killing.

blot *n.* a mark caused by ink spilt or dropped on paper. *v.* make a mark by dropping ink or crossing out words. **blotter** *n.* a book containing sheets of blotting paper; a piece of wood on which blotting paper has been fixed. **blotting paper** soft paper used to soak up ink.

blouse *n.* a shirt worn mainly by women, tucked into a skirt or trousers at the waist.

blow *v.* drive, force, move, flow (of air or wind); move by blowing. *n.* a hard stroke; a shock or dreadful happening. **blow over** pass away. **blow up** damage or destroy completely by causing an explosion.

bluff *v.* make others afraid by pretending to be strong or clever. *n.* talk intended to mislead others.

blunder (blun-der) *v.* make a mistake; move here and there in a clumsy way. *n.* a mistake.

blunt *a.* with no point or sharp edge; honest, speaking plainly. *v.* make blunt, take away the point or edge.

blush *v.* turn red in the face from shame or confusion. *n.* a redness of the face caused by shame or shyness.

bluster (blus-ter) *v.* blow strongly and violently; talk noisily and with threats. *n.* noisy, threatening words.

boar *n.* a male pig.

board *n.* a long, flat, thin piece of wood; a flat piece of wood for a special purpose (chess, diving etc.); meals supplied and paid for, usually by the week; persons appointed to take charge of a business or other activity. *v.* live at another person's house, paying for food; get on to a ship or train etc. **on board** (see **aboard**) on or in a ship or train etc.

boast *v.* praise the things one does or talk too much about the things one has. *n.* something to talk proudly about. **boastful** *a.* continually boasting.

boat *n.* a small vessel for travelling on water, using oars, by steam or with a motor.

bob *v.* move up and down. *n.* a style of short haircut for women and children.

bobbin (bob-bin) *n.* a small roller on which thread is wound.

bobsleigh (bob-sleigh) *n.* a racing sledge carrying two people, with two pairs of runners, used in tobogganing.

bodice (bod-ice) *n.* the upper part of a woman's dress, fitting the body.

body *n.* a human being or animal; the trunk of a human body; a dead person or animal; a large quantity of matter; a number of people. **bodily** *adv.* as a whole, without taking a thing apart. **bodyguard** *n.* a man who goes about with a person to protect him from harm.

bog *n.* a marsh or swamp. **boggy** *a.* soft, wet, swampy, marshy.

boisterous (bois-ter-ous) *a.* rough, loud, violent (of winds, crowds etc.).

bolt *n.* a metal bar which fastens a door or window; a metal pin on which a nut can be screwed; a shaft of lightning (often called a thunderbolt). *v.* fasten with a bolt; run away in alarm; swallow (food etc.) quickly.

bomb *n.* a hollow container filled with explosive material. *v.* drop bombs on. **bomber** *n.* a plane made specially for dropping bombs.

bond *n.* an agreement to pay money in return for a loan; something which brings people closer together; anything that binds a person. **bondage** *n.* slavery.

bone *n.* one of the many parts which make up the skeleton of a person or an animal. *v.* take the bones out of. **bony** *a.* full of bones.

bonfire (bon-fire) *n.* a large fire in an open space.

bonnet (bon-net) *n.* a close-fitting covering for the head, often tied under the chin; the metal covering over the front part of a motor-car.

bonny or **bonnie** *a.* handsome, pretty, healthy.

bonus (bo-nus) *n.* a payment of money in addition to what is usually paid.

boo *int.* an expression of dislike, sometimes used to animals. *v.* use such an expression.

book *n.* written, printed or blank sheets of paper fastened together in a cover. *v.* give or receive an order for seats at a theatre or concert; write down somebody's name, especially that of a footballer who has committed a foul or other offence. **booklet** *n.* a thin book. **bookmaker** (or **bookie**) *n.* a person who takes people's bets at horse races or in a shop.

boom *n.* a long, deep sound; a quick increase in prices giving larger profits. *v.* prosper, become rich, speed up (of trade).

boomerang (boo-me-rang) *n.* a bent, or curved piece of hard wood which when thrown returns to the person who throws it. Boomerangs are used by Australian aborigines.

boost *v.* lift or raise by pushing from behind or below; raise, increase (in prices etc.). *n.* a rise (in prices etc.).

boot *n.* a heavy shoe reaching above the ankle; a place for baggage usually at the rear of a motor car.

booth *n.* a small room or compartment for a telephone or for voting; a stall for the sale of goods in a street market.

border (bor-der) *n.* a side, edge or margin; a dividing line or boundary between lands. *v.* act as a boundary.

bore *v.* pierce, make a narrow, deep hole, drill; tire people with talking too much. *n.* a dull, tiresome person.

born *v.* one form of the word bear, having come into the world by birth; having some great talent or fault.

borne *v.* past tense of the word bear, meaning endured, carried.

borrow (bor-row) *v.* take a thing, promising to give it back at a later time to its owner.

boss *n.* an employer, a person who sees that other persons do their work. *v.* order others to do things.

both *pron.* the one and the other, the two.

bother (both-er) *v.* annoy, cause trouble; take the trouble to do something. *n.* worry, trouble.

bottle (bot-tle) *n.* a container, usually of glass, with a narrow neck. *v.* put into bottles to store. **bottleneck** *n.* a narrow strip of road where traffic often has to wait to get through; a large amount of road or rail traffic causing delays.

bottom (bot-tom) *n.* the lowest part; the bed of a lake, sea, river etc.; the seat of a chair or the part of the body that sits on it. *a.* lowest.

bough *n.* (rhymes with *now*) a large branch growing from the trunk of a tree.

bounce *v.* spring back after hitting a wall or a floor; make a thing bounce; jump up and down.

bound *a.* going in the direction of. *v.* be limited by, next to; spring, jump. *n.* a boundary line or limit. **boundary** *n.* a dividing line or border; the hitting of a cricket ball to the boundary of the field by which a score of 4 or 6 is made.

bouquet (bou-quet) *n.* (pronounced *bo-kay*) a bunch of flowers.

bow *n.* (rhymes with *so*) a knot made with one or more loops; a strip of wood, curved by a string stretched between its ends, used for shooting arrows; a slender stick with horse hair stretched from end to end, used to play the violin or other musical instrument which has strings. **bow-legged** *a.* with legs curved outwards at the knees. **bow-tie** *n.* a neck-tie fastened with a bow.

bow *v.* (rhymes with *now*) bend down; stoop to express greeting, shame or surrender. *n.* the front part of a boat; the action of bending down.

bowel (bow-el) *n.* part of the digestive system of the body; inward parts (of the earth etc.).

bowl *n.* a hollow dish; the contents of a bowl. *v.* send a ball to a person who is batting in the game of cricket. **bowler** *n.* the person who bowls the ball to the one who is batting; a hard rounded hat, usually black. **bowling alley** see alley. **bowling green** an area of short grass on which the game of bowls is played.

box *n.* a container, usually of wood, cardboard, metal or plastic; what a box holds; a small compartment for a few people in a theatre, separated from all others. *v.* fight with the fists. **boxer** *n.* a boy or man who boxes; a dog related to the bull-dog with a smooth coat.

boy *n.* a child who will one day be a man. **boyish** *a.* like a boy.

boycott (boy-cott) *v.* join with others in having nothing to do with a person or a group of persons; refuse to accept the products of another country.

brace *n.* an appliance used to hold tight or give support; straps worn over the shoulders to support the trousers; a tool which holds another tool called a bit and which can be turned to make holes. *v.* strengthen, make firm.

bracelet (brace-let) *n.* a band of metal or other material worn as an ornament about the wrist.

bracket (brack-et) *n.* a support of wood or metal for a shelf, a lamp or other article on a wall; one of two marks ( ) used in writing or print to enclose words or figures.

brag *v.* boast, talk too much about oneself, the things one has or what one can do.

braid *v.* divide into parts and plait. *n.* hair, silk etc., woven into a plait or band sometimes used for the edge or trimming of cloth or a garment.

brain *n.* a mass of grey matter inside the skull of a human being or animal. **brainwashing** *n.* a method of forcing a person to give up his beliefs and accept those pressed on him. **brainwave** *n.* a sudden bright idea.

brake *n.* a device used to make vehicles slow down or stop. *v.* slow down or stop in a vehicle.

bramble (bram-ble) *n.* a bush which carries long, prickly shoots and bears blackberries.

bran *n.* the outer covering of grains, sometimes separated from the grain before it is ground.

branch *n.* a limb of a tree which grows from the trunk or from another branch; a division of a river, road, railway, mountain range, a family or organization.

brand *v.* mark with a hot iron. *n.* the mark which is branded on; a trade name of a particular product.

brandy (bran-dy) *n.* a strong alcoholic drink usually made from grapes.

brass *n.* a bright yellow metal which is a mixture of copper and zinc.

brave *a.* not afraid to face danger or pain. *v.* face, meet. *n.* an American Indian warrior. **bravely** *adv.* with courage. **bravery** *n.* courage.

bray *n.* the cry of a donkey; the loud sound of a trumpet. *v.* make a loud, harsh cry or sound.

bread *n.* a food made with flour and yeast, mixed, kneaded and baked in an oven. **breadwinner** *n.* the person who works to support a family.

break *v.* smash or be smashed; make useless; crush, abandon; interrupt; change in some way. *n.* an interval; a new start. **breakfast** *n.* the first meal of the day which breaks the fast of the night before.

breast *n.* chest; the upper front part of the human body or an animal's body.

breath *n.* air taken into and sent out of the lungs; movement of air. **breathless** or **out of breath**, panting, breathing hard and quickly through exertion. **breathe** *v.* take air into the lungs and send it out again; tell (a secret).

breeches (breech-es) *n.* short trousers reaching to just below the knees.

breed *v.* keep for producing young; produce young, multiply; cause. *n.* a kind or variety of animal, bird, insect etc.

breeze *n.* a gentle wind.

brew *v.* make by boiling and fermenting or by scalding; bring about, form.

briar or **brier** *n.* a plant with sharp thorns along the stem; a wild rose on which cultivated varieties are grown.

bribe *n.* money, favours or gifts made to a person to get him to do something which may be wrong or dishonest. *v.* give a bribe to. **bribery** *n.* the giving or taking of bribes.

brick *n.* a piece of clay shaped and baked hard, used in building; anything shaped like a brick (ice cream etc.); a building toy.

bride *n.* a woman newly married or about to be married. **bridegroom** *n.* a man newly married or about to be married. **brides-**

maid *n.* a young girl who attends the bride at the wedding.

bridge *n.* a structure built over a river, road or railway for people and vehicles to cross; a platform across the deck of a ship used by the captain and officers; a game played with cards; a thin piece of wood used to support the strings of a violin or other stringed instrument. *v.* make a bridge over.

bridle (bri-dle) *n.* the part of a horse's harness that fits over the head and includes the bit, the straps and the reins.

brief *a.* short. *n.* shorts or underpants without legs; a short summary or plan of action given in advance to the crew of an aircraft or to anybody going on a mission.

brigade (bri-gade) *n.* a part of an army consisting of several regiments. a group of people organized for special work.

brigand (brig-and) *n.* a member of a gang of robbers, a bandit.

bright *a.* shining, giving light; cheerful and happy; very clever. **brighten** *v.* make bright.

brilliant (bril-liant) *a.* very bright, sparkling; very clever. **brilliance** *n.* great brightness.

brim *n.* the part of a hat which turns outwards at the bottom of the crown; the top edge of a cup, bowl or glass. *v.* (of a vessel) be full almost to overflowing.

brine *n.* water containing a great deal of salt.

bring *v.* come with something; carry or lead; cause.

brisk *a.* active, quick, lively.

bristle (bris-tle) *n.* one of the short, stiff hairs in brushes or in the coats of animals.

broad *a.* large, wide across.

broadcast (broad-cast) *v.* send out in all directions as in spreading news (especially by radio) or sowing seed.

bronco (bron-co) *n.* a wild or half-tamed horse used in western North America.

bronze *n.* a yellowish metal made by melting copper and tin together.

brooch *n.* an ornament for the dress which has a pin at the back to make it fast.

brood *n.* all the young birds hatched at the same time in a single nest; a popular expression for a mother's children. *v.* think sadly about one's troubles.

brook *n.* a small stream.

broom *n.* a stiff brush with a long handle; a shrub with yellow flowers which grows on sandy soil. **broomstick** *n.* the handle of a broom.

broth *n.* the water in which meat or fish has been boiled. Thickened with vegetables it is served as soup.

brother (broth-er) *n.* the son of the same parents as another person. **brotherhood** *n.* a group of men who consider themselves as dear to each other as brothers; an organization. **brother-in-law** *n.* the husband of one's sister or the brother of one's husband or wife.

brow *n.* eyebrow; the arch of hair above the eye; forehead.

bruise *n.* an injury to one's body caused by a blow or bump which turns the skin a dark colour but does not break it; *v.* cause a bruise.

brunette (bru-nette) *n.* a person with dark or brown hair, eyes and skin.

brush *n.* a tool with stiff hairs or bristles. *v.* clean with a brush; rub against when passing.

brute *n.* a savage, cruel or unkind person; any animal (not including man). **brutal** *a.* cruel, savage.

bubble (bub-ble) *n.* a ball of liquid containing air or gas which floats in the air and on liquids. *v.* form bubbles.

buck *n.* a male deer, goat, hare or rabbit. *v.* jump with arched back and all four feet off the ground.

bucket (buck-et) *n.* a vessel of wood, metal, canvas or plastic with a handle for carrying coal, water, milk etc.

buckle (buck-le) *n.* a fastener of metal, bone or plastic with a spike which goes through a hole in a belt or strap. *v.* fasten with a buckle; crumple up because of a heavy weight or strain.

bud *n.* a leaf or flower before it unfolds. *v.* form buds.

budgerigar (bud-ge-ri-gar) or **budgie** *n.* a small Australian bird of the parrot family.

budget (bud-get) *n.* a written document showing how much money was received and spent last year, and how much it is believed will be received and spent next year.

buffalo (buf-fa-lo) *n.* a term used to describe the bison of North America, the Cape Buffalo of Africa and the Wild and Water Buffalo of Asia.

buffer (buf-fer) *n.* two rods on springs put on vehicles to lessen the blow when they stop or touch each other.

buffet (buf-fet) *v.* knock against. *n.* a blow; a number of blows; a counter or table where food and drink may be bought and consumed (pronounced *boo-fay*).

buffoon (buf-foon) *n.* a jester, a clown or a person who behaves like one.

bugle (bu-gle) *n.* a small brass horn used by soldiers, sailors and boy scouts.

build *v.* make by putting together many parts. **builder** *n.* a person who constructs or helps to construct buildings. **building** *n.* a house or other construction of stone, bricks, wood, concrete etc.

bulb *n.* a thick root, often round, which may be fit to eat, a hollow-shaped object of glass.

bulge *v.* swell outwards; *n.* a swelling.

bull *n.* the male of an animal, especially of the ox family, the elephant, rhinoceros etc.

bullet (bul-let) *n.* a shaped piece of lead that is fired from a gun or revolver.

bulletin (bul-le-tin) *n.* a short statement of news, put out for the information of the public.

bully (bul-ly) *n.* a blustering, boastful person who terrifies those who may be weaker. *v.* use one's strength to frighten, rob or hurt others.

bump *n.* a swelling on the body caused by a knock or blow. *v.* hit, strike or knock against something else. **bumper** *n.* a bar fixed to the front and back of a motor vehicle to lessen the damage which might be done by a collision. **bumpy** *a.* full of raised places and hollows.

bun *n.* a small, sweet roll or cake, often containing currants.

bunch *n.* a number of things growing or held together, a cluster. *v.* crowd together (of people).

bundle (bun-dle) *n.* a number of things bound, tied or fastened together. *v.* wrap, bind or put together; send somebody rudely and quickly to a place (or away).

bungalow (bun-ga-low) *n.* a house with only one storey.

bungle (bun-gle) *v.* do a piece of work badly. **bungler** *n.* a person who is continually making mistakes.

bunk *n.* a narrow bed, usually fixed to a wall or the floor.

bunting (bun-ting) *n.* brightly coloured cloth used to make flags and decorations.

buoy *n.* (pronounced *boy*) a floating object used to mark a channel and to guide ships; a floating object used to prevent a person from sinking.

bur or **burr** *n.* a rough part of a plant which contains seeds. A bur sticks to people's clothes and the coats of animals.

burden (bur-den) *n.* a load; something that must be borne; the weight of cargo a ship can carry.

bureau (bu-reau) *n.* a writing desk with drawers; a branch or department of government which deals with one activity **bureaucracy** *n.* a government of paid officials called bureaucrats who go by the rules and against whom there is often no remedy for unfair treatment.

burglar (bur-glar) *n.* a person who breaks into a building to steal. **burglary** *n.* robbery from buildings.

burn *v.* use for light or heat; be on fire; be hurt by fire; make burn, set on fire; sting. *n.* an injury or mark made by something hot.

burrow (bur-row) *v.* dig a hole in the ground. *n.* a nest or home made in the ground by an animal which burrows.

burst *v.* break apart, explode; rush suddenly; start suddenly.

bury (bur-y) *v.* put under the ground; cover up with something. **burial** *n.* the act or ceremony of burying.

bus *n.* a public vehicle with a long body and seats for passengers. **bus stop** the place where passengers get on and off the bus.

busby (bus-by) *n.* a tall fur hat worn by certain regiments in the British Army.

bush *n.* a low plant with a hard stem and many branches rising from the ground; a stretch of land covered with bushes and small trees, chiefly in Australia and New Zealand. **bushy** *a.* thick with bushes or with hair.

business (bus-i-ness) *n.* buying and selling; a firm consisting of one or more people; one's duty, what one has to do.

busy (bus-y) *a.* active, fully occupied; full of activity and work.

butcher (butch-er) *n.* a man who keeps a shop in which he cuts up meat and sells it to the public.

butter (but-ter) *n.* the cream from milk which when beaten or churned becomes a soft, light yellow solid; certain substances like butter, such as cocoa butter and peanut butter. *v.* spread butter on. **buttermilk** *n.* the liquid left after butter has been made from the cream. **butterscotch** *n.* a sweet made by boiling butter and sugar together.

button (but-ton) *n.* a knob or disc of brass, pearl, bone or plastic which acts as a fastening or a decoration on clothing; a small object that looks like a button and which is pressed to make something work. *v.* fasten with buttons. **buttonhole** *n.* the hole in clothing through which a button goes.

buy *v.* acquire something by paying money. **buyer** *n.* a person who buys a

thing or who buys goods to be sold in a large store.

buzz *n.* a low humming sound like that of bees. *v.* make a buzzing noise

by *adv. & prep.* at the side of, near; through the use of or the doing of; along; as soon as; not later than; past. **by and by** later on **bygone** *a.* in past time. **bypass** *n.* a road that goes round a town. **bystander** *n.* a person standing near.

C

cab *n.* a taxicab or taxi; the covered part of a locomotive or lorry where the driver sits

cabaret (ca-ba-ret) *n.* (pronounced *cab-aray*) an entertainment provided in a restaurant or night-club while guests are dining.

cabin (ca-bin) *n.* a small house or hut; a small room in a ship; the enclosed space in an aircraft designed for crew, passengers or cargo.

cabinet (cab-i-net) *n.* a piece of furniture consisting of shelves, drawers or places for holding things of value, letters, pottery etc.; a piece of furniture which holds a radio, record player or television; the body of ministers which governs a country. **filing cabinet** a case in which letters and other documents are kept in order.

cable (ca-ble) *n.* a thick, strong rope, often made of several wires twisted together; a similar rope of twisted wire used for conducting electricity; *v.* send a message by cable. **cablegram** (or **cable**) *n.* a message sent by cable. **cable railway** a railway on which cars are hauled by a moving cable.

cadet (ca-det) *n.* a young person who is being trained to become an officer in the army, navy, air force or police. **cadet corps** (pronounced *core*) a group of persons being trained for one of these services.

café (ca-fe) *n.* (pronounced *cafay*) a room or building where refreshments or meals are served. **cafeteria** *n.* a restaurant where people serve themselves from a long counter.

cage *n.* an enclosed space like a box made with wires or bars in which birds or animals are kept.

calculate (cal-cu-late) *v.* find out by working with numbers. **calculation** *n.* the result of calculating.

calendar (cal-en-dar) *n.* a list of the days, weeks and months of the year showing the number of each day in the month and the most important days in the year.

calf *n.* the young of a cow and of certain other animals; the fleshy and muscular part of the back of the human leg between knee and ankle.

callous (cal-lous) *a.* without pity, caring nothing for the suffering of others.

calm *a.* (of the weather) quiet, with no wind. (of living beings) not excited. *v.* make or become calm. *n.* a time when everything is peaceful and quiet.

calorie (cal-o-rie) *n.* an amount of heat, an amount of energy supplied by food. An ounce of white bread supplies 69 calories.

camel (cam-el) *n.* an animal with a long neck and either one or two humps on its back.

camera (cam-e-ra) *n.* a machine for taking photographs. **cameraman** *n.* a person who works a camera in a film or television studio.

camouflage (cam-ou-flage) *n.* a way of disguising men, guns, ships etc., so that an enemy cannot see them; the means to make anything, animals etc., hard to see.

camp *n.* a group of tents, caravans or other simple buildings where people can live, usually for a short time. *v.* live in a camp or a tent for a time.

campaign (cam-paign) *n.* a plan of action to defeat an enemy, to get money or for any other purpose. *v.* take part in such a plan.

camphor (cam-phor) *n.* a white, strong-smelling substance used in medicine and for making celluloid.

can *n.* a metal container for oil, fruit, fruit juices, vegetables, fish etc. *v.* put into a can and sealed so that no air can get in; know how to, have the strength, ability or right to do a thing.

canal (ca-nal) *n.* a channel dug by men either for boats or for taking water to fields where crops are growing. **canal boat** a boat specially made to carry loads on canals.

canary (ca-na-ry) *n.* a small bird, usually yellow, which sings sweetly.

cancel (can-cel) *v.* cross out, draw a line through; make a mark on postage stamps to show that they have been used; state that something decided on will not be done or take place.

cancer (can-cer) *n.* a tumour on or in the body which grows and may cause death.

candidate (can-di-date) *n.* a person who is being put forward or is putting himself forward for a certain position.

candle (can-dle) *n.* a stick of wax with a wick or string through it. When the wick is lit it slowly burns up the wax to give light. **candlestick** *n.* a holder for a candle.

cannabis (can-na-bis) *n.* a drug made from parts of the Indian hemp plant.

cannibal (can-ni-bal) *n.* a person who eats human flesh.

cannon (can-non) *n.* a large gun fixed to the ground or on wheels.

canoe (ca-noe) *n.* a light boat which is propelled by hand-paddles.

canopy (can-o-py) *n.* a covering of cloth or other material fixed on a frame or held over a person by hand.

canteen (can-teen) *n.* a place to which soldiers, factory workers, schoolchildren etc. can go to buy and eat food; a box or chest of silver or cutlery.

canvas (can-vas) *n.* strong, coarse cloth used for tents, sails, bags or coverings.

canvass (can-vass) *v.* go from door to door asking for votes, subscriptions, or orders for goods etc. **canvasser** *n.* a person who canvasses.

canyon (can-yon) *n.* a very deep valley with steep sides, through which a stream or river may flow.

cap *n.* a small covering worn on the head; a small cover for bottles, jars, car radiators etc.; small pieces of thin paper which hold gunpowder for use in toys; a special headdress worn by soldiers etc. *v.* put a cap or cover on; award a cap to a scholar, footballer etc.

capable (ca-pa-ble) *a.* able, having knowledge, strength or skill to do a thing well.

capacity (ca-pac-i-ty) *n.* the power to hold or contain; the power to do.

capital (cap-i-tal) *n.* the city where the government of a country is seated; money or property which can be used in business. *a.* letters of the alphabet which are large and formed differently from small letters. **capitalist** *n.* a person who has capital and uses it in business.

capitulate (ca-pit-u-late) *v.* give in, surrender.

capsize (cap-size) *v.* (of a boat or ship) turn over or make turn.

capsule (cap-sule) *n.* a small case for seeds in a flower; a tiny container of medicine taken like a pill, which dissolves in the body; the compartment of a rocket in which the astronauts live.

captain (cap-tain) *n.* a leader; a commanding officer in the army or navy; the person in charge of a ship.

capture (cap-ture) *v.* make a prisoner of, take or seize. *n.* the act of capturing or being caught. **captive** *n.* a prisoner. **captivity** *n.* being held captive.

car *n.* a vehicle moving along the road under its own power, an automobile; the coach of a railway train.

caramel (car-a-mel) *n.* a kind of soft toffee; burnt sugar used for flavouring.

caravan (car-a-van) *n.* a covered cart or wagon used by people to live in; a company of people going together for safety through desert country.

carcass (car-cass) *n.* the dead body of an animal.

card *n.* a piece of thick paper, blank or printed, used for brief messages; one of the 52 cards used for games such as whist or poker. **cardboard** *n.* a thick stiff paper used for making boxes etc.

cardigan (car-di-gan) *n.* a knitted woollen jacket buttoning up the front.

care *v.* like; be interested in. *n.* attention, thought; sorrow, anxiety. **careful** *a.* paying attention, being watchful. **care for** *v.* look after. **careless** *a.* thoughtless, paying little attention. **caretaker** *n.* a person who is paid to look after a building.

career (ca-reer) *n.* a method of earning a living for which one has to be trained.

cargo (car-go) *n.* goods carried by ship or plane.

carnival (car-ni-val) *n.* a time when people make merry and feast, with processions, dancing etc.

carpenter (car-pen-ter) *n.* a workman who makes anything, especially parts of buildings and furniture, from wood.

carpet (car-pet) *n.* thick material of wool, hair or man-made fibre for covering floors; a covering of grass, leaves, ferns etc. *v.* cover smoothly as with a carpet.

carriage (car-riage) *n.* a vehicle for carrying people usually with four wheels, pulled by horses; a compartment of a railway train; a manner of holding the head and body.

carry (car-ry) *v.* move something from one place to another by hand, with a vehicle etc.; keep, possess; win a position, pass a motion by voting; hold the head and body in a certain manner. **carry on** *v.* continue to do something.

cart *n.* a two-wheeled vehicle for carrying loads. *v.* take away or carry away in a cart.

carton (car-ton) *n.* a box of stiff paper or cardboard.

cartridge (car-tridge) *n.* a case of metal or cardboard which holds explosives; something shaped like a cartridge, which contains ink for some types of pens.

carve *v.* cut a design on or cut into shape; cut meat into pieces. **carver** *n.* a person who carves things; a knife used for carving meat.

case *n.* a box, carton or container; a condition, how things are, a state of health; a matter to be settled by law. **casing** *n.* a covering, wrapping or frame.

cash *n.* money in coins or notes. *v.* give or get cash for. **cashier** *n.* a person who looks after money in a bank or a large store.

casket (cas-ket) *n.* a small box for holding valuable things.

cassock (cas-sock) *n.* a long garment worn by some priests, or singers in church choirs.

cast *v.* throw; pour into a mould to make a shape. **cast iron** iron which has been shaped in this way. **cast-offs** *n.* clothing which the owner does not wish to wear again.

castle (cas-tle) *n.* a large building or group of buildings once used as a fort or dwelling-place; a large house or mansion; one of the pieces in a game of chess, the upper part of which is shaped like the tower of a castle.

casual (cas-u-al) *a.* happening by chance, not thought of before. **casualty** *n.* a person injured by accident or in battle.

cat *n.* a small animal with a coat of fur, kept as a pet and to catch mice; an animal of the cat family which includes lions, tigers, panthers and leopards; a whip with nine knotted lashes once used to flog soldiers, sailors and prisoners (short for cat-o-nine-tails). **cat's eye** a small reflector placed in the middle of the road to guide motorists in the dark.

catalogue (cat-a-logue) *n.* a book or list with brief notes on the names, articles etc. listed. *v.* make a list.

catamaran (cat-a-ma-ran) *n.* a small craft made up of two hulls fastened side by side.

catapult (cat-a-pult) *n.* a device for throwing large stones or small pellets; a device which launches planes from the deck of an aircraft carrier.

cataract (cat-a-ract) *n.* a waterfall which drops from a great height; a growth on the eye which prevents people from seeing well.

catch *v.* take and hold on to something which moves; surprise, discover; become ill (cold, influenza etc.); become entangled with, prevented from moving. *n.* something which fastens; a trick to deceive. **catch fire** begin to burn. **catch up** *v.* follow and come level with.

cater (ca-ter) *v.* provide anything people require, such as food and entertainment. **caterer** *n.* a person or firm supplying and sometimes serving food and drink for a party or entertainment.

caterpillar (cat-er-pil-lar) *n.* a small insect which later develops into a moth or butterfly; a tractor which runs by means of a steel belt working on two or more wheels.

cathedral (ca-the-dral) *n.* the chief church in the district controlled by a bishop.

Catholic (Cath-o-lic) *n.* a person who belongs to the Roman Catholic Church. *a.* (with a small c) universal, involving all.

cattle (cat-tle) *n.* cows, bulls, calves and steers.

cauliflower (cau-li-flower) *n.* a cultivated plant which has in the centre a mass of solid white flowers.

cause *v.* produce, make happen. *n.* reason; a thing which people believe in and are working for.

caution (cau-tion) *n.* care, being on the alert; a warning. *v.* warn. **cautious** *a.* careful.

cavalry (cav-al-ry) *n.* soldiers who fight on horseback. **cavalier** *n.* a soldier on horseback; (with a capital C) one who fought for King Charles I in the English Civil War.

cave *n.* a hollow place underground or in the side of a cliff. **cavity** *n.* an empty or hollow space. **cave in** fall or sink, give way.

cease *v.* stop; come to an end; finish.

ceiling (ceil-ing) *n.* the overhead surface inside a room; the highest point anything may reach (as in prices); the highest distance overhead which an aircraft can go.

celebrate (cel-e-brate) *v.* do something to show that a day or happening is important; honour and think well of. **celebrated** *a.* well-known. **celebration** *n.* an occasion when some person or special event is celebrated.

cell *n.* a small room in a prison or monastery; one of the many separate spaces or parts; a device which makes electricity and is part of a battery.

cellar (cel-lar) *n.* a room under the ground used for storing things.

celluloid (cel-lu-loid) *n.* a plastic material used for making combs, buttons, film for cameras and many other articles.

cement (ce-ment) *n.* a substance made by burning lime and clay which is soft when mixed with water but then becomes very hard. It is used for building, making roads and laying floors; any material that sets hard, fills holes and sticks things together. *v.* join firmly together.

cemetery (cem-e-ter-y) *n.* a burial ground or graveyard not part of a church.

censor (cen-sor) *n.* an official who examines books, letters, plays, films etc. to make sure that anything not thought to be suitable is left out.

census (cen-sus) *n.* a counting of all the people living anywhere.

centigrade (cen-ti-grade) *a.* according to a scale on the thermometer showing 100 degrees between the freezing and boiling points of water.

centipede (cen-ti-pede) *n.* a long active animal like an insect whose body has many sections, each with a single pair of legs.

centre (cen-tre) *n.* the middle point; an important place to which people go. *v.* keep in the centre, put in the centre. **centre forward** and **centre half** (back) two important positions in a football team. **central** *a.* middle or chief.

century (cen-tu-ry) *n.* one hundred years; a hundred runs scored by one man in a game of cricket.

cereal (ce-re-al) *n.* any kind of grain used for food.

certain (cer-tain) *a.* sure; of which there is no doubt; referring to a person or thing not named. **certainly** *adv.* without doubt.

certificate (cer-tif-i-cate) *n.* a printed or written statement which can be produced as evidence that a certain thing is true.

chain *n.* many links or rings fastened together to make an unbroken line; a number of things or events linked together in some way. *v.* make fast with a chain.

chalk *n.* a soft white powdery material made from limestone. *v.* write, draw or mark with chalk.

challenge (chal-lenge) *n.* an invitation to take part in a contest of strength, skill etc.; a call to fight. *v.* make or send out a challenge.

chamber (cham-ber) *n.* a private room, especially a bedroom; a large room where parliament or a town council meets; a committee which exists for a special purpose; the part of a rifle or gun in which the cartridge or shell is placed before firing.

chamois (cham-ois) *n.* (pronounced *shamwah*) a goatlike antelope which lives in mountainous regions of Europe and south-western Russia. **chamois** (pronounced *shammy*) **leather** a piece of soft leather used for cleaning windows.

champion (cham-pi-on) *n.* the person who wins or takes first place in a game or contest. **championship** *n.* the position of a champion.

chance *n.* accident, something that had not been expected; an opportunity. *v.* happen by chance.

chandelier (chan-de-lier) *n.* a branched support for lights hanging from the ceiling.

change *v.* put in place of; make different. *n.* a difference; money in coins of small value. **changeable** *a.* likely to change.

channel (chan-nel) *n.* a stretch of water joining two seas; a line of deeper water in a river or harbour; a passage through which anything passes.

chapel (chap-el) *n.* a place used for worship, usually smaller than a parish church; a small place for prayer inside a church; a place of worship used by some Christians who do not belong to the Church of England. **chaplain** *n.* a priest or clergyman who takes services in a chapel.

character (char-ac-ter) *n.* the things in a person's disposition that make him different from others; all the good qualities that make for excellence in a person; a person who is noted for special deeds or behaviour; a person in a book or play.

charcoal (char-coal) *n.* a black substance made by burning wood slowly until it is black.

charge *v.* accuse; ask as a price for; make a record of something to be paid later; rush forward, attack; load, fill. *n.* something one is charged with; the price asked for; the amount of powder put into a gun or used to make an explosion; work given as a duty. **charger** *n.* a horse on which a knight in olden times rode to war.

charity (char-i-ty) *n.* help given to the poor and sick; a society organized to give help; kindness, willingness to forgive.

charm *n.* power to give pleasure; something believed to have magic power. *v.* please, give pleasure, use magic on.

chart *n.* a sheet of paper on which a list or diagram gives information on weather, prices, temperature etc.; a map used by sailors to show where rocks and lighthouses are. *v.* put on a chart.

chase *v.* run after in order to capture or drive away. *n.* the act of chasing.

chassis (chas-sis) *n.* (pronounced *shassi*) the framework on which a motorcar or the parts of a radio are mounted.

check *v.* compare; hold back or stop; investigate. *n.* a pattern of lines making squares of different colours.

cheek *n.* the two sides of the face below the eyes; impudence.

cheer *v.* shout encouragement; make glad; give comfort or happiness. *n.* a shout of joy or encouragement; gladness. **cheerful** *a.* happy, bringing happiness. **cheery** *a.* lively and gay.

cheese *n.* solid food made by separating the thick part of milk and shaping it into a cake.

chemist (chem-ist) *n.* a scientist who studies how substances are made up and how they change when put with other substances; a person who sells medicines, drugs, toilet articles and prepares medicines prescribed by the doctor. **chemistry** *n.* the study of how substances behave when treated in different ways.

cheque *n.* (pronounced *check*) a written order to a bank to pay money to the person who presents it.

cherish (cher-ish) *v.* look after a person or a thing with care; hold on to a belief or a hope.

chess *n.* a game for two players played on a black and white check board of 64 squares with pieces called chessmen.

chest *n.* a large box with a lid and sometimes drawers, used to store tools, linen, clothes or jewellery; the upper front part of the body.

chestnut (chest-nut) *n.* a tree with a smooth, reddish-brown nut; the nut of the chestnut tree.

chew *v.* crush, cut and grind into tiny pieces with one's teeth.

chicken (chick-en) *n.* a young fowl often

bred for its meat and its eggs. **chickenpox** *n.* an illness in which a person breaks out in many small red spots.

chief *n.* a leader, a person placed over others. *a.* most important, placed over others. **chiefly** *adv.* mainly.

child *n.* a boy or girl who has not yet grown up; a son or daughter.

chill *v.* make cold, become cold. *n.* an illness brought on by cold; coldness. **chilly** *a.* cool, rather cold. **chilblain** *n.* a painful swelling on hand or foot caused by cold.

chime *n.* a series of notes sounded on bells; the bells giving these notes. *v.* ring, show the time by ringing. **chime in** interrupt people who are talking.

chimney (chim-ney) *n.* a structure like a long tube built into a house to draw the fumes of a fire up and out of the building. **chimney-pot** *n.* a pipe fixed to the top of a chimney.

chin *n.* the lowest part of the face, below the mouth.

china (chi-na) *n.* white clay which has been baked, glazed and made into cups, saucers, plates and dishes; things made out of china.

chink *n.* a narrow crack, split or opening through which one may peep or through which the wind blows.

chip *n.* a small piece broken or cut off; a thin strip of wood used for making baskets; a finger of fried potato cut from a slice and fried with others. *v.* cut or break pieces off.

chiropodist (chi-rop-o-dist) *n.* a person who looks after other people's feet and treats their complaints.

chirp *v.* make light, short, sharp sounds.

chisel (chis-el) *n.* a tool with a sharp steel edge at one end. *v.* trim or cut with a chisel.

chloroform (chlo-ro-form) *n.* a thin colourless liquid which easily turns to vapour and which can be used to make persons unconscious before operations.

chocolate (choc-o-late) *n.* a substance made by grinding the seeds of the cacao tree and which can be drunk or made into small blocks to eat. *a.* the colour of chocolate, dark brown. **choc-ice** *n.* ice cream to which chocolate has been added.

choice *n.* something chosen or picked; the right or chance to choose. *a.* the very best.

choir *n.* a number of people who sing together; the part of a church where the church choir is situated.

choke *v.* be unable to breathe because the throat is blocked; spoil by filling up; stop somebody breathing because of fumes or pressure on the throat.

choose *v.* pick or select a thing, or what one wants to do.

chop *v.* cut by striking with a knife or axe. *n.* a slice of meat with the bone in it. **chopsticks** *n.* the two sticks used by Chinese for eating.

chord *n.* three or more notes of music played together in harmony.

chore *n.* a small duty which one does, usually in the home.

chorus (cho-rus) *n.* music for a choir or a large number of singers; the part of a song which comes after the verse and is sung by everybody.

Christian (Christ-ian) *n.* a follower of Jesus Christ who believes in his teachings. *a.* according to Christ's teachings. **Christianity** *n.* the teachings of Christ. **christen** *v.* give a first (or Christian) name when baptized in a church. **Christmas** *n.* 25 December, the anniversary of the birth of Christ.

chromium (chro-mium) *n.* a bright substance which shines like silver and is used for making pigments in photography, and for plating taps and car fittings.

chrysanthemum (chrys-an-the-mum) *n.* a garden flower with small petals which blooms in autumn and early winter.

chubby (chub-by) *a.* round and plump (usually of little children).

chuckle (chuck-le) *n.* a low, quiet laugh. *v.* laugh softly and quietly.

chunk *n.* a large piece.

church *n.* a building to which Christians go for public worship; a body of Christians who worship in the same way. **churchyard** *n.* the ground around the church.

churn *n.* a tub in which cream is shaken to make butter. *v.* shake and beat cream in butter-making.

cigar (ci-gar) *n.* tobacco leaves made into a tight roll for smoking. **cigarette** *n.* shreds of tobacco rolled in a piece of thin paper for smoking.

cinder (cin-der) *n.* a small piece of coal or other material partly burned.

cipher (ci-pher) *n.* the figure 0 which represents nought; a method of writing in code so that it can be understood only by those who know the code.

circle (cir-cle) *n.* a perfectly round line on which every point is the same distance from the centre; a number of people who meet to do things together. *v.* move in a circle.

circular (cir-cu-lar) *a.* round, the shape of a circle. *n.* a letter or notice sent out to many people. **circulate** *v.* go round or send round. **circulation** *n.* sending round, the number sent round.

circumference (cir-cum-fer-ence) *n.* the outer boundary.

circumstance (cir-cum-stance) *n.* a state or condition; a group or set of facts.

circus (cir-cus) *n.* a show in which clowns, performing animals and acrobats take part; a place, originally circular, where many streets meet.

cistern (cis-tern) *n.* a water tank from which pipes run to taps.

city (cit-y) *n.* a large town whose people are given special rights to govern themselves. **citizen** *n.* a person belonging to a city or to a country who has the right to vote and take part in its government.

civilization (ci-vi-li-za-tion) *n.* the development of a people from a primitive or simple society to an advanced one with art, science, education and government; the way in which a nation or race lives and thinks; a nation or part of the world at a certain point in its history. **civilize** *v.* train and educate people to a higher level of behaviour and culture.

claim *v.* demand something as a right; say that something is true; take up time or attention. *n.* a right.

clamber (clam-ber) *v.* climb with difficulty, using hands and feet.

clamp *n.* an appliance for holding things together; a heap of potatoes stored for the winter under straw, earth and rubbish. *v.* fasten with clamps.

clank *n.* a loud sound as of metals banging together. *v.* make a clanking noise.

clash *v.* make a loud, harsh noise; disagree, have different opinions from others. *n.* a loud, harsh noise.

clasp *n.* a device, usually of metal, for fastening things together; *v.* hold tightly, fasten with a clasp.

class *n.* a group of persons taught together; a group of things which are of the same kind. *v.* put into a class or group. **classroom** *n.* a room in which a class of students is taught.

clatter (clat-ter) *n.* a loud rattling noise as if hard objects are being knocked together. *v.* make a clatter.

claw *n.* a sharp nail, usually curved, on an animal's foot. *v.* tear, scratch, pull as if with claws.

clay *n.* a kind of earth which is soft and sticky when wet and becomes hard when dry. It is used to make tiles, bricks and many kinds of pottery.

clean *a.* free from dirt, smoke, wrongdoing or anything impure; skilful. *v.* remove dirt from, make clean. **cleaner** *n.* a person or anything which cleans.

clear *a.* easy to see through, bright; easy to understand; easy to see and hear. *v.* free oneself from anything which is in the way. *adv.* away, not touching.

clergyman (cler-gy-man) *n.* a Christian minister qualified to take religious services.

clerk *n.* (pronounced *clark*) a person who works in an office such as a bank, copying statements and keeping accounts; an important officer who looks after the business affairs of a government or a large company.

clever (clev-er) *a.* quick to learn, skilful, smart.

click v. make a short, sharp sound. n. a short, sharp sound.

cliff n. the face or front of a high, steep rock.

climate (cli-mate) n. the general weather conditions of a region of a country or the world.

climb v. go up, grow up. n. an ascent by climbing.

cling v. hold tightly to.

clinic (clin-ic) n. a place where medical treatment may be given.

clip n. a wire metal device for holding tightly; an ornament which clips on a garment. v. fasten with a clip; cut or cut off with scissors or shears; punch a hole.

clippers n. a tool with small knives in it like scissors, for cutting hair, hedges etc.

cloak n. a loose outer garment, usually without sleeves. **cloakroom** n. a place where hats and coats may be left; a lavatory.

clock n. an instrument by which one can tell the hour of the day or night.

close adv. (rhymes with *dose*) near a place or person; near in time; nearly equal. a. nearly equal; short of fresh air making breathing difficult; loved, trusted; strict, very careful (watch, supervision). **closely** adv. well, strictly.

close v. (rhymes with *those*) shut; bring or come to an end. n. end.

cloth n. material made by weaving threads of wool, silk, hair, flax, cotton or other fibre; a piece of cloth. **clothe** v. dress. **clothes** n. articles of dress or coverings. **clothing** n. clothes.

cloud n. a large body of vapour or ice particles floating in the sky; smoke or dust or a collection of insects floating in the air. v. become dark or dim as if by a cloud. **cloudless** a. having no clouds. **cloudy** a. filled with clouds, not clear.

clown n. a man who performs in a circus, paints his face, dresses comically and does amusing tricks.

club n. a group of persons who have joined together either to help each other or to follow some sport or pastime; one of the four sets of cards in a pack; a stick with a metal head used in playing golf; a heavy wooden stick, thick at one end, used as a weapon. v. hit with a stick or other weapon.

clue n. an idea, a happening or something left behind which helps to solve a problem.

clumsy (clum-sy) a. awkward, not having much skill in movement.

cluster (clus-ter) n. a number of things of the same kind growing or held together. v. come together in a cluster.

clutch v. seize with the hands or claws; hold tightly. n. mastery of one person over another; a device for joining two working parts of a machine, putting the machine in or out of action.

coach n. a closed carriage with four wheels, pulled by horses; a railway carriage; a bus which travels long distances; a teacher who has only one or two pupils at a time. v. teach a small number.

coal n. a black mineral sold in chunks and burned to give heat; a piece of wood or coal which is burning. **coalfield** n. a district where coal is dug from under the ground.

coarse a. rough, not fine or smooth to the touch; vulgar, common.

coast n. land lying along the side of water. v. move without effort.

coat n. an outer garment with sleeves; anything (paint etc.) that covers; the hair or fur of an animal. v. cover.

coax v. persuade somebody to do or say something by being kind and patient.

cobbler (cob-bler) n. a man who mends shoes.

cock n. the male of the farmyard fowl and of many other kinds of birds. v. turn upwards. **cocksure** a. so confident that one boasts about one's strength or cleverness.

cocoa (co-coa) n. powdered chocolate mixed with hot milk and water and usually taken as a hot, sweet drink.

coconut (co-co-nut) *n.* the large brown fruit of the coco palm tree, with a hard shell, a layer of white nut and milky juice inside.

cocoon (co-coon) *n.* the silky case or covering made by a caterpillar to protect itself during the winter before it changes into a moth or butterfly.

cod (also **codfish**) *n.* a large fish caught in the northern seas. **cod-liver oil** the oil from the liver of the cod, used as a medicine and a source of vitamins A and D.

code *n.* a system of signs or secret writing used for sending messages; a rule or set of rules or laws by which people live.

co-education (co-ed-u-ca-tion) *n.* education of boys and girls in the same school and in the same class.

coffee (cof-fee) *n.* a drink made with the roasted and ground seeds of the coffee plant.

coffin (cof-fin) *n.* a box or case in which the dead body of a person is placed for burial.

coil *v.* wind into rings one above the other. *n.* a continuous ring or spiral made by winding round and round.

coin *n.* a piece of metal money. *v.* make coins from metal; make up new words or phrases.

coincide (co-in-cide) *v.* fit; agree in every way; happen at the same time.

coincidence *n.* something which agrees with another, just by chance.

cold *a.* not warm or hot; unkind, not friendly. *n.* an illness of the nose and throat which makes one cough and sneeze.

collapse (col-lapse) *v.* fall in, come tumbling down.

collar (col-lar) *n.* a bend, or that part of a garment worn round the neck; a band of metal which joins two pipes.

colleague (col-league) *n.* one of a group of persons who work together.

collect (col-lect) *v.* bring together, gather together, come together; gather together and keep (things). **collection** *n.* a group of things or people.

college (col-lege) *n.* a place where people can study subjects to a higher level than in school.

collide (col-lide) *v.* come together with great force. **collision** *n.* when two things collide.

colonel (colo-nel) *n.* (pronounced *kernel*) an officer in the army who commands a regiment.

colony (col-o-ny) *n.* a country or state founded by people who have left their own country; people from one country who live together in a small part of another country; a number of animals or plants living or growing together. **colonial** *a.* having to do with colonies.

colour (col-our) *n.* how the light from the things we see strikes the eye. *v.* put colour on. **colours** *n.* any ribbon, dress, badge or flag used for identification. **colour-blind** *a.* not able to tell the difference between certain colours. **colourless** *a.* without colour.

colt *n.* a young male horse under the age of about five years.

column (col-umn) *n.* a tall pillar or post used as a support in buildings; a long line or row.

comb *n.* a piece of metal, plastic etc., with teeth for straightening hair or wool; a structure of wax made by bees for storing honey. *v.* straighten by using a comb; search everywhere.

combat (com-bat) *n.* a fight, struggle. *v.* fight. **single combat** a fight between two persons.

combine (com-bine) *v.* join or put together. **combination** *n.* two or more things put together.

come *v.* move forward; happen, occur; reach; become; amount to. **coming** *a.* happening or to happen soon.

comedian (com-e-di-an) *n.* an actor who makes people laugh, an amusing person.

comedy (com-e-dy) *n.* a play or film which ends happily, contains very little sadness and is sometimes humorous.

comet (com-et) *n.* a bright body going round the sun in an orbit, and trailing a tail of light.

comfort (com-fort) *v.* soothe or cheer. *n.* being at ease, having what one wants. **comfortable** *a.* giving comfort or being in comfort.

comic (com-ic) *a.* funny, humorous. *n.* a paper for children containing stories illustrated with numerous pictures. **comical** *a.* amusing, humorous.

comma (com-ma) *n.* a punctuation mark which shows a slight break in a sentence. **inverted commas** marks ('') which show the beginning and end of speeches.

command (com-mand) *v.* order. *n.* an order. **commander** *n.* a person in charge, a naval officer ranking below a captain. **in command** in charge.

commence (com-mence) *v.* begin.

commerce (com-merce) *n.* trade, buying and selling goods. **commercial** *a.* having to do with commerce.

commit (com-mit) *v.* perform, do; give up, put into the care of. **committee** *n.* a small body of people appointed to do a certain piece of work.

common (com-mon) *a.* usual, frequent, often occurring; belonging to all, shared. **House of Commons** the body elected by the people of Great Britain and Northern Ireland as one part of Parliament. **in common** shared by two or more persons. **commonwealth** *n.* the body of people making up a state; (with a capital C) all the peoples of the world connected with Britain and once part of the British Empire.

communicate (com-mu-ni-cate) *v.* pass on or exchange news, feelings etc.; make known. **communication** *n.* news sent from place to place.

community (com-mu-ni-ty) *n.* people living together in a town, country, village or settlement.

company (com-pa-ny) *n.* persons who have joined together in business; people who take part in a play or entertainment; being with others; a unit of soldiers commanded by a captain; the name of a business or firm. **companion** *n.* a friend, one who keeps company with another. **companionship** *n.* association of companions.

compare (com-pare) *v.* examine things to

find out how they are alike and how they differ. **comparison** *n.* likeness or difference.

compass (com-pass) *n.* an instrument with a magnetized needle which points north, used for showing direction. **pair of compasses** an instrument for drawing circles and measuring distances.

compete (com-pete) *v.* take part in any contest. **competition** *n.* a contest. **competitor** *n.* one who competes.

complain (com-plain) *v.* say that something is wrong. **complaint** *n.* a statement that something is not right; an illness.

complexion (com-ple-xion) *n.* appearance, natural colour of skin, hair, eyes etc.

complicate (com-pli-cate) *v.* make more difficult. **complicated** *a.* made up of many parts; difficult to do or understand. **complication** *n.* the result of becoming complicated; a difficulty.

compliment (com-pli-ment) *n.* an expression of praise; a greeting. *v.* praise, congratulate.

compose (com-pose) *v.* make up, arrange, put together (of materials, music etc.); become or make calm. **composition** *n.* something put together; the parts of which something is made.

comprehensive (com-pre-hen-sive) *a.* taking everything in. **comprehensive school** a school which replaces separate grammar and secondary modern schools, taking all senior pupils.

computer (com-pu-ter) *n.* an electronic machine able to program information and, if questioned on it, produce the correct answer.

conceal (con-ceal) *v.* hide, keep secret. **concealment** *n.* hiding, keeping things secret.

conceit (con-ceit) *n.* exaggerated pride in oneself and what one can do.

concern (con-cern) *v.* have to do with, have an effect on; be unhappy, make unhappy or anxious. *n.* something one is very interested in ; a business or firm.

concert (con-cert) *n.* a musical entertainment.

condition (con-di-tion) *n.* a state of things, affairs, business, health, repair etc. **on condition that** only if.

conduct (cón-duct) *n.* behaviour; the way one acts.

conduct (con-dúct) *v.* guide, lead; take charge of; direct and lead a choir, orchestra or band.

conductor (con-duc-tor) *n.* the leader of a choir, band or orchestra; a person in charge of passengers on a bus, train or other vehicle who collects fares and issues tickets; a substance that allows heat or electricity to pass through it.

cone *n.* a solid figure with a circular base and which comes to a point at the top; the pod of an evergreen tree containing the seeds; a hollow wafer which is filled with a portion of ice-cream.

confer (con-fer) *v.* give or grant; meet and discuss. **conference** *n.* a meeting for discussion.

confess (con-fess) *v.* admit that one has done wrong or is at fault; tell one's sins to a priest. **confession** *n.* a statement admitting that one is at fault.

confide (con-fide) *v.* tell something to somebody knowing that it will be kept secret. **confidence** *n.* faith in oneself or others. **confident** *a.* having faith in oneself or others. **confidential** *a.* secret.

confuse (con-fuse) *v.* mix up, jumble; mistake one for another. **confusion** *n.* disorder.

congratulate (con-grat-u-late) *v.* say that one is pleased about a person's good

fortune or success. **congratulation** *n.* an expression of pleasure at this.

congregate (con-gre-gate) *v.* meet together. **congregation** *n.* all those, except for the minister and choir, attending a church service.

conjurer or **conjuror** (con-ju-rer) *n.* one who practises magic and entertains people with clever tricks, usually with his hands. **conjure** *v.* perform such tricks.

connect (con-nect) *v.* join or put together; be joined; think of different things as being related. **connection** (or **connexion**) *n.* the state of being connected; something joining one thing to another.

conquer (con-quer) *v.* overcome; take possession of by force. **conquest** *n.* the act of conquering.

conscious (con-scious) *a.* awake; able to notice what is going on. **consciousness** *n.* being conscious.

consent (con-sent) *v.* agree, permit. *n.* permission.

conserve (con-serve) *v.* keep, save, preserve. **conservation** *n.* official preservation of natural resources. **conservative** *a.* having a tendency to preserve existing conditions, institutions etc. *n.* (with a capital C) one of the political parties of Great Britain.

consider (con-sid-er) *v.* think about; bear in mind; think well or badly of a thing or person. **considerable** *a.* very large.

consist (con-sist) *v.* be made up of.

consonant (con-so-nant) *n.* any letter of the alphabet except a, e, i, o, u (and sometimes y); any letter which is not a vowel.

constable (con-sta-ble) *n.* a policeman.

constellation (con-stel-la-tion) *n.* a group of stars first named by people in ancient times (The Great Bear, Orion etc.)

constitution (con-sti-tu-tion) *n.* the rules by which a group, a town or a country is governed; the bodily structure or make-up of a person.

construct (con-struct) *v.* build, put together, make. **construction** *n.* a building, something made or built; the way in which words are arranged in a sentence.

consult (con-sult) *v.* get information or advice from; join together to think about something. **consultant** *n.* an expert in some branch of medicine or surgery. **consultation** *n.* a meeting for consulting.

consume (con-sume) *v.* use up, eat, drink up; destroy. **consumption** (con-sumption) *n.* the amount consumed; a disease which destroys part of the body.

contact (con-tact) *n.* touch; the state of touching or coming together; connection (or connexion) for electric current. *v.* get in touch with.

contagious (con-ta-gious) *a.* spreading through touch (of a disease).

contain (con-tain) *v.* hold within itself; be equal to; keep one's feelings under control. **container** *n.* a box, bottle, barrel etc. purposely made to contain things.

content (con-tént) *a.* satisfied with things as they are. *v.* satisfy, make content.

contents (cón-tents) *n.* what is contained in a vessel, a container, a book etc.

contest (con-tést) *v.* fight, argue, try to win. (cón-test) *n.* a fight, a struggle.

continent (con-ti-nent) *n.* one of the chief land masses of the world; (with a capital C) Europe without Great Britain. **continental** *a.* belonging to, or similar to what is on the Continent.

continue (con-tin-ue) *v.* go on being or doing, proceed; start again where something has been left off. **continual, continuous** *a.* going on all the time.

contract (cón-tract) *n.* an agreement to supply goods or do work at a fixed price.

contract (con-tráct) *v.* agree by making a contract; make or become smaller.

contrary (con-tra-ry) *a.* opposite, against; stubborn, refusing to give in to others (often pronounced *contrairy*).

contribute (con-trib-ute) *v.* give money, help etc. **contribute to** be one of the causes of something. **contribution** *n.* something given.

control (con-trol) *n.* power to order, a device that helps to operate a machine. *v.*

manage, direct; keep back; make more or less.

convenient (con-ven-i-ent) *a.* handy, suitable. **convenience** *n.* being free from difficulty or trouble. **public convenience** a public lavatory, usually in a street or square.

convent (con-vent) *n.* a society of women known as nuns, living in a place apart from others, and devoting their lives to the service of God; the building in which nuns live; a school where children are taught by nuns.

convention (con-ven-tion) *n.* a meeting of members of a society, political party, trade union, religious denomination etc., for a special purpose.

conversation (con-ver-sa-tion) *n.* talk between two or more people.

convict (con-víct) *v.* declare in a court of law that somebody has committed an offence.

convict (cón-vict) *n.* a person found guilty of a crime and serving a prison sentence as a punishment.

cook *v.* prepare food by heating in some way. *n.* a person who cooks either in the home or as a profession. **cooker** *n.* a stove on which food is cooked.

cool *a.* between warm and cold; calm, not afraid; not very friendly or interested. *v.* make or become cool.

coop *n.* a small cage, usually for poultry. *v.* be forced to stay in a place, not able to leave.

cooperate (co-op-er-ate) *v.* work together. **cooperation** *n.* working together. **co-op** *n.* a shop owned by a cooperative society, an organization for buying and selling run by its own members.

copper (cop-per) *n.* a reddish brown metal, one of the best conductors of electricity. *a.* copper-coloured.

copy (cop-y) *n.* a piece of art, a paper, a

letter etc. made exactly like another. *v.* make a copy of; take answers for examination questions from another person's work.

coral (co-ral) *n.* a hard substance built on the sea bed from the shells of small creatures.

cord *n.* a length of thick string or thin rope; part of the body which is like a cord (the spinal cord; the vocal cords).

core *n.* the hard, centre part of apples, pears and of some other fruit. *v.* to take out the core.

cork *n.* the bark of the cork tree, used to make lifejackets, stoppers for bottles and many other things. *v.* put in the cork or stopper. **corkscrew** *n.* an instrument with a metal spiral used for drawing out corks.

corn *n.* the seed of any grain, plant or cereal; a hard, painful growth of skin on the foot.

corner (cor-ner) *n.* a point where two lines, surfaces, edges, streets etc. meet; a hiding place or secret place; a kick in association football, from the corner of the field towards the goal of the opposing side. *v.* put into a position from which it is impossible to get out; buy up as much as possible of something so as to control its supply to the public and make greater profits.

cornet (cor-net) *n.* a musical instrument like a trumpet with three keys; a biscuit shaped like a cone which holds ice cream.

coronation (co-ro-na-tion) *n.* the ceremony of crowning a king, queen or emperor.

corporal (cor-po-ral) *n.* a soldier in the army, ranking below a sergeant.

corpse *n.* a dead body, usually of a man, woman or child.

correct (cor-rect) *a.* true, right; proper, showing good manners or taste. *v.* put or

make right. **correction** *n.* something done to put right a mistake.

correspond (cor-res-pond) *v.* be in agreement with, be right for; be alike, be equal to; communicate, exchange letters with. **correspondent** *n.* one with whom a person communicates; a person who is employed by a newspaper or magazine to send reports regularly.

corridor (cor-ri-dor) *n.* a passage connecting various parts of a building, compartments of a railway train etc.

cost *v.* be worth; end in losing something (a job, reputation etc.). *n.* the price paid for something; what has to be sacrificed to achieve or obtain something.

costume (cos-tume) *n.* dress or clothes made in a certain style; a woman's suit; a dress of a special kind (bathing, historical, highland etc.).

cottage (cot-tage) *n.* a small house, usually in the country.

cotton (cot-ton) *n.* a soft, white fluff which grows round the seeds of the cotton plant; the cloth made from it. *a.* made from cotton. **cotton wool** cotton from the plant cleaned and used for pads and bandages.

couch *n.* a piece of furniture for seating two or more people, usually with a back and armrests.

cough *v.* (pronounced *coff*) send out air from the lungs through the throat with a sudden sharp sound. *n.* an illness which makes one cough.

council (coun-cil) *n.* a group of persons chosen by others to make rules or carry out plans. **councillor** *n.* a member of a council, usually a town council.

count *v.* recite numbers one after the other; think, consider; rely, depend; be valuable. *n.* addition (of votes etc.).

counter *n.* the long table or bench in a shop behind which the assistant stands to serve the customer.

counterfeit (coun-ter-feit) *a.* made in imitation of something, not genuine. *v.* make counterfeit, especially of money.

country (coun-try) *n.* land lived in by a nation, the land in which one was born; any kind of land (desert, mountainous etc.); land with large open spaces mainly used for farming, and away from towns.

county (coun-ty) *n.* a division of Great Britain having its own name (Kent, Somerset etc.).

couple (cou-ple) *n.* two persons or things, generally associated; a husband and a wife; a pair of partners. *v.* fasten, join or connect two things.

courage (cour-age) *n.* bravery. **courageous** *a.* brave, fearless, possessing or showing courage.

courier (cou-ri-er) *n.* a messenger carrying important news; a person employed, sometimes by a travel agency, to arrange all the details of a journey.

course *n.* a movement forward; a ground for certain sports (golf, racing etc.); a series of talks, classes, lectures, medical treatments etc.; one of many parts of a meal. *v.* run (of blood, tears etc.). **of course** certainly, without doubt.

court *n.* the place where law cases are heard and decided; the place where a great ruler lives, as well as the people who live there or go there for special occasions; a space marked out for certain games (tennis, squash etc.); an open space wholly or partly enclosed by walls or buildings. *v.* try to gain the affection of a woman in the hope of marrying her; do things in order to bring about (popularity, danger etc.). **courtier** *n.* a person who attends the court of a king or sovereign.

court-martial *n.* a special court for trying members of the armed forces by military law.

courteous (cour-te-ous) *a.* polite, showing good manners. **courtesy** *n.* politeness.

cousin (cou-sin) *n.* the son or daughter of one's aunt or uncle.

cover (cov-er) *v.* place one thing over another; sprinkle with; protect; travel a distance; present a gun at, holding it in position; report (an event). *n.* the thing that covers; a wrapper; the thick outside leaf or binding of a book or magazine; a place giving shelter; a place laid for a meal; a position of a fielder in a cricket game.

cow *n.* a common dairy animal kept on a farm to supply milk; the female of the bull or ox; the female of the seal, elephant and some other animals. **cowboy** *n.* a man who rides a horse and looks after large herds of cattle in some parts of the United States. **cowshed** or **cowhouse** *n.* a building in which cows are kept and where they are milked.

coy *a.* shy or pretending to be shy.

crack *n.* a long thin line where something is split but not broken off; a sudden sharp sound. *a.* excellent, very clever. *v.* make something crack or break; become harsh (of a voice).

crackle (crack-le) *n.* a cracking sound. *v.* make a cracking sound. **crackling** *n.* the crisp skin of pork that has been well roasted.

cradle (cra-dle) *n.* a child's small bed or cot on rockers. *v.* hold in one's arms as in a cradle.

craft *n.* work requiring some skill or art; a boat or small ship; cheating, cunning, trickery. **craftsman** *n.* one who does skilled work. **crafty** *a.* full of craft or cunning.

cram *v.* fill a thing as full as possible; fill one's memory with facts for an examination.

cramp *n.* a sudden pain in a muscle, often caused by cold or overwork. *v.* prevent movement or hinder progress.

crane *n.* a large wading bird; a machine for lifting heavy weights. *v.* stretch (the neck).

crank *n.* a bar shaped like an L and used to set a machine in motion; a person with strange habits and ideas. *v.* make a machine go with a crank.

crash *v.* fall down making a loud noise; be

wrecked; meet disaster; break into a party uninvited. *n.* a fall, blow, explosion or collision; the noise made by a fall, collision etc. **crash-helmet** *n.* a helmet worn for protection in case of a crash. **crash-land** *v.* land when partly out of control (of aircraft).

crate *n.* a large container made of basketwork or wood. *v.* put in a crate.

crater (cra-ter) *n.* the mouth or hole at the top of a volcano; a hole in the ground made by the explosion of a shell or bomb.

crawl *v.* move slowly, pulling the body along the ground; move on hands and knees; go very slowly; be covered with (insects etc.). *n.* a stroke in swimming which gives great speed.

crayon (cray-on) *n.* a stick or pencil of coloured chalk, charcoal or wax. *v.* draw with crayons.

crazy (cra-zy) *a.* foolish, insane; excited about something; enthusiastic about something; unsafe (of buildings). **crazy paving** a pavement made up of many irregular pieces.

creak *n.* a harsh squeaking sound. *v.* make a harsh, squeaking sound.

cream *n.* the fatty part of milk which rises to the top and is made into butter; a substance or food resembling cream (ice cream, shaving cream etc.); the best part. *v.* take the cream off milk; take away the best part. *a.* yellowish white.

crease *n.* the line made on paper or cloth by pressing; the white line which marks the position batsmen and bowlers should take in cricket. *v.* mark or wrinkle by folding.

create (cre-ate) *v.* cause to be, produce. **creation** *n.* something created, the act of creating. **creature** *n.* an animal or human being.

credit (cred-it) *n.* approval, recognition; the amount of money one has in the bank; something added to; a good reputation or name. *v.* believe in or put trust in.

creek *n.* a narrow stream of water; an inlet on the seashore or a river bank.

creep *v.* move quietly with the body close

to the ground; grow along the ground or up walls (of plants); move slowly.

crest *n.* a small bunch or tuft of feathers on a bird's head; the top of a hill or of a large wave; a decoration, once resembling feathers on a hat or helmet or shown on a coat of arms.

crew *n.* a group of persons in charge of running a ship or aircraft; any group of people working together on a task, a gang.

crib *n.* a baby's bed often made of wickerwork and lined with a soft material such as muslin; a translation of a work to help students. *v.* copy the work of another person dishonestly.

cricket (crick-et) *n.* an outdoor game played in summer with eleven players on each side; a small brown insect like a grasshopper which jumps and makes a chirping sound by rubbing its legs together.

crime *n.* an evil act punishable by law. **criminal** *n.* a person who commits a crime.

crimson (crim-son) *a.* deep red.

crinkle (crin-kle) *n.* a tiny wrinkle in paper, cloth or other material. **crinkly** *a.* with crinkles; very curly (of hair).

cripple (crip-ple) *n.* a person unable to walk properly through injury or weakness. *v.* make weak, damage seriously, injure.

crisp *a.* hard and dry, easy to break; cold, frosty (of the weather). **potato crisps** *n.* thin slices of potato fried, dried and sold in packets.

critic (crit-ic) *n.* a person skilled in judging the merits of something artistic, and who writes reviews about new books, films, plays, music etc. **criticize** *v.* point out the good and bad parts of something, find fault with. **criticism** *n.* a statement criticizing something. **critical** *a.* finding fault; likely to find fault; dangerous, at a point where things might get better or much worse.

croak *n.* a low, hoarse sound. *v.* make this kind of sound; speak in a croaking voice.

crochet (cro-chet) *n.* (pronounced *cro-shay*) a kind of needlework done by making loops and pulling the thread through with a hook.

crocodile (croc-o-dile) *n.* a large reptile with four legs, a long body, powerful jaws and a tail which lives in tropical waters and marshes.

crook *n.* a stick or staff used by a shepherd; a bend or curve; a dishonest person. *v.* bend into the shape of a crook. **crooked** *a.* not straight, not honest.

crop *n.* the amount of corn, hay or fruit that has been produced; a pouch-like enlargement of a bird's throat in which its food is partly digested; a thick growth (hair etc.). *v.* cut off the ends or a part of something; cut short. **crop up** appear unexpectedly.

cross *n.* a mark made by drawing one line across the middle of another; a medal shaped like a cross; a stake or post with another fixed across it; a mixture of breeds (of animals etc.). *v.* go or place across; go against, oppose; pass in a journey or in the post. *a.* in a bad temper.

crouch *v.* sink down, bending the knees and body in fear, in order to hide or in readiness to spring.

crow *n.* a large black bird; a shrill cry. *v.* make a shrill cry; cry out happily; boast about, express triumph over.

crowd *n.* many people close together. *v.* come close together; put or push close together.

crown *n.* a head-dress worn by kings, queens and some nobles; the power of a king, queen or emperor; a wreath to put on the head; the top of the head or of a hat. *v.* put on a crown; reward.

crucify (cru-ci-fy) *v.* put to death by fastening a person to a cross by his hands and feet.

crude *a.* raw, just as it is taken from the earth or harvested; rough, not complete, not properly finished; uncivilized, not polite.

cruel (cru-el) *a.* taking pleasure in the pain and suffering of others; causing pain or suffering. **cruelty** *n.* treatment which is cruel.

cruise *v.* travel from place to place. *n.* a voyage, usually by boat. **cruiser** *n.* a fast warship, a fast boat.

crumb *n.* a small piece of bread, cake or biscuit; a small amount. **crumble** *v.* break or fall into very small pieces.

crumple *v.* crush into small creases; become full of folds and creases.

crunch *v.* crush noisily with the teeth; be crushed noisily. *n.* the act of crunching; the noise made by crunching.

crusade (cru-sade) *n.* one of the wars fought long ago by Christians against the Muslims or Mohammedans to win back the Holy Land; any struggle for a worthwhile cause or idea. **crusader** *n.* a person who went on a crusade or who takes up a cause.

crush *v.* squeeze out of shape or break; become full of creases, lose shape; defeat completely. *n.* a crowd of people or things pushed or pressed together.

crust *n.* the surface of a loaf or pie baked hard; a hard covering, a hard surface.

crutch *n.* a long stick or staff to support a lame person.

cry *v.* shout; weep, shed tears; call out loudly. *n.* a loud call; a fit of weeping.

crystal (crys-tal) *n.* a substance like glass which is clear and shines. *a.* made of clear shining glass.

cub *n.* a young lion, bear, fox, wolf etc.; a junior scout between the ages of 8 and 11.

cube *n.* a solid figure which has six square sides all of equal size; the produce of a number multiplied by itself twice ($3 \times 3 \times 3 = 27$, the cube).

cucumber (cu-cum-ber) *n.* a creeping

plant which bears a long green fruit; the fruit of this plant eaten as a vegetable and in salads.

cud *n.* that part of the food which the cow, ox and other animals which have two stomachs bring up from the first stomach to be chewed again.

cuddle (cud-dle) *v.* hug, hold lovingly in the arms; lie close and comfortably.

cue *n.* a long straight wooden rod, thin at one end and tipped with a leather pad, used by billiard players to strike the ball; the last part of one actor's speech which shows the next actor when to begin his own speech; a hint on how to behave.

cuff *n.* the band around the bottom of a sleeve of a skirt or coat, fastening round the wrist; a blow. *v.* give a blow with the hand. **cufflink** *n.* a link for fastening a cuff.

culprit (cul-prit) *n.* someone who has done wrong, a guilty person.

cultivate (cul-ti-vate) *v.* prepare land for sowing and help crops to grow; try to bring something into being (friendship etc.). **cultivation** *n.* the act of cultivating. **cultivator** *n.* a machine for cultivating the land.

cunning (cun-ning) *a.* sly, clever at deceiving others. *n.* slyness, craft, skill.

cup *n.* a small container with a handle, used with a saucer for drinking; what a cup holds, a cupful; a vessel of some metal (gold, silver etc.) given as a prize. *v.* shape like a cup (of the hands). **cupboard** *n.* a piece of furniture with shelves and drawers (so-called because it was once used for cups). **cup tie & cup final** stages in the competition in some sport in which a cup is won.

curator (cu-ra-tor) *n.* an official in charge of a museum or art gallery.

curb *v.* keep in check, control. *n.* a strap of leather which passes under the jaw of a horse, used as a means of control.

curd *n.* the thick, soft part of sour milk. **curdle** *v.* to become so sour that the curds become separated (of milk).

cure *v.* make well after an illness; treat substances like food, leather and tobacco so as to preserve them. *n.* something one does or takes to become well.

curfew (cur-few) *n.* the ringing of a bell in the evening telling people to cover their fires and put out lights; in modern times

under martial law, a signal to all people to remain indoors.

curious (cu-ri-ous) *a.* eager to learn, to find out; strange, hard to understand. **curiosity** *n.* a desire to learn; an unusual thing.

currant (cur-rant) *n.* a small, sweet dried grape grown mostly in California and Greece, often used in cakes.

current (cur-rent) *n.* water, air, gas etc. flowing in a stream; the flow of electricity through a wire. *a.* in use today. **current account** an account with a bank out of which money may be drawn without giving notice.

curse *n.* a wish that somebody be punished, injured or destroyed; a cause of damage. *v.* make a wish that somebody be punished etc.; use bad language.

curtain (cur-tain) *n.* a hanging piece of cloth in front of a window or door; a hanging screen of heavy cloth to hide a stage from the audience.

curve *n.* a line without angles that changes direction gradually. *v.* bend in a curve; make something do this.

cushion (cush-ion) *n.* a small bag filled with feathers, air, sponge, rubber or other soft material to sit or kneel on. *v.* supply with cushions.

custody (cus-to-dy) *n.* care; care of the police. **custodian** *n.* a caretaker; a person who has custody of a public building.

custom (cus-tom) *n.* a way of behaving which people consider and accept as correct; something done by a person or a group over a long period of time; always buying from the same shop, person or firm; taxes due to a government when foreign goods are brought into a country; the government department set up to collect these taxes. **customary** *a.* usually done. **customer** *n.* a person giving his custom to a firm or shop.

cut *v.* divide into pieces; make an opening with a sharp instrument; make shorter by cutting; purposely avoid speaking to a person. *n.* a shorter way to go. **cutlery** *n.* knives, forks, spoons, scissors etc. **cutlet** *n.* a piece of meat cut from a larger joint for cooking. **cutting** (cut-ting) *n.* something cut from a newspaper or magazine; part of a plant cut off and re-planted to take root; a way or road dug by removing part of a hill.

cyclone (cy-clone) *n.* a violent storm during which the wind blows round and round.

cygnet (cyg-net) *n.* a young swan.

cylinder (cyl-in-der) *n.* a solid or hollow object, circular at both ends. Hollow cylinders are used in engines to provide power.

cymbal (cym-bal) *n.* one of a pair of round brass plates used as a musical instrument.

D

dab *v.* touch, put on gently. *n.* a very small quantity dabbed on.

dagger (dag-ger) *n.* a short pointed knife with two edges used as a weapon, mainly for stabbing.

dairy (dai-ry) *n.* a place, room or building where milk and cream are made into butter and cheese; a shop or company which sells milk, butter, cheese etc

dam *n.* a barrier, wall or bank to stop water flowing or to make a pond, reservoir etc. *v.* stop water flowing with a dam or bank.

damage (dam-age) *n.* harm or injury that spoils something; money paid to a person or persons for injury done. *v.* injure or harm, resulting in spoiling something.

damp *a.* moderately wet, moist, not quite dry. *v.* make damp.

dance *v.* move with the feet or body, usually in time to music; move quickly; *n.* a number of movements done in time with music; a party mainly for dancing.

danger (dan-ger) *n.* a chance that harm or

injury will happen; a possible cause of harm or injury. **dangerous** *a.* liable or likely to cause danger.

dare *v.* have enough courage to do a thing; challenge a person to do something. **daredevil** *n.* a person who is bold and takes great risks. **daring** *a.* bold.

dark *a.* with very little or no light; having little colour; almost black; secret, hidden; sad, gloomy, without hope. *n.* absence of light. **darken** *v.* make or become dark. **darkness** *n.* being dark.

darn *v.* mend clothes by crossing and weaving threads to fill up a hole, usually by means of a needle. *n.* a place where a thing has been darned

dart *v.* move, spring, run suddenly and swiftly. *n.* a running or springing movement, a small weapon with a sharp point thrown at a board in the game of darts.

date *n.* the time (day, month, year or period) when something happened or existed; a meeting by arrangement; the small sweet fruit of the date palm which grows in North Africa and south-east Asia. *v.* go out with a person of the opposite sex **out of date** no longer used or usable. **up-to-date** the very latest in use.

daughter (daugh-ter) *n.* a female child of her parents. **daughter-in-law** *n.* the wife of one's son.

day *n.* the light period between the rising and setting of the sun; the period between midnight and the next midnight — twenty-four hours; a period of time. **daybreak** *n.* dawn. **daydreams** *n.* pleasant thoughts when the mind wanders. **daylight** *n.* the light of the sun. **daily** *a.* happening or coming every day.

daze *n.* not knowing what to do, not thinking clearly. *v.* make stupid or unable to think clearly.

dazzle (daz-zle) *v.* make it difficult for somebody to see, act or think clearly. *n.* brilliant lights which dazzle, especially from an approaching car.

dead *a.* no longer living; no longer in use. **deaden** *v.* make fainter or decrease. **deadly** *a.* tending to cause death. **deadlock** *n.* a point in time when two sides can no longer agree.

deaf *a.* unable to hear; unwilling to listen. **deaf-aid** *n.* a small appliance used to improve the hearing of deaf people. **deafen** *v.* make so much noise that others cannot hear. **deafness** *n.* being deaf.

deal *n.* a quantity, an amount; a bargain or agreement. *v.* give out (cards etc.); trade, do business; have to do with. **dealer** *n.* one who buys and sells.

dear *a.* loved; high in price, charging high prices; a word used at the beginning of a letter; a word used to show surprise and sometimes annoyance (Oh dear!). **dearly** *adv.* greatly, at great cost.

death *n.* the end of life. **deathbed** *n.* the bed on which one dies. **deathtrap** *n.* a situation which may cause death.

debate (de-bate) *n.* a discussion, especially at a meeting of people. *v.* discuss or argue about something.

decay (de-cay) *v.* go bad. *n.* rotting, going bad.

deceive (de-ceive) *v.* mislead, make a person believe something which is not true. **deceit** *n.* deceiving. **deceitful** *a.* full of deceit.

decent (de-cent) *a.* respectable; in good taste; good, satisfactory; kind, likeable. **decency** *n.* good manners; good treatment of others.

decide (de-cide) *v.* settle a question; judge in a dispute; make up one's mind what to do. **decision** *n.* the act or result of deciding.

decimal (dec-i-mal) *a.* having to do with tens or tenth parts. **decimal fractions** parts of whole numbers written in this way after the decimal point. **decimal system** money or weights reckoned in tens. **decimalization** *n.* the changing of money, weights, measurements etc. into the decimal system.

declare (de-clare) *v.* make known to all; make a statement about goods brought into the country, one's income etc.; close an innings in cricket before all the side has batted. **declaration** *n.* something declared.

decline (de-cline) *v.* refuse, say no to; fall in strength or amount. *n.* a falling in strength, amount etc.

decorate (dec-o-rate) *v.* make more gay, pretty or beautiful; paint (a building), put paper etc. on the inside walls; reward a person with a medal. **decoration** *n.* the painting of a building; the medal given to a person. **decorator** *n.* a person who decorates houses and other buildings especially their interiors, for a living.

decrease (de-crease) *v.* become less or smaller. *n.* the amount by which something decreases.

dedicate (ded-i-cate) *v.* give up time or money to some special purpose; print in a book that it has been written in honour of a person the author loves or respects; declare that a building or monument is for a certain purpose. **dedication** *n.* words used in dedicating a book; the act of dedicating a building.

deep *a.* going far down; low in sound; dark in colour; coming from far down. **deep-freeze** *n.* a refrigerator which keeps food very cold to preserve it for long periods.

defeat (de-feat) *v.* overcome in contest or battle. *n.* the act of defeating or being defeated.

defect (dé-fect) *n.* fault, want, lack, imperfection. (de-féct) *v.* desert one side in a quarrel or conflict and join the other. **defective** *a.* faulty, having defects.

defend (de-fend) *v.* fight for, work for the defence of; speak or write in support of. **defendant** *n.* the person or persons against whom a charge is brought in a court of law.

define (de-fine) *v.* explain what something means; show or state very clearly. **definite** *a.* clear, easy to see, exact. **definition** *n.* the act of explaining, explanation, the amount of detail (in a picture or photograph).

defy (de-fy) *v.* challenge the power of, resist; refuse to obey; be too difficult. **defiance** *n.* refusal to obey, resistance. **defiant** *a.* refusing to obey.

degree (de-gree) *n.* one 360th part of a complete turn; one unit in measuring temperature; a small amount, a small space of time; a title given after a university course.

dejected (de-ject-ed) *a.* sad, unhappy. **dejection** *n.* a state of sadness.

deliberate (de-lib-er-ate) *a.* done on purpose; slow, careful. *v.* think about, talk about. **deliberation** *n.* careful thought and discussion.

delicate (del-i-cate) *a.* soft, tender; fine, cleverly made; easily made ill or broken; easily able to detect changes (of a scientific instrument etc.). **delicacy** *n.* any kind of exotic, expensive or delicious food. **delicatessen** *n.* a shop selling exotic foods, chiefly foreign; the foods sold.

delicious (de-li-cious) *a.* pleasing and delightful in every way.

delight (de-light) *n.* great pleasure, enjoyment. *v.* give great pleasure, take pleasure. **delightful** *a.* giving pleasure.

delinquent (de-lin-quent) *a.* doing wrong *n.* a person who does wrong. **delinquency** *n.* wrongdoing.

demand (de-mand) *v.* ask for; need; a wish to have or get. *n.* something demanded or asked.

democracy (de-moc-ra-cy) *n.* a government in which all adult citizens take part, usually by electing members to their parliaments; a country which has this kind of government. **democrat** *n.* a person who believes in democracy as the best form of government. **democratic** *a.* having to do with democracy.

demolish (de-mol-ish) *v.* pull down, destroy. **demolition** *n.* pulling down, destroying.

demonstrate (dem-on-strate) *v.* show to others; proclaim opinions in public. **demonstration** *n.* any kind of showing; a procession in the streets in favour of some cause.

dense *a.* close together, not easily seen through; stupid, not clever. **density** *n.*

being dense (fog, trees etc.).

dentist (dent-ist) *n.* a person who takes out, fills and cares for people's teeth. **dental** *a.* having to do with teeth. **dentifrice** *n.* tooth-powder or toothpaste. **denture** *n.* a plate of artificial teeth which fits on to the gums.

deny (de-ny) *v.* declare that something is not true; say 'no' to a request. **denial** *n.* the act of denying.

deodorant (de-o-do-rant) *n.* a substance that destroys odours, often sprayed in a room or on the body.

depart (de-part) *v.* go away, leave. **departure** *n.* the act of going away.

department (de-part-ment) *n.* a division of an organization, a government, a business or a country.

depend (de-pend) *v.* need; trust; rely. **dependent** *a.* depending on. **dependant** *n.* someone who depends on another for support or favour.

deport (de-port) *v.* send a person by force out of a country; behave in a certain way. **deportation** *n.* the sending of undesirable persons and others out of a country. **deportment** *n.* behaviour, the way a person acts, stands, walks etc.

deposit (de-pos-it) *v.* put, lay, place; store to keep safe. *n.* money paid in part payment for an article one is buying; matter, earth, precious stones etc. laid down by floods and other natural happenings.

depress (de-press) *v.* push or pull down; make sad.

depression (de-pres-sion) *n.* sadness, being depressed; a hollow or a place where a surface has sunk; a lessening of air pressure in the atmosphere which usually brings clouds and rain.

deprive (de-prive) *v.* take away from

somebody. **deprivation** *n.* depriving or being deprived.

depth *n.* distance from top to bottom; the deepest, worst, lowest or most distant. **depth-charge** *n.* a bomb thrown into the sea to be used against enemy submarines.

deputy (de-pu-ty) *n.* a person chosen to act for or represent somebody else. **deputize** *v.* act as a deputy.

descend (de-scend) *v.* go or come down; be the children, grand-children etc. of; attack (with on). **descendant** *n.* one who is descended from. **descent** *n.* going down, being handed down, attack.

describe (de-scribe) *v.* say what something or somebody is like; mark or draw (in geometry). **description** *n.* a statement about what somebody or something is like.

desert (de-sért) *v.* go, run away from; leave without money or help. **deserter** *n.* one who has deserted from the army, navy, air force etc. **desertion** *n.* leaving, abandoning.

desert (dés-ert) *n.* a large area of land without water or trees, with very few inhabitants.

deserve (de-serve) *v.* merit something because of conduct, actions etc.

design (de-sign) *n.* drawing, plan or pattern. *v.* make designs for.

desire (de-sire) *n.* a great longing for. *v.* long greatly for. **desirable** *a.* to be desired. **desirous** *adv.* wishing to be or have.

despair (des-pair) *n.* having lost all hope. *v.* lose or give up all hope. **desperate** *a.* in despair; ready to do anything; dangerous.

despise (des-pise) *v.* think badly of; feel contempt for.

destine (des-tine) *v.* be set apart for some work. **destination** *n.* the place to which somebody is going. **destiny** *n.* a power which is believed to decide a person's future.

destroy (des-troy) *v.* ruin, bring to nothing, break to pieces. **destruction** *n.* de-

stroying, the result of destroying or being destroyed. **destructive** *a.* causing or liable to cause destruction; fond of destroying.

detail (de-tail) *n.* a small part, a small fact *v.* give a special task to.

detain (de-tain) *v.* keep back, make to wait. **detention** *n.* being detained; being kept late at school.

detect (de-tect) *v.* find something out. **detection** *n.* discovery. **detective** *n.* a person whose work is to find and arrest criminals.

deter (de-ter) *v.* hinder or discourage somebody from performing an action. **deterrent** *n.* something which may deter.

detergent (de-ter-gent) *n.* a substance which cleans and which removes dirt.

determine (de-ter-mine) *v.* decide on; be the fact which decides. **determination** *n.* the power to decide and carry out.

detonate (de-to-nate) *v.* explode with a great noise. **detonator** *n.* the part of a bomb which causes it to explode.

develop (de-vel-op) *v.* grow or cause to grow; treat a photographic film with chemicals so that a picture can be made from it.

device (de-vice) *n.* something made to carry out a special purpose; a plan or scheme.

devil (de-vil) *n.* an evil spirit which does wicked things; Satan, the chief of all evil spirits (in the Bible); a cruel, wicked person; a poor unfortunate person.

devote (de-vote) *v.* give up one's time, energy etc. to one thing; be mainly concerned with. **devoted** *a.* loving, loyal. **devotion** *n.* being devoted to, having great love for.

devour (de-vour) *v.* eat greedily; read, look at, hear, listen with great attention; destroy.

dew *n.* the drops of water which form on

grass in the evening and on chilly mornings.

diagram (di-a-gram) *n.* a drawing or plan which explains how a building, a piece of machinery etc. is to be built or made.

dial (di-al) *n.* a flat surface on which numbers or letters and sometimes pointers show the time, weight, temperature, gas or electricity consumed.

dialect (di-a-lect) *n.* a way of speaking used in one part of a country.

diamond (di-a-mond) *n.* a precious stone used in jewellery, which sparkles brightly; one of the four suits in a pack of cards. **diamond wedding** the 60th anniversary of a wedding. **rough diamond** a kind-hearted person with rough manners.

diary (di-a-ry) *n.* a written record of what a person does or thinks each day. **diarist** *n.* a person who keeps a diary.

dictate (dic-tate) *v.* say words aloud so that another person may write them down; give orders to others. **dictation** *n.* saying words aloud, to be written down or to be recorded by a machine. **dictator** *n.* a powerful ruler who must be obeyed. **dictaphone** *n.* a machine used in an office which records words for a typist to copy later.

dictionary (dic-tion-a-ry) *n.* a book which gives the meanings of words in one language, or translations of words from one language into another. **diction** *n.* the way a person speaks.

die *v.* cease to live, come to the end of life. *n.* a block of metal with a design on it for making coins, medals, and stamping designs on paper and other materials.

diet (di-et) *n.* the food we usually eat; the food one may be limited to eating.

differ (dif-fer) *v.* be unlike in any way. **difference** *n.* the way in which people or things differ from each other. **different** *a.* differing one from another.

difficult (dif-fi-cult) *a.* hard, not easy; hard to please. **difficulty** *n.* something difficult.

digest (di-gest) *v.* change or be changed inside the body (of food); take into the mind so that it can be remembered and used later. **digestion** *n.* the power or act of digesting.

diligent (dil-i-gent) *a.* taking care and making efforts in what one does. **diligence** *n.* effort, continued steady work.

diligently *adv.* in a diligent manner.

dim *a.* faint, weak, not bright, not easy to see; not able to see clearly. *v.* make or grow dim.

dimension (di-men-sion) *n.* measurement, length, width, depth, height or area. **three dimensional** (of a picture) giving the appearance of depth as well as height and breadth, like a view of the actual thing.

diminish (di-min-ish) *v.* become smaller or less; make smaller or less.

dine *v.* have dinner. **dining-room** *n.* the room in which one dines.

dinghy (din-ghy) *n.* a small boat; a boat made of rubber or some material that can be expanded and filled with air used by people in an aircraft when forced down over water.

dingy (din-gy) *a.* looking dirty, dark.

dinner (din-ner) *n.* the main or chief meal of the day taken either at noon or in the evening; a party at which people dine, a banquet. **dinner-jacket** *n.* a black jacket worn in the evening by men for dinners and other occasions. **dinner-service** *n.* set of plates, dishes etc. for dinner.

diocese (di-o-cese) *n.* the district under the care of a bishop.

dip *v.* put into and take out again; go or bring down (headlights of a car). *n.* a quick bathe.

diphtheria (diph-the-ri-a) *n.* a serious disease of the throat. Diphtheria is infectious and when it breaks out the authorities should be notified.

direct (di-rect) *a.* straight, not turning to one side or the other. *v.* show the way; address a letter or parcel; order, manage or control; turn (one's attention etc.). **direction** *n.* the way in which a person or thing is going; instructions for doing, using etc.; management, control of an organization or of people. **directly** *adv.* quickly, straight. **director** *n.* a person who directs or manages the affairs of a business or other organization.

disable (dis-a-ble) *v.* injure, make unable to do things. **disabled** *n.* persons crippled in war, through accident, illness etc. in such a way that they are unable to do certain things.

disagree (dis-a-gree) *v.* fail to agree, have different opinions; not be good for. **disagreeable** *a.* not pleasant.

disappear (dis-ap-pear) *v.* go away, go out of sight. **disappearance** *n.* vanishing, going out of sight; loss of a thing or a person.

disappoint (dis-ap-point) *v.* fail to do what has been promised or what one wishes. **disappointment** *n.* being disappointed; something that disappoints.

disarm (dis-arm) *v.* take weapons away; cut down the size of armies, navies and air forces. **disarmament** *n.* the act of disarming, being disarmed.

disaster (dis-as-ter) *n.* any sudden great misfortune that happens to a person or a number of people (flood, earthquake etc.); loss of money or fortune. **disastrous** *a.* causing disaster.

discharge (dis-charge) *v.* give out, send out; fire (a weapon); dismiss, send away from work; do a duty, pay a debt. *n.* carrying out (duties etc.); the act of giving out, firing or dismissing.

disciple (dis-ci-ple) *n.* one of the twelve men who first personally followed Jesus Christ; a person who follows the teachings of another.

discipline (dis-cip-line) *n.* training of the mind, body and the character to fit one for life; control (of children, animals etc.).

discontent (dis-con-tent) *n.* a state of unhappiness about something. **discontented** *a.* not satisfied, unhappy.

discontinue (dis-con-tin-ue) *v.* stop, put an end to; come to an end.

discourage (dis-cour-age) *v.* lose or take away hope or confidence. **discourage-**ment *n.* loss of hope, something that discourages.

discover (dis-cov-er) *v.* find out, obtain knowledge of. **discovery** *n.* the act of discovering; something that is discovered.

discus (dis-cus) *n.* a round plate of metal or stone thrown in athletic contests in ancient Greece and Rome, also an event in the Olympic Games.

discuss (dis-cuss) *v.* talk about, argue about, examine by talking. **discussion** *n.* an argument, talk, examination by discussing.

disease (dis-ease) *n.* any illness of human beings, animals or plants. **diseased** *a.* suffering from disease.

disgrace (dis-grace) *n.* shame, loss of the respect of others. *v.* bring shame upon. **disgraceful** *a.* bringing or causing disgrace.

disguise (dis-guise) *v.* do something to change the appearance, sound etc.; mislead or conceal who or what one is. *n.* things done and used to change the appearance of a thing or person.

disgust (dis-gust) *n.* a feeling of strong dislike or anger. **disgusting** *a.* causing dislike or disgust.

dish *n.* a shallow container for holding food; food brought in a dish; something very good to eat. **dishes** *n.* all the crockery. **dish up** put into a dish to serve for a meal.

dishonest (dis-hon-est) *a.* not honest, prepared to cheat others. **dishonesty** *n.* not being honest; a dishonest act.

disinfect (dis-in-fect) *v.* keep free from germs so that disease does not spread. **disinfectant** *n.* a substance that kills germs.

dismal (dis-mal) *a.* sad, dark, gloomy; miserable (of a place or person).

dismiss (dis-miss) *v.* send away; discharge from employment; put a batsman out (of cricket). **dismissal** *n.* the act of dismissing.

disobey (dis-o-bey) *v.* refuse to do what one is ordered to do. **disobedience** *n.* refusal to obey. **disobedient** *a.* refusing to obey.

disorder (dis-or-der) *n.* absence of order, confusion; disturbance (among crowds); an illness. **disorderly** *a.* with no order.

display (dis-play) *v.* show; spread out so that everybody can see. *n.* a show or exhibition.

dispose (dis-pose) *v.* get rid of; set out or place in order. **disposal** *n.* getting rid of. **be disposed** be willing to do something.

dispute (dis-pute) *v.* challenge; argue, debate, quarrel about something; resist. *n.* an argument, a debate.

disqualify (dis-qua-li-fy) *v.* deprive of the right or ability to do something. **disqualification** *n.* the act of disqualifying or being disqualified.

dissolve (dis-solve) *v.* melt into something and become a part of it, as sugar in tea.; put a solid into a liquid so that it dissolves.

distance (dis-tance) *n.* the amount of space between two points; a place farther away or a long way off. **distant** *a.* far away in space, time or relationship.

distinct (dis-tinct) *a.* plain, clear, easily seen or heard; different, not like, apart from. **distinction** *n.* difference from others; a mark of honour which makes a person different from others.

distinguish (dis-tin-guish) *v.* recognize the difference between; make oneself famous or well known. **distinguished** *a.* famous.

distract (dis-tract) *v.* draw the attention away from. **distracted** *a.* confused, anxious about things. **distraction** *n.* anxiety amounting almost to madness.

distress (dis-tress) *n.* pain, sorrow, suffering; danger, difficulty. *v.* cause distress.

distribute (dis-trib-ute) *v.* hand out, give out, send out; spread out. **distribution** *n.* the act or the manner of giving out or distributing.

district (dis-trict) *n.* a part of a country or town. *a.* having to do with a district (district nurse, organizer etc.).

distrust (dis-trust) *v.* doubt, have no trust in. *n.* want of trust, suspicion of. **distrustful** *a.* unwilling to trust.

disturb (dis-turb) *v.* break the quiet or peace; cause to worry; put out of the right order. **disturbance** *n.* something that disturbs, disorder.

ditch *n.* a long, narrow channel in the ground, often between fields or along the side of a road.

divide (di-vide) *v.* separate or be separated into parts; cause to disagree. **division** *n.* the act of dividing; a process in arithmetic. **divisible** *a.* something that can be exactly divided.

divine (di-vine) *a.* from God, like God or like a god; very good, excellent. *v.* discover, guess, learn about hidden things. **diviner** *n.* a person who can discover where water, precious metals etc. are to be found.

divorce (di-vorce) *v.* end a marriage by law. *n.* the ending of a marriage in this way.

dizzy *a.* having a feeling of giddiness, as if unable to keep one's balance. **dizziness** *n.* being dizzy.

do *v.* perform an action; make; work at; carry out; be good, satisfactory; be suitable; cook until ready for a meal; a verb used with other verbs as 'Do you like chocolate? I once did but I don't like it now.'

dock *n.* a platform or platforms built on a river or on the seashore where ships may be loaded, unloaded or repaired; that part of a court of law where an accused person stands to be tried. *v.* (of a ship) go, be brought or taken into a dock.

dockyard *n.* an enclosed place where there are many docks. **dry dock** a dock from which water may be pumped out.

doctor (doc-tor) *n.* a person who has received the highest degree of a university; a person who has been trained in medicine and treats people who are ill. *v.* treat for illness; alter something dishonestly.

document (doc-u-ment) *n.* a written or printed paper giving evidence or proof. **documentary** *n.* a film or television programme showing some special aspect of life.

dog *n.* an animal kept by man as a pet or to guard the house, work with the police, with shepherds etc. **dog-fight** *n.* a battle in which a number of aircraft take part. **dog-tired** *a.* tired out, exhausted.

doll *n.* a child's toy made in the likeness of a baby or other human being.

dollar (dol-lar) *n.* a unit of money used in the United States of America, Canada, Australia, Mexico and other countries.

dome *n.* a rounded roof with a circular base such as we see on St Paul's Cathedral.

domestic (do-mes-tic) *a.* having to do with the home and the family; having to do with one's own country; kept by man (of animals). **domesticate** *v.* tame (animals).

dominate (dom-i-nate) *v.* have control over, have authority over; overlook (of a high place). **domination** *n.* dominating, or being dominated.

donkey (don-key) *n.* an ass, an animal with long ears and coarse hair.

doom *n.* fate or destiny; death; ruin or some future evil. *v.* condemn (to death,

disappointment etc.). **doomsday** *n.* the last day of the world's existence.

door *n.* a moveable barrier of wood or some other material designed to close up an entrance; a house in a street or row (next door etc.). **doorway** *n.* the opening leading into a room or house.

dope *n.* a thick liquid used as varnish; a harmful drug. *v.* give a drug to make sleepy, unconscious or more wideawake. **dopey** *a.* sleepy, as though drugged; stupid (slang).

dormitory (dor-mi-to-ry) *n.* a room for sleeping, usually with many beds, most commonly found in a school or similar institution.

dose *n.* a quantity of medicine to be taken at one time. *v.* give a dose to oneself or another person.

dot *n.* a small round mark made with a pencil or pen; mark with a dot. **dotted** *a.* sprinkled as if with dots. **dotted line** a line of dots.

double (dou-ble) *a.* twice as much in weight, strength, quality, goodness, cost etc. *v.* make or become double; fold in two.

doubt *v.* be uncertain in opinion; distrust. **doubtful** *a.* feeling or causing doubt. **doubtless** *a.* without doubt.

dough *n.* (pronounced *doe*) flour or meal mixed with water and made into paste for making bread, cake, pastry etc. **doughnut** *n.* a small cake of dough fried in deep fat, shaped like a ring or ball.

dove *n.* a bird of the pigeon family; a symbol of peace. **dovetail** *n.* a joint for two pieces of wood, the parts of which are fitted together so as to lock.

down *adv.* from higher to lower; from an earlier to a later time. *v.* bring, put, knock down. *n.* the soft feathers of young birds, the soft hair on some plants or seeds, or other fine, soft hair. **downcast** *a.* sad, depressed. **downfall** *n.* a heavy fall of rain, a fall from riches or power. **downward** *a.* moving, pointing etc. to what is lower. **downwards** *adv.* towards what is lower.

doze *v.* sleep lightly. *n.* a short, light sleep

dozen (doz-en) *n.* twelve.

draft *n.* plan, sketch or outline; a small number of people taken from a larger body for some special work (especially members of the forces). *v.* make a plan, choose men for a draft.

drain *n.* a ditch or pipe for carrying away water or waste liquids; something that uses up strength, time, money etc. *v.* make drier by allowing water or other liquids to flow away through a drain; use up strength, time, money etc.

drama (dra-ma) *n.* a play for a theatre, film or television; plays in general, their construction and writing. **dramatic** *a.* having to do with drama; exciting such as one gets in drama. **dramatize** *v.* make a play of.

drape *v.* hang cloth, curtains etc. in folds round or over something. **draper** *n.* a person who sells cloth, linen and other materials for curtains, table-cloths or clothing. **drapery** *n.* goods sold by a draper.

draught *n.* (pronounced *draft*) a strong current of air in an enclosed space; the depth of water needed to float a ship; the amount one can drink at one time. **draughty** *a.* causing draughts. **draughts** *n.* a game for two players, played with round pieces on a board of black and white squares.

dread *n.* fear of something; great anxiety. *v.* fear greatly. **dreadful** *a.* causing dread, unpleasant.

dream *n.* the things we seem to see and hear when we are asleep. *v.* have dreams, see or hear something in a dream.

dreamy (of a person) not keeping one's thoughts on one's work.

dreary (drear-y) *a.* dull, dark, gloomy; uninteresting; long (of speeches etc.).

dredge *n.* a machine for making channels and ditches deeper. *v.* clear a lake channel or stream with such a machine. **dredger** *n.* a boat which carries a dredge.

drench *v.* wet something all over, soak through and through.

drift *v.* be carried along by the wind, the breeze or running water. *n.* something caused by drifting (snowdrift etc.).

drill *n.* a tool or machine for making holes; training or exercise, often done by repeating things again and again. *v.* make holes with a drill; train or be trained to do something.

drip *v.* fall or let fall in drops. **dripping** *a.* very wet, wet through. *n.* fat melted out of meat which has been roasted.

drive *v.* make an animal or a person move by force; operate a machine, an engine, bus or car; direct or guide a plough or cart; travel in a vehicle; carry in a vehicle; move with force; compel, force to do something or into a certain position or state. *n.* a journey in a vehicle; a private road; the hitting of a ball very swiftly in golf, cricket, tennis etc. **driver** *n.* a person who drives.

droop *v.* bend over because of tiredness or want.

drop *n.* a very small quantity of a liquid that forms a tiny round ball as it falls; something shaped like a drop, movement from higher to lower. *v.* fall or make fall; come to an end; make something come to an end.

drown *v.* die or cause to die in water through not being able to breathe; make a noise loud enough to prevent other sounds from being heard.

drug *n.* a substance used to prevent or cure a disease; a substance that causes sleep or any kind of intoxication. *v.* give drugs to. **druggist** *n.* a chemist, a person who sells drugs.

drunk *v.* past tense of the word drink; *a.* intoxicated through drinking liquids containing alcohol. *n.* a person who is drunk. **drunkard** *n.* a person who is often drunk.

due *a.* to be paid, to come; right, fair. *n.* money to be paid for membership of an organization. **due to** caused by.

duel (du-el) *n.* a fight between two persons with weapons, fought under agreed rules in the presence of other persons called seconds.

duet (du-et) *n.* a piece of music specially written for two people to sing or play.

dull *a.* not bright or clear; slow to learn; not interesting. *v.* make or become dull.

dumb *a.* unable to speak; silent for a short time. **dumb-bell** *n.* a short bar which has weights at both ends used for exercising the muscles.

dunce *n.* someone who learns very slowly; a stupid person.

dungeon (dun-geon) *n.* a dark cell or room under the ground in which prisoners used to be kept.

duplicate (du-pli-cate) *v.* make an exact copy of. *n.* one thing which is exactly like another. **duplicator** *n.* a machine which produces exact copies of something written or printed.

durable (du-ra-ble) *a.* lasting a long time. **duration** *n.* the time during which something exists.

dusk *n.* the short time towards the end of daylight when the sky is becoming dark. **dusky** *a.* dark-coloured, dim.

duty (du-ty) *n.* something one must do; a tax on things exported out of or imported into a country. **dutiful** *a.* doing one's duty well.

dwarf *n.* a person, animal or plant much smaller than others of the same kind. *v.* prevent from growing; make to appear small when put against other objects.

dye *v.* make a different colour, usually by dipping in coloured liquid. *n.* liquid or powder used for dyeing.

dynamite (dy-na-mite) *n.* a substance specially made to explode with great force. *v.* blow up with dynamite.

E

eager (ea-ger) *a.* keen, wanting to do, be or have. **eagerly** *adv.* in an eager manner. **eagerness** *n.* very great desire.

ear *n.* an organ of the body by which sounds are heard; power to hear and distinguish between sounds; the part of a grain plant on which the seeds appear. **earphone** *n.* that part of a receiver placed over the ear by which one can hear sounds by telephone and radio.

early (ear-ly) *a.* near to the beginning of a period of time; before the usual time.

earn *v.* gain or deserve; receive something in return for work. **earnings** *n.* what one receives in return for work.

earnest (ear-nest) *a.* serious, determined to do or be. **earnestly** *adv.* in an earnest manner. **in earnest** in a serious manner.

earth *n.* the planet on which we live; the ground on which we stand; soil, dirt. **earthen** *a.* made of baked earth. **earthenware** *n.* jugs, jars and other pots made from baked earth. **earthworm** *n.* a worm that lives in the soil. **earthquake** *n.* a sudden shaking of the earth's surface causing buildings to fall or be damaged.

east *n.* the direction in which the sun rises; lands lying in that direction. *a.* coming from the east. **easterly** *a.* from the east. **eastern** *a.* in the part lying in the east.

eccentric (ec-cen-tric) *a.* behaving in a strange unusual manner; not having the same centre.

echo (ech-o) *n.* sound which comes back, reflected from a wall, a rock etc. *v.* send back an echo; repeat the words of another.

eclipse (e-clipse) *n.* the hiding of sunlight from the earth when the moon passes in front of the sun (a solar eclipse); the complete or partial disappearance of the moon when the earth passes between it and the sun (a lunar eclipse). *v.* make something seem dull, small or unimportant when compared with something else.

ecology (e-col-o-gy) *n.* that part of science which deals with the habits of living beings and the effect their surroundings have on them.

economy (e-con-o-my)· *n.* saving, not wasting things, making the best use of what one has; the management of the finances of a community or country. **economics** *n.* the study of how goods and materials are made and distributed to all parts of the world. **economize** *v.* make the best use of what one has.

edit (ed-it) *v.* prepare a book, newspaper or film for publication or presentation. **edition** *n.* the form in which a book or newspaper is published. **editor** *n.* a person who does this or who is in charge of this work.

educate (ed-u-cate) *v.* teach, train. **education** *n.* instruction, training.

effect (ef-fect) *n.* result; how something is seen, felt or heard. *v.* cause. **effective** *a.* having an effect.

efficient (ef-fi-cient) *a.* able to do things well. **efficiency** *n.* the state of being efficient.

effort (ef-fort) *n.* the use of physical or mental power; trying hard. **effortless** *a.* making no effort, without effort.

elaborate (e-lab-o-rate) *a.* worked or done very carefully. *v.* describe in great detail.

elbow (el-bow) *n.* the joint where the upper and lower parts of the arm meet; that part of a sleeve which covers the elbow; a joint which brings two pipes together at an angle. *v.* force one's way with the elbows. **elbow-room** *n.* room to move freely.

elder (el-der) *a.* older (of two people). *n.* an officer in some Christian churches. **elders** *n.* people who are older. **elderly** *a.* becoming old. **eldest** *a.* oldest (of three or more people).

elect (e-lect) *v.* choose; decide. **election** *n.* choosing, being elected. **elector** *n.* one who elects.

electric (e-lec-tric) *a.* worked by or having to do with electricity. **electrical** *a.*

having to do with electricity. **electrician** *n.* a person who works with electrical apparatus. **electricity** *n.* a force that gives light, heat and power and which can be sent or distributed through wires. **electrify** *v.* put electricity into. **electrocute** *v.* kill by means of electricity.

elegant (el-e-gant) *a.* handsome, graceful, well-dressed.

element (el-e-ment) *n.* one of the simplest substances of which matter is composed and which cannot be split into others; one of the parts of the universe usually earth, water, air and fire; the simplest part of anything; the surroundings, occupation or hobby which make one feel happy. **elementary** *a.* simple, in its very simplest form.

elephant (el-e-phant) *n.* the largest four-footed animal now living, with thick skin, a trunk and ivory tusks.

elevate (el-e-vate) *v.* lift up, raise, improve. **elevation** *n.* height, altitude.

elevator *n.* a machine that lifts things on a belt with buckets; a building for lifting and storing grain.

eliminate (e-lim-in-ate) *v.* get rid of, take or put away.

ellipse (el-lipse) *n.* an oval. **elliptic** *a.* oval-shaped.

elocution (el-o-cu-tion) *n.* good speech, especially in public.

eloquence (el-o-quence) *n.* clever use of language to appeal to an audience.

embark (em-bark) *v.* go on board ship, take people or things on board; start something new. **embarkation** *n.* embarking or being embarked.

embarrass (em-bar-rass) *v.* make anxious, shy or uncomfortable. **embarrassment** *n.* something which makes uncomfortable.

emblem (em-blem) *n.* a sign; something drawn, written or made which represents something else (the rose for England, the thistle for Scotland etc.).

embroider (em-broi-der) *v.* decorate cloth with stitches of various colours and designs. **embroidery** *n.* stitching in colours and designs.

emerge (e-merge) *v.* come out; become known. **emergency** *n.* a sudden happening which makes it necessary to act quickly.

emigrate (e-mi-grate) *v.* leave one's own country to live in another. **emigrant** *n.* a person who emigrates.

eminent (em-i-nent) *a.* famous, well-known; among the very best. **eminence** *n.* being among the best; a high place.

emotion (e-mo-tion) *n.* strong feeling, excitement of mind. **emotional** *a.* feeling strong emotion, causing deep emotion in others.

emperor (em-per-or) *n.* the ruler of a number of countries. **empire** *n.* all the countries under the rule of one person or one country.

emphasis (em-pha-sis) *n.* stress laid on a word or anything else of importance. **emphasize** *v.* lay stress on.

employ (em-ploy) *v.* give work to. **employer** *n.* one who gives work. **employment** *n.* work. **employment exchange** an office of the government which helps people to find employment.

empty (emp-ty) *a.* having nothing inside.

enchant (en-chant) *v.* fill with joy and pleasure; use magic on (in fairy tales). **enchanting** *a.* magical; delightful.

enclose (en-close) *v.* shut in on all sides; put in a parcel or envelope. **enclosure** something (land, a letter etc.) enclosed.

encourage (en-cour-age) *v.* help, inspire, give courage to. **encouragement** *n.* help, words or actions which help.

encyclopaedia (en-cy-clo-pae-dia) *n.* a book or a number of books which give information about all branches of knowledge.

end *n.* the last part; what remains; the finish. *v.* come to an end. **ending** *n.* the finish (of a word, story, life etc.).

endeavour *n.* effort, attempt. *v.* try, attempt to do something.

enemy (en-e-my) *n.* a person who tries to harm another; one army which is fighting another; anything which may harm.

energy (en-er-gy) *n.* power to do things; liveliness. **energetic** *a.* full of energy.

engage (en-gage) *v.* employ for a short time; promise or agree to marry; be busy. **engagement** *n.* promise, agreement to marry; arrangement to be at a place or to meet somebody. **engagement ring** a ring worn by those who are engaged to be married.

engine (en-gine) *n.* a machine that produces power for driving other machinery. **engineer** *n.* a person who designs, repairs or looks after engines, builds bridges, railways or docks etc.

enjoy (en-joy) *v.* get pleasure from, like, have as an advantage or benefit. **enjoyable** *a.* giving pleasure or happiness. **enjoyment** *n.* pleasure, happiness.

enlighten (en-light-en) *v.* give information or knowledge. **enlightenment** *n.* knowledge.

enlist *v.* join or be taken into, especially into one of the armed forces; obtain (sympathy, help etc.).

enormous (e-nor-mous) *a.* huge, large, very great.

enough (e-nough) *a.* as large, as many or

as much as is needed or wanted.

enquire (en-quire) v. ask. **enquiry** n. question; investigation into something that has happened.

entangle (en-tan-gle) v. catch by a snare or among obstacles; get into difficulties. **entanglement** n. the act of entangling; a snare.

enter (en-ter) v. come or go into; become a member of; take part in (conversation etc.); write (names, figures etc.). **entrance** n. door or gate for going in; the act of going in. **entry** n. coming or going in; an item put into a book or on a list.

enterprise (en-ter-prise) n. something done which needs special courage or boldness; the courage required to do it. **enterprising** a. having the necessary courage or boldness; adventurous.

entertain v. receive as guests; interest or amuse in any way; be ready to consider something (an offer etc.). **entertainment** n. the way a person is received and looked after; a public performance.

enthusiasm (en-thu-si-asm) n. great interest, eagerness over something. **enthusiastic** a. full of enthusiasm. **enthusiast** n. a person who is interested in some pursuit (politics, sport etc.).

entire (en-tire) a. whole, complete. **entirely** adv. completely.

envelop (en-vel-op) v. wrap, cover on every side. **envelope** n. a paper cover specially made to hold letters and papers.

environment (en-vi-ron-ment) n. surroundings, conditions under which one lives and works; the land, water and air around us. **environs** n. the districts surrounding a town.

envy (en-vy) n. a feeling of unhappiness because others are richer, more intelligent, healthier, better looking etc.; a person or object which causes envy. v. feel envy. **envious** a. full of envy.

epidemic (ep-i-dem-ic) n. a disease which spreads among many people at the same time.

episode (ep-i-sode) n. an event or description of an event in a series of events or in a person's life etc.; one section of a story or of a play.

equal a. the same in size, amount, number, quality etc. **equal to** having courage, strength etc. to do a thing.

equip (e-quip) v. supply, provide with what is needed for a special purpose. **equipment** n. the things needed for a purpose (expedition, experiment etc.).

erase (e-rase) v. rub out. **eraser** n. something, usually a piece of rubber, used to erase. **erasure** n. a place where something has been erased.

erect (e-rect) a. upright, standing on one end. v. set up, build. **erection** n. setting up of something, something set up (a building, memorial etc.).

errand (er-rand) n. a short journey to take, bring or convey a message; the purpose of such a journey.

error (er-ror) n. a mistake, something done wrong. **in error** having made one or more mistakes.

escape (es-cape) v. slip away, free oneself (from prison etc.); find a way out; keep free from. n. the act of getting free; the act of finding a way out; a means of escape (fire-escape etc.).

escort (es-cort) n. a person, ship or aircraft accompanying others to give protection or prevent from escaping. v. go with, as an escort.

especial (es-pe-cial) a. great, main, particular. **especially** adv. very, particularly.

essay (es-say) n. a short piece of writing, usually on one subject. **essayist** n. a writer who produces essays.

essence (es-sence) n. the most important part or quality of something; that part of a substance which remains when everything not needed has been removed. **essential** a. most important; most necessary.

establish (es-tab-lish) v. set up, organize; settle a person or oneself in a particular place, office etc. **establishment** n. an organization (school, business, shop, church etc.).

estate (es-tate) n. a piece of property composed of land; all a person's property. **estate car** a car with an enlarged body made to carry goods or passengers.

esteem (es-teem) v. think very well of,

respect greatly. *n.* respect, high opinion of.

estimate (es-ti-mate) *v.* judge or calculate the size, thickness, weight, value, cost etc.; form a judgment about. *n.* a rough calculation, idea or judgment.

etc. (short for et cetera) and other things; and so on.

eternal (e-ter-nal) *a.* lasting or seeming to last for ever; always seeming to be present. **eternity** *n.* time that has no end or seems to have no end.

ether (e-ther) *n.* a colourless liquid used to make people unconscious; the substance once believed to fill the space between stars, through which heat, light and electricity passed.

evacuate (e-vac-u-ate) *v.* remove oneself or remove other people from a place because of danger. **evacuee** *n.* a person who has been evacuated.

evaporate (e-vap-o-rate) *v.* turn into vapour or steam; vanish (of hopes, expectations etc.). **evaporation** *n.* the act or result of evaporating.

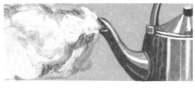

even (e-ven) *a.* level, flat; regular, the same. *n.* a number which can be divided by 2. *adv.* still, yet. **evenly** *adv.* regularly (of events in time, placing things in space etc.).

evening (eve-ning) *n.* that part of the day between sunset and bedtime. *a.* done, appearing, taken etc. in the evening (meal, star, paper etc.).

event (e-vent) *n.* anything that happens; one of the competitions or races in a sports meeting. **eventful** *a.* full of important happenings.

evergreen *n.* a plant whose leaves do not drop in winter.

evidence (ev-i-dence) *n.* anything that proves what happened at a certain time or place; a mark or trace of something. **evident** *a.* plain, clear.

evil (e-vil) *a.* bad, wicked, sinful; unfortunate (times, days). *n.* wrongdoing; bad things, thoughts, deeds etc.

evolution (ev-o-lu-tion) *n.* growth, development; the belief that one form of life has descended from another simpler and more primitive form. **evolve** *v.* develop, cause to develop, unfold.

exaggerate (ex-ag-ger-ate) *v.* describe something as better, larger, worse, louder etc. than it really is. **exaggeration** *n.* the giving of such descriptions.

example (ex-am-ple) *n.* something which shows or illustrates; a person or object to be copied; a warning. **for example** as an illustration.

excavate (ex-cav-ate) *v.* dig, usually in order to find something. **excavation** *n.* digging. **excavator** *n.* a machine or a person who digs.

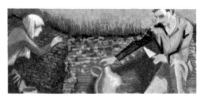

exceed (ex-ceed) *v.* be greater than; go faster than; go beyond what is necessary, allowed or wise. **exceedingly** *adv.* very, extremely.

excel (ex-cel) *v.* do or be better than; do very well at a certain thing. **excellence** *n.* being very good. **excellent** *a.* very good.

except (ex-cept) *prep.* but, leaving out. **exception** *n.* something which has not been or is not included.

exchange (ex-change) *v.* give back for something else. *n.* the act of exchanging; what has been exchanged; a place where goods, money etc. are exchanged. **telephone exchange** the building where telephone lines are connected.

excite (ex-cite) *v.* stir up the feelings of. **excitable** *a.* easily excited (of people or animals). **excitement** *n.* the state of being excited.

exclaim (ex-claim) *v.* cry out suddenly. **exclamation** *n.* a sudden, short cry. **exclamation mark** a punctuation mark (!) put after an exclamation in writing.

excursion (ex-cur-sion) *n.* a short journey or trip, usually taken for pleasure. **excursion ticket** a special ticket at a cheap rate covering return journeys.

excuse (ex-cuse) *v.* forgive; set a person

free from some duty, debt etc. **excuse** *n.* a reason for one's conduct.

execute (ex-e-cute) *v.* do, carry out; put to death, usually by cutting off the head; carry out the terms of a will. **execution** *n.* carrying out (of orders etc.); putting to death.

exercise (ex-er-cise) *n.* something done again and again to make a person skilful; movements of troops, ships etc. to keep them alert and fit for battle. *v.* take exercise; move ships, troops etc.; use (judgment etc.). **exercise book** a book used for exercises in any subject.

exert (ex-ert) *v.* use (strength, powers etc.); try (always used with self). **exertion** *n.* using strength, skill etc.

exhaust (ex-haust) *v.* use up, tire out. *n.* the tube in the engine from which waste, petrol fumes etc. are sent out. **exhaustion** *n.* being tired out, unable to move or go further.

exhibit (ex-hib-it) *v.* show in public. *n.* something shown publicly; something produced as evidence in a law court.

exhibition *n.* a public or private show.

exist (ex-ist) *v.* be; continue to be or live. **existence** *n.* being, way of living.

exit (ex-it) *n.* a way out; departure of an actor from the stage; a stage direction meaning 'goes out'.

exotic (ex-o-tic) *a.* of foreign character, exciting and unusual (of plants, fashions etc.); foreign and strange in style.

expect (ex-pect) *v.* think something will happen. **expectation** *n.* what may be expected.

expedition (ex-pe-di-tion) *n.* a journey for a special purpose; people who go on such a journey. **expeditionary** *a.* intended to go on an expedition (of an army).

expel (ex-pel) *v.* send, force or drive out; send away in disgrace.

expense (ex-pense) *n.* cost or charge. **expend** *v.* spend money, time etc. **expenditure** *n.* spending; the amount spent.

experience (ex-pe-ri-ence) *n.* knowledge obtained by seeing or doing things; the things which happen to a person, or any single thing happening. *v.* meet with, see, feel.

experiment (ex-per-i-ment) *n.* a test to discover what will happen if certain things are done. *v.* make such a test. **experimental** *a.* founded on or used for experiments.

explain (ex-plain) *v.* tell the meaning of; account for, give reasons why. **explanation** *n.* the act of explaining; the statement made when explaining.

explode (ex-plode) *v.* burst with a loud noise. **explosion** *n.* the loud noise caused by something exploding. **explosive** *a.* that may explode *n.* a substance which may explode.

explore (ex-plore) *v.* travel through a new area to find out about it; examine a problem in an attempt to solve it; look into something closely. **exploration** *n.* the act or result of exploring. **explorer** *n.* a person who travels in order to make discoveries.

export (ex-port) *v.* send goods to another country to be sold. *n.* the business of exporting; something exported to be sold.

expose (ex-pose) *v.* uncover, leave uncovered; show, bring to the notice of all; allow light to enter a camera to make a photograph or film. **exposure** *n.* the act of exposing or being exposed.

express (ex-press) *v.* say or tell in words or by actions. *n.* a train which goes very quickly; a service for carrying goods. **expression** *n.* a way of saying something; a word or phrase.

extend (ex-tend) *v.* make longer; stretch out, reach (of land, roads etc.). **extension** *n.* a part added on. **extent** *n.* length or area.

extinguish (ex-tin-guish) *v.* put out (a fire). **extinguisher** *n.* a device used to put out fires. **extinct** *a.* no longer burning, having died out.

extra (ex-tra) *a.* additional, beyond what was required or agreed.

extract (ex-tract) *v.* take out, press out, copy out from a book etc. *n.* something taken out, pressed out or copied out.

extraction *n.* the act or result of taking out.

extraordinary (ex-traor-di-nar-y) *a.* not usual, out of the ordinary. **extraordinarily** *adv.* extremely, very, surprisingly.

extravagance (ex-trav-a-gance) *n.* waste, spending too much (money, effort, time etc.). **extravagant** *a.* wasteful, spending more money than one ought to.

extreme (ex-treme) *a.* farthest; very great; belonging to either end (hot—cold, love—hate, height—depth etc.). **extremely** *adv.* very. **extremity** *n.* extreme point, end.

F

fable (fa-ble) *n.* a short story, often with animals as characters. **fabulous** *a.* absurd, not possible to believe; wonderful.

fabric (fab-ric) *n.* cloth or other material which is woven, knitted or made of felt.

fact *n.* something that is true; what has really happened. **factual** *a.* not fiction, having to do with fact.

factor (fac-tor) *n.* a whole number (except 1) by which a larger number can be divided; a fact which helps to arrive at a certain result.

factory (fac-to-ry) *n.* workshop; a building in which things are made.

faculty (fac-ul-ty) *n.* the power to do things; one of the departments of learning in a university.

fade *v.* lose colour, become less bright; grow dim, faint, go out of sight or hearing.

faint *a.* not clear, not easy to hear or see; weak, exhausted. *v.* lose consciousness. *n.* a temporary loss of consciousness.

fair *a.* just, honest; neither bad nor good, just average; fine (of the weather); light in colour, pale; beautiful. *n.* a large market, often with shows and entertainment.

faith *n.* a strong belief; a system of religious belief (e.g. Christianity, Buddhism). **faithful** *a.* keeping faith; true to the facts.

fall *v.* come or go down; collapse; be defeated. *n.* autumn.

false *a.* wrong, not true; lying; not loyal; not real (teeth, hair etc.). **falsehood** *n.* a lie, lying.

falter (fal-ter) *v.* move, walk, act or speak slowly with hesitation.

fame *n.* being known by many; talked about by many. **famous** *a.* known by many.

familiar (fa-mil-i-ar) *a.* well known; knowing something well; friendly (with people). **familiarity** *n.* being familiar with.

family (fam-i-ly) *n.* parents and children, grandparents, uncles, aunts etc.; all the people descended from one person; a group of living beings related to each other (the family of man). *a.* having to do with a family (party, resemblance etc.).

famine (fam-ine) *n.* a shortage of food; any kind of shortage (water, cotton, potatoes etc.).

far *adv.* at a distance; *a.* distant, more distant.

farce *n.* a play for acting, full of ridiculous events, specially written to make people laugh; a series of events or situations, with so little sense as to be laughable.

fare *n.* money charged for making a journey; a person who rides in a hired vehicle; food provided at table. *v.* make progress, get on. **farewell** *int.* (may you fare well) goodbye.

farm *n.* a piece of land used for raising animals and growing food. *v.* use land for this purpose. **farmer** *n.* a person who owns or manages a farm. **farmyard** *n.* that part of a farm round which the buildings, barns and sheds stand.

fascinate (fas-ci-nate) *v.* charm, attract, hold the attention. **fascinating** *a.* having charm and attraction. **fascination** *n.* power to interest or charm.

fashion (fash-ion) *n.* a way of doing something; a way of dressing which most people like and admire. *v.* make. **fashionable** *a.* in fashion; worn by, visited by people.

fast *a.* firmly·fixed, not moved easily;

quick, rapid; before time (of a clock or watch). *adv.* firmly; quickly. *v.* go without food. *n.* a period spent without eating (certain) food. **fasten** *v.* make fast.

fat *n.* a white or yellowish substance found in meat, milk and the bodies of animals. *a.* having much flesh on the body. **fatten** *v.* make fat. **fatty** *a.* with much fat.

fate *n.* a power which is thought to make things happen in a way that cannot be changed; death. **fatal** *a.* ending in death. **fatality** *n.* an event which ends in death.

father (fath-er) *n.* the male parent; God; a priest in a church. **father-in-law** *n.* the father of one's wife or husband.

fatigue (fa-tigue) *n.* the state of being very tired; a tiring task.

fault *n.* something which is imperfect or wrong; responsibility for having done something. **faultless** *a.* having no faults. **faulty** *a.* having a fault or faults.

favour (fa-vour) *n.* an act of kindness; approval; a badge, ribbon or rosette. *v.* support, show favour to; do things for. **favourable** *a.* approving, helpful.

favourite *n.* one to whom favour is shown; one who is believed able to win a race or competition.

fear *n.* the feeling one has when danger may be near. *v.* be afraid of. **fearful** *a.* terrible, having fear. **fearless** *a.* having no fear.

feat *n.* a difficult deed which needs great skill, strength, courage etc.

feather (feath-er) *n.* one of the light quills that cover a bird's skin.

feature (fea-ture) *n.* a part of the face; a part which is most noticed; an important article in a newspaper, magazine, radio or television programme. *v.* bring to one's notice as being very important.

fee *n.* money paid for some service.

feeble *a.* weak. **feeble-minded** *a.* weak in mind.

feed *v.* give food, supply material to a machine in a factory. *n.* food for animals; the pipe to carry fuel to a machine.

feel *v.* learn about by touching and handling; notice through something touching; be in a certain condition (well, ill, warm, faint etc.); think. **feeler** *n.* one of two long arms like hairs which an insect uses to feel, find food, find its way etc. **feeling** *n.* pain, pleasure, anger etc. which one feels.

fellow (fel-low) *n.* a man or boy; somebody belonging to the same group, class, nation etc. **fellowship** *n.* a group of friends; friendly meeting and companionship.

felt *n.* wool or hair pressed hard to make a thick cloth. *v.* past tense of the verb feel.

female (fe-male) *n.* a woman, girl or she-animal. *a.* having to do with women, girls etc. **feminine** *a.* female; suitable for women and girls.

fence *n.* a wall or barrier made of wooden sticks, metal or wire to keep animals apart or to keep people out; a receiver of stolen goods. *v.* surround by a fence; fight with long thin swords or blunt thin swords called foils.

fender (fen-der) *n.* a metal guard in front of a fireplace; a guard of metal or other material to lessen the shock when two vehicles collide.

ferment (fer-ment) *v.* change or be changed by the addition of certain substances. *n.* the change which takes place when certain substances are added together (e.g. yeast and dough make bread).

fern *n.* a plant with green feathery leaves which has no flowers.

ferro-concrete (fer-ro-con-crete) *n.* concrete which has inside it iron or steel bars to strengthen it and prevent it cracking under strain.

ferry (fer-ry) *n.* a place from which a boat or aircraft may carry people across water. *n.* the boat or aircraft which crosses. *v.* take people or goods across water by ferry.

fertile (fer-tile) *a.* rich, producing good crops (of land); having many ideas (of people); producing young in numbers (of animals); producing good seeds (of plants). **fertility** *n.* being fertile. **fertilize** *v.* make fertile. **fertilizer** *n.* a substance used to fertilize soil.

festival (fes-ti-val) *n.* a time for feasting

and rejoicing ; a series of performances of music, drama etc. usually held once a year. **festive** a. having to do with festivals and feasting. **festivity** n. merry-making, joyful happenings.

fetch v. go for and bring back; bring in money from a sale.

fete n. a festival or open-air entertainment. v. honour a person by giving a dinner or a party.

fever (fe-ver) n. a high temperature of the body caused by some illness or other; a disease belonging to a certain group in which high temperature occurs; great excitement.

few a. not many, a small number of. **quite a few** a good few, a number of.

fiancé (fi-an-cé) n. a man to whom a woman is engaged to be married. **fiancée** n. a woman to whom a man is engaged to be married.

fibre (fi-bre) n. one of the thin hairs which make up wool, cotton and other materials. **fibreglass** n. fibres of glass looking rather like cotton wool and used to prevent heat leaking out of rooms etc.

fickle (fick-le) a. never the same, always changing.

fiction (fic-tion) n. something untrue; imaginative writing, consisting of stories which have been invented.

fiddle (fid-dle) n. a violin; a dishonest act. v. play the violin; act dishonestly to get things for oneself.

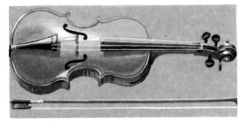

fidget (fid-get) v. never stop moving. n. a person who fidgets.

field n. a piece of land, usually with a wall or fence round it; an area bounded by the limits of sight; a piece of ground where cricket or other sports are played; a place .where a battle has been fought; a battlefield. v. stop a ball after it has been hit by a batsman (in cricket).

fierce a. savage, cruel, violent.

fig n. a small fruit shaped like a pear which has small seeds and is soft and sweet inside. Figs grow in warm countries and those eaten in colder lands have been dried.

fight v. struggle against an animal, person, another country or nation etc. n. a struggle, the act of fighting.

figure (fig-ure) n. a sign that represents a number; a shape in geometry; arithmetic (figures); the shape of a living being, of the human body; a well-known or great person. v. work out or understand; play a part.

fill v. make full, become full; hold a position and do all the work needed in it. n. a full supply, as much as is needed.

filly (fil-ly) n. a female foal or colt.

film n. a thin coat or layer; specially prepared material which is rolled and is put into cameras to take pictures; a motion picture. v. take a motion picture.

filth n. dirt which is very unpleasant, things written or printed which are obscene. **filthy** a. very dirty; disgusting.

fin n. that part of a fish which is used when it swims; anything shaped like a fin or used in the same way.

final (fi-nal) a. last. n. the last match which decides who shall have a prize or trophy (cup final); the last edition of a newspaper. **finalist** n. a person who has won all the rounds and plays in the final finally adv. lastly.

finance (fi-nance) n. money. a. having to do with money (company, house etc.) **financial** a. of money. **financially** adv with regard to money. **financier** n. a person who deals in money.

find v. look for and get back something lost; supply; obtain. n. something found

fine n. a sum of money paid as a punishment. v. make a person pay a fine. a. bright, clear (weather); handsome, splendid, enjoyable, excellent; in very small pieces; very narrow.

finger (fin-ger) n. that extreme part of the hand used for handling, pointing, touching etc.; there are five fingers on each hand. **fingerprint** n. a mark made by pressing the finger on a flat surface, used to detect criminals.

finish (fin-ish) v. bring to an end; come to an end; do well, put a finish or fine surface on. n. a fine, smooth surface; the last part, the end.

fir *n*. an evergreen tree which bears cones and has small sharp leaves like needles.

fire *n*. the state of burning, being burnt; things burning; the heat and light given off from things burning; shots from guns etc. *v*. shoot from a gun, catapult or bow. **firearm** *n*. a gun, pistol, rifle or revolver. **fireproof** *a*. that does not burn. **firing-line** *n*. the front line (of trenches) most exposed to enemy fire.

firm *a*. solid, not moving; not changing, steady, always the same. *n*. a group of persons who carry on a business. **firmly** *adv*. in a firm manner.

fish *n*. an animal living in water, breathing through gills and having fins for swimming. *v*. catch fish. **fisherman** *n*. a man who earns his living by fishing. **fishery** *n*. an area of the sea where fishing is carried on.

fist *n*. the hand tightly closed.

fit *a*. right, suitable for. *v*. be the right size and shape; put something on or in a special place. *n*. a short attack, a sudden brief illness; a sudden attack of illness in which one falls and moves violently. **fitter** *n*. a person who in dressmaking cuts and fits garments; a workman who fits together pipes and parts of machines.

fizz *v*. make a hissing sound. **fizzle** *v*. make a soft fizzing sound. **fizzle out** *v*. come to an end without achieving anything.

flabby (flab-by) *a*. soft, weak (of the muscles).

flag *n*. a piece of cloth with a design on it to show the country or organization to which it belongs, or used to give a signal. *v*. become weak; give a signal by waving a flag. **flagstone** *n*. a square or oblong piece of stone laid for people to walk on.

flake *n*. a small, thin, flat piece. *v*. peel off in flakes.

flame *n*. the part of a fire which blazes up. *v*. burn with a flame; become red (of the face).

flank *n*. the soft part of the body between ribs and hip; a position on the right or left side of a person or an army. *v*. be on the flank of.

flannel (flan-nel) *n*. a soft woollen cloth; a cloth for washing the face and body.

flap *v*. wave up and down, move from side to side. *n*. a piece of cloth, wood, paper etc., that folds over, covering an opening.

flare *v*. burn brightly and unsteadily, the flame rising and falling quickly; suddenly become angry. *n*. a device for making a light which flares; the side of a long skirt which spreads or widens gradually.

flash *n*. a bright light that comes suddenly and then goes out; a thought that occurs suddenly. *v*. burst suddenly into light; send a sudden light as a signal. **flashlight** *n*. a small electric torch which has a battery inside it; a device that gives a sudden flash to take photographs where there is not enough light.

flask *n*. a bottle with a narrow neck used in a laboratory or for holding wine or spirits.

flat *a*. level; dull, without interest. *n*. a stretch of flat land; a dwelling, usually part of a larger building. *adv*. at full length, spread out. **flatten** *v*. make flat.

flatter (flat-ter) *v*. compliment, praise too much; show a thing or person looking better than they really do. **flattery** *n*. praise which is not meant.

flavour (fla-vour) *n*. taste. *v*. give flavour to. **flavouring** *n*. something which gives flavour.

flaw *n*. something that spoils, makes a thing worth less. **flawless** *a*. having no faults, perfect.

flax *n*. a plant with a blue flower; the thread which is made from the fibres of the flax plant. **flaxen** *a*. the colour of the thread of flax; pale yellow.

flea *n*. a small, wingless insect that feeds

on human or animal blood and is able to leap a long way.

flee v. run or hurry away from.

fleece n. the wool cut all in one piece from a sheep. v. swindle; strip of money.

fleet n. a number of ships which sail together under the command of a single officer; aircraft or buses under one firm or working together. a. moving quickly. **fleeting** a. passing quickly.

flesh n. the soft part of the body covering the bones; the body as contrasted with the spirit.

flex v. bend. n. the wire which bends easily and is used for conducting electricity to lights. **flexible** a. bending easily.

flicker (flick-er) v. burn unsteadily. n. a faint flash of light; the smallest measure.

flight n. a flying movement through the air; a journey by air; a number of birds moving through the air; a number of steps; running, flying, driving away (from danger etc.).

flinch v. draw back, move back quickly.

fling v. throw with great force; move quickly and violently. n. a lively Scottish dance, the Highland Fling.

flip v. throw something quickly; toss in the air by a movement of the thumb and finger.

flipper (flip-per) n. the fin or foreleg of certain sea animals (seals, penguins, turtles); special footwear which look like flippers, worn by frogmen.

flit v. fly quickly, dart.

float v. rest on the surface of water or other liquids; make float; start a business. n. anything that floats; money given to the treasurer of an organization to meet daily expenses; a wagon or cart which is drawn in a procession.

flog v. beat severely with a rod or whip.

flood n. water flowing over a place that is usually dry; a large number (people, tears, complaints etc.). v. cover with water; arrive in great numbers.

florist (flor-ist) n. a person who sells flowers and plants in a shop.

floss n. soft threads of silk before being spun. **candy floss** sugar spun into fine threads and eaten off the end of a short stick.

flour n. wheat or other grain ground fine and used for baking.

flourish (flour-ish) v. grow quickly and well, be healthy; be alive at a certain time. n. a waving of something such as a sword for show; fancy handwriting.

flow v. move along as a river does; hang down (of dresses, hair etc.). n. movement (of water, the tides etc.).

flower (flow-er) n. the blossom of a plant, the part that produces seeds; the best or finest part of anything. v. produce flowers.

flue n. a tube or pipe which carries smoke out of a building by way of a chimney.

fluid (flu-id) n. a liquid substance. a. able to flow as liquids do; easily changed, not fixed.

flush v. pour water over or through; blush, become red in the face. n. a rush of blood to the face. a. level with.

flute n. a musical wind instrument like a recorder, consisting of a tube closed at one end, and with holes in the side which are stopped by the fingers.

flutter (flut-ter) v. move or beat the wings without flying; move or beat in an irregular way. n. a feeling of excitement.

fly v. move through the air with or without wings; move in the air; be blown here and there; go quickly. n. an insect with wings, especially the one which lives in the house; an artificial fly used for fishing.

foal n. a young horse. v. give birth to a foal.

foam n. a white liquid made up of many tiny bubbles forming on the surface through being stirred. v. make foam. **foam**

rubber rubber made like sponge and used for upholstering furniture.

focus (fo-cus) *n.* a point where rays of light or heat meet; a central point of attraction, attention on activity. *v.* fix an instrument so that rays of light or heat come together at a point; keep one's attention on something.

foe *n.* enemy; a person fighting or working on the opposite side.

fog *n.* water vapour in the air which makes it difficult to see and is thicker than mist; a time when fog is about.

foil *v.* prevent another from carrying out his plans. *n.* metal rolled very thin and used for several purposes, especially wrapping and cooking; a very light sword with a button at the point, used for fencing.

fold *v.* bend (paper, cloth etc.) so that two surfaces are next to each other; cover, wrap. *n.* that which can be folded; the place where a thing is folded; an enclosed space where sheep are kept. **folder** *n.* a holder of paper or cardboard for keeping papers or drawings in.

foliage (fol-i-age) *n.* the leaves of trees and plants.

folk *n.* people. *a.* having to do with the customs of a part of a country. **folklore** *n.* the study of the beliefs, tales and customs of a people.

follow (fol-low) *v.* come, go or be after; go along; understand; work at a certain trade; come as a result. **follower** *n.* a person who follows or supports. **following** *n.* people or things which follow.

folly (fol-ly) *n.* foolishness, foolish ideas, beliefs, actions; anything which is ridiculous.

fond *a.* taking pleasure in, full of affection or love for; loving. **fondle** *v.* touch or stroke lovingly. **fondness** *n.* being fond.

font *n.* the basin in a church which holds water for the ceremony of baptism.

food *n.* something that can be eaten by human beings or animals or that can be used to make plants grow. **foodstuff** *n.* material used as food.

fool *n.* a person without much sense; one who is stupid; a clown who is paid to make people laugh; a jester; a person who has been deceived or tricked. *v.* behave like a fool; cheat others. **foolhardy** *a.* taking unnecessary risks. **foolish** *a.* not wise.

foot *n.* that part of the body below the leg, on which people and animals walk; the lowest part (of a ladder, hill etc.); twelve inches. **footstep** *n.* the sound of a person walking.

forbid (for-bid) *v.* order not to do something or that a thing shall not be done.

force *n.* strength; something that causes changes or movement; a body of men employed for a certain purpose; a body of trained people armed by their government; power, action. *v.* use force; make plants grow more quickly.

ford *n.* a place where a river is shallow enough to be crossed on foot or by wading through water. *v.* cross water by means of a ford.

fore *a.* the front (part); *n.* well known or best known positions. **forecast** *n.* an account of what will probably happen **forefathers** *n.* ancestors. **foreman** *n.* a man who is in charge of or leads others. **foremost** *a.* the very first. **foresee** *v.* see something which is about to happen. **foresight** *n.* the ability to foresee. **forestall** *v.* prevent another person doing a thing by doing it first. **foretell** *v.* say that something is going to happen. **forethought** *n.* the power to plan ahead, to think of what may happen.

foreign (for-eign) *a.* in, from or belonging to another country; strange, to which one is not accustomed; brought in or coming in from outside. **foreigner** *n.* a person belonging to another country.

forest (for-est) *n.* land covered with trees, much larger than a wood. **forester** *n.* a man who looks after a forest or an area where there are woods.

forfeit (for-feit) *v.* lose or give up something as a result of doing wrong or not obeying rules. *n.* something forfeited.

forge *n.* a special fireplace where a blacksmith softens iron so that it can be hammered into shape; a building in which metals are shaped and worked into articles of use. *v.* shape something by heating and hammering; make a copy of another person's handwriting, or printing in order to deceive. **forger** *n.* a person who forges signatures, money etc. **forgery** *n.* forging.

forget (for-get) *v.* fail to remember; not pay attention to. **forgetful** *a.* often forgetting.

forgive (for-give) *v.* pardon; say that you do not wish to punish; give up all claim for payment. **forgiveness** *n.* pardon; forgiving.

formula (for-mu-la) *n.* symbols used for writing in science, chemistry and mathematics; a number of directions for making or putting together.

fort or **fortress** (for-tress) *n.* a building, groups of buildings or town made strong for defence against an enemy.

fortnight (fort-night) *n.* two weeks, 14 days.

fortune (for-tune) *n.* chance, luck good or bad; money, property, wealth, success. **fortune-teller** *n.* a person who claims to be able to foretell the future. **fortunate** *a.* lucky.

forward (for-ward) *a.* towards the front; making good progress. *v.* send (a letter or parcel) to a new address. **forwards** *adv.* in a forward direction.

fossil (fos-sil) *n.* an animal or plant which has been buried for millions of years and has become hardened like rock.

foul *a.* smelling or tasting bad; filthy; evil, wicked; not fair (of the weather). *n.* an action in a game which is against the rules. *v.* dirty or make dirty.

found *v.* start (a building, city, organization etc.); past tense of the verb find. **foundation** *n.* the founding of a building etc.; the grounds for a belief. **foundations** *n.* the parts of a building which are below the ground and on which it is based. **founder** *n.* a person who founds an organization etc.

foundry (found-ry) *n.* a place where metal is melted and moulded into various shapes.

fountain (foun-tain) *n.* a continual spring of water made to spurt up from a pipe or pipes and then allowed to drop back.

fowl *n.* a bird; one of the larger birds, a farmyard cock or hen.

fox *n.* a small, wild animal resembling a dog.

fraction (frac-tion) *n.* a part of something larger; a number that is not a whole number.

fracture (frac-ture) *n.* a break or crack; a crack in a bone in the body. *v.* break, crack.

fragile (frag-ile) *a.* delicate, easily broken.

fragment (frag-ment) *n.* a piece broken off, a small piece. **fragmentation bomb** a bomb which breaks up into small fragments when it explodes.

fragrance (fra-grance) *n.* a sweet, pleasant smell. **fragrant** *a.* sweet-smelling, pleasant.

frail *a.* fragile, easily broken, weak.

frailty *n.* being frail, weak.

frame *n.* the skeleton of a building or an animal, which holds it together; the wooden, metal or other border round a picture, door or window. *v.* put a frame round; make a false charge against a person. **framework** *n.* the skeleton on which a thing is constructed.

frank *a.* open and honest in speech, saying what one thinks. *v.* cancel the stamps on letters as they pass through the post office.

frantic (fran-tic) *a.* excited, wild with joy, rage or fear, frenzied.

fraternal (fra-ter-nal) *a.* like a brother. **fraternity** *n.* brotherhood, people who are joined together by similar interests or occupations.

fraternize *v.* mix with people who are or have been enemies.

fraud *n.* cheating, deceiving others. *n.* a person who cheats or deceives others; a thing that deceives. **fraudulent** *a.* acting with deceit; got by deceit.

freak *a.* unusual or odd. *n.* an animal or person not like any others of the same kind.

freckle (freck-le) *n.* a small light brown spot on a person's skin. *v.* become covered with freckles.

free *a.* able to do as one pleases; without any payment or cost; not busy. *v.* make free, set at liberty. **freedom** *n.* being free. **free-for-all** *n.* a fight in which anybody can join. **freelance** *n.* a person who does not work for any one employer for a wage or salary. **free trade** trade between countries free from customs and duties. **freewheel** *v.* ride a bicycle downhill without using the pedals.

freeze *v.* become or make so cold that a liquid or gas becomes solid; preserve food by making it very cold; feel cold. *n.* a period when the weather is very cold; a period when wages or prices are not allowed to rise or fall.

freezer *n.* a machine or a special room for freezing food.

freight *n.* goods carried from one place to another; money charged for carrying goods. **freighter** *n.* a ship which carries goods.

frenzy (fren-zy) *n.* wild or violent excitement; fury. **frenzied** *a.* very excited, furious.

frequent (fré-quent) *a.* happening often. **frequent** (fre-quént) *v.* go often to. **frequency** (fré-quenc-y) *n.* rapid occurrence; a number of repetitions in a given time (of electric current etc.).

friction (fric-tion) *n.* the rubbing of one thing against another; quarrelling between persons.

friend *n.* a person, not a relative, whom one knows well and respects; a person

who helps other people or supports a cause. **friendless** *a.* having no friends. **friendly** *a.* acting or ready to act as a friend. **friendship** *n.* the feeling that exists between friends.

fright *n.* sudden fear; a ridiculous looking person or thing. **frighten** *v.* give a fright to. **frightful** *a.* not pleasant, awful.

frigid (frig-id) *a.* very cold; not friendly; showing no sympathy.

frill *n.* a trimming on cloth gathered at one edge. **frilled** *a.* having a frill or frills.

fringe *n.* an ornamental border of threads which hang loose; the edge (of a crowd etc.); the front part of the hair which falls over the forehead and is cut straight. *v.* put a fringe on; act as a fringe to.

frisk *v.* jump and run as if in play; search a person for hidden weapons. **frisky** *a.* in a frisking manner, playful, lively.

fritter (frit-ter) *v.* waste time, money, energy etc.; *n.* a small cake made of fried batter, sometimes containing fruit or jam.

frog *n.* a small, cold-blooded animal living on land and in water which has long back legs and moves by jumping; a fastener like a long wooden or plastic button which is put through a loop to fasten coats, cloaks etc. **frogman** *n.* a person who swims under water, wearing a special suit and flippers on his feet.

frolic (frol-ic) *v.* frisk playfully. *n.* an amusing joke, lively play. **frolicsome** *a.* lively, wanting to play.

front *n.* the side which faces forwards; the place where the fighting is in a war; a promenade by the sea or a lake. *a.* at the front. **frontier** *n.* the part of a country which faces another country.

frost *n.* a state of the temperature which causes water to turn to ice; frozen vapour like a white powder which forms on very cold days. *v.* cover with frost or something like frost; give a frost-like surface. **frosty** *a.* very cold. **frostbite** *n.* injury to a part of the body from frost.

froth *n.* foam, numbers of small bubbles

on the top of a liquid; make froth.

frown *v.* wrinkle the forehead to look displeased or in deep thought. *n.* a frowning look.

fruit *n.* that part of a tree or plant containing the seeds, which is used by man or animals; a result, reward. **fruiterer** *n.* a person who sells fruit. **fruitful** *a.* bringing good results. **fruitless** *a.* bringing no results. **fruity** *a.* tasting like fruit.

fry *v.* cook or be cooked in hot fat. *n.* the young of fishes, hatched in large numbers. **small fry** unimportant people; young children.

fuel (fu-el) *n.* material used for burning. *v.* supply with fuel, put fuel into the tank of an engine (refuel).

fugitive (fu-gi-tive) *n.* a person who runs away or flees (from an enemy, justice, danger etc.).

fulfil (ful-fil) *v.* do, carry out (a duty, a mission etc.).

full *a.* able to hold no more; complete; as fast, long, high etc. as possible. **full-back** *n.* the football player nearest to the goalkeeper who helps to defend the goal. **fully** *adv.* completely.

fumble (fum-ble) *v.* feel about clumsily with the hands; handle awkwardly or nervously.

fume *n.* smoke, gas or vapour which smells strong. *v.* give off fumes; show anger or irritation. **fumigate** *v.* treat a room, a building, a tree etc. with fumes to kill germs or pests.

fun *n.* playfulness, amusement; something or some person causing fun. **for fun** as a joke. **funny** *a.* causing fun; strange, surprising.

function (func-tion) *n.* the special work of a person or thing; a public event.

fund *n.* a supply of money for some special purpose; some quality of character or knowledge (stories, humour etc.).

funeral (fu-ner-al) *n.* burying or burning a dead body and the service connected with it. *a.* having to do with a funeral.

fungus (fun-gus) *n.* a plant that grows on other plants or on decaying matter. Some fungi are edible and others are highly poisonous.

funnel (fun-nel) *n.* a tube which opens at the top like a cone, down which liquids can be poured into a container; the tube serving as an outlet for smoke in a ship or an engine.

fur *n.* the soft hair which covers certain animals such as the fox, cat beaver and rabbit; the skin of an animal which has fur, used as a garment; the crust left inside a kettle through the boiling of water. **furrier** *n.* a tradesman who makes and sells furs. **furry** *a.* like fur.

furlough (fur-lough) *n.* a short holiday, especially for such people as soldiers, missionaries and others who live abroad.

furnace (fur-nace) *n.* a structure specially built to contain a fire, used mostly to heat buildings, produce metals etc.

furnish (fur-nish) *v.* provide with things or services; fix up a house with the necessary appliances. **furnisher** *n.* a person who sells furniture. **furniture** *n.* all those things that can be moved in a house — beds, tables, chairs etc. used to furnish a room or other space.

furrow (fur-row) *n.* a long deep cut or ditch made in the ground by a plough; a deep wrinkle on the face. *v.* make wrinkles in.

further (fur-ther) *adv.* farther, to a greater distance; more (supplies, information etc.). *v.* help forward (plans).

fury (fu-ry) *n.* violent anger; frenzy, fierceness. **furious** *a.* full of fury, without control.

fuse *n.* the string or tube which carries the flame to set off an explosive charge; a piece of metal which allows electricity to pass through it but melts if too much is passed, thus stopping the current. **fuse wire** special kinds of wire used for fuses.

fuselage (fu-se-lage) *n.* the body of an aircraft.

fusilier (fu-si-lier) *n.* a soldier who once carried a light musket.

fuss *n.* a useless display of anxiety; attention which may not be necessary. *v.* show worry. **fussy** *a.* in the habit of fussing or making a fuss.

future (fu-ture) *n.* time which will come after the present. *a.* having to do with the future (plans, life etc.).

fuzz *n.* soft fluff or down, very fine hair.
fuzzy *a.* covered with down; indistinct.

G

gable (ga-ble) *n.* a three-cornered outside wall of a building enclosed by two sloping roofs and the line between their lowest points. **gabled** *a.* having a gable.

gag *n.* something thrust into the mouth to prevent a person speaking. *v.* put something into a person's mouth to prevent speech; deprive people of free speech, prevent newspapers publishing certain pieces of news.

gaiety (gai-e-ty) *n.* cheerfulness, merry-making; bright appearance.

gain *v.* get, obtain; get nearer or reach; increase (numbers, profit, weight etc.); go ahead of the correct time. *n.* something obtained by work, trade etc.

gait *n.* the way in which a person walks.

gala (ga-la) *n.* an occasion of public merrymaking and festivity.

galaxy (gal-ax-y) *n.* a large number of stars forming a light band in the sky but which cannot be seen separately; a brilliant company of persons.

gale *n.* a strong wind; a sudden loud noise made by one or more persons, usually cheerful.

gallant (gal-lant) *a.* brave, stately, good-looking, fine, beautiful; showing special concern and respect to ladies.

gallery (gal-le-ry) *n.* a room in which pictures and other works of art are displayed; a platform extending from the inner walls of a church, theatre or hall; a room specially set apart for shooting.

gallon (gal-lon) *n.* a measure of liquids. 1 gallon equals 4·5 litres approximately.

gallop *n.* the fastest speed a horse can go; a period when one rides at such a pace. *v.* move very fast by leaps.

gallows (gal-lows) *n.* the wooden frame of uprights and cross pieces used for hanging criminals.

gamble (gam-ble) *v.* play games for money; take great risks in the hope of a favourable result; lose money by gambling. *n.* something done with great risk of loss.

game *n.* sport played according to rules; the materials for playing such games; complete games sold in shops; a series of contests in which people compete in all kinds of sports; a cunning plan; wild animals that are hunted or shot. *a.* brave, ready to go on fighting or working.

gammon (gam-mon) *n.* the lower end of a side of bacon including the hind leg.

gander (gan-der) *n.* a male goose.

gang *n.* a group of persons working together; a group of criminals. **gangplank** a moveable way which can be placed against the side of a ship to allow passengers to come ashore. **gangster** *n.* a member of a group of criminals. **gangway** *n.* a passage between seats or walls along which people may walk.

gaol *n.* (pronounced *jail*) *n.* a prison; a period spent in prison. *v.* send a person to prison. **gaoler** *n.* a person who looks after prisoners.

gap *n.* an opening in a wall, hedge etc.; an empty space between objects (teeth, books etc.); a space or period of time not filled in.

gape *v.* open the mouth wide; yawn; stare in surprise with the mouth open. *n.* a yawn; an open-mouthed stare. *a.* wide open (of cracks, holes etc.).

garage (ga-rage) *n.* a building in which cars are kept; an establishment where cars are stored and repaired. *v.* put a car into a garage.

garbage (gar-bage) *n.* scraps of uneaten food put aside for pigs and other animals to eat; general waste and rubbish.

garden (gar-den) *n.* a piece of ground where flowers, shrubs and vegetables are grown; part of the name of a street; a public park. *v.* look after a garden. **gardener** *n.* a person who looks after a garden.

gargle (gar-gle) *v.* wash the throat by holding liquid in the back of one's mouth and breathing through it; *n.* a liquid used for gargling; the action of gargling.

garland (gar-land) *n.* flowers or leaves made into a circle or crown and used as a personal ornament or decoration. *v.* decorate or crown with a garland.

garlic (gar-lic) *n.* a plant like an onion which has a very strong taste and smell.

garment (gar-ment) *n.* an article of clothing.

garnish (gar-nish) *v.* decorate food for the table. *n.* something used in the decoration of food for the table.

garret (gar-ret) *n.* a room on the top floor of a house under the sloping roof, an attic; a poor, wretched room.

garrison (gar-ri-son) *n.* a force of soldiers stationed in a town or fort; *v.* station soldiers in a town or fort to live for long periods.

garter (gar-ter) *n.* a band worn round the leg for holding up stockings; (with a capital G) the badge of the highest order of English knighthood.

gas *n.* any substance that is not solid or liquid at ordinary temperatures; one of the gases used for lighting or heating buildings; gas or gases which are poisonous (in mines, warfare etc.). *v.* poison or overcome by gas. **gas-fitter** *n.* a workman who puts in and repairs apparatus for supplying gas in homes and factories.

gash *n.* a long deep cut or wound. *v.* make or suffer a deep cut, often by accident.

gasp *v.* breathe quickly as one does after running hard; struggle for breath; speak in a breathless way. *n.* a short quick breath.

gate *n.* an opening in a wall, hedge, fence etc. that can be closed with a moveable barrier; the moveable part by which it is opened or closed. **gate-crasher** *n.* a person who enters without ticket or invitation. **gate-way** *n.* a way that can be opened or closed by a gate.

gather (gath-er) *v.* put, get, come or bring together; pick (flowers etc.); understand from what is said, read etc.; pull into small folds and sew together. **gathering** *n.* a meeting of people; a swelling on the body containing pus.

gauge *n.* (pronounced *gage*) an instrument for measuring (steam, rain etc.); the width between a pair of railway lines. *v.* form a judgment of character, size, depth etc.

gaunt *a.* thin, lean from hunger, illness or suffering; grim, bare and deserted (of a place).

gay *a.* merry, cheerful, light-hearted, full of fun; looking bright and cheerful (of dresses, scenes etc.). **gaily** *adv.* in a gay manner.

gaze *v.* look long and steadily. *n.* a long, steady look.

gazette (ga-zette) *n.* the name of certain newspapers; an official journal published by the government containing lists of appointments and promotions, bankruptcies etc.

gear *n.* a set of wheels working together to make a machine run; machinery used for a special purpose; everything one needs for a special purpose. **in gear** with the gears adjusted so that the motor will turn the wheels and the vehicle can move.

gelatine (gel-a-tine) *n.* a substance added to water which makes jelly.

gelignite (gel-ig-nite) *n.* a substance made from various chemicals and used as an explosive.

gem *n.* a precious stone; something thought much of because of its great beauty or value.

gendarme (gen-darme) *n.* a member of the police force in France and some other countries.

gender (gen-der) *n.* a grammatical means of grouping words; in English, masculine (of males), feminine (of females) and neuter (of things).

general (gen-er-al) *a.* affecting all people or things; rough, not in detail. *n.* an army officer next in rank above a lieutenant-general and below a field-marshal. **generally** *adv.* in most cases, as a general rule.

generation (gen-er-a-tion) *n.* one step in the descent of a family; people born about the same time; the average period between the ages of parents and children.

generator (gen-er-a-tor) *n.* a machine used for making steam, electric current etc.

generous (gen-er-ous) *a.* willing to share with others; ready to give (money, time etc.); plentiful. **generosity** *n.* being generous.

genial (ge-ni-al) *a.* pleasant, kindly, warm, sympathetic and sociable; helping growth (of climate).

genius (gen-i-us) *n.* someone who is outstandingly brilliant at some kind of work. *n.* great brilliance, ability in one or more subjects or pursuits.

gentle (gen-tle) *a.* kind, friendly; mild, not violent or rough.

gentleman (gen-tle-man) *n.* a man who acts honourably and considers other people in everything he does. **gentlefolk** *n.* persons of gentle (or high) birth.

genuine (gen-u-ine) *a.* real, true; what a thing is said to be; not imitation.

geography (ge-og-ra-phy) *n.* the study of the earth's surface — mountains, rivers, climate, population etc.

geology (ge-ol-o-gy) *n.* the study of the earth's crust and its rocks, their construction and history.

geometry (ge-om-e-try) *n.* that part of mathematics which deals with lines, angles, surfaces and solid bodies.

geranium (ge-ra-ni-um) *n.* a plant with either red, pink or white flowers which has a strong scent.

germ *n.* a small organism or microbe that can be seen only with a microscope, which may live in an animal's body and cause disease. **germicide** *n.* a preparation made specially to kill germs.

gesture (ges-ture) *n.* a movement of the hand, head or other part of the body to show feelings, needs, ideas, intentions etc.

get *v.* receive, be given; procure, have something done; obtain; go from one place to another; bring, take or place; pass from one condition to another; hear or understand; become ill with.

geyser (gey-ser) *n.* a hot spring which sends up water; an apparatus for producing hot water, usually in a bathroom or kitchen.

ghost *n.* the spirit of a dead person which haunts living people; the very smallest. **The Holy Ghost** the spirit of God; the third Person of the Trinity.

giant (gi-ant) *n.* a very large, strong man. *a.* very large, much larger than others of the same kind. **gigantic** *a.* very large.

giddy (gid-dy) *a.* feeling that everything is whirling round; that one cannot stand firmly; too fond of pleasure.

gift *n.* something given as a present; a special ability in some pursuit, art or science; *a.* having to do with gifts (shop, token etc.). **gifted** *a.* having great ability.

giggle (gig-gle) *v.* laugh in a silly way. *n.* a short, light laugh.

gild *v.* cover with a thin coating of gold or gold paint; make bright like gold. **gilt** *n.* a thin coating of gold.

gill *n.* the organ with which a fish breathes under water; one quarter of a pint of liquid (pronounced *jill*).

gimlet (gim-let) *n.* a small tool used for making holes in wood.

gin *n.* a trap for catching animals; a drink containing alcohol, flavoured with juniper berries, orange peel etc.; a machine for separating cotton from its seeds; a trap or snare for catching animals.

ginger (gin-ger) *n.* the root of the ginger plant, preserved and eaten or ground and put into cakes. *a.* looking or tasting like ginger, of a reddish-brown colour. **gingerbread** *n.* cake or biscuit flavoured with ginger.

gipsy (gip-sy) – or **gypsy** *n.* someone belonging to a minority race who lives in a caravan and wanders about the country earning a living by dealing in scrap metal, basket-making, peg-making and other work of the same kind.

giraffe (gi-raffe) *n.* a tall African animal with a very long neck, long front legs and dark spots on a yellow skin.

girdle (gir-dle) *n.* a belt or cord worn round the waist; anything that goes round anything else in a circle. *v.* put a girdle round.

girl *n.* a young woman, a female child, a daughter. **Girl Guide** a member of an organization for girls, to develop health,

character and home-making ability. **girlhood** *n.* the time or state of being a girl. **girlish** *a.* like a girl.

give *v.* make a present of; hand over in exchange; provide; cause; perform an action; become less strong or firm. **give up** *v.* stop trying, lose hope.

glacier (gla-cier) *n.* a mass of ice that moves very slowly down the side of a mountain and melts only when it reaches the warmer land below.

glad *a.* happy, pleased; causing happiness; bringing joy or pleasure. **gladness** *n.* joyfulness, cheerfulness.

glamour (glam-our) *n.* the power to charm or fascinate others. **glamorous** *a.* possessing the power to charm.

glance *v.* look quickly; slip or slide off (a blow, an arrow etc.); shine brightly. *n.* a quick look, turning of the eyes.

gland *n.* an organ of the body which takes substances from the blood and helps the body to keep healthy.

glare *n.* a strong light; an angry look. *v.* shine with a strong light; stare or glance fiercely or angrily.

glass *n.* a hard substance which can be seen through; certain things which are made of glass; the quantity or contents of a drinking glass. **glasses** *n.* more than one glass for drinking; spectacles. **glassware** *n.* articles made of glass.

glaze *v.* cover with or put in glass; cover with substances to make shine like glass (e.g. pottery).

gleam *n.* a beam or flash of light; a fragment, the very slightest bit (hope, joy etc.). *v.* send out gleams, shine brightly.

glee *n.* feeling of great joy, delight or pleasure; a song for three or four parts, sung in harmony.

glen n. a narrow valley with steep sides.

glide v. move along continuously without effort (of a stream, a boat etc.). **glider** n. an aeroplane that flies without an engine.

glimmer (glim-mer) n. a faint gleam which comes and goes; a fragment (as in gleam). v. give a faint gleam.

glimpse n. a very quick look; an imperfect view. v. catch a very quick look or imperfect view of.

glisten (glis-ten) v. shine brightly, sparkle.

glitter (glit-ter) v. shine brightly or sparkle with quick flashes of light.

globe n. a large round object, especially one which shows a map of the world; a glass vessel in the shape of a sphere (e.g. a lampshade or fishbowl).

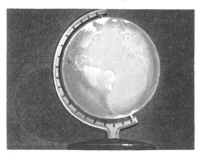

gloom n. almost total darkness; a feeling of sadness, despair or hopelessness. **gloomy** a. dark, dismal, depressing.

glory (glo-ry) n. honour and praise given to a person who has done something great; great splendour. v. be proud about something. **glorify** v. give honour and glory to. **glorious** a. excellent, admirable in every way.

gloss n. a smooth, bright surface. **glossy** a. having a polished surface.

glove n. a covering for the hand with separate parts for each finger.

glow v. shine with heat but without flame; show pleasure, pride, good health etc. n. a gentle, dim light; an expression of emotion, pleasure, pride or embarrassment.

glue n. a sticky substance made specially to fasten things together. v. make things fast, stick things with glue; look fixedly at something.

glum a. sad, gloomy.

glut n. more than is needed. v. give, have, supply more than is needed; eat too much. **glutton** n. one who eats too much.

glycerine (glyc-er-ine) n. a clear, sweet liquid made from oils, used in medicine and the manufacture of explosives.

gnat n. (pronounced *nat*) a small insect that has two wings, feelers and a sting.

gnaw v. (pronounced *nor*) wear something down with constant biting as a dog does with a bone.

gnome n. (pronounced *nome*) a small elf or goblin, a make-believe being said to live under the ground and guard treasure.

go v. move from one place to another; change; reach (a place); leave a place; be put, find a place; disappear, be used up; have certain words or music. n. an attempt at something. **go to** v. attend (a school, church etc.).

goal n. in a football match, the space between the posts through which the ball has to pass in order to score; the point given to the team which succeeds in getting the ball through the opening between the posts of the opposite side; what one hopes to be or do. **goalkeeper** n. the football player whose task is to defend his team's goal.

goat n. a domestic animal with horns, kept for its meat and milk, and in some parts of the world for its hair.

gobble (gob-ble) v. gulp, eat noisily and quickly; make the cry of a turkey-cock. n. the cry of a turkey-cock.

goblet n. a drinking glass with a stem and a base, but without a handle.

goblin (gob-lin) n. an ugly, mischievous elf or spirit supposed to harm human beings.

god n. the Maker and Governor of the world and the whole universe (with a capital G); a being that is worshipped; a person or thing which people love, praise or value greatly. **goddess** n. a female god. **godfather, godmother** (or **godparents**) n. persons who promise when a child is baptized to make sure it is brought up as a Christian. **godly** a. very religious. **godsend** n. a piece of good fortune.

goggles (gog-gles) n. spectacles with specially thick rims and frames worn so as to protect the eyes from injury.

gold n. a precious yellow metal used for making jewellery and coins. a. the colour of gold. **golden** a. made of gold, the colour of gold. **golden wedding** the 50th anniversary of a wedding. **goldfish** *n.* a small golden-coloured fish. **goldsmith** *n.* a craftsman who makes or sells articles of gold.

golf *n.* an outdoor game in which a small white ball is driven with a club, the object being to get it into a hole in as few strokes as possible. **golfer** *n.* a person who plays golf. **golf course** or **golf links** the specially prepared ground on which the game of golf is played.

gong *n.* a piece of metal shaped like a saucer which gives out a sound when struck.

good *a.* satisfactory; doing what is needed; helpful; satisfying; pleasant; well-behaved. *n.* that which is good, the good actions done by a person or persons. **goodbye** *int.* farewell (said by people on parting). **good-humoured** *a.* always cheerful. **goodwill** *n.* a feeling of friendliness to people. **goods** *n.* property, things owned.

goose *n.* a large bird like a duck but heavier and with a longer neck; the flesh of the bird used as food.

gorge *n.* a very narrow valley between high hills. *v.* eat greedily; fill oneself (with).

gorgeous (gor-geous) *a.* magnificent, richly coloured, giving great pleasure and satisfaction.

gorilla (go-ril-la) *n.* the largest of all the apes, which lives on the ground and climbs trees.

gospel (gos-pel) *n.* the teaching of Jesus Christ; the rules of conduct and behaviour in which one believes and on which one acts; one of the four books of the New Testament giving an account of the life of Christ.

gossip (gos-sip) *v.* talk too much about other people's private affairs. *n.* a person who is fond of gossip and does this.

gouge *n.* (pronounced *gowge*) *n.* a chisel with a sharp curved edge used for making grooves in wood. *v.* cut out with a gouge.

govern (go-vern) *v.* rule or control the affairs of a state. **government** *n.* the body of persons who govern a state. **governor** *n.* a person who governs a province, or who manages with others the affairs of a school, society etc.

gown *n.* a dress worn by a girl or a woman; a loose, flowing outer garment worn by judges, members of universities etc.

grab *v.* grasp quickly and roughly, snatch. *n.* a quick snatch; a mechanical device for taking up and lifting things.

grace *n.* a beautiful movement which pleases and attracts others; a prayer of thanks for food, said before and sometimes after meals; the way of addressing a duke, a duchess or an archbishop. **graceful** *a.* full of grace, showing grace.

gracious (gra-cious) *a.* kind, showing pleasure, merciful.

grade *n.* rank; a step in rank, quality, value etc. (high, low, first etc.); a step in a course of instruction; a division in a school's course; *v.* sort out into different qualities.

gradient (gra-dient) *n.* a measure of the steepness of a slope.

gradual (grad-u-al) *a.* rising or falling in small amounts; not steep (of a slope).

grain *n.* the small hard seed of plants used for food; a single seed of such a plant; a very small hard piece; the tiniest bit; the way in which the fibres of wood go.

gram or **gramme** *n.* a unit of weight in the metric system.

grammar (gram-mar) *n.* the study of words and how they make up a language. **grammar school** an English secondary school in which Latin was once the chief subject taught; more recently a school for children who passed the eleven-plus examination. **grammatical** *a.* having to do with grammar.

gramophone (gram-o-phone) *n.* a machine which reproduces sound which has been previously recorded on records.

grand *a.* splendid, large, most important; magnificent, fine, enjoyable; very highly respected. **grandfather, grandmother, grandparents** *n.* the parents of one's father or mother. **grand-children, granddaughter, grandson** etc. the children of one's sons and daughters.

granite (gran-ite) *n.* very hard rock used for buildings, monuments etc.

grant *v.* allow; give; agree, admit to be true. *n.* something given, usually money from a government or organization.

granule (gran-ule) *n.* a small grain. **granulated** *a.* in the form of small grains.

grape *n.* the black, brown or green berry or fruit that grows in bunches on a vine and which can be eaten or made into wine. **grapevine** *n.* the plant on which grapes grow.

grapefruit (grape-fruit) *n.* a large acid-tasting fruit with a juicy pulp which can be eaten, and a yellow skin.

graph *n.* a diagram ruled with lines which show how things are related to each other.

grapple (grap-ple) *v.* seize and struggle with.

grasp *v.* seize and hold firmly; try to seize; understand. *n.* a firm hold; understanding of something.

grass *n.* a green plant with narrow leaves, growing close to the ground; other plants of the same kind with long narrow leaves.

grasshopper (grass-hop-per) *n.* an insect remarkable for its powers of leaping and the chirping noise produced by the males.

grate *n.* a frame of iron or steel for holding the fuel in a fireplace. *v.* rub against a rough piece of metal and break into small pieces; make a harsh sound by rubbing. **grater** *n.* a rough sheet of metal pierced with holes for grating.

grateful (grate-ful) *a.* thankful, showing thanks. **gratify** *v.* give pleasure, make grateful.

gratitude (grat-i-tude) *n.* thankfulness.

grave *n.* a hole dug in the ground for burying a dead body. *a.* solemn, serious.

gravel (grav-el) *n.* large numbers of small stones mixed with sand, used to make paths and roads.

gravity (grav-i-ty) *n.* the force which draws objects to the centre of the earth; seriousness (see **grave**).

graze *v.* eat grass in fields; scrape in passing. *n.* a mark or place where the surface is broken through.

grease *n.* oil or fat from plants, animals or any other source. *v.* put on or apply grease. **greasy** *a.* covered with grease; having too much grease in it.

great *a.* much better than the average; famous, very able, worthy of being remembered; very large; very enjoyable. **greatness** *n.* importance; being great.

greed *n.* a desire to have more of something than is necessary or good for one. **greedy** *a.* having greed.

greet *v.* receive with words expressing good wishes or friendship. **greeting** *n.* words spoken on meeting a person or, written, expressing good wishes.

grenade (gre-nade) *n.* a small bomb either thrown, or fired from a rifle.

grid *n.* a system by which electricity is carried over the country by cables stretched between high pylons; a network of lines on a map; a grating.

grief *n.* deep sorrow. **grieve** *v.* cause to be filled with grief. **grievance** *n.* something which causes one to grieve or be unhappy. **grievous** *a.* severe.

grill *v.* cook by keeping directly under a flame or heat; question very closely for a long period. *n.* a room in a restaurant in which grilled dishes are served; a kitchen utensil with iron bars used for grilling food. **grille** *n.* a barred gate enclosing a cell, a prison, a counter etc.

grim *a.* solemn, stern, severe.

grime *n.* dirt which coats the surface of an object. **grimy** *a.* dirty, covered with grime.

grind *v.* crush into small pieces; sharpen by rubbing on stone. **grindstone** *n.* a circular stone turned on an axle on which tools are sharpened.

grip v. grasp and hold firmly. n. a tight hold; something which grips; power, mastery over things or persons.

gristle (gris-tle) n. whitish, tough tissue found in meat.

grit n. minute particles of sand or stone; courage, pluck. **grit the teeth** keep the jaws close together.

grizzled (griz-zled) a. having grey hair. **grizzly** n. a large, fierce grey bear living in North America.

groan v. make a low sound, usually caused by pain; make a sound resembling a groan. n. the low sound made by groaning.

grocer (gro-cer) n. a person who keeps a shop, selling tea, sugar, flour and other articles of household use. **groceries** n. all the things a grocer sells. **grocery** n. the trade of a grocer.

groom n. a person who takes charge of horses; a man who has just been married or is about to be married. v. feed, brush and care for a horse.

groove n. a long, hollow cut into the surface of metal or wood; the line cut into the surface of a gramophone record along which the needle slides to produce the sound.

grope v. feel one's way or search for things one cannot see.

ground n. the surface of the earth, the soil; land set apart for a special purpose; reasons for saying or doing something; the surface on which a design has been drawn; fundamental knowledge of a subject. v. touch the bottom of the sea; touch or remain on the land. **groundless** a. without reason.

group n. a number of persons or things placed together. v. put or gather into groups.

grouse n. a wild bird which lives on moors and is shot for sport. v. grumble or sulk.

grow v. become larger, increase in size; cultivate, allow to grow; change from one state to another.

growl v. make a deep, fierce sound in the throat; say something in a deep unpleasant voice n. a fierce sound; an angry exclamation.

grub n. larva of certain insects. v. dig something out of the ground.

grudge v. be unwilling to give or grant. n. a feeling of dislike, jealousy or spite against a person.

gruesome (grue-some) a. making one shudder with horror.

gruff a. harsh and deep in sound.

grumble (grum-ble) v. complain and find fault in a bad-tempered way. n. a complaint or complaints made in a bad temper.

guarantee (guar-an-tee) n. a promise that something supplied will be satisfactory or that things will be done; something offered to make sure that payment will be made. v. promise to do something should another person fail.

guard v. protect from danger or interference; take care to protect. n. a person or persons keeping watch; a person employed to look after a train; an object designed to protect people or objects from harm or damage. **guardian** n. a person who is legally responsible for someone under age or not able to look after his property.

guerrilla (guer-ril-la) n. a person fighting for a cause who is not a member of a regular army. **guerrilla war** a war carried on by people who are not members of regular armies.

guess v. give an opinion based not on what one knows but on what one thinks may be true. n. an opinion formed in this way.

guest n. a person staying for a meal or for a period of time at another person's home; a person staying at an hotel, inn or boarding house. **paying guest** a person staying at a private home and paying for board.

guide n. a person who shows others the way; a person who shows others round a building, exhibition etc.; anything that helps to influence actions; a book or other reading matter to help one to find one's way. v. act as a guide. **guidance** n. guiding, being guided.

guilt *n.* having done wrong; a feeling of sorrow for having done wrong. **guilty** *a.* to blame for a wrong.

guitar (gui-tar) *n.* a musical instrument having six strings which are plucked with the fingers.

gulf *n.* a part of the sea surrounded by land.

gull *n.* a large sea-bird with large webbed feet.

gullet (gul-let) *n.* the passage through which food passes from the mouth to the stomach.

gully (gul-ly) *n.* a small valley cut by rainwater; a gutter specially made to carry water off a building.

gulp *v.* swallow quickly and greedily. *n.* a single act of swallowing.

gum *n.* a sticky substance used mainly for sticking paper together; the flesh in the mouth covering the base of the teeth.

gun *n.* a weapon which may be small enough to fire bullets or large enough to fire shells and rockets. **gunman** *n.* a man who uses a gun to attack and rob people. **gunpowder** *n.* powder used to fire guns and cause explosions. **gunner** *n.* a soldier in the artillery; a naval officer or a member of an air-crew in charge of guns.

gurgle (gur-gle) *n.* a sound like that of bubbles rising through water. *v.* make a bubbling sound.

gush *v.* rush or burst out suddenly. *n.* a sudden flow or outburst.

gust *n.* a sudden blast of wind.

gutter (gut-ter) *n.* a channel which carries away water.

gymnasium (gym-na-sium) or **gym** *n.* a room which contains all kinds of apparatus for exercise and body-building.

gypsy see **gipsy.**

H

habit (hab-it) *n.* something which a person does often, and may find it difficult to give up; a dress worn for a special purpose.

hack *v.* cut or chop clumsily. **hacksaw** *n.* a saw used for cutting metal. **hacking cough** a deep, harsh cough.

haggard (hag-gard) *a.* looking pale and worn as if from want, hunger, overwork or suffering.

hail *v.* salute or greet, welcome; originally come from; fall as hail or like hail. *n.* frozen rain falling from the sky; a shower of anything.

hair *n.* the natural covering of the human head and on the skins of some animals and plants.

half *n.* one of two equal parts. *adv.* up to, down or about half; partly. **half-back** *n.* (in football or hockey) one who plays between the forwards and the backs. **half-brother, half-sister** *n.* a brother or sister by one parent only. **half-time** *n.* the short space of time between the two halves of a game. **halfway** *adv.* half the distance up etc.

hall *n.* space at the entrance of a building which opens on to various rooms; a large building or room where public functions are held; a large medieval country house.

halt *v.* come to a stop; bring to a stop. *n.* a stop. *int.* stop!

halter (halt-er) *n.* a rope or strap put round the head of a horse so that it can be led; a rope used for hanging a person.

ham *n.* the upper part of a pig's back leg, often eaten salted and smoked.

hamlet (ham-let) *n.* a small village or group of houses, often without a church.

hammer (ham-mer) *n.* a tool with a metal head for breaking things and driving in nails. *v.* strike with a hammer, with fists or other objects.

hammock (ham-mock) *n.* a hanging bed or couch made of canvas or netting which may be swung by means of ropes at each end.

hamster (ham-ster) *n.* a small, short-tailed animal kept as a pet by children.

hand *n.* the part of the body at the end of the arm, consisting of the palm, the thumb and four fingers; someone who is employed to work with his hands; a pointer on a dial; style of handwriting; a number of cards in a card game given to one person. *v.* give, pass. **handy** *a.* skilful, easy to reach.

handle (han-dle) *n.* the part of a tool or utensil by which it may be held; *v.* hold or touch with the hands; control, manage; buy and sell.

handsome (hand-some) *a.* good-looking; generous (of gifts etc.).

hang *v.* attach something so that it is held only from above; place something so that it hangs; be put to death or die by hanging with a rope round the neck. **hanger** *n.* a frame on which clothes are hung.

happy (hap-py) *a.* pleased, content. **happiness** *n.* being happy or pleased, gladness.

harass (har-ass) *v.* trouble, torment, worry; attack again and again.

harbour (har-bour) *n.* a stretch of water along the shore where ships may shelter. *v.* give shelter or refuge to; keep in mind.

hard *a.* firm, solid; difficult, not easy to understand; involving energy; full of unhappiness or suffering; strict; *adv.* with determination; with force. **harden** *v.* make or become hard. **hardship** *n.* suffering. **hardware** *n.* metal goods such as nails, pans, kettles, locks etc.

hardy *a.* strong and healthy, bold and daring.

harm *n.* hurt, injury, damage. *v.* hurt or injure. **harmful** *a.* causing harm. **harmless** *a.* causing or doing no harm.

harmonica (har-mon-i-ca) *n.* a mouth organ, producing notes by blowing and sucking through small holes.

harmony (har-mo-ny) *n.* notes sounded together to give a pleasing effect; colours put together to give a pleasing effect; agreement between the tastes, feelings, opinions etc. of people. **harmonious** *a.* in harmony. **harmonize** *v.* bring things into or make harmony.

harness (har-ness) *n.* the straps by which an animal is attached to a cart, plough or other vehicle. *v.* put on harness; use rivers, tides, the atom etc. to serve human needs.

harp *n.* a musical instrument consisting of strings on a frame and played with the fingers. **harpsichord** *n.* a musical instrument resembling a piano, the strings of which are plucked by leather or quill points moved by keys.

harpoon (har-poon) *n.* a spear with barbs that stick backwards from the point. *v.* strike with a harpoon.

harsh *a.* rough and disagreeable to the eye, the ear, the touch or the taste, severe, cruel.

harvest (har-vest) *n.* the time for taking in the crops; the amount of grain, hay etc collected. *v.* take in the crops. **harvester** *n.* a person or a machine that takes in the crops.

hash *n.* meat chopped up and re-cooked. **make a hash of** do something very badly.

hatch *n.* an opening in a door, wall or in a floor which can be closed and covered. *v.* cause young to break out of an egg; make a plot or scheme.

hatchet (hatch-et) *n.* a small axe with a short handle.

hate *v.* dislike very much. **hatred** *n.* great dislike.

haughty (haugh-ty) *a.* proud, showing that one has a high opinion of oneself.

haul *v.* move by pulling. *n.* a good pull; the amount taken through effort.

haunt *n.* visit often after death as a spirit or ghost; return often to the thoughts. *n.* a place often visited.

have *v.* possess, own; take, get; cause to be done; hold; meet with; a word showing an action that is or is not yet past (have read, have done etc.); receive. **have to** must.

hawk *n.* a large strong bird that eats other birds and animals. *v.* go from house to house selling things.

hazard (haz-ard) *n.* a risk or danger. *v.* risk.

haze *n.* slight mist. **hazy** *a.* rather misty; vague, confused in mind.

he *pron.* a word used instead of the name of a boy, man or male animal.

head *n.* the part of the body above the neck which contains eyes, ears, nose and mouth; that side of a coin on which the head of the ruler or other important person appears; ability; the part of an article which is like a head; the top; chief; a point of land jutting out into the sea; the place where a boil bursts. *v.* be at the head. **heading** *n.* the title or words at the top of a piece of written or printed matter. **headline** *n.* the top line on a newspaper sheet, usually in large print. **headlong** *adv.* head first. **headmaster** *n.* the master in charge of a school. **headway** *n.* progress.

health *n.* the condition of the body or mind. **healthy** *a.* in good health, bringing good health.

heap *n.* a pile, a great quantity. *v.* pile up.

hear *v.* notice a sound with the ears; attend to, listen to; learn about, have news of. **hearing** *n.* the ability to hear.

hearse *n.* a carriage specially made to carry a coffin at a funeral.

heart *n.* the muscular organ that pumps the blood throughout the body; the centre of feelings or emotions; courage; the centre; one of the four suits of playing-cards. **hearty** *a.* strong, large, cheerful. **by heart** from memory. **heart failure** when the heart suddenly ceases to beat.

hearth *n.* the floor of a fireplace; the fireplace.

heat *n.* the state of being hot; feeling, emotion. *v.* make hot. **heater** *n.* a device for heating.

heath *n.* a stretch of wild, flat, uncultivated land, often covered with small shrubs, coarse grass and heather. **heather** *n.* a small plant with tiny white or purple flowers.

heave *v.* lift with force; lift and throw; utter (sighs etc.); rise and fall regularly. *n.* a pull, a throw.

heavy (heav-y) *a.* weighing a great deal; very great, with more than the usual size, amount, force etc.

hedge *n.* a line of small trees or bushes planted together to form a fence. *v.* put a hedge round; prevent a person doing what he wishes. **hedgehog** *n.* a small animal covered with spines that eats insects.

heed *v.* listen, pay attention. *n.* attention. **heedless** *a.* paying no attention.

heel *n.* the back part of the foot. *v.* repair the heel of a sock or shoe; (of a ship) lean to one side (with over).

hefty (hef-ty) *a.* big, strong.

heifer (heif-er) *n.* a young cow that has not had a calf.

height *n.* the distance from bottom to top; a high place; the greatest degree of.

heir *n.* a person who has the right to the property of another when that person dies. **heiress** *n.* a woman who is heir to property. **heirloom** *n.* a valuable article handed down from one generation to another.

helicopter (hel-i-cop-ter) *n.* an aircraft that flies by means of large blades which revolve above it. **heliport** *n.* a place where helicopters can land passengers, refuel and fly off again.

hell *n.* a place or state of punishment of the wicked after death; the opposite to heaven; a state of great misery and suffering.

hello *int.* a friendly greeting; a cry made to attract attention; a word used when one picks up a telephone receiver.

helm *n.* the wheel used to steer a boat. **helmsman** *n.* the man who steers the boat.

helmet (hel-met) *n.* a covering worn to protect the head.

help *v.* do part of another person's work to make it easier; keep from doing, prevent. *n.* assistance; a person or thing which has helped. **helpful** *a.* giving help. **helpless** *a.* without help; unable to help oneself.

hem *n.* the edge of a piece of cloth, folded back and sewn, especially the bottom of a dress, skirt etc. *v.* put up a hem.

hemisphere (hem-i-sphere) *n.* half a sphere, ball or globe; half the earth.

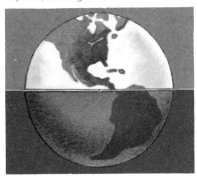

hemstitch *n.* an ornamental stitch made by gathering threads together and tying them.

hen *n.* the female of the barnyard fowl, the female of a named bird (moorhen, guinea-hen, peahen etc.).

her *pron.* a word used instead of the name of a girl, woman or female animal. *a.* belonging to her. *pron.* hers.

herald (her-ald) *n.* a person who, in olden days, carried messages from one ruler to another; something which announces. *v.* announce.

herd *n.* a large number of cows, bison, deer and similar animals feeding or travelling together; a person who looks after cattle and other animals. *v.* gather animals together.

here *adv.* at or to this place. **hereabouts** *adv.* near this place. **hereafter** *adv.* after this time.

hermit (her-mit) *n.* a person who lives alone, away from all others, to lead a religious or quiet life. **hermitage** *n.* the dwelling-place of a hermit.

hero *n.* a man or boy who has done some brave deed; the chief character in a story or play. **heroic** *a.* like a hero, brave.

heroism *n.* great valour, courage. **heroine** *n.* a female hero.

herring (her-ring) *n.* a small fish caught in the sea and used for food.

hesitate (hes-i-tate) *v.* doubt, stop for a short time as if not certain whether or not to go on. **hesitation** *n.* the act of hesitating.

hibernate (hi-ber-nate) *v.* sleep all through the winter as some animals do.

hiccup (hic-cup) or **hiccough** *n.* a sudden stopping of the breath which sounds like a light cough. *v.* make a hiccup.

hieroglyph (hi-er-o-glyph) *n.* a picture of an object representing a sound, word or part of a word. **hieroglyphic** *a.* written in hieroglyphs.

high *a.* having an extent upwards; excellent, chief; near the top of the scale in music; expensive, costing money or effort; going bad. **high-fidelity** *n.* (of radio etc.) giving a sound as near as possible to the original (shortened to **hi-fi**). **highlands** *n.* country far above sea level. **high-pitched** *a.* sounding high up the musical scale. **highroad, highway** *n.* a main road. **highwayman** *n.* a robber stopping travellers on the highway. **Highness** *n.* the title of honour given to royal persons.

hike *n.* a long walk in the country. *v.* walk long distances. **hiker** *n.* one who hikes.

hill *n.* a place where the ground rises above the surrounding land; a slope; a heap of earth made by ants, moles etc. **hilly** *a.* having many hills.

hilt *n.* the handle of a sword or dagger.

him *pron.* a boy, man or male animal.

hind *a.* (of wheels, legs, parts etc.) the back. **hindmost** *a.* furthest behind, nearest the back.

hinder (hin-der) *v.* delay, get in the way of. **hindrance** *n.* something which delays.

hinge *n.* a joint on which a door, a gate or a lid can be made to open or shut. *v.* depend.

hint *v.* suggest something without mentioning it directly. *n.* a piece of advice.

hip *n.* the part of the body where the legs are joined to the trunk.

hippopotamus (hip-po-pot-a-mus) *n.* a large, plant-eating animal with a huge head, short legs and thick, hairless skin that lives in and near the rivers, lakes etc. of Africa.

hire *v.* obtain something or the help of somebody for a fee. *n.* money paid for the use of goods or services.

his *a. pron.* belonging to him.

hiss *v.* make a sound like that of a long 'sss'; show dislike. *n.* a hissing sound.

history (his-to-ry) *n.* the story or record of what has happened in the past; a book or account of past events; the story of a person or a thing. **historian** *n.* a person who writes about history. **historic** *a.* important in history. **historical** *a.* relating to history; true, not imagined or in fiction.

hit *v.* strike with force; find; score in cricket. *a.* wounded, damaged. *n.* a blow; a successful performance.

hitch *v.* pull up; fasten, tie or become tied. *n.* a kind of knot used by sailors; a short delay. **hitch a lift** stop motorists and ask for a lift. **hitch-hiker** *n.* a hiker who hitches lifts.

hive *n.* a box specially made for bees to live in; a number of busy people.

hoard *n.* a secret store. *v.* store secretly.

hoarding (hoard-ing) *n.* a temporary wooden fence round a building which is being erected; a board on which advertisements and notices are posted.

hoax *v.* play a mischievous trick on somebody. *n.* a mischievous trick.

hobby *n.* something one does out of interest in spare time.

hoe *n.* a tool for use in the garden. *v.* work with a hoe.

hoist *v.* lift up, usually with ropes and

pulleys. *n.* a device for lifting things.

hold *v.* keep the body or part of the body in one position; take something and keep it for a while; contain; keep back; organize, conduct; remain as it is or was; fasten; occupy, be in possession of. *n.* the act of holding; something that gives a place to hold or grasp; the part of a ship where cargo is stored. **holder** *n.* an article specially made to hold something.

holiday (hol-i-day) *n.* a day when all work is suspended; a day or period when one does not go to work.

hollow (hol-low) *a.* with an empty space inside; sounding as if it comes from something hollow. *n.* a little valley. *v.* make a hollow in.

holster (hol-ster) *n.* a leather holder for a pistol or revolver, attached to a belt or saddle.

holy (ho-ly) *a.* having to do with God or religion; having given oneself up to religion; sacred.

home *n.* the place where one lives; a place where people or animals are cared for; a place where an animal or plant lives and grows. *a.* having to do with a house; having to do with one's own country. *adv.* at or to one's home or one's own country. **homeless** *a.* having no home. **homely** *a.* simple, making one think of home. **homesick** *a.* sad at being away from home. **homeward** *a. & adv.* towards home. **homework** *n.* the part of a lesson to be prepared outside school hours.

honest (hon-est) *a.* telling the truth, not cheating, fair. **honesty** *n.* being honest.

honey (hon-ey) *n.* the sweet, sticky liquid made by bees. **honeycomb** *n.* the small six-sided cells made of wax in which bees store their honey. **honeymoon** *n.* the holiday taken by a newly married couple. **honeysuckle** *n.* a climbing plant with sweet-smelling flowers.

honour (hon-our) *v.* respect, admire; pay respect. *n.* high respect; good character; a polite title. **honourable** *a.* deserving of honour.

hook *n.* a piece of metal or other material which is curved so that things can be caught and held on it. *v.* fasten or catch with a hook.

hooligan (hool-i-gan) *n.* a member of a gang of boys or men who make trouble in streets and other public places.

hoop *n.* a circular band of wood, wire or

metal; a circular frame once used to make skirts stand out; a circular ring over which paper has been stretched.

hoot *n.* the cry made by an owl *v.* make such a cry; make fun of, mock.

hope *n.* a wish for something to happen and a feeling that it will happen. *v.* expect and wish. **hopeful** *a.* believing that a thing will happen. **hopeless** *a.* having no hope, giving no reason to hope.

horizon (ho-ri-zon) *n.* the line where sky and earth or sea appear to meet.

horizontal *a.* in line with or parallel to the horizon; level, flat.

horn *n.* a hard point or spike, sometimes curved, growing out of the heads of cattle and some other animals; an instrument played by blowing. *a.* made of horn. **hornpipe** *n.* an English dance once danced by sailors to an instrument called a hornpipe.

horoscope (hor-o-scope) *n.* a diagram of the position of the stars at the time of a person's birth, believed to show his or her character or future.

horrible (hor-ri-ble) or **horrid** *a.* terrible. **horrify** *v.* fill with horror. **horror** *n.* something that makes a person terrified.

horse *n.* a large animal employed to carry a rider or as a beast of burden; a frame or block on legs used for a special purpose (to dry clothes, vaulting etc.).

hose *n.* a flexible tube through which water can be forced; stockings or tights. **hosier** *n.* a person who sells underwear, socks etc. **hosiery** *n.* articles sold by a hosier.

hospital (hos-pi-tal) *n.* a building where the sick and injured are treated. **hospitality** (hos-pi-tal-i-ty) *n.* the generous reception and entertainment of guests.

hospitable *a.* always ready to offer hospitality to others.

host *n.* a person who receives and entertains guests; a person who keeps an inn; a large number, an army. **hostess** *n.* a woman acting as a host. **air-hostess** *n.* a woman who sees to the comfort of passengers in an aeroplane.

hostage (host-age) *n.* a person taken by an enemy as a guarantee that an agreement will be kept.

hostel (host-el) *n.* a building in which students, workmen etc. being trained may live at a cheap rate.

hotel (ho-tel) *n.* a building where people may have meals and stay the night.

hound *n.* a dog with a keen sense of smell, used for tracking and racing. *v.* follow, worry, persecute a person.

hour *n.* 60 minutes; the time of day; a period of time. **hourly** *adv.* every hour, at any hour.

house *n.* a building in which people live; a building used for a special purpose; a family; the audience in a theatre. *v.* have room for people or goods. **household** *n.* everybody living in a house. **housekeeper** *n.* a woman employed to manage the affairs of a household. **housewife** *n.* a woman who looks after her house and her family's welfare.

hover (hov-er) *v.* stay in or near one place in the air. **hovercraft** *n.* a vehicle which moves on a cushion of air and can travel over land or water.

howitzer (how-itz-er) *n.* a cannon with a short muzzle which fires shells high into the air to hit the required target.

howl *n.* a long, loud cry. *v.* make such a cry; cry with howling sounds.

hub *n.* the central part of a wheel into which the spokes fit; the important centre of an industry etc.

huddle (hud-dle) *v.* crowd close together.

hue *n.* colour.

hug v. hold tightly in the arms; keep close. n. a close embrace.

huge a. very large indeed.

hull n. the covering of some fruits and seeds, especially peas and beans; the body of a ship. v. take off the outer covering of.

hum v. make a sound like that of bees; sing with the lips closed; move about busily. n. a humming noise.

human (hu-man) a. about people or like people. **humane** a. merciful, kind-hearted.

humble (hum-ble) a. modest, not showing pride in oneself or what one does; of low rank. v. make a person feel humble; lower his opinion of himself.

humid (hu-mid) a. damp (of a climate). **humidity** n. dampness, amount of moisture in the air.

humour (hu-mour) n. power to cause amusement or to be amused; temper, state of mind. v. agree with, give way to. **humorous** a. having humour.

hump n. a round lump, a raised place.

hunch n. a hump; a suspicion. v. form a hump with one's back. **hunchback** n. a person with a hump on his back.

hunger (hun-ger) n. the need for food; a need or desire. v. have such a need. **hungry** a. needing food or some other satisfaction.

hunt v. chase wild animals either for food or for sport; seek something. n. a chase after a person or animal; a search. **hunter** n. a person who hunts. **huntsman** n. a man who has charge of the hounds during a hunt.

hurdle (hur-dle) n. a frame of wood which can be moved from place to place to fence in animals; a frame specially made to be jumped over in certain races; a hindrance, a difficulty.

hurl v. throw with great force.

hurricane (hur-ri-cane) n. a violent tropical storm.

hurry (hur-ry) n. great haste. v. move with great haste.

hurt v. cause injury or pain; damage. n. harm, injury. **hurtful** a. causing hurt or injury.

husband (hus-band) n. a married man. v. save, keep ready for use.

hush v. make quiet, become quiet. n. quietness, stillness. **hush money** money paid to a person to keep quiet.

husk n. the dry outer covering of some seeds.

husky (hus-ky) a. big and strong; rough and hoarse (of the voice). n. a dog used by Eskimos to draw sledges.

hustle (hus-tle) v. push roughly. n. movement and activity.

hut n. a small building or shelter.

hutch n. a small box or cage in which rabbits are kept.

hydrant (hy-drant) n. a large water pipe, usually in the street, to which a hose can be fitted for cleaning, or in case of fire.

hydraulic (hy-drau-lic) a. worked by water power.

hydrogen (hy-dro-gen) n. a gas which has no colour, taste or smell and burns with a faint blue flame. **hydrogen bomb** the most powerful bomb known.

hygiene (hy-giene) n. the science of healthy living. **hygienic** a. free from germs or anything that may cause disease.

hymn n. a song of praise to God or to a god.

hyphen (hy-phen) n. a small stroke used to connect two words together.

hypnotize (hyp-no-tize) v. put into a state of sleep in which a person's acts can be directed by someone else. **hypnotism** n. the science that makes a person fall asleep or into a trance. **hypnotic** a. having to do with hypnotism. **hypnosis** n. sleep produced by the hypnotist. **hypnotist** n. a person who practises hypnotism.

hypocrite (hyp-o-crite) *n*. a person who pretends to be better or more virtuous than he really is. **hypocrisy** *n*. being a hypocrite.

hypodermic (hy-po-der-mic) *a*. having to do with injecting substances under the skin. **hypodermic needle** *a*. needle used with a syringe to inject under the skin.

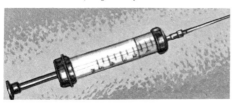

I

idea (i-dea) *n*. knowledge; a plan; an opinion.

ideal (i-deal) *a*. perfect; what one would like to be or have.

idiot (id-i-ot) *n*. a person so feeble in mind as to need caring for by others; an absent-minded or foolish person. **idiotic** *a*. foolish.

idle (i-dle) *a*. doing nothing, not working; lazy, worthless. *v*. be idle; run slowly (of an engine). **idleness** *n*. being idle. **idler** *n*. a person who idles.

idol (i-dol) *n*. an image of a god; a person very much loved or admired. **idolize** *v*. make an idol of; love very much.

if *conj*. granted that, given that; whether; though.

ignorance (ig-no-rance) *n*. not knowing **ignorant** *a*. not knowing, lacking knowledge. **ignore** *v*. take no notice of.

ill *a*. not in good health; bad, harmful. *adv*. badly. **illness** *n*. being ill.

illegal (il-le-gal) *a*. against the law.

illuminate (il-lu-mi-nate) *v*. give light to; decorate with bright lights of many colours; decorate lettering with designs and colours. **illumination** *n*. lighting, being lit or decorated.

illusion (il-lu-sion) *n*. something seen or thought which does not exist or which is unreal or false.

illustrate (il-lus-trate) *v*. decorate with pictures; explain. **illustration** *n*. a picture or diagram in a book or magazine; an example which explains something.

imagine (i-mag-ine) *v*. make a picture in the mind. **imaginary** *a*. existing in the mind but not real. **imagination** *n*. the power to imagine. **imaginative** *a*. having a good imagination, done from the imagination.

imitate (im-i-tate) *v*. copy the behaviour or actions of others. **imitation** *n*. a copy. *a*. not real.

immediate (im-me-diate) *a*. coming at once; nearest (relative, neighbour etc.). **immediately** *adv*. at once.

immense (im-mense) *a*. extremely large, boundless, very great. **immensely** *adv*. enormously.

immigrate (im-mi-grate) *v*. come from a foreign land into another country and settle there (the opposite of emigrate). **immigrant** *n*. a person coming from a foreign land to settle.

immortal (im-mor-tal) *a*. living for ever; remembered for ever. **immortality** *n*. the condition or state of being immortal; fame or remembrance.

impact (im-pact) *n*. a collision; force, strength.

impassable (im-pass-a-ble) *a*. not possible to travel on or cross.

impatient (im-pa-tient) *a*. not patient or willing to wait. **impatience** *n*. unwillingness to wait.

imperfect (im-per-fect) *a*. having a fault; not as good as possible. **imperfection** *n*. a fault.

imperial (im-pe-ri-al) *a*. having to do with an empire or an emperor. **imperialism** *n*. a belief in the value of a large empire. **imperialist** *n*. a person who believes in extending an empire.

impersonate (im-per-son-ate) *v*. pretend (either in play or real life) to be somebody else.

impertinent (im-per-ti-nent) *a*. insolent,

not showing respect. impertinence *n.* being insolent.

implement (im-ple-ment) *n.* a tool, an instrument for doing something. *v.* fulfil a promise or a contract.

impolite (im-po-lite) *a.* not polite, not showing good manners. impoliteness *n.* being impolite, rudeness.

import (im-port) *v.* bring goods from a foreign country into one's own country. imports *n.* goods brought in from another country.

important (im-por-tant) *a.* meaning a great deal, to be treated as serious; having a position of power. importance *n.* being important, worth serious thought.

impose (im-pose) *v.* put on (a tax); put in force (a law); take advantage of (with on). imposition *n.* something imposed; a task given in school, sometimes as a punishment.

impossible (im-pos-si-ble) *a.* not possible; which cannot be done.

impress (im-press) *v.* mark or stamp by pressing something on; fix in the mind; produce an effect on the mind. impression *n.* the effect produced by impressing on materials or on persons.

imprison (im-pris-on) *v.* put or keep in prison. imprisonment *n.* being imprisoned.

improve (im-prove) *v.* become or make better; make use of (time etc.). improvement *n.* getting better; something that makes another thing or condition better.

impudent (im-pu-dent) *a.* rude, not polite, not showing respect. impudence *n.* being impudent, insolence.

impure (im-pure) *a.* not pure or clean. impurity *n.* something which makes impure or unclean.

in *prep. & adv.* showing a place; showing a movement or direction into; showing time; showing what is around (rain, dark, cold etc.); showing shape or position (rows, blocks, dozens etc.); showing manner (smiles, tears etc.); here, at home; showing what one does (industry, the police etc.); of a game — showing what one side or the other is doing.

incense (in-cense) *n.* a substance which when burnt gives off a sweet smell. *v.* make angry.

inch *n.* a measure of length; one twelfth part of a foot; a small amount of space. *v.* move very slowly and carefully.

inclination (in-cli-na-tion) *n.* a slope; a nod (of the head); a bending forward of the body; a desire to do or have. incline *v.* slope or slant; dispose or be disposed to do something. *n.* a slope, a bending.

include (in-clude) *v.* count in or be counted in. inclusion *n.* being included. inclusive of including.

income (in-come) *n.* money received for work, supplying goods etc. income tax a tax based on a person's income.

incorrect (in-cor-rect) *a.* not correct, wrong.

increase (in-crease) *v.* make or become greater or larger. *n.* a growing greater or larger.

incurable (in-cur-a-ble) *a.* that cannot be cured.

indecent (in-de-cent) *a.* vulgar, offending against good taste or good behaviour.

indeed (in-deed) *adv.* really, in truth. *int.* is that so!

independence (in-de-pen-dence) *n.* freedom; not being dependent. independent *a.* free, not being controlled by others.

index (in-dex) *n.* a list at the end of a book which gives the names of subjects dealt with in alphabetical order and the pages on which they are to be found; a list giving levels of wages and prices compared with an earlier date. index finger the finger next to the thumb with which we point. card index a number of cards in alphabetical order which show where information or objects are to be found.

indicate (in-di-cate) *v.* point out, show. indication *n.* a sign, something which shows or is intended to show. indicator *n.* something (a dial, clock etc.) which shows.

indigestion (in-di-ges-tion) *n.* difficulty in digesting food. indigestible *a.* hard or impossible to digest.

indigo (in-di-go) *n.* a deep blue dye made from a plant of that name.

indirect (in-di-rect) *a.* not straight, roundabout; not intended or aimed at.

indistinct (in-dis-tinct) *a.* not clearly seen, heard or understood.

individual (in-di-vid-ual) *a.* for or of one person only. *n.* any one human being (contrasted with society, the state etc.). **individually** *adv.* separately.

indoors (in-doors) *adv.* inside or into a house or other building.

industry (in-dus-try) *n.* hard work; a branch of trade or manufacture; the manufactures of a district, a country, a continent, the world. **industrial** *a.* having to do with industry. **industrious** *a.* hard-working, diligent.

inexpensive (in-ex-pen-sive) *a.* not costing much.

infant (in-fant) *n.* a child during the earliest part of its life. *a.* having to do with an infant or infants. **infancy** *n.* the time when one is an infant.

infantry (in-fant-ry) *n.* soldiers who march and fight on foot.

infect (in-fect) *v.* pass disease germs from one to others; pass on ideas or moods. **infection** *n.* a disease which has been passed on. **infectious** *a.* spread by being carried through the atmosphere.

infirm (in-firm) *a.* weak in body or in mind. **infirmary** *n.* a building in which people who are ill may be treated, a hospital. **infirmity** *n.* some kind of illness or weakness.

inflame (in-flame) *v.* become red, swollen and tender; become angry, filled with rage. **inflammation** *n.* being inflamed; an inflamed place on the body.

inflate (in-flate) *v.* blow up, fill with air or other gas. **inflation** *n.* a blowing up (of a balloon etc.); a rising of prices caused by an expansion in the supply of money or bank credit.

inflict (in-flict) *v.* cause suffering or pain to another person. **infliction** *n.* a painful or troublesome experience.

influence (in-flu-ence) *n.* the power to alter or change the actions of others. *v.* have an effect on. **influential** *a.* having influence.

inform (in-form) *v.* give knowledge to; tell the police. **information** *n.* something communicated or told. **informative** *a.* containing much information. **informer** *n.* a person who gives evidence to the police against another person.

informal (in-for-mal) *a.* without special dress or ceremony.

inhabit (in-hab-it) *v.* live or dwell in (a place). **inhabitant** *n.* a person or animal inhabiting a place.

inherit (in-he-rit) *v.* receive property, rights, titles etc. from one's ancestors; receive certain qualities of appearance and character from one's ancestors. **inheritance** *n.* the things and qualities that one inherits.

initial (in-i-tial) *a.* the first. *n.* the first letter of a word or name. *v.* put one's initials on (a document etc.).

inject (in-ject) *v.* force a liquid into a part of a living body with a needle and syringe. **injection** *n.* the act of injecting; the substance injected.

injure (in-jure) *v.* damage, hurt. **injured** *a.* hurt or offended. **injurious** *a.* harmful. **injury** *n.* damage; an injured condition.

inlet (in-let) *n.* a strip of water extending into the land from a larger body of water; a piece of material inserted into a garment; a way in (to a reservoir etc.).

inn *n.* a public house supplying meals and beds for the night.

inner (in-ner) *a.* inside, of the inside. **inner tube** the tube filled with air inside the cover of a bicycle or motor car tyre.

innings (in-nings) *n.* the time in some games when a team takes its turn in batting; the time a single person is batting.

innocent (in-no-cent) *a.* not guilty; doing no harm; foolish and simple. **innocence** *n.* being innocent.

inoculate (in-oc-u-late) *v.* give an injection to a person to prevent disease. **inoculation** *n.* the action of being inoculated, the substance with which one is inoculated.

insane (in-sane) *a.* mad, senseless. **insanity** *n.* madness; being insane.

insect (in-sect) *n.* a tiny animal with six legs, and a body made up of three parts. **insecticide** *n.* a substance, often in powder form, for killing unwanted insects.

insert (in-sert) *v.* put in, fit or place in. **insertion** *n.* something put in; a piece of lace or embroidery inserted in a dress.

inside (in-side) *n.* the side that is in anything, the inner surface; the stomach and bowels. *adv.* in or on the inside of anything.

insincere (in-sin-cere) *a.* not honest or sincere; not meaning what one says. **insincerity** *n.* not being sincere.

insist (in-sist) *v.* say something or make a statement with great force. **insistent** *a.* said with great force; demanding attention. **insistence** *n.* insisting on a request, fact or a demand.

insolent (in-so-lent) *a.* insulting, offensive in manner. **insolence** *n.* being insolent, offensive.

inspect (in-spect) *v.* examine very closely and carefully to see that everything is correct. **inspection** *n.* being inspected; inspecting. **inspector** *n.* a person whose work is to inspect. **police inspector** a rank in the police force next above a sergeant.

inspire (in-spire) *v.* fill with hope, trust, enthusiasm or other good feelings. **inspiration** *n.* something that inspires, a sudden bright idea leading to action. .

install (in-stall) *v.* put in, fix in place; hold a ceremony to give a person an important office or post. **installation** *n.* installing; the ceremony of installing a person.

instalment (in-stal-ment) *n.* part of a story which is to be continued in the next issue of a magazine; part of a debt which is to be paid at fixed times.

instance (in-stance) *n.* an example, a fact which may support a statement. **for instance** as an example.

instant (in-stant) *n.* a moment in time. *a.* happening in a moment, at once; specially made to be prepared quickly (of

coffee etc.). **instantaneous** *a.* happening in an instant.

instead (in-stead) *adv.* in place (of somebody or something).

instep (in-step) *n.* the arched upper part of the foot between the toes and the ankle; the part of a shoe which covers this.

institution (in-sti-tu-tion) *n.* a building used as a school or hospital or for charitable purposes. **institute** *n.* an organization for a special purpose (e.g. education or social life). *v.* start (an enquiry, legal proceedings etc.).

instruct (in-struct) *v.* teach; command. **instruction** *n.* teaching; directions for doing things. **instructor** *n.* a person who instructs others.

instrument (in-stru-ment) *n.* a tool or apparatus; an instrument specially made for the production of music. **instrumental** *a.* acting as an instrument or means of doing something; of or for musical instruments. **instrumentalist** *n.* one who plays a musical instrument.

insulate (in-su-late) *v.* protect by special coverings from loss of heat or electricity. **insulating tape** tape specially made to wrap round electric wire to prevent anything touching the metal inside.

insult (in-sult) *v.* act or speak in a way that hurts or offends another person. *n.* an action or remark which insults others.

intelligence (in-tel-li-gence) *n.* the power to understand and learn things; news, especially with regard to important happenings. **intelligent** *a.* having or showing intelligence. **intelligible** *a.* that can be understood.

intercept (in-ter-cept) *v.* take, catch or seize something between its departure and its arrival at its destination. **interceptor** *n.* something (especially an aeroplane) that intercepts.

interest *n.* the state of wanting to know,

being curious about something; something that makes one concerned or curious; what one is concerned in doing, seeing, hearing, reading etc.; money paid for the use of other money borrowed. *v.* make a person interested in something. **interesting** *a.* arousing, holding the interest and attention.

interfere (in-ter-fere) *v.* show too much interest or break in on the affairs of other people without being asked to do so. **interference** *n.* interfering, the state of being interfered with (also applied to radio and television reception).

interior (in-te-ri-or) *a.* inside. *n.* the inside of an object, the inland areas of a country.

internal (in-ter-nal) *a.* having to do with the interior or inside. **internal combustion** the source of power by which a petrol engine is driven.

international (in-ter-na-tion-al) *a.* happening, existing, being carried on between nations.

interpret (in-ter-pret) *v.* explain, make clear; show by performing, painting, acting etc.; translate, usually by word of mouth. **interpretation** *n.* a meaning given by explanation or performance. **interpreter** *n.* a person who translates from another language, who interprets.

interrupt (in-ter-rupt) *v.* make a break in; break in on the work or conversation of other people. **interruption** *n.* the act of breaking in in this way.

interval (in-ter-val) *n.* time between two events or two points in time; space between two objects or points; a difference in pitch between two notes in a musical scale.

intervene (in-ter-vene) *v.* come between events in time; interfere between persons in a dispute. **intervention** *n.* intervening, especially between countries.

interview (in-ter-view) *n.* a meeting between an employer and a person applying for a post; a meeting between an important person and a reporter who wishes to know his views. *v.* have an interview with.

intimate (in-ti-mate) *a.* close and familiar; private; (of something one has studied) well-known. **intimacy** *n.* close friendship or knowledge of someone.

intoxicate (in-tox-i-cate) *v.* make a person drunk; excite a person so that he

cannot think clearly or control himself. **intoxicant** *n.* something that intoxicates. **intoxication** *n.* being intoxicated.

introduce (in-tro-duce) *v.* make persons known to each other; make use of something (machinery, ideas etc.) for the first time; bring forward (ideas, schemes, bills in Parliament etc.) for the first time; put in, insert into.

introduction (in-tro-duc-tion) *n.* introducing or being introduced; making persons known to each other; the first paragraph or sentence of a book or a speech. **introductory** *a.* which introduces, by way of introduction.

invade (in-vade) *v.* enter another country and try to take it by force of arms. **invader** *n.* a person who invades. **invasion** *n.* invading or being invaded.

invalid (in-va-lid) *n.* a person who is weak through illness or injury. *a.* having to do with an invalid. *v.* take people out of the forces because they are unfit. **invalid** (in-vá-lid) *a.* of no force or value.

invent (in-vent) *v.* make or plan something that has not existed before; make up (excuses etc.). **invention** *n.* inventing; something that has been invented. **inventor** *n.* a person who invents.

invest (in-vest) *v.* put money into a bank, a building society etc.; surround a town with armed forces. **investment** *n.* the money invested; the act of investing.

investigate (in-ves-ti-gate) *v.* examine; enquire into, find out about. **investigator** *n.* a person who investigates. **investigation** *n.* an examination or enquiry.

invite (in-vite) *v.* ask somebody to attend at a place, or to do a thing; tempt, encourage to do something. **inviting** *a.* tempting. **invitation** *n.* the act of inviting, something that invites.

iodine (i-o-dine) *n.* a dark brown substance obtained from seaweed and used as an antiseptic and germicide.

iron (i-ron) *n.* a hard, heavy metal from which steel is made; an article made of iron (fire-irons, gridiron etc.); a device for pressing cloth under heat. *v.* smooth cloth with an iron; clear up a difficulty. *a.* strong (of nerves, the will etc.). **iron curtain** a phrase first used by Sir Winston Churchill to denote the closed border between the West and the communist countries allied to Russia. **iron lung** an air-tight case fitted over the body to help a sick person breathe.

irregular (ir-reg-u-lar) *a.* not straight or even, not regular in shape etc.; against the rules, contrary to what has been customary.

irrigate (ir-ri-gate) *v.* supply crops with water by means of artificial ditches, overhead pipes etc. **irrigation** *n.* the act of irrigating.

irritate (ir-ri-tate) *v.* annoy, make angry; make sore and uncomfortable or inflamed. **irritation** *n.* irritating; being irritated.

island (is-land) *n.* (rhymes with *highland*) a piece of land surrounded by water; a platform in a busy road for the safety of people who wish to cross. *a.* having to do with an island or islands. **isle** *n.* another word for an island.

issue (is-sue) *v.* come out, go out, flow out, put out; publish. *n.* the putting out or publishing of something; the thing put out or published; the result of a previous happening or condition.

isthmus (isth-mus) *n.* a strip of land joining two larger bodies of land.

item (i-tem) *n.* a separate article on a list; a separate piece or paragraph of news. **itemize** *v.* write down every detail of something.

ivory (i-vo-ry) *n.* a white, bone-like substance forming the tusks of elephants and used 'for making ornaments, piano keys etc.

ivy (i-vy) *n.* a climbing clinging evergreen plant with dark, shiny leaves.

J

jack *n.* a device for lifting heavy weights, especially cars and other vehicles; a small ball at which the players aim in the game of bowls; the knave in a pack of playing cards, ranking between the ten and the queen; a flag. *v.* raise a weight with a jack. **jackass** *n.* a male ass; a foolish person. **jackpot** *n.* the chief prize in a lottery and in some games.

jacket (jack-et) *n.* a coat which reaches just below the hips, with short or long sleeves; an outside covering (of a book, a potato, a water-heater etc.).

jag *v.* cut or tear unevenly. **jagged** *a.* with rough, uneven edges.

jam *v.* crush, be crushed; become fixed so that a machine cannot work; crowd tightly together, interfere with a radio programme broadcast from another station. *n.* many things or people crowded together; an awkward or difficult situation; a preserve made by boiling fruit with sugar.

jangle (jan-gle) *v.* give out a harsh, loud clanging sound. *n.* such a sound.

jar *v.* give unpleasant feelings, have an unpleasant effect, conflict, be out of harmony with. *n.* a shock, a thrill; a sudden harsh sound or vibration; a vessel, often made of glass, with a wide opening at the top.

javelin (jave-lin) *n.* a long light spear thrown by hand, especially in sports events.

jaw *n.* one of the two bones which form the frame of the mouth.

jealous (jeal-ous) *a.* feeling resentment

against another person who is more successful, wealthier etc. **jealousy** *n.* an instance of this, an act which shows that one is jealous.

jeer *v.* mock, cry out or laugh rudely; *n.* a jeering remark; mockery, rude laughter.

jelly (jel-ly) *n.* a food made by boiling sugar and fruit juice which, when cool makes a soft, transparent substance; a portion of this substance turned out of a mould on to a dish; any substance resembling jelly. **jelly-fish** *n.* a fish whose body resembles a soft, circular piece of jelly.

jerk *n.* a sudden movement, a push, pull, twist, throw etc. done quickly. *v.* give a jerk to something; move with a jerk. **jerky** *a.* moving in jerks.

jersey (jer-sey) *n.* a woollen garment which covers the body down to the waist and has sleeves; a cow belonging to the breed which once came from Jersey, the largest of the Channel Islands.

jet *n.* a stream of liquid or gas coming from a small opening; a hard, black mineral which can be highly polished. **jet aircraft** aircraft driven by jet engines. **jet propulsion** power given to an aeroplane through an engine which sends out jets of gas.

jewel (jew-el) *n.* a precious stone such as a diamond or pearl; something highly valued. **jeweller** *n.* a person who sells or makes jewels. **jewellery** *n.* rings, brooches, pendants and other ornaments often set with jewels.

jig *n.* a quick, lively dance; music for this kind of dance; a device for holding a piece of work and guiding the tools that are used on it. *v.* dance a jig, move up and down in a jerky manner.

jingle (jin-gle) *n.* a light ringing or tinkling sound; an attractive little rhyme which is easily remembered. *v.* make a light ringing sound.

job *n.* a piece of work being done or completed; an employment or post; a difficult task. **jobber** *n.* a dealer on the Stock Exchange. **jobbing** *v.* doing whatever jobs are given.

jockey (jock-ey) *n.* a person, usually a professional, who rides in horse races. **jockey for position** push or jostle others to get a better place.

join *v.* put together, fasten together, unite; come together; become a member of a society or organization. *n.* a place where two things are put or fastened.

joint *n.* a place where two things are joined together; a piece of meat for cooking; a place in the body where the bones come together. *a.* having to do with two or more people (efforts, ownership etc.).

joke *n.* something done or said to make people laugh. *v.* make jokes. **joker** *n.* a person who is fond of making jokes; an extra playing card, the 53rd always included in a pack but seldom used in games.

jot *v.* make a short note of something. *n.* the least bit. **jotter** *n.* a book in which one scribbles down rough notes. **jottings** *n.* rough notes.

journal (jour-nal) *n.* a daily record of events; a newspaper, magazine or other periodical. **journalism** *n.* the work of writing or publishing newspapers, magazines etc. **journalist** *n.* a person who writes, edits or publishes journals.

journey (jour-ney) *n.* a voyage from one place to another; the time taken in making such a voyage. *v.* make journeys, especially to distant places.

joy *n.* great pleasure, gladness; a person, thing or happening that causes joy. **joyful** *a.* having or causing joy. **joyless** *a.* having no joy. **joyous** *a.* full of joy, with joy.

jubilee (ju-bi-lee) *n.* the celebration of an anniversary; a period of gaiety and merrymaking. **jubilation** *n.* great joy and merrymaking.

judge *n.* a person who gives the final decision in a court of law; a person who decides the result of a match or competition. *v.* act as a judge; form an opinion. **judgment** (or **judgement**) *n.* a decision; wisdom.

judo (ju-do) *n.* the art of self-defence first practised in Japan.

jug *n.* a deep vessel or pitcher with a handle and lip; what a jug holds.

juggle (jug-gle) v. do tricks with balls, plates, hoops, furniture etc. entertain people; deceive by trickery. **juggler** n. a person who juggles.

juice n. the liquid part of fruit, vegetables or meat; the liquids in the body that help to digest food; the digestive juices. **juicy** a. full of juice.

jumble (jum-ble) v. mix or be mixed up. n. a confusion, mixture, disorder. **jumble-sale** n. a sale of second-hand articles, usually organized to raise funds for some society or charity.

jump v. leap, rise in the air by suddenly stretching the legs; go over something by jumping; move with a sudden jerk. n. the act of jumping; the distance jumped; a sudden jerk of the body; a sudden rise (prices, fares etc.). **jumper** n. somebody or something that jumps; a garment pulled over the head, usually made of wool.

junction (junc-tion) n. a place where roads or routes, railway lines etc. meet; a place where anything is joined.

jungle (jun-gle) n. land in hot countries covered by trees, bushes and creeping plants so close together that it is difficult to pass through.

junior (ju-nior) a. younger, lower in rank (also used of a son who has the same first name as his father, or the younger of two brothers in a school etc.). n. a younger person.

jury (ju-ry) n. a body of people (twelve in Great Britain) chosen to listen to cases in court and then give a decision of guilty or not guilty; a body of persons chosen to decide or award a prize in a competition.

just adv. very recently; now; only; barely; a word emphasizing something ('Just look!') a. fair, reasonable.

justice (just-ice) n. fair and reasonable conduct; lawfulness (of a cause etc.); the decision of the law; a judge, a magistrate.

jut v. stand out, be out of line with what is around.

juvenile (ju-ve-nile) n. a young person. a. suitable, fitting for a young person (to wear, say, do etc.).

K

kaleidoscope (ka-lei-do-scope) n. a tube containing many pieces of coloured glass, through which one can see colourful, changing patterns; a scene which is continually changing.

kangaroo (kan-ga-roo) n. a marsupial animal found in Australia and New Guinea with powerful hind-legs, that moves in long jumps and carries its young in a pouch.

keel n. the frame of wood or metal on which the hull of a boat is constructed.

keep v. have in one's possession; observe, be true to; celebrate, possess and look after; remain (in a state or a place); go on, continue to do something; remain good, fit to eat. n. food, lodging and attendance. **keeper** n. a person who looks after something. **keeping** n. care (safe-keeping etc.). **keepsake** n. something which one keeps and by which one remembers another person.

keg n. a small barrel, usually of less than 10 gallons.

kennel (ken-nel) n. a small hut in which a dog is kept. **kennels** n. a place where dogs may be left to be cared for.

kernel (ker-nel) n. that part of a seed inside any fruit; the softer part inside the shell of a nut, which can be eaten; the most important part of a discussion or problem.

kettle (ket-tle) n. a metal container with a lid, spout and handle, in which to boil water.

key n. a piece of metal designed for opening a door, winding up a clock, a machine etc.; a list of answers to problems, or a translation from a foreign language to help students; that part of a machine or musical instrument pressed down by the finger; a group of notes all related to each other and based on one of the notes in the musical scale; something which helps to solve a puzzle. **keyboard** n. the rows of keys on a typewriter, a piano, organ, accordion etc. **keynote** n. the note on which a musical key is based.

keyhole n. the hole into which a key is inserted. **keystone** n. the stone at the top of an arch which holds all the others in place.

kick v. strike with the foot; move the foot as if to strike; dismiss, send out with force; jerk suddenly when fired (of a gun). n. the act of or result of kicking. **kick off** v. start a game of football and resume after half-time. **kick-off** n. the start of the game.

kid n. a young goat; a child, a childish person. v. (in slang) deceive, play a joke on.

kidnap (kid-nap) v. steal or carry someone away by force illegally, often with a demand for ransom.

kidney (kid-ney) n. an organ of the body, one of a pair, which separates the waste matter from the blood and passes it out of the body in the form of urine.

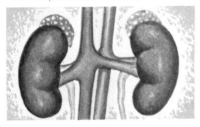

kill v. put to death, put an end to life. n. the act of killing (especially in hunting etc.); the animals killed.

kiln n. an oven for burning lime, baking pottery etc.

kilo n. a kilogram. **kilogram** n. a thousand grams. **kilolitre** n. a thousand litres. **kilometre** n. a thousand metres. **kilowatt** n. a thousand watts (in electricity).

kilt n. the short pleated skirt worn by some people in Scotland.

kin n. people related to each other. **kinship** n. relationship by birth. **kinsman, kinswoman, kinsfolk** n. relatives by birth. **next of kin** the nearest relative (or relatives).

kind n. sort, variety, class; character. a. showing thoughtfulness and love for others. **in kind** (of payment or gifts) not in money but in goods. **kindhearted** a. sympathetic, having a kind heart. **kindly** adv. in a kind manner. **kindness** n. being kind.

kindergarten (kin-der-gar-ten) n. a school for very young children.

kindle (kin-dle) v. catch fire, start a fire burning; rouse or be roused to a state of feeling (anger, enthusiasm etc.).

kindred (kin-dred) n. relationship by birth; all one's relatives. a. springing from the same source. **kindred spirit** a person with similar tastes to someone else.

king n. a male ruler of a country a very important person in some business; the principal piece in a game of chess; a playing card with a picture of a king's head on it.

kingdom (king-dom) n. a country ruled over by a king or queen; one of the three great groups of the natural world: the animal, vegetable and mineral kingdoms.

kingfisher (king-fish-er) n. a small bird which catches fish in rivers and lakes.

kiosk (ki-osk) n. a small building for a special purpose such as selling newspapers, telephoning etc.

kipper (kip-per) n. a herring which has been cleaned, salted and dried in the air or in smoke.

kiss v. touch with the lips to show affection or to greet. n. a touch with the lips.

kit n. the equipment needed by a soldier, sailor, workman or for some sport. **kitbag** n. a long canvas bag which a workman needs to carry equipment.

kitchen (kit-chen) n. the room in a house or building used for cooking. **kitchen garden** a garden in which herbs and vegetables are grown for the kitchen.

kite n. cloth or paper stretched out on a light framework which can be thrown into the air and flown at the end of a long string; a bird belonging to the hawk family.

kitten (kit-ten) n. a young cat.

knack n. (pronounced nack) cleverness; a clever way of doing something.

knapsack (knap-sack) n. (pronounced napsack) a bag of canvas or leather carried on the back and containing the things one needs on a walk, a march or in war.

knave n. (pronounced nave) a dishonest man; the card between the 10 and the queen in a pack of playing cards, the jack. **knavery** n. dishonesty.

knead v. (pronounced need) make flour and water into a firm paste called dough by working it with the hands; massage parts of the body, the muscles etc., as if making dough.

knee *n.* (pronounced *nee*) the joint which connects the upper and lower part of the leg; the part of a garment covering the knee. **kneecap** *n.* the oval bone that protects the joint of the knee. **kneel** *v.* sink down on one's knees, be on one's knees.

knell *n.* (pronounced *nell*) the solemn sound of a bell, rung when a person has died.

knickerbockers (knick-er-bock-ers) *n.* (pronounced *nickerbockers*) loose breeches gathered in at the knees.

knife *n.* (pronounced *nife*) a sharp metal blade fixed to a handle and used for cutting. *v.* cut or stab with a knife.

knight *n.* (pronounced *night*) a brave man in the Middle Ages who commanded a body of soldiers; a nobleman in old legends; a man who has been honoured by the monarch for his services and has the title 'Sir' before his name; a piece in the game of chess.

knit *v.* (pronounced *nit*) form stitches, usually with wool, so that they join to make a garment; join together firmly (of broken bones etc.). **knitting** *n.* the action of knitting, or the material made as a result of this.

knock *v.* (pronounced *nock*) hit, strike. *n.* a hit; the sound of knocking. **knock-out** *n.* (in boxing, pronounced *nock-out*) when one of the contestants cannot rise to his feet in time to carry on the fight.

knot *n.* (pronounced *not*) a place where pieces of rope, string etc. have been tied together; a piece of ribbon or material tied in a certain way; a hard part in wood where a branch has once grown from another branch, or from the trunk of a tree; a number of persons standing close together; a measure of the speed of a ship; a mode of measuring distances at sea. *v.* make a knot or knots, tie rope or string together with knots. **knotty** *a.* (pronounced *notty*) full of knots; difficult to solve (of a problem).

know *v.* (pronounced *no*) understand, have learnt; be acquainted with a person; understand through experience; be able to distinguish. **know of** *v.* be informed about. **knowledge** *n.* understanding, being familiar with or aware of.

knuckle (knuck-le) *n.* (pronounced *nuckle*) a joint in the finger, or between the fingers and the hand; the joint between the foot and leg of an animal.

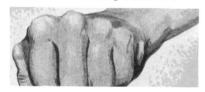

L

label (la-bel) *n.* a small piece of paper, wood, cardboard, cloth, plastic or metal which can be attached to an article or substance giving information about it. *v.* fix on a label.

laboratory (lab-or-a-to-ry) *n.* a room in which people do scientific experiments, especially in chemistry and physics.

labour (la-bour) *n.* work; those who work; a government department or political party having to do with workers. *v.* try hard, work; move with difficulty. **labourer** *n.* a worker.

labyrinth (lab-y-rinth) *n.* a maze of roads, paths or passages from which it is very difficult to free oneself.

lace *n.* a fabric made of threads joined by knots and making many patterns, used for trimming dresses, covers and uniforms; a piece of cord used to draw parts of an article of clothing together. *v.* fasten by means of laces; tighten with laces.

lacquer (lac-quer) *n.* a varnish that dries quickly, giving a hard, shiny surface. *v.* coat with lacquer, brush on lacquer.

lad *n.* a young man.

ladder (lad-der) *n.* a set of steps that can be moved, consisting of two long pieces with crosspieces for the feet to rest on; a place in a garment where a thread has broken leaving a tear. *v.* make a ladder (in a stocking etc.).

ladle (la-dle) *n.* a large spoon with a long handle. *v.* remove from one vessel to another with a ladle.

lady (la-dy) *n.* a woman; a girl or woman with good manners; a title, a peeress, the wife of a nobleman. **Our Lady** the Virgin Mary. **Lady-Chapel** a chapel in a church dedicated to the Virgin Mary. **ladybird** *n.* a reddish brown flying beetle with black spots on its wings.

lag *v.* move slowly, fall behind the rest of the party; wrap hot water pipes with material to protect them against frost. *n.* a falling behind in time.

lagoon (la-goon) *n.* a body of shallow water separated by low banks from the sea or connected with it by a narrow strait.

lair *n.* the den or resting-place of a wild animal.

lake *n.* a large body of water surrounded by land.

lamb *n.* a young sheep; the flesh of the lamb used as food.

lame *a.* crippled, injured; not able to walk properly because of an injury; not satisfactory (of an excuse).

lament (la-ment) *v.* mourn, show or feel great sorrow. *n.* an expression of grief or sorrow in verse, song or music.

laminate (lam-i-nate) *v.* separate or split into thin layers; cover with thin metal plates. **laminated plastic** (or hardboard) sheets of closely pressed paper or board, covered with hard resin and made to shine.

lamp *n.* a container with oil and a wick for giving light; any device for giving light (gas, electricity etc.). **lamplight** *n.* the light from a lamp. **lampshade** *n.* an article made of glass, paper, plastic, cloth etc. which can be placed over a lamp to dim its light.

lance *n.* a long spear with a pointed metal head used by knights in the Middle Ages. *v.* cut open with a lancet. **lancet** *n.* a small sharp instrument used by doctors and surgeons.

land *n.* the solid part of the earth's surface; earth used for farming; a country. *v.* come to land, put on land, bring (a ship, aircraft etc.) to land. **landlord, landlady** *n.* the man, woman or body of people who own property and let it for rent to others.

landing (land-ing) *n.* coming or bringing to land; a platform at the top of or between two flights of stairs.

lane *n.* a narrow road; the name of a street; a route used by ships crossing the oceans; a part of a road marked out for traffic.

language (lan-guage) *n.* a means of communication by words, signs or symbols; the manner in which a person uses words.

lantern (lan-tern) *n.* a case with transparent sides for enclosing a light and protecting it from the wind.

lap *n.* the front part of a person's body from waist to knees, when seated; a single time round a racecourse; the sound of water moving. *v.* take up with the tongue (of animals).

lapel (la-pel) *n.* the front edge of the coat or jacket that folds back to make the collar.

lapse *n.* a slight mistake in speech or behaviour; a slight failure from accepted standards (of conduct etc.); an interval of time. *v.* neglect what is good; pass out of existence through not being used.

larceny (lar-ce-ny) *n.* stealing, the wrongful taking away of another person's goods.

lard *n.* the fat of pigs melted down and prepared for cooking.

larder (lard-er) *n.* a room or cupboard where meat and other kinds of food are stored.

large *a.* of great size or amount. **large-scale** *a.* thorough, covering a large area. **at large** free (of wild animals, escaped criminals etc.). **largely** *adv.* to a large extent.

larva (lar-va) *n.* an insect immediately after it has come from the egg, and appears like a small worm.

larynx (lar-ynx) *n.* that part of the windpipe where the vocal cords are. **laryngitis** *n.* inflammation of the larynx.

lash *v.* beat, strike with violence; rouse (to anger, fury etc.); fasten tightly with rope. *n.* that part of a whip which can be swung to give the stroke; the hairs on the edge of the eyelid.

lass *n.* a girl or young woman.

lasso (las-so) *n.* (rhymes with *shoe*) a long rope with a slip-knot and noose, used by cowboys for catching horses and cattle *v.* catch with a lasso.

last *a.* final, after all others; coming just before the present; the only one (or ones) left. *v.* go on, be enough for. *n.* a piece of iron or wood shaped like a foot on which shoes are made or stretched. **lasting** *a.* continuing for a long time.

latch *n.* a device to hold a door or gate shut; a small lock with a spring inside it, opened from the outside with a latchkey. *v.* fasten with a latch.

late *adv.* after the time fixed or expected; near the end (of the week, year, performance etc.). *a.* recent, that has just happened; recently dead. **lately** *adv.* recently.

lath *n.* (rhymes with *path*) a long, thin strip of wood, used for such things as trellis, plastering walls and the making of certain kind of blinds.

lathe *n.* a machine in which a piece of wood or metal can be fixed and shaped by turning.

lather (lath-er) *n.* the mass of white foam which forms as, for instance, when soap is rubbed with water. *v.* make and apply lather; foam (at the mouth).

latitude (lat-i-tude) *n.* the number of degrees north or south of the Equator; freedom to act or speak as one wishes.

latter (lat-ter) *a.* belonging to the later part of a certain period; the second of two things already mentioned.

laugh *v.* make sounds with the voice and movements of the face to show joy or merriment. *n.* the act of laughing, the sound made by laughing. **laughter** *n.* laughing.

launch *v.* float a boat or a ship; start a scheme, an action or a project. *n.* a small motor-driven boat which carries passengers on short journeys; the act of launching a boat or ship.

laundry (laun-dry) *n.* a place where clothes are washed and ironed; linen or clothes which are to be washed and ironed. **launder** *v.* wash and iron. **laundrette** *n.* a place to which people may take their clothes and have them washed in a machine while they wait.

lava (la-va) *n.* molten rock which is thrown or which flows out of a volcano.

lavatory (lav-a-to-ry) *n.* an apparatus which gets rid of the waste products from a human being, a toilet; a room in which one may wash one's hands and face.

law *n.* a rule by which the behaviour or way of life of the people of a country or town are controlled; all the laws of a country; what is sure to happen under certain conditions. **lawful** *a.* allowed by law. **lawless** *a.* not obeying the law. **lawyer** *n.* a person who has studied law and deals with matters having to do with it; a solicitor.

lay *v.* put in a certain position; produce (of birds and some animals); put or keep down (carpets, lino etc.); arrange (the table, the fire etc.); put on (a tax); put down (money for bets etc.). **lay-by** *n.* a place at the side of a main road where cars and lorries may park for a limited time.

layer (lay-er) *n.* one thickness of material laid over another; the shoot of a plant fastened down to the ground to take root. *v.* fasten down the shoot of a plant.

lazy (la-zy) *a.* not willing to work; not working properly (the eye etc.). *n.* a time when one is not working. **laziness** *n.* being lazy.

lead *n.* (rhymes with *said*) a soft, heavy metal used for making roofs and pipes, and for mixing with other metals; a name commonly given to graphite, the material used in 'lead' pencils. **leaden** *a.* made of lead or looking like lead.

lead *v.* (rhymes with *need*) guide, show the way, take by the hand or by a strap, rope etc.; direct by example (a choir, an orchestra); go first; be a way to, a road to; go through, spend, live (life); put down the first card in a part of a game; *n.* the act of guiding or leading; the first place; a strap for leading (animals etc.); an electric flex for taking current to the place where it is needed; the principal part in a play. **leader** *n.* a person who leads.

league *n.* a group of nations, societies or persons working for a common cause; a group of clubs playing the same sport.

leak *n.* a crack or a hole through which gas or liquid may escape or enter. *v.* pass in or out through a leak. *n.* the passing of secret information. **leakage** *n.* a leak (especially of secrets).

lean *a.* containing no fat, not fat; poor, producing little in the way of harvest, returns or profit. *v.* be or put into a sloping position (backwards, forwards etc.); be or put into a sloping position against something; depend (on a person).

leap *v.* jump, jump over, make (an animal etc.) jump over. *n.* a jump. **leap-frog** *n.* a game in which players leap over others who are stooping. **leap-year** one year in four in which February has 29 days.

learn *v.* come to know through effort, study, practice, being taught or from books, radio etc.

leash *n.* a leather strap for holding a dog; a lead.

leather (leath-er) *n.* material for clothes, shoes and other articles of use made from the skins of animals. **leatherjacket** *n.* the grub of the crane-fly, often responsible for damaging lawns and cricket-pitches.

ledge *n.* a narrow shelf; a reef or line of rocks under the sea or under other bodies of water.

ledger (led-ger) *n.* a book in which the accounts of a business are kept.

leg *n.* one of the limbs on which a human being or an animal walks; that part of a garment which covers the leg; one of the supporters of a piece of furniture; that part of a cricket field to the left rear of a batsman; a stage or any given distance in a relay race or a journey. **-legged** *a.* having legs (long-legged etc.). **legless** *a.* having no legs. **leggings** *n.* coverings for the legs.

legacy (leg-a-cy) *n.* a gift of property given to a person through the will of another person who has died. **legatee** *n.* somebody who receives a legacy.

legal (le-gal) *a.* connected with the law; allowed, required or authorized by the law.

legend (le-gend) *n.* a story made up in the past which is believed by some to be true. **legendary** *a.* told about in legend.

legible (leg-i-ble) *a.* capable of being read easily. **legibly** *adv.* in a legible manner.

legislate (leg-is-late) *v.* make laws. **legislation** *n.* laws, the making of laws. **legislature** *n.* the body of people making the laws (in Great Britain, Parliament).

leisure (lei-sure) *n.* spare time; time when one is not working. **leisurely** *adv.* with no haste or hurry.

lemon (lem-on) *n.* a pale yellow fruit with very sour juice, used for flavouring. **lemonade** *n.* a drink made from lemon juice, sugar and water.

lend *v.* give something for a certain length of time on condition that it is returned.

length *n.* how long anything is; how long something lasts; a piece of cloth (usually for making up into a garment etc.). **lengthen** *v.* make longer.

lenient (le-nient) *a.* merciful, not inclined to punish.

lens *n.* a piece of glass specially made with one or both sides curved, for use in spectacles, telescopes, cameras etc.

Lent *n.* the period of forty days before Easter, set aside for fasting and worship and observed by many Christians.

lentil (len-til) *n.* a plant with a seed like a

small bean; the seed of the lentil plant, used for food.

leopard (leop-ard) *n.* a large, fierce animal of the cat family, living in Africa and southern Asia. The leopard has a yellowish coat with spots.

leper (le-per) *n.* a person suffering from a disease of the skin which eats into the body and slowly destroys parts of it. **leprosy** *n.* the disease from which lepers suffer.

less *a. adv.* not so much, a smaller quantity.

lesson (les-son) *n.* something to be learnt or taught; the period of time (usually in minutes) given to learning one subject; a passage from the Bible read as part of a church service.

lest *conj.* for fear that; in case (after fear, be afraid) that.

let *v.* allow to; hire, rent (house, room etc.). **let in** *v.* allow to come in **let off** *v.* excuse, fire off (a weapon etc.).

lethal (leth-al) *a.* causing, intended or liable to cause death.

letter (let-ter) *n.* a sign representing a sound; one character in an alphabet; a written message. **lettering** *n.* printed or written words. **letterhead** *n.* the printed name and address of a person or firm at the top of a sheet of paper.

lettuce (let-tuce) *n.* a garden plant with large tender green leaves used in salads.

level (lev-el) *n.* a horizontal line or surface. *a.* having such a surface. *v.* make or become level or flat; raise (a gun etc.). **level crossing** a place where a road and a railway cross each other, usually protected by barriers. **spirit level** an instrument containing an air bubble which shows when a surface is exactly level.

lever (le-ver) *n.* a bar or other instrument used for lifting weights, forcing open

doors etc. *v.* move or open something with a lever.

levy (lev-y) *v.* impose, put on (a tax etc.); collect by authority. *n.* a tax or fine. **levy war upon** make war after levying or collecting men and supplies.

liable (li-a-ble) *a.* responsible by law; subject to (fines, danger etc.); likely to (do something).

liberal (lib-er-al) *a.* generous, giving freely; plentiful (of supplies, food etc.); *n.* a member of the Liberal Party; a British political party. **liberality** *n.* generosity, an inclination to give freely.

liberty *n.* the condition of being free, not captive or imprisoned; freedom (to speak, think etc.).

library (li-bra-ry) *n.* a place where books are kept; a book borrowed from a lending library; a room in a private house for writing or reading. **librarian** *n.* a person who looks after a library.

licence (li-cence) *n.* a statement giving permission to a person or persons to do something or own something e.g. driving, keeping a dog. **license** (li-cense) *v.* give a licence to. **licensed premises** places such as hotels, restaurants, public houses etc. licensed to sell alcoholic drinks.

lieutenant (lieu-ten-ant) *n.* (pronounced *leftenant*) a junior officer in the army next below a captain, and in the navy next below a lieutenant-commander. **flight-lieutenant** *n.* a rank in the Royal Air Force above a flying officer and below a squadron leader.

life *n.* that which lives, grows and produces young; a human being; a way of living; the time between birth and death; the biography of a person; energy, interest, activity. **lifetime** *n.* the length of time one lives.

light *a.* the opposite of dark, so that things can be seen; of a pale colour; gentle (of touching, a breeze etc.); not deep (of sleep); *n.* that which makes it possible to see things; anything that gives light; a flame; knowledge, information; an opening in a wall letting in light. **light-headed** *a.* dizzy. **light-hearted** *a.* cheerful. **light-fingered** *a.* clever at stealing.

lighten (light-en) *v.* make or grow lighter; make brighter. **lightning** *n.* flashes of light in the sky produced by electricity in the atmosphere. **lightning conductor** a rod of metal which, by taking lightning down to the ground, prevents it doing damage to buildings.

like *v.* be fond of, enjoy; desire to have or do something. *a.* similar to, resembling. **likeable** *a.* pleasant, friendly. **likely** *a. & adv.* probable, probably. **liking** *n.* fondness. **likeness** *n.* resemblance, portrait.

lily (li-ly) *n.* a plant, of which there are many kinds, growing from a bulb.

lily-of-the-valley *n.* a small white flower with a sweet scent.

limb *n.* the leg or arm of a human being or an animal; the branch of a tree.

lime *n.* a white powder made by burning limestone, used for making cement and whitewash; a tree with sweet-smelling yellow blossom and fruit resembling a lemon. **lime-kiln** *n.* an oven specially made for burning limestone. **quick-lime** *n.* burnt lime before water is added. **slaked lime** lime after the addition of water. **limelight** *n.* a powerful white light for lighting the stage of a theatre. **in the limelight** the object of public interest.

limit (lim-it) *n.* a boundary line; a point beyond which one must not go. *v.* put a limit on. **limitless** *a.* without limit. **limited company** (shortened to Ltd.) a company whose members are liable only to the amount of money they hold in shares.

limp *a.* not stiff, drooping. *v.* walk in a lame fashion. *n.* a jerky movement.

line *n.* a length of thread, wire, rope or string; a long mark made by a pen, pencil, brush etc., a row of persons or things; a railway track or route; a method of doing something; a succession of kings, members of families etc.; military posts joined together for defence; some kind of work or activity; a row of words on a page or of notes in music; any goods to be bought or sold. *v.* mark with lines; cover the inside of. **liner** *n.* a ship or aircraft travelling on a certain route or line. **linesman** *n.* a person who watches the boundary line of a football pitch or a tennis court and judges when the ball is out of play. **lining** *n.* a layer on the inner side of something such as a coat, box etc.

linen (lin-en) *n.* cloth made from flax; articles made from linen. *a.* made from linen.

link *n.* one ring of a chain; a torch once used to light people along the streets, often carried by a link-boy; something or an event which connects others. **links** *n.* a golf course.

lion (li-on) *n.* a large animal of the cat family found in Africa and southern Asia. **lioness** *n.* a female lion.

lip *n.* the fleshy fold above and below the mouth; part of the edge of a vessel which sticks out so that liquids may be poured from it. **lip-reading** *n.* a method used by the deaf of watching the lips to find out what others are saying. **lipstick** *n.* a stick of some coloured substance used for colouring the lips.

liquid (liq-uid) *n.* a substance such as water or oil that flows freely and can be poured out. *a.* in the form of a liquid. **liquefy** *v.* turn into a liquid. **liquidate** *v.* bring to an end, kill. **liquor** *n.* a drink containing alcohol. **liquorice** *n.* a substance taken from the root of a plant, used in drinks, medicine and sweets.

list *n.* a number of names or figures in a row or column. *v.* make a list; lean over to one side.

listen (lis-ten) *v.* try to hear; pay attention. **listen in** *v.* listen to a radio broadcast; eavesdrop. **listener** *n.* one who listens, especially to the radio.

literature (lit-er-a-ture) *n.* stories, poems, essays, biographies etc. published in books; written material sent out as advertisements. **literary** *a.* having to do with the writing of books etc. **literate** *a.* able to read and write. **literacy** *n.* ability to read and write.

litter (lit-ter) *n.* all kinds of waste paper, bottles etc. scattered about; straw used as bedding for animals; the young of an animal immediately after birth; a couch or a stretcher used to carry people. *v.* leave odds and ends about.

little (lit-tle) *a.* small; short; not much, a small quantity or amount. *adv.* slightly.

live *v.* (rhymes with *give*) be alive; dwell; feed, keep alive by means of; pass one's life. **living** *n.* a means of keeping alive, a way of life. **living room** the room which a family uses during the day for recreation and entertaining. **live** *a.* (rhymes with *hive*) being alive, having life; burning hot, unexploded; carrying electricity, not recorded (of a broadcast programme). **lively** *adv.* bright, gay, exciting.

liver (liv-er) *n.* an organ of the body which helps in the digestion of food; the liver of an animal used as food.

load *n.* that which is placed in or on anything to be carried; the amount that can be carried. *v.* put loads on to a person, an animal or a vehicle; put a bullet into a gun or a film into a camera. **load-shedding** cutting off or cutting down the supply of electric current from a power station.

loaf *n.* a large piece of bread baked in a special shape; meat, sugar etc. prepared and shaped like a loaf. *v.* waste time idly.

loathe *v.* be disgusted by; dislike. **loathsome** *a.* disgusting.

lobby (lob-by) *n.* an entrance hall, a large room in the House of Commons where visitors may interview members. *v.* try to persuade members of the House of Commons to aid or prevent the passing of a bill.

lobe *n.* the lower part of the ear.

local (lo-cal) *a.* having to do with a certain district; concerning a part and not the whole. **locality** *n.* a certain place. **locate** *v.* find the position of. **location** *n.* the place where a thing happens; a place other than the film studio, where a film is photographed.

lock *n.* a means of shutting a door etc. so that it cannot be opened without a key; an enclosed part of a canal where boats can be raised or lowered by changing the level of the water. *v.* fasten with a lock; become fixed, jammed, not able to be moved. **locker** *n.* a small cupboard where things can be locked. **locket** *n.* a small case for a portrait or a lock of hair. **lockkeeper** *n.* a person who looks after the machinery of a lock in a canal. **locksmith** *n.* a man who makes and mends locks.

locomotion (lo-co-mo-tion) *n.* the power to move from place to place. **locomotive** *n.* a railway engine.

locust (lo-cust) *n.* a winged insect living in parts of Africa and Asia which flies in great swarms and devours crops and vegetables.

lodge *n.* a small house at the entrance to the grounds of a country estate; a house used during the hunting or shooting season; the room used by a porter at the entrance to a college, factory, block of flats etc.; the place where members of a society meet. *v.* receive as a guest; pay for bed and board at another person's house; become fixed in a place; place a statement with the authorities. **lodger** *n.* a person who lodges in another person's house. **lodging** *n.* a room or rooms in which one lives.

loft *n.* a room in the highest part of a house, stable or barn, used for storing things; part of a church.

logic (log-ic) *n.* the study of methods of reasoning; the ability to convince people by clear reasoning. **logical** *a.* arrived at through reasoning.

loiter (loi-ter) *v.* go slowly towards a place, stand about, loaf.

lonely (lone-ly) *a.* alone, with no company; not often visited. **loneliness** *n.* being lonely.

long *a.* having great distance from one end to the other; having much time from one point to another. *v.* desire very much. **longing** *n.* a great desire. **long-sighted** *a.* able to see things far away but not near to the eyes. **long-winded** *a.* inclined to talk for a very long time.

longitude (lon-gi-tude) *n.* distance east or west in degrees, from Greenwich.

loom *n.* a machine for weaving cloth. *v.* appear indistinctly.

loop *n.* a rope, thread, wire, line etc. which curves and crosses itself. *v.* make a loop. **loop the loop** fly an aeroplane in a loop.

loose *a.* free from restraint, not kept in check, on a lead, in a purse, box, prison etc.; not tight. **loosen** *v.* make free, make less tight.

loot *n.* something stolen or taken away by force. *v.* steal, take away by force.

lose *v.* cease having something and be unable to find it; fail to do or get something; be defeated; go slow (of a clock or watch); waste (time, chances etc.).

loss *n.* being lost; not winning, waste; something lost or destroyed.

lotion (lo-tion) *n.* a liquid used for healing and cleansing the skin.

lottery (lot-ter-y) *n.* a scheme for raising money by the sale of tickets, some of which, picked out by chance after the sale, give their owners the right to claim prizes.

loud *a.* noisy, not soft; bright, vivid (of colours). **loudly** *adv.* in a loud manner.

lounge *v.* stand, sit or lie about lazily; *n.* a room with comfortable chairs etc.

love *n.* feeling of great fondness and affection for people, things or activities. *v.* have a feeling of affection for; enjoy. **lovely** *a.* beautiful, enjoyable. **lover** *n.* a person who loves. **lovingly** *adv.* in a loving manner.

low *a.* not high, of little height; not as high as normal; small; neither loud nor high in tone; almost gone (of supplies, savings etc.); in a low position. **lower** *v.* bring or come down.

loyal (loy-al) *a.* true to somebody or some cause.

lubricate (lu-bri-cate) *v.* put oil or grease into parts of a machine to make it work smoothly. **lubrication** *n.* lubricating, being lubricated.

luck *n.* chance; good or bad fortune. **lucky** *a.* having or bringing good luck.

luggage (lug-gage) *n.* bags, trunks etc. used when one goes on a journey.

lull *v.* make quiet. *n.* an interval of quiet. **lullaby** *n.* a song sung by a mother to lull a child to sleep.

lumber (lum-ber) *v.* move heavily and noisily; fill or load with useless articles. *n.* timber sawn and split into planks; useless and old articles stored away.

luminous (lu-mi-nous) *a.* giving out light, reflecting light.

lump *n.* a piece of solid matter without regular shape; a swelling. *v.* put together in one heap.

lunatic (lu-na-tic) *n.* a mad person. *a.* mad, very foolish. **lunacy** *n.* madness, mad or foolish actions.

lunch *n.* a meal taken at midday or shortly after. *v.* have lunch.

lung *n.* one of the two organs with which human beings and animals breathe.

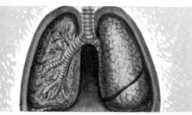

lunge *n.* a thrust as in fencing. *v.* make a lunge.

lurch *v.* suddenly lean or roll to one side *n.* a sudden roll.

lurk *v.* remain in hiding, waiting to attack.

luscious (lus-cious) *a.* very pleasing to taste, rich and sweet to taste or smell.

lustre (lus-tre) *n.* brightness, especially of a surface; glory, distinction (of a deed, a person or a name).

luxury (lux-u-ry) *n.* having and enjoying costly food, clothing and everything that is pleasant; much more than one needs; something not really needed but which gives very great pleasure. **luxurious** *a.* enjoying luxury, supplying luxury.

lynch *v.* kill someone without authority.

lyric (lyr-ic) *n.* a verse composed for setting to music for singing.

M

macadam (ma-cad-am) *n.* broken stone, crushed and rolled, used to surface a road. **macadamize** *v.* construct a road of macadam.

macaroni (mac-a-ro-ni) *n.* wheat flour mixed with water and made into long hollow tubes.

macaroon (mac-a-roon) *n.* a sweet cake or biscuit made of the whites of eggs, sugar, a little flour and almond paste or coconut.

mace *n.* a heavy club covered with spikes and used as a weapon by soldiers in the Middle Ages; an ornamental staff carried before the mayor of a town or an important official as a symbol of his office; a spice made from nutmegs.

machine (ma-chine) *n.* a device made up of many parts, all working together to do a task more quickly than a person could do it by hand. **machinery** *n.* machines or mechanical devices. **machinist** *n.* a person who works a machine.

mackerel (mack-er-el) *n.* a fish found in the North Atlantic which is caught for food.

mackintosh (mack-in-tosh) *n.* a rain-proof coat.

mad *a.* diseased in mind, insane; furious and violent (of animals); foolish. **madness** *n.* being mad. **madden** *v.* make mad or angry.

magazine (mag-a-zine) *n.* a book with a paper cover coming out at regular periods, which contains articles and stories; a place where ammunition and explosives are stored; that part of a gun which holds the cartridges; that part of a camera which holds the film.

magic (mag-ic) *n.* the supposed power of making things happen by the help of spirits or mysterious beings; tricks done by a conjurer. *a.* able to produce magic, mysterious. **magician** *n.* a person who is believed to have magic power or who does conjuring tricks.

magistrate (mag-is-trate) *n.* a person, called a Justice of the Peace, who acts as judge in a police court.

magnet (mag-net) *n.* a piece of iron which has the property of attracting other pieces of iron or steel. **magnetic** *a.* having to do with a magnet, having power to attract. **magnetic field** the area round a magnet, affecting objects near it. **magnetic needle** a magnetized steel rod which, if left to swing freely, points north and south. **magnetic tape** tape made specially for use in a tape-recorder. **magnetism** *n.* the force exerted by a magnet. **magnetize** *v.* transfer magnetic force to a piece of iron or steel.

magnificent *a.* splendid; superb. **magnify** *v.* increase the apparent size of. **magnifying glass** a glass which makes things look larger.

mahogany (ma-hog-a-ny) *n.* a tropical tree with a reddish-brown wood.

maid, maiden *n.* a young unmarried woman; a girl who works as a servant for a family. **maiden aunt** unmarried aunt. **maiden name** the surname of a woman before she marries. **maiden over** (in cricket) an over of six balls from which no runs are scored.

mail *n.* the government organization for collecting and delivering parcels and letters between one place and another; the letters etc. carried; armour of metal links worn by soldiers in the Middle Ages.

maintain (main-tain) *v.* keep, preserve; support, provide with food, clothing etc.; hold on to an argument, insist; keep in repair.

majesty (maj-es-ty) *n.* a condition, appearance or sound of great splendour. **majestic** *a.* splendid in every way.

major (ma-jor) *n.* an army officer ranking between a captain and a lieutenant-colonel. *a.* greater. **majority** *n.* the greater number.

make *v.* construct; earn; bring about, cause; cause to be or do; be or become; amount to; raise to a certain position. *n.* kind of manufacture. **make off** *v.* go away. **make for** *v.* go in the direction of. **make up** *v.* put together. **make-up** *n.* cream, lipstick etc. that a woman puts on her face. **maker** *n.* the person making a thing; (with capital M) God.

malady (mal-a-dy) *n.* a disease or illness.

malaria (ma-lar-i-a) *n.* a fever introduced into the body by the sting of the mosquito. **malarial** *a.* giving or causing malaria.

male *n.* a man, boy or the 'he' of any animal. *a.* belonging to the male sex.

malice (mal-ice) *n.* the wish to cause injury or suffering to other persons. **malicious** *a.* showing malice.

malignant (ma-lig-nant) *a.* showing a desire to cause injury; causing danger to life (of diseases).

mallet (mal-let) *n.* a tool like a hammer, usually made of wood.

malnutrition (mal-nu-tri-tion) *n.* weakness caused through not eating enough food.

mammal (mam-mal) *n.* one of the class of animals of which the female feeds its young with milk from the breast and which is warm-blooded.

mammoth (mam-moth) *n.* a huge elephant with a hairy coat and long tusks, that once lived on earth. *a.* very great, very large.

manage *v.* handle, control; be able to do, to live etc. **management** *n.* the handling of an institution, business etc.; the

people who handle affairs. **manager** *n.* a person who controls or manages a business.

mane *n.* the long hair that grows on the neck of a horse, and round the head of a lion.

manger (man-ger) *n.* a long trough or box open at the top, from which horses eat.

mangle (man-gle) *v.* crush, damage, tear, injure badly; put garments etc. through a mangle. *n.* a machine with rollers through which clothes are passed after washing to smooth and dry them.

mania (ma-nia) *n.* great excitement or enthusiasm; madness accompanied by violence and great excitement. **maniac** *n.* a madman.

manicure (man-i-cure) *n.* care, or professional care, of the hands and fingernails. *v.* care for the hands and nails. **manicurist** *n.* a person whose occupation is manicure.

manifest (man-i-fest) *v.* appear; show. **manifesto** *n.* a public declaration by a ruler, political party or revolutionary group.

manipulate (ma-nip-u-late) *v.* handle skilfully; arrange things, sometimes unfairly, to gain certain ends.

manner (man-ner) *n.* the way a thing is done; a way of behaving among people.

manoeuvre (ma-noeu-vre) *n.* a planned movement of troops or war vessels; planned movements in the training of military forces. *v.* change the position of.

mantle (man-tle) *n.* a loose cloak without sleeves; something that covers; a hood or cover fixed over a flame which becomes hot and glows, giving light.

manual (man-u-al) *a.* done with hands. *n.* a small book of instructions, a handbook; the keyboard of an organ.

manufacture (man-u-fac-ture) *v.* make by machinery; the making of goods by machinery, the things that are made. **manufacturer** *n.* a person or firm manufacturing something.

manure (man-ure) *n.* animal waste or other manufactured substances spread on the ground to make it more fertile. *v.* spread manure on the soil.

manuscript (man-u-script) *n.* a book, piece of music or an article for a journal, written out by hand or with a typewriter.

map *n.* a diagram or drawing of the earth, a part of the earth, the moon, a planet or the heavens. *v.* make a map of.

marauder (ma-raud-er) *n.* a person who robs and plunders.

marble (mar-ble) *n.* limestone, often white, sometimes with coloured markings, used for building and making statues; a small ball made of glass or baked clay used by children in the game of marbles.

march *v.* walk in time, taking steps of the same length; make a person or persons march. *n.* the act of marching; a piece of music to which one marches.

mare *n.* a female horse.

margin (mar-gin) *n.* the blank space between the writing or printing and the edge of a page; the difference between buying and selling prices; an amount over and above what is necessary.

marine (ma-rine) *a.* having to do with the sea. *n.* a soldier who may serve on board ship. **mercantile** (or **merchant**) **marine** all the merchant ships of a country. **mariner** *n.* a sailor.

mark *n.* a line, dent, scratch, stain etc.; a sign; a printed sign indicating a brand name; a grade; something aimed at; the place where a race starts; a unit of German money. *v.* put a mark or marks on; have marks on.

market (mar-ket) *n.* a place to which people may go to buy and sell; trade in a certain kind of produce; a place or a country where one may sell goods. *v.* take to a market to sell. **market garden** a garden where vegetables, fruit, salad plants etc. are grown to be sold at market. **marketplace** *n.* an open space, usually in the centre of a town, where markets are held on certain days.

marriage (mar-riage) *n* the ceremony at which a man and a woman become husband and wife; the state of being married. **marry** *v.* take in marriage.

marsh *n.* an area or expanse of low, wet land.

marshal (mar-shal) *n.* a military officer of the highest rank in the army, known as a fieldmarshal; an officer responsible for arranging important state functions.

marsupial (mar-su-pi-al) *n.* a mammal whose young are born when they are only partly developed, and are then transferred to a pouch on the mother's stomach.

martial (mar-tial) *a.* having to do with war.

martyr (mar-tyr) *n.* one who suffers death rather than give up his religion or some important belief. *v.* put a person to death. **be a martyr to** suffer from. **martyrdom** *n.* death or suffering.

marvel (mar-vel) *n.* something to be wondered at. *v.* wonder at, be surprised at. **marvellous** *a.* wonderful.

mascot (mas-cot) *n.* a person, animal or thing that is supposed to bring good luck.

masculine (mas-cu-line) *a.* of or like a man. *n.* a class of words in grammar.

mask *n.* a covering for the face worn as a disguise or to hide the features; a breathing apparatus to protect the wearer against smoke and poisonous gases. *v.* put on or wear a mask.

mason (ma-son) *n.* a person who builds or works in stone. **masonry** *n.* stonework.

masquerade (mas-quer-ade) *n.* a party or ball at which all the guests wear masks. *v.* pretend by disguise or other methods, to be another person.

mass *n.* a large quantity; a large lump or number without shape. *v.* join or come together. **Mass** *n.* the celebration of holy communion in a Roman Catholic church. **mass meeting** a large number of people meeting to give their views about something. **mass production** the making of large numbers of articles, all alike, with machines.

massacre (mass-a-cre) *n.* the merciless killing of large numbers of innocent people. *v.* carry out a massacre.

massage (mas-sage) *n.* treatment of the body by rubbing and pressing to make the muscles and joints less painful. *v.* rub, knead and press the muscles and joints.

mast *n.* a tall upright pole which supports the sail of a boat or ship.

master (mas-ter) *n.* a person who rules and controls; a person whose skill at a certain kind of work is recognized; the captain of a merchant ship; the way of addressing a boy or young man; a male teacher; the holder of a university degree above that of bachelor. *v.* learn a subject thoroughly; control. **masterpiece** *n.* a picture, poem, novel, piece of music etc., recognized by all as being extremely good. **masterful** *a.* liking to control or order others. **mastery** *n.* complete control of some activity.

mastiff (mas-tiff) *n.* a large, powerful dog, used mainly as a watchdog.

mat *n.* a piece of material, usually woven, for covering floors, putting under ornaments, on the dining table etc. *v.* tangle or be tangled together.

mate *n.* a ship's officer below the rank of captain; one of a pair of animals or birds. *a.* become one of a pair or couple (of animals).

material (ma-te-ri-al) *n.* the substances out of which a thing is made or with which things are done. *a.* having to do with the body and its needs; very important (of the law etc.). **materialize** *v.* become real.

maternal (ma-ter-nal) *a.* having to do with a mother.

mathematics (math-e-mat-ics) *n.* the study of numbers and measurements (length, breadth, area, time, amount).

mathematical *a.* having to do with mathematics.

matinée (mat-i-née) *n.* the afternoon performance at a theatre or cinema.

matter (mat-ter) *n.* all material things of which the universe is composed; something to think or talk about; things printed or written; importance; something wrong. *v.* be important.

mattress (mat-tress) *n.* a large thick pad which may be of wool and contain springs, or of feathers, foam rubber etc., made specially to sleep on.

mature (ma-ture) *v.* ripen, become ready for use, become fully developed. *a.* fully grown up, adult; well thought out.

maul *v.* injure by rough treatment.

maximum (max-i-mum) *a.* the greatest (number, quantity, amount etc.).

may *v.* possibly, have been, will etc.; be allowed to; hope that.

mayor (rhymes with *fair*) the chief officer and head of the corporation of a town or city. **mayoress** *n.* the wife of a mayor; the woman a mayor or lady mayor chooses as companion in office for the year.

maze *n.* a confusing network of paths; anxiety or confusion of mind.

meadow (mead-ow) *n.* a field where grass is grown, usually for making hay.

mean *v.* plan, think of doing; intend to say; be of value. *a.* looking poor or weak; of low rank; selfish. **means** *n.* money, the way in which things are done.

measure (meas-ure) *n.* the size, weight, amount etc.; something with which size, amount, weight etc. is found; laws or actions to bring about a result. *v.* find the size, weight or amount; be a certain size etc. **measurement** *n.* the figures found by measuring.

meat *n.* the flesh of animals (not including that of fish and birds); food in general.

mechanic (me-chan-ic) *n.* a skilled workman who makes and repairs machinery. **mechanical** *a.* having to do with machinery; done without thought. **mechanism** *n.* the working parts of a machine.

medal (med-al) *n.* a badge, usually a flat piece of metal with a design on it, given to a person for long service, bravery or for some other reason.

meddle (med-dle) *v.* busy oneself in other people's affairs without being asked.

mediate (me-di-ate) *v.* act as go-between or peace-maker, succeed in making peace by doing this.

medicine (med-i-cine) *n.* the study of the means of preventing or curing disease; the substances taken to help cure illnesses. **medical** *a.* having to do with medicine.

medieval (med-i-e-val) *a.* having to do with the Middle Ages (about 800 to 1500 A.D.).

mediocre (me-di-o-cre) *a.* not very good, not bad, about average.

meditate (med-i-tate) *v.* think about. **meditation** *n.* silent, deep thought, reflection.

medium (me-dium) *n.* the means by which something is done; a person who acts as a link, especially in spiritualism. *a.* not too much, not too little.

meet *v.* come upon, come face to face with; get to know, be introduced to; come together by arrangement; satisfy; pay; join (of lines, roads etc.) **make both ends meet** have enough to live on. **meeting** *n.* coming together by chance or arrangement.

megaphone (meg-a-phone) *n.* a large horn into which one speaks and which magnifies the voice so that it can be heard a long distance away.

melancholy (mel-an-cho-ly) *a.* sad. *n.* sadness.

melody (mel-o-dy) *n.* a tune; tunefulness; the chief part when two or more sing or play. **melodious** *a.* sweet-sounding.

memory (mem-o-ry) *n.* the power to bring back to mind things that have happened in the past; a period of time which a person can remember. **memorial** *n.* something chosen or made to remind people. **memorize** *v.* learn by heart, commit to memory.

menace (men-ace) *n.* danger, threat. *v.* threaten.

menagerie (me-nag-e-rie) *n.* a place where wild animals are brought together

in cages, especially in a travelling circus.

mend *v.* repair; become better in health. **invisible mending** the repair of clothes so that no trace of the hole or tear can be seen.

mental (men-tal) *a.* having to do with the mind.

mention (men-tion) *v.* speak or write about something. *n.* reference to or notice of a thing (in speeches, newspapers etc.).

menu (men-u) *n.* a list of the courses being served in a meal.

mercenary (mer-ce-na-ry) *n.* a professional soldier who is paid to fight in a foreign army.

merchant (mer-chant) *n.* a trader who buys and sells goods; a person who deals in a certain kind of goods. *a.* having to do with merchants and trading. **merchandise** *n.* goods in which merchants deal.

mercury (mer-cu-ry) *n.* a heavy liquid that shines like silver.

mercy (mer-cy) *n.* a decision not to punish a person for his offence; pity. **merciful** *a.* showing mercy. **merciless** *a.* showing no mercy.

mere *a.* being nothing more than. **merely** *adv.* only, simply.

merge *v.* join together. **merger** *n.* the joining of two or more businesses etc.

merit (mer-it) *n.* some quality that deserves praise; worth. *v.* deserve.

mermaid (mer-maid) *n.* a maiden described in fairy tales, who has the tail of a fish instead of legs, and lives in the sea.

merry (mer-ry) *a.* gay, bright, happy, joyful. **merriment** *n.* being merry.

mess *n.* dirt, filth, disorder; trouble; *n.* the place used in the army and navy to eat and for entertainment.

message (mes-sage) *n.* news, information; an errand; an important statement. **messenger** *n.* a person carrying a message.

metal (met-al) *n.* any hard substance such as tin, copper, lead, iron or gold, which comes from ore dug from the ground.

meteor (me-te-or) *n.* a shooting star, a solid body rushing from outer space into the earth's atmosphere and causing a bright streak in the sky as it burns up. **meteorite** *n.* a piece of stone or metal that has fallen to earth from outer space.

meter (me-ter) *n.* an apparatus for recording measurements on a dial. *v.* measure with a meter. **parking meter** an apparatus measuring the amount of time a car has been parked in one place.

method (meth-od) *n.* a way of doing things; order in doing something. **methodical** *a.* doing things in an orderly way.

metre (me-tre) *n.* a unit of length equal to 39·37 inches; a poetic measure. **metric** *a.* having to do with the metre or with metre. **metric system** the system of measurement based on the metre.

metropolis (me-trop-o-lis) *n.* the most important city in any country. **metropolitan** *a.* having to do with a metropolis.

mew *n.* the sound made by a cat. *v.* make the sound (of a cat etc.).

micro (mi-cro) a word meaning small, from which we form other English words. **microbe** *n.* a tiny living creature too small to be seen. **microphone** *n.* an instrument which changes sound into electricity so that it can be sent great distances. **microscope** *n.* an instrument to enlarge things too small to be seen with the naked eye.

midget (mid-get) *n.* a very small person. *a.* very small.

might *n.* great strength, great power. **mighty** *a.* having great strength, powerful.

migrate (mi-grate) *v.* go from one place to another to live; travel to another part of the world to live during certain seasons of the year (mainly of birds). **migration** *n.* the movement of people or birds to other places.

mild *a.* gentle in manner and speech towards others; not strong or sharp in flavour; not too cold (of the weather); not severe (of illness, punishment etc.).

mile *n.* a measure of distance, just over 1,609 metres. **milestone** *n.* a stone set up by the roadside giving distances to the most important places.

military (mil-i-ta-ry) *a.* having to do with soldiers, armies or land battles. **militarism** *n.* a belief in the importance of military strength. **militant** *a.* ready and willing to fight for a cause.

million (mil-lion) *n.* one thousand thousand. **millionaire** *n.* a very rich man who is worth a million or millions (of pounds, dollars, francs etc.).

mimic (mim-ic) *n.* a person who is clever at imitating other persons or animals. *v.* imitate, especially for a joke. **mime** *n.* a play in which few words are spoken, and in which imitation is the most important part.

mince *v.* cut or chop up into small pieces. **mincemeat** *n.* currants, raisins, sugar, apples, suet and spices mixed together; minced meat.

mind *n.* brain; that part of the person which remembers, thinks and directs the actions of the body; intention. *v.* be careful about; be troubled by, object.

mine *pron.* the possessive form of I; *n.* a hole or tunnel in the earth for digging out coal, iron or minerals; a metal case filled with explosive which blows up when disturbed. *v.* dig for coal or other minerals; lay explosive mines; sink with mines. **minefield** *n.* an area of land on which explosive mines have been placed. **miner** *n.* a person who works in a mine. **mineral** *n.* a substance such as iron, lead or copper dug from the earth by mining.

mingle (min-gle) *v.* mix (of things or people).

miniature (min-i-a-ture) *n.* a very small portrait of a person or a scene. *a.* on a very small scale; tiny.

minimum (min-i-mum) *n.* the very smallest amount or number of. *a.* very smallest (wage, temperature etc.).

mink n. a small, weasel-like animal living near the water whose fur is very valuable.

minor (mi-nor) a. less important; the younger of two brothers (e.g. Jones minor); a person under the age of 18. **minor scale** the scale beginning and ending with 'lah' (lah, te, doh, ray, me, fah, soh, lah). **minority** n. the smaller number; a small number of foreign people living in a country.

minstrel (min-strel) n. a person who sings and tells funny stories; one of a class of medieval musicians.

mint n. a plant which has a pleasant smell and which is used in the making of sauces and flavourings; a place where coins are made. v. make coins.

minus (mi-nus) a. less.

minute (min-ute) n. the sixtieth part of an hour. **minutes** n. the record of what has been said and decided on in a meeting. **minute** (pronounced my-newt) a. very small.

miracle (mir-a-cle) n. something that cannot be explained by the laws of nature; a most fortunate happening, hard to explain. **miraculous** a. like a miracle, as if done by a miracle.

mirage (mi-rage) n. the appearance of a sheet of water in the desert, which is really not there; a hope that cannot be realized.

mirror (mir-ror) n. a surface which reflects objects, once made of polished metal but now usually of glass; a looking glass. v. reflect.

mischief (mis-chief) n. things done without thought, which cause annoyance to others; damage; a person who is fond of mischief but who does not usually intend to do harm. **mischievous** a. causing mischief, full of mischief.

miser (mi-ser) n. a person who loves money for its own sake and hoards it, spending as little as possible.

miserable (mis-er-a-ble) a. very unhappy; bad, poor. **misery** n. being miserable, suffering.

misfortune (mis-for-tune) n. bad luck; something bringing bad luck; an unfortunate happening.

mislead (mis-lead) v. lead or guide wrongly; cause others to do the wrong things.

missile (mis-sile) n. something which is thrown or shot. **guided missile** a missile which can be shot into the air and guided to its destination.

mission (mis-sion) n. a number of persons sent out to do a special piece of work; a body of religious teachers sent to convert people to a religion; the work one feels one has to do in life. **missionary** n. a member of a religious mission.

mist n. water vapour in the air through which it is difficult to see. v. be covered with mist or vapour. **misty** a. having mist.

mistake (mis-take) n. a wrong idea or deed. v. make a mistake or error. **mistaken** a. in error.

mistress (mis-tress) n. a woman who is in charge of a house, a family or a school.

mix v. put together and stir so that one substance cannot be distinguished from another; carry on more than one activity at the same time. **mixed up** confused in mind. **mixture** n. various things put together.

moan n. a low sound of pain; a low sound. v. speak with groans, complain.

moat n. a deep, wide ditch round a castle, a fort or a large house, dug out and filled with water to defend it against enemies.

mob *n*. a disorderly crowd of people. *v*. crowd round to attack in great numbers, or to cheer.

mobile (mo-bile) *a*. able to move or be easily moved; moving, changing. *n*. a structure with many hanging parts which is moved continually by currents of air.

mock *v*. make fun of by copying. *a*. not real or genuine. **mockery** *n*. mocking, an offensive imitation.

model (mod-el) *n*. a small copy; a pattern to be copied; something of which many copies are to be made; a person who poses for artists or sculptors; a person employed to wear clothes for buyers to see. *v*. shape from clay or some other soft substance; copy the ways of another person. **modelling** *n*. the art of making models.

moderate (mód-er-ate) *a*. neither too small nor too great, too little nor too much. **moderate** (mod-er-áte) *v*. keep oneself, one's wishes, needs etc. from becoming extreme; become less extreme. **in moderation** not too much, not too little.

modern (mod-ern) *a*. of present and recent times; the very latest. **modernize** *v*. bring up to date.

modest (mod-est) *a*. not thinking too highly of oneself or one's own abilities; not large in size or amount. **modesty** *n*. being modest.

modify (mod-i-fy) *v*. change, make different; reduce, make more suitable. **modification** *n*. modifying, being modified; an alteration to suit new conditions.

moist *a*. damp, slightly wet. **moisten** *v*. make moist. **moisture** *n*. damp, vapour.

mole *n*. a small dark spot on the human skin; a small dark-grey animal covered with fur which burrows under the ground. **molehill** *n*. a pile of soft earth which the mole throws up while burrowing.

molecule (mol-e-cule) *n*. the smallest particle of matter that can exist unchanged.

molest (mo-lest) *v*. interfere with or annoy.

moment (mo-ment) *n*. a very short period of time; a point in time. **momentary** *a*. lasting for a very short time.

momentum (mo-men-tum) *n*. speed increased by movement.

monarch (mon-arch) *n*. a ruler, a king, queen, emperor etc. **monarchist** *n*. a person who believes that the head of a country should be a monarch (and not, for instance, a president or a dictator).

monastery (mon-as-ter-y) *n*. a building in which monks live.

money (mon-ey) *n*. metal coins or printed pieces of paper used by people when buying and selling; amounts of money in banks. **monetary** *a*. having to do with money.

mongrel (mon-grel) *n*. a dog whose parents are of different breeds; any plant or animal of mixed origin.

monitor (mon-i-tor) *n*. a child who helps a teacher with special tasks such as keeping order or supervising work; a kind of receiving set for radio and television etc. on which programmes are checked. *v*. act as a monitor.

monk *n*. a man living as a member of a religious group apart from the world in a building called a monastery.

monkey (mon-key) *n*. an animal that is one of a group of higher primates, the most closely related to the mammals and man, found in Africa, Asia and South America. *v*. play, behave mischievously.

monsoon (mon-soon) *n*. a seasonal wind which blows over India and the southern parts of Asia.

monster (mon-ster) *n*. a mis-shaped animal or plant, person etc.; a thing of extraordinary size or shape; a person who is in some way evil. **monstrous** *a*. evil, causing horror, very large; absurd, unbelievable, scandalous.

month *n*. one of the twelve parts into which the year is divided; a period of about 28 days or 4 weeks. **monthly** *a*. happening once a month.

monument (mon-u-ment) *n*. a statue, pillar etc., usually set up as a memorial to a great person or to celebrate some event

monumental *a.* having to do with a monument; of outstanding value, genius, brilliance etc.

mood *n.* state of mind or feeling. **moody** *a.* having moods that change quickly.

moon *n.* the satellite nearest the earth and which moves round it, whose light is reflected to the earth at night; a heavenly body moving round one of the planets. *v.* move about lazily with nothing special to do. **moonbeam** *n.* a ray of light from the moon.

moor *n.* an area of uncultivated land, often covered by heather and rough grass. *v.* make a boat or ship fast to a quay or a landing-stage. **moorings** *n.* the place at which a boat is moored.

moral (mo-ral) *n.* a lesson taught by a story. *a.* having to do with right and wrong, good and evil. **morals** *n.* standards of behaviour accepted by society. **morality** *n.* the kind of morals one believes in and practises. **morale** *n.* the state of discipline and the spirit of an army, a school, a team etc.

morbid (mor-bid) *a.* unpleasant, unhealthy (of ideas and thoughts).

more *a., n. & adv.* greater in number, amount, size; greater in extent or degree; again; a greater amount, number etc.

morning (mor-ning) *n.* the early part of the day before noon. *a.* having to do with the morning (walk, break, coffee etc.).

morose (mo-rose) *a.* bad-tempered, sulky; sullen, gloomy in appearance and manners.

morphia (mor-phia) *n.* a drug made from opium which is given to relieve pain.

mortal (mor-tal) *a.* certain to die, causing death. *n.* a human being. **mortality** *n.* number of deaths caused; death-rate. **mortuary** *n.* a building in which corpses are kept until the time of burial.

mortar (mor-tar) *n.* a mixture of cement, lime, sand and water used to hold bricks and stone together in a building; a bowl of hard material in which drugs etc. are powdered with a pestle; a very short cannon which throws shells at high angles into the air so that they drop at the place intended.

mortgage (mort-gage) *n.* a written agreement to take a loan on property promising to give up the property if the debt is not paid at the time stated. *v.* make such an agreement.

mosquito (mos-qui-to) *n.* a small flying insect the female of which feeds on the blood of living beings.

most *a. & adv.* the greatest in number, quantity, quality etc.; the greater number, the greater part of; very. **mostly** *adv.* chiefly, nearly all.

moth *n.* a winged insect resembling a butterfly. **moth-eaten** *a.* eaten by moths and full of holes. **mothproof** *a.* proof against moths.

mother (moth-er) *n.* the female parent. *v.* care for, as a mother does, with love and attention. **mother-in-law** *n.* the mother of one's husband or wife. **mother tongue** the language one has spoken from birth. **mother country** one's native land.

motion (mo-tion) *n.* movement; a certain way of moving, a gesture; an item for discussion in a meeting, proposed by one of the members. *v.* make a movement. **motionless** *a.* with no movement.

motive (mo-tive) *a.* causing motion. *n.* something causing action. **motivation** *n.* what causes a person or persons to do certain things.

motor (mo-tor) *n.* an engine, a machine that supplies power to make other machines work. *v.* travel by car. **motorist** *n.* a person who drives a car. **motorway** *n.* a road for the use of motor vehicles only.

mould *n.* a growth of small fungi on food when it starts to decay; a container into which molten material (lead, jelly etc.), is poured so that it will take its shape when solid; v. give a shape to something (a model, a person's character). **mouldy** a. covered with mould.

mound n. a small pile of earth, a small hill.

mount v. go up, get on (an animal or vehicle); grow in size or amount; put something into position (a jewel, a photograph etc.). n. the article or animal on which a certain person or thing is mounted; a mountain, especially when named (e.g. Mount Everest).

mourn v. feel great sorrow for. **mourner** n. one who mourns another who has died.

mournful a. sad. **mourning** n. sadness; black clothes worn by relatives and friends when a person has died.

moustache (mous-tache) n. hair growing on the upper lip of a man.

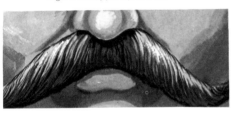

mouth n. the opening in the face through which human beings and animals take in food and by which sounds and speech are made; the entrance or outlet of many other objects. **mouthful** n. as much as the mouth will hold. **mouth-organ** n. a harmonica. **mouthpiece** n. the part of a pipe or a musical instrument which is placed in or against the mouth.

move v. put a thing in a different place; change position; go to live in another place; cause strong feelings of pity, sorrow etc. in others; put forward a subject (see **motion**) to be decided or discussed in a meeting. n. a change of position in a game.

movement (move-ment) n. a changing from one position to another; that part of a machine which moves; the effort of a group of people to change conditions; a section of a musical composition.

mow v. cut down, cut the grass, destroy (in battle etc.). **mower** n. a machine that mows.

Mr (shortened form of **mister**) the title placed before a man's name. **Mrs** (short-

ened form of **missis**) the title placed before the name of a married woman. **Messrs** the shortened form of the French word **Messieurs**, used in English as the title placed before the names of more than one man.

mud n. wet, soft, sticky earth. **muddy** a. covered with mud. **mudguard** n. a device put over the wheel of a bicycle etc. to prevent mud from flying up from the wheels.

muddle (mud-dle) v. bring to disorder and confusion. n. a confusion of things and ideas.

mule n. an animal which is the young of a mare and a male donkey; a flat slipper which leaves the heel exposed; a machine for spinning cotton and wool.

multiply (mul-ti-ply) v. add a number to itself a certain number of times; increase in number, make greater in number. **multiple** a. having many parts. **multiplication** v. multiplying, being multiplied.

multitude (mul-ti-tude) n. a great number (especially of people gathered in one place).

mumble (mum-ble) v. speak indistinctly so that people can hardly hear.

mummy (mum-my) n. the dead body of a human being preserved by the use of spices and chemicals; mother. **mummify** v. embalm and dry a dead body so as to preserve it.

mumps n. a disease in which the glands of the neck swell painfully.

munch v. chew; eat with much movement of the jaws.

municipal (mu-ni-ci-pal) a. having to do with a town or city (library, building etc.). **municipality** n. a town or city which governs itself.

munitions (mu-ni-tions) n. guns, shells, bombs, rockets etc. for use in war.

murder (mur-der) n. the unlawful killing of a person. v. kill a person unlawfully. **murderer** n. a person who murders.

murky (mur-ky) a. dark, dismal, gloomy (of the weather, darkness etc.).

murmur (mur-mur) n. a low, soft, continuous sound (of a brook etc.); soft spoken words. v. make such a sound, speak softly.

muscle (mus-cle) n. the strong tissues of the body of an animal which control the movements. **muscular** a. having to do with muscles.

museum (mu-se-um) *n.* a building in which interesting objects are displayed, especially those relating to art, history etc.

mushroom (mush-room) *n.* a fungus that can be cultivated and eaten. *v.* gather mushrooms.

music (mu-sic) *n.* sounds made by the human voice or by instruments which create melody and harmony, usually giving pleasure to those who listen; written signs which consist of instructions as to what to sing or play. **musical** *a.* enjoying or making music. **musician** *n.* a person skilled in composing or performing music.

musket (mus-ket) *n.* an old type of gun which could be fired from the shoulder. **musketeer** *n.* a soldier whose chief weapon was the musket.

muslin (mus-lin) *n.* a fine cotton cloth from which light dresses, curtains, sheets and pillowcases are often made.

mussel (mus-sel) *n.* a small creature protected by a black shell, living in the sea.

must *v.* have to; need to; may be supposed to.

mustard (mus-tard) *n.* a plant with yellow flowers and hard seeds in pods; the seeds of the mustard plant, ground and made into a hot-tasting sauce.

muster (mus-ter) *n.* an assembly or parade of soldiers. *v.* call troops together for inspection or for action; summon, call forth (energy etc.).

mute *a.* silent, not speaking; not sounded (of a letter in a word); made to sound more softly (as with a musical instrument). *n.* a piece of bone or metal put over the strings of a stringed instrument or a pad put into the bell of a wind instrument to muffle the sound; a person who is unable to speak.

mutilate (mu-til-ate) *v.* injure or damage a person or animal by breaking, tearing or cutting. **mutilation** *n.* the act of mutilating, being mutilated.

mutiny (mu-ti-ny) *n.* a rebellion of soldiers, sailors, prisoners etc. against those who are in charge of them. *v.* rebel against authority. **mutineer** *n.* a person who has mutinied.

mutter (mut-ter) *v.* mumble, say something in a low voice so that it can hardly be heard. *n.* a muttered utterance or sound.

mutton (mut-ton) *n.* the meat from sheep, used as food.

mutual (mu-tu-al) *a.* shared, held in common (opinions etc.).

muzzle (muz-zle) *n.* the mouth of a gun or pistol; the end from which the shot comes; the jaw, mouth and nose of an animal; a device of straps and wires placed over an animal's mouth to prevent it from biting. *v.* put such a device in place; stop newspapers or people from saying what they think.

mystery (mys-ter-y) *n.* something impossible to understand. **mysterious** *a.* full of mystery.

myth *n.* a story handed down from olden times, usually about superhuman beings such as gods, fairies and legendary heroes. **mythical** *a.* existing only in myths; imaginary. **mythology** *n.* the study of myths; the collected myths of people.

N

nag *v.* continually ask, scold or find fault with. *n.* an old, tired-looking horse.

nail *n.* a hard plate growing on the tops of and at the ends of fingers and toes; a thin pointed piece of metal used for hammering into wood etc. *v.* fasten with a nail or nails.

naked (na-ked) *a.* without clothes; with

no covering; not disguised in any way.

napkin (nap-kin) *n.* a piece of cloth used during a meal to protect the clothing and to wipe one's hands and lips; a towel, usually of cloth, folded and fastened between a baby's legs.

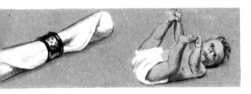

nappy (nap-py) *n.* a baby's napkin.

narrow (nar-row) *a.* neither wide nor broad, measuring little in width compared with length; near, close. **narrow-minded** *a.* not tolerant of the opinions or behaviour of other people.

nasty (nas-ty) *a.* dirty, unpleasant; bad-tempered; dangerous; having done harm (accident etc.).

nation (na-tion) *n.* a body of people who have the same government, usually speak the same language and have similar customs and ways of life. **national** *a.* having to do with a nation. **nationalism** *n.* a love of one's own nation, sometimes a desire to fight for its independence. **nationality** *n.* being a member of a nation. **nationalize** *v.* put under the control of the government of a nation.

natural (nat-u-ral) *a.* having to do with or produced by nature; being such (a musician, a footballer etc.) by nature, without having to learn a great deal from instructors. **naturalist** *n.* a person who studies animals and plants. **naturalization papers** the papers which prove that a person has taken another nationality. **naturalize** *v.* give a person the right to become a citizen of a country other than the one in which he was born. **naturally** *adv.* by nature, in a natural way.

nature (na-ture) *n.* the universe — the earth, sea, sky and all that are in them are part of nature; simple life not using many of the things man has made; qualities that belong to certain persons, animals or things.

navigate (nav-i-gate) *v.* manage and steer a boat or aircraft; sail over (an ocean .c.). **navigation** *n.* the art and science of

navigating; the act of navigating. **navigator** *n.* a person who navigates.

navy *n.* a country's warships and those who man them. **naval** *a.* having to do with a navy.

neat *a.* tidy; liking tidiness; clever; with nothing added (of intoxicating drinks).

nebula (neb-u-la) *n.* a cluster of stars resembling a cloud of light. **nebulous** *a.* like clouds; vague and not thoroughly worked out.

necessary (nec-es-sa-ry) *a.* having to be done. *n.* that which is important and cannot be ignored. **necessitate** *v.* make necessary, be necessary. **necessity** *n.* something necessary.

neck *n.* that part of the body which connects the head to the trunk; the neck of an animal used for food; something like a neck (bottleneck, neck of the woods etc.); part of a piece of clothing that covers the neck.

nectar (nec-tar) *n.* the drink of the gods in Greek mythology; the sweet liquid collected from flowers by bees; any sweet drink.

need *n.* a want, a lack of something; poverty, misfortune. *v.* want, require. **needy** *a.* poor; in need.

negative (neg-a-tive) *a.* expressing a refusal usually with 'no' or 'not'. *n.* an answer meaning 'no'; a photographic plate or film on which the light parts of the object are dark and the dark parts are light.

neglect (neg-lect) *v.* fail to give time and care to; omit to do something. *n.* the state of being neglected. **neglectful** *a.* in the habit of neglecting things. **negligence** *n.* the habit of neglecting. **negligent** *a.* neglectful.

negotiate (ne-go-ti-ate) *v.* talk about something with others in order to come to a decision; conclude, arrange (a sale, treaty, rent or loan). **negotiation** *n.* the act of negotiating.

Negro (ne-gro) *n.* a member of one of the black-skinned races which came originally from central and southern Africa.

neigh *v.* (pronounced *nay*) whinny, make the cry of a horse. *n.* the cry of a horse.

neighbour (neigh-bour) *n.* a person who lives near another; a person (sitting etc.) near another; a country which is near another. **neighbourhood** *n.* a district, a district near to.

neither (nei-ther) *a. & pron.* not one or the other. *adv.* nor.

nephew (neph-ew) *n.* the son of one's brother or sister.

nerve *n.* one of the small fibres carrying messages between the brain and all parts of the body; boldness, courage. **nervous** *a.* of the nerves; easily frightened, restless.

nest *n.* the place in which birds, animals or insects choose to lay and hatch their eggs; a number of things that fit together (tables etc.); a hiding-place. *v.* make a nest. **nestle** *v.* lie close and in a comfortable position.

net *n.* material made by knotting string, wire, hair etc., for various purposes such as fishing. *v.* catch with a net. *a.* remaining when everything extra has been taken away (net profit, net price, net weight). **netball** *n.* a game played mainly by girls in which a ball has to be thrown into a net hung from a pole. **network** *n.* lines, rivers, railways, roads, crossing each other.

neuralgia (neu-ral-gia) *n.* pains along the path of a nerve especially in the face and head. **neurosis** *n.* a nervous illness.

neutral (neu-tral) *a.* on neither side in a war or quarrel. *n.* a neutral country; a person on neither side. **neutrality** *n.* being neutral. **neuter** *a.* (in grammar) the gender which is neither masculine nor feminine.

new *a.* never known, possessed, seen or heard before; coming or beginning again; existing but not known or know-

ing before. **newborn** *a.* just born. **newcomer** *n.* a new arrival.

news *n.* fresh information as to what has happened. **newsagent** *n.* a shopkeeper who sells newspapers and periodicals. **newspaper** *n.* a journal giving news. **newsprint** *n.* paper for printing newspapers on.

newt *n.* small amphibian like a lizard, living mainly in water but also on land, which feeds on larvae and tiny water creatures.

nibble (nib-ble) *v.* bite off small bits; bite gently. *n.* a small bite.

nice *a.* pleasant, agreeable; friendly; clever, needing skill and accuracy. **nicely** *adv.* very well, cleverly.

niche *n.* a place shaped out of a wall in which ornaments may be put; a place in life or in one's work where one is happy and doing well.

nick *n.* a small cut made by a knife or axe in wood, or cut out of stone. *v.* make a nick or cut a notch in. **nickname** (nick-name) *n.* a name which is not a person's real name, but is used by friends. *v.* give such a name.

niece *n.* the daughter of one's brother or sister.

night *n.* the dark period of time between sunset and sunrise on the following day. **nightdress, nightgown** *n.* a loose garment worn in bed. **night-light** *n.* a small light, either candle or electric bulb, used to light a bedroom during the dark hours. **nightingale** *n.* a small bird of the thrush family that sings sweetly both day and night.

nimble (nim-ble) *a.* moving quickly; having a quick mind. **nimbly** *adv.* in a nimble manner.

nip *v.* press hard between finger and thumb; pinch or bite; stop something growing by taking off or damaging the growing end. *n.* a biting quality (in the air, in taste etc.).

nitrogen (ni-tro-gen) *n.* a gas which forms four-fifths of the air we breathe.

no *a.* not one, not any; the opposite of 'yes'.

noble (no-ble) *a.* good, righteous, of excellent character; splendid, admirable. *n.* a person of high rank or birth. **nobly** *adv.* admirable, in a noble or excellent way.

nobody (no-bod-y) *pron.* no person.

nod *v.* make a sign of agreement or greet a

person by bowing the head slightly; let the head fall forward as if going to sleep; move backwards and forwards as if with the wind. *n*. a nodding of the head.

noise *n*. a sound of any kind; a loud, harsh, unpleasant sound. **noiseless** *a*. making no noise, with no noise. **noisy** *a*. with much noise, making much noise.

nomad (no-mad) *n*. a person, usually one of a tribe which wanders from place to place, having no fixed home.

nominate (nom-i-nate) *v*. to appoint a person to a duty or an office; put a person forward to be elected. **nomination** *n*. the process or the result of nominating. **nominee** *n*. a person who has been nominated.

non- a prefix which indicates a negative — not being or doing something: **non-alcoholic** *a*. not containing alcohol; **non-destructible** *a*. which cannot be destroyed; **nondescript** *a*. not easy to describe; of no special kind; **non-edible** *a*. that cannot be eaten. **non-inflammable** *a*. not catching fire. **non-intoxicating** *a*. not making a person intoxicated. **nonsense** *n*. foolish talk or behaviour.

none *pron*. not any, not one.

noon *n*. the middle of the day. 12 o'clock.

noose *n*. a loop in a rope or a piece of string with a slip knot tied in it.

normal (nor-mal) *a*. regular, usual. *n* the usual state, level, number etc.

north *n*. the direction in which the left arm points when one faces the rising sun; one of the points of the compass. *a*. situated in the north, from the north (wind etc.). *adv*. to, from or at the north (facing, travelling etc.). **north-east** *n*., *a. & adv*. halfway between north and east. **north-easter** *n*. the wind blowing from the north-east. **north-west** *n*., *a. & adv*. halfway between north and west. **northerly** *adv*. in from or towards the north. **northern** *a*. having to do with the north.

nose *n*. that part of the face just above the mouth through which one breathes and is able to smell; a good sense of smell. **nostril** *n*. one of the openings of the nose.

not *adv*. a word used to make another word or words have an opposite, negative meaning (not here, not going etc.).

notable (no-ta-ble) *a*. worth noticing; famous, outstanding. *n*. a well-known or famous person.

notch *n*. a nick, a small V-shaped cut. *v*. make notches on a stick to keep count.

nothing *n*. not a thing, not anything. *adv*. not at all, in no way (nothing like etc.).

notice (no-tice) *n*. information about something; a warning of a coming event within a fixed time; attention. *v*. see, hear, observe. **notice-board** *n*. a board on which announcements are fixed.

notify (no-ti-fy) *v*. give notice about. **notification** notice given.

notion (no-tion) *n*. idea, opinion, feeling.

nought *n*. nothing; the figure 0 indicating nothing.

noun *n*. the name of a person, place, thing or quality (goodness, size etc.).

nourish (nour-ish) *v*. feed, keep alive and make grow. **nourishment** *n*. food, anything which nourishes.

novel (nov-el) *n*. a long, fictional story. *a*. new, not thought of before. **novelty** *n*. newness; something new, not known before. **novelties** *n*. various manufactured things such as toys, ornaments etc., which do not cost much.

now *adv*. the present time; the present moment. **nowadays** *adv*. in our own time. **now and then** from time to time.

nowhere (no-where) *adv*. in no place, not anywhere.

nozzle (noz-zle) *n*. the metal pipe at the end of a hose or a pair of bellows etc. through which water or air can flow.

nuclear (nu-cle-ar) *a*. concerned with a nucleus. **nuclear reactor** an apparatus which produces nuclear energy. **nucleus** *n*. the central part of anything around which other parts are grouped, especially the central part of an atom.

nude *a*. naked, not dressed. **nudity** *n*. nakedness.

nudge *n*. a light touch or push. *v*. give a slight push.

nugget (nug-get) *n*. a lump, usually of metal, especially gold.

nuisance (nui-sance) *n*. something or

somebody causing offence to others.

numb *a.* not able to feel. *v.* make numb; deaden feeling.

number (num-ber) *n.* quantity, a few, many; one issue of a magazine or journal; a single part of a stage performance. *v.* give a number to; count; consider a person or thing (to be etc.).

numeral (nu-mer-al) *n.* a word or figure standing for a number. **numerous** *a.* very many, great in number.

nun *n.* a woman living apart from society as a member of a religious group, in a building called a nunnery or convent.

nurse *n.* a trained person who works in a hospital or visits homes, taking care of the sick and injured. *v.* take charge of people who are sick; hold a child or an animal close and fondle it; give special care to. **nursery** *n.* a room in which small children are looked after; an establishment where young plants are grown.

nut *n.* the hard fruit of certain trees, enclosed in a shell; a hollow piece of metal into which a bolt can be screwed. **nutmeg** *n.* the hard seed of the fruit of an East Indian tree.

nymph *n.* a goddess of Greek and Roman mythology who lived in the sea, on hills, among trees etc.

O

oak *n.* a large tree with very hard wood, used for making furniture, ships and floors; the wood of the oak. **oaken** *a.* made of oak.

oar *n.* a long pole with a blade at one end used for rowing a boat. **oarsman, oarswoman** *n.* a rower, usually for sport or pastime.

oasis (o-a-sis) *n.* a place in the desert where water is to be found and where trees grow.

oat *n.* a grass-like plant used for food for men and animals. **oatmeal** *n.* meal made from oats.

oath *n.* a promise to do something, with the help of God; a declaration made with God as a witness that what one is about to say is true; a swear-word. **on oath** having sworn on the Bible to tell the truth.

obey (o-bey) *v.* do what one is told to do. **obedience** *n.* obeying. **obedient** *a.* obeying, willing to do what one is told to do.

object (ób-ject) *n.* something that can be seen or touched; an aim; something which appears strange, uncommon or pitiful. **object** (ob-ject) *v.* not to be in favour of something. **objection** *n.* the statement or act of objecting. **objectionable** *a.* not liked, unpleasant.

oblige (o-blige) *v.* force; bind by a promise, a rule or an oath. **obliged** *a.* forced (to be or do); grateful. **obliging** *a.* always ready to help. **obligation** *n.* something that ought to be done. **obligatory** *a.* that has or have to be done.

oblique (ob-lique) *a.* slanting, sloping, not vertical, not at a right angle.

oblivion (ob-liv-i-on) *n.* the state of being forgotten. **oblivious** *a.* forgetting; not knowing about.

oblong (ob-long) *a.* having four straight sides and four right-angles. *n.* a figure having this shape.

obscene (ob-scene) *a.* indecent, disgusting. **obscenity** *n.* being disgusting; disgusting action or language.

obscure (ob-scure) *a.* dark, not easy to see; not easy to understand. *v.* hide, make a thing obscure (by mists, clouds etc.). **obscurity** *n.* being obscure; something obscure or indistinct.

observe (ob-serve) *v.* see and notice;

mention; keep, celebrate. **observation** *n.* observing, being observed, the act of noticing, remarking, celebrating. **observer** *n.* one who observes, the name of certain newspapers.

obstacle (ob-sta-cle) *n.* something which makes an act or acts difficult or stops progress.

obstinate (ob-sti-nate) *a.* not willing to give way or yield to others. **obstinacy** *n.* being obstinate.

obtain (ob-tain) *v.* acquire, get, buy, borrow etc.

obvious (ob-vi-ous) *a.* clear, easy to understand.

occasion (oc-ca-sion) *n.* a time when something happens; a reason. **occasional** *a.* happening from time to time.

occupy (oc-cu-py) *v.* live in, be in; take possession of; fill space; fill time; fill the mind; fill a post or position. **occupation** *n.* taking possession; what one does for a living or to fill one's time.

occur (oc-cur) *v.* happen; come to one's mind; be found. **occurrence** *n.* something that happens.

ocean (o-cean) *n.* a large body of water, larger than a sea. *a.* having to do with an ocean. **oceanic** *a.* of, like or living in the ocean.

octave (oc-tave) *n.* in music, the space between one doh and the next higher doh (C to C. D to D etc.).

octopus (oc-to-pus) *n.* a sea animal with an oval body and eight arms, each ending in a sucker.

oculist (oc-u-list) *n.* a specialist who examines and treats diseases of the eye.

odd *a.* not even, a number which will not divide by 2; being one of a set apart from all the others; being one of a pair when the other is not there; not regular (jobs etc.); strange, not normal. **oddity** *n.* something which is unusual or odd.

offence (of-fence) *n.* crime, sin, wrongdoing. **offend** *v.* irritate in mind or feelings. **offender** *n.* a person who offends, usually against the law. **offensive** *a.* irritating, causing offence.

offer (of-fer) *v.* say that one is willing to give or pay for something. *n.* the act of offering; something that is offered.

office (of-fice) *n.* a place of business; a government department; a position of power and authority. **officer** *n.* a person commanding others in the forces or who is in a position of authority.

official (of-fi-cial) *n.* a person holding a position of responsibility in a society or in government. *a.* having to do with a position of authority or with a formal ceremony. **officiate** *v.* carry out an official duty.

oil *n.* grease and fat obtained from animals and plants, or liquid from the ground that does not mix with water and which usually burns. *v.* apply oil. **oil-cake** *n.* food for cattle made from seeds after the oil has been pressed out. **oilfield** *n.* an area where oil is found, usually by drilling into the earth. **oilskin** *n.* a coat made of cloth treated with oil to keep out water. **oily** *a.* like oil, having oil on; unpleasantly smooth in manner.

ointment (oint-ment) *n.* a paste made from medicines with oil or grease, and used for putting on the skin to heal sores and bruises.

omen (o-men) *n.* something which is regarded as a sign of future good or bad fortune. **ominous** *a.* threatening.

omit (o-mit) *v.* miss out; not do something. **omission** *n.* a missing out; something not done.

once *adv.* at some time in the past; at one time. **at once** immediately.

one (one) *n.* the sign of figure 1; *pron.* any person; *a.* a single person. *a.* a single; the same. **one another** each other.

onion (on-ion) *n.* a vegetable with a round bulb and a strong smell, used as food; the onion plant.

only (on-ly) *a., adv. & conj.* no more than (only one); a single (only friend); merely, simply (only came for etc.). *conj.* but.

opaque (o-paque) *a.* that cannot be seen through.

open *a.* letting things and persons in or through; without cover or roof; spread out (of a book etc.); public, admitting all people; able to be changed (of the opinion) *v.* make open; extend, spread out; let people know that a place is open; become open; begin. **opening** *n.* a gap; beginning; a vacant position. **openly** *adv.* publicly.

opera (op-e-ra) *n.* a play in which the players sing all the words and are accompanied by an orchestra.

operate (op-er-ate) *v.* work or make work; cut into the body to treat a disease or the result of an accident. **operation** *n.* a piece of work to be done; the way in which a thing works; the movement of military forces; an act performed by a surgeon on a living body. **operator** *n.* a person who manages a mechanical device.

opinion (o-pin-ion) *n.* the way a person thinks.

opportunity (op-por-tu-ni-ty) *n.* a chance, time when a chance arises.

oppose (op-pose) *v.* be against. **opposition** *n.* being opposed, resistance; the people or force opposing.

opposite (op-po-site) *adv.* facing; completely different. *n.* something completely different.

oppress (op-press) *v.* rule with cruelty; be oppressed; feel uncomfortable in body or mind. **oppression** *n.* oppressing; being oppressed. **oppressive** *a.* unjust; hard to bear.

optical (op-ti-cal) *a.* having to do with the eyes and sight. **optician** *n.* a person who makes and sells optical instruments (spectacles etc.).

optimist (op-ti-mist) *n.* a person who is always hopeful and inclined to look on the bright side of things.

option (op-tion) *n.* the right and power of choosing; what is or may be chosen; the

right to buy or sell something at a certain price within a certain time.

oracle (or-a-cle) *n.* a statement given by a priestess at a shrine in ancient Greece as the answer of a god to an enquiry; a person who can be trusted to give good advice.

orange (or-ange) *n.* a round, thick-skinned juicy fruit growing in tropical lands; a reddish-yellowish colour.

orator (or-a-tor) *n.* a public speaker of great skill.

orbit (or-bit) *n.* the path followed by a satellite or planet around a body such as the earth or sun; the path followed by an earth satellite round the earth.

orchestra (or-ches-tra) *n.* a group of performers on various musical instruments playing compositions together.

ordinary (or-di-na-ry) *a.* usual, average; not bad, not good. **ordinarily** *adv.* in the ordinary way.

ore *n.* rock or earth from which metals can be extracted.

organ *n.* a single part of the body which does its own special work; a musical instrument with a keyboard and pedals often placed in churches and large assembly halls. **organism** *n.* any form of animal or plant life. **organist** *n.* a person who plays an organ.

organize (or-gan-ize) *v.* form and put into working order. **organization** *n.* the process of organizing; an organized body. **organizer** *n.* one who organizes.

Orient (o-ri-ent) *n.* the East; the countries east of the Mediterranean Sea. **Oriental** *a.* of the Orient.

origin (or-i-gin) *n.* the beginning. **original** *a.* first; new, not seen etc. before. **originally** *adv.* at first. **originate** *v.* begin.

ornament (or-na-ment) *n.* an object that makes something more beautiful. *v.* make more beautiful by adding ornaments. **ornamental** *a.* used for ornament.

other (o-ther) *n., adj. & pron.* not the same (one); the second of two; a different one.

ought *v.* should.

ounce *n.* a unit of weight used in Great Britain, one-sixteenth c. a pound.

out *adv.* not at home; not in; at another place; not a secret any longer; into the open, showing; not burning; ended; loudly (of speaking etc.); in error (of calculating); without (of supplies etc.);

apart, away from the rest. **outbreak** *n.* the start of some trouble, a war etc. **outburst** *n.* a bursting forth of temper, rage etc. **outcast** *n.* a person cast out, turned away from family, society etc. **outcome** *n.* the result. **outdistance** *v.* go faster than others. **outdoor** *n.* the open air. **outgrow** *v.* grow too big for. **outhouse** *n.* a small building near or joined to a main building. **outlive** *v.* live longer than. **outnumber** *v.* be more in number than. **outpatient** *n.* a patient of a hospital who travels from home for treatment. **output** *n.* the things produced in industry or any single concern. **outset** *n.* beginning. **outward** *adv.* to the outside, on the outside. **outwit** *v.* get the better of others by cunning or by a trick.

outcry (out-cry) *n.* a general protest.

outing (out-ing) *n.* a trip for pleasure, a holiday away from home.

outlay (out-lay) *n.* expenditure, money put down to start a business.

outlet (out-let) *n.* a way out for liquids, water etc.; a way of releasing (energy etc.).

outline (out-line) *n.* a line showing the shape of an object; a short summary giving the main features of something. *v.* give an outline.

outlook (out-look) *n.* the view, the prospect.

outpost (out-post) *n.* an observation post for soldiers some distance from the main army; a distant part of a country or empire.

outrage (out-rage) *n.* a cruel or violent act; a shocking act. *v.* treat with violence; commit an outrage on.

outside (out-side) *n.* the outer side. *a.* of, on or nearer the outer side; out of doors.

outstanding (out-stand-ing) *a.* easily noticed; not yet attended to; still to be done.

oval (o-val) *a.* having the general form of an egg.

oven (o-ven) *n.* an enclosed space shaped like a box in which food can be cooked or heated.

over *adv.* from a standing position, falling on one side or the other; to or from (come over, go over etc.); left, remaining (of money and articles); more than (of weight, height, quantity etc.); ended; above; governing, in charge of (other persons); again (of doing things); across

(streams, roads, stiles etc.). **overboard** *adv.* over the side of a ship. **overcoat** *n.* a coat put on over all one's other clothes. **overcrowd** *v.* put too many in too small a space. **overdo** *v.* do too much. **overdue** *a.* late; should have already arrived. **overflow** *v.* flow over the edges. **overhang** *v.* hang over. **overhead** *adv.* above. *a.* raised above the ground. **overhear** *v.* hear things one is not intended to hear. **overnight** *adv.* through the night (stay etc.). **overrule** *v.* decide against a decision given by another or others. **overrun** *v.* conquer and occupy a country. **oversight** *n.* something not seen, neglected. **overtake** *v.* catch up and pass. **overthrow** *v.* defeat and put an end to. **overtime** *n.* time worked longer than the normal hours. **overweight** *n.* weight in excess of what is usual. *a.* being more than the weight usual or allowed. **overwhelm** *v.* cover over, crush completely. **overwork** *v.* work too hard or too long.

overcome (o-ver-come) *v.* be too strong for, get the better of; make weak (fumes, alcohol etc.).

overdraw (o-ver-draw) *v.* take a cheque out of a bank which represents more money than one has in that bank. **overdraft** *n.* an amount of money by which a person's bank account is overdrawn.

overgrown (o-ver-grown) *a.* covered with something that has grown over it; having grown too fast.

overhaul (o-ver-haul) *v.* examine (an engine etc.) to find out what is wrong and to put it right; catch up and pass another in a race.

overlook (o-ver-look) *v.* see from above; pay no attention to a thing, fail to notice it; superintend other people's work; pass over some fault without punishing the culprit.

overturn (o-ver-turn) v. upset; turn over; cause to turn over.

owe v. be in debt to another; need to pay to another (money, duty etc.).

owl n. a bird that comes out only at night and lives on small birds and animals.

own v. possess; have as one's property; a. belonging to a person. pron. a thing belonging to a person. v. agree, confess to an action or a state.

oxygen (ox-y-gen) n. a gas with no taste, smell or colour, present in the air and necessary for all forms of life.

oyster (oy-ster) n. a small flat shellfish that is cultivated to eat or for the pearls which some varieties produce.

P

pace n. the distance covered in one step; the speed at which one walks. v. walk slowly and regularly. **pacemaker** n. a person who in a race sets the pace for a competitor by running etc. beside him; an electrical device put into the human body to help the heart to keep beating.

pacify (pac-i-fy) v. make quiet and calm.

pack n. a bundle; a number of dogs kept for hunting; a number of wolves travelling together; a set of 52 playing cards. v. put things together into a container, suitcase, trunk etc.; crowd closely together; put paper or other material round fragile things to keep them safe. **package** n. a parcel or bundle. **packet** n. a small parcel.

pad n. soft material made into a small cushion to give comfort or protection; a guard for the leg when playing certain games; sheets of writing paper fastened together at one edge; the soft part under the feet of certain animals; a small cushion of absorbent material soaked with ink for inking rubber stamps. v. put a pad or pads on or into something.

paddle (pad-dle) n. a short oar held in both hands and used to move a canoe through the water. v. send a canoe or other craft through the water with a paddle; walk in the water with bare feet.

paddock (pad-dock) n. a small field where horses are exercised and where they are brought together before a race.

page n. one side of a leaf of paper in a book, journal or newspaper; a boy who served at court in the Middle Ages, and was in training to become a knight; a boy who serves in a hotel or a club. v. call a person's name aloud in a hotel, club or public place.

pageant (pag-eant) n. an outdoor entertainment in which scenes from history are usually shown; a great celebration in which there is a procession of people wearing costumes of past ages etc. **pageantry** n. great display with scenery, costume and entertainment.

pail n. a bucket of metal, wood or plastic; a pail filled with something; what a pail holds.

pain n. suffering through illness or injury; threat (of death, torture etc.) while in captivity. v. hurt, give pain, mental or physical. **pains** n. effort, care in doing work. **painful** a. giving pain. **painkiller** n. something to take pain away. **painless** a. with no pain.

paint n. colouring matter that can be put on a surface with a brush, spray or by other means. v. spread paint on; make a picture by painting. **painter** n. a person who paints, an artist. **painting** n. a picture or design done in paint.

pair n. two things of a kind, matched together; two parts of an article joined together (scissors etc.); two married persons. **pair off** v. group in twos, go two by two.

palace (pal-ace) n. the official residence of a ruler, archbishop, bishop etc.; a large house; a large building for shows and entertainment.

palate (pal-ate) n. the roof of the mouth. **palatable** a. pleasant to the taste.

pale a. of a whitish appearance, without much colour; light in colour. n. a long pointed stick put in the ground and used as part of a fence. **paling** n. a fence of pales.

palm n. that part of the inner surface of the hand between the wrist and the fingers; a tree that grows in warm climates. **palmist** n. a person who claims to be able to tell fortunes and read the character by looking at the palm of the hand.

pamphlet (pamph-let) n. a thin paper-covered book, usually on a subject of general interest. **pamphleteer** n. a person who writes pamphlets.

pan n. a metal dish, usually shallow and sometimes with a handle, used for cooking; what a pan holds. **pancake** n. a thin, flat cake of eggs, flour and milk, fried in a pan.

panda (pan-da) n. a mammal from the Himalayas and central China, with a black and white body and large black patches around its eyes.

pane n. a single sheet of glass in a window; a thin sheet of wood, part of a door or of panelling.

panel (pan-el) n. a separate part of the surface of a door, wall or ceiling, framed like a picture; a piece of material put into a dress, of a different colour or pattern from the rest; a body of speakers answering questions or taking part in a game, usually with an audience. **panelled** a. with panels. **panelling** n. panels on a wall.

panic (pan-ic) n. fear and terror spreading to everybody. v. be struck with terror; rush about in confusion.

panorama (pan-o-ra-ma) n. a view over a wide area; a scene which is constantly changing.

pant v. breathe hard and quickly as one does after exertion. n. a short, quick breath, a gasp.

pantomime (pan-to-mime) n. a kind of play with music usually based on a fairy tale.

pantry (pan-try) n. a small room in a house where food is kept.

paper (pa-per) n. material made from wood, rags etc. pressed into thin sheets to be used for writing, printing, drawing and wrapping; a newspaper; a set of examination questions; an essay, usually read out to an audience; a document. v. paste paper on to a wall or ceiling.

parable (par-a-ble) n. a story told for the purpose of teaching a lesson.

parachute (par-a-chute) n. a device which when dropped from the air opens like an umbrella and is used for landing troops, supplying provisions and in displays.

parade (pa-rade) v. gather together for inspection, drilling, marching etc. n. a gathering together; a display (fashion, military etc.); a promenade by the sea, in public gardens etc.

paradise (par-a-dise) n. heaven; a place of extreme beauty and happiness; a state of perfect happiness.

paraffin (par-af-fin) n. oil obtained from coal and petroleum, used for burning. a. using paraffin (of a lamp, stove etc.). **paraffin wax** a kind of wax used for making candles, polishes etc.

paragraph (par-a-graph) n. a group of

sentences dealing with one subject; a short item in a newspaper.

parallel *a.* (of lines) being the same distance apart throughout their length. *n.* a line of latitude. **parallelogram** *n.* a figure whose opposite sides are parallel.

paralyze (par-a-lyze) *v.* make unable to move or feel with part or all of the body. **paralysis** *n.* being paralyzed. **paralytic** *a.* accompanied by paralysis; *n.* a person who is paralyzed.

parasite (par-a-site) *n.* an animal or plant that lives in or on another and gets its nourishment from it.

paratroops (par-a-troops) *n.* soldiers specially trained to be landed by parachute.

parcel (par-cel) *n.* something wrapped and tied up for storing, carrying, sending etc. **parcel post** a department of the Post Office dealing with the posting of parcels.

parch *v.* make dry; dry up with heat, especially the heat of the sun.

parchment (parch-ment) *n.* the skin of sheep, goats etc., dried and prepared for use as a writing material.

pardon (par-don) *n.* forgiveness. *v.* forgive; excuse from further imprisonment or from punishment.

pare *v.* take away the outer part. **parings** *n.* pieces or parts pared off.

parent (par-ent) *n.* a father or mother. **parentage** *n.* fatherhood, motherhood, ancestry. **parental** *a.* having to do with parents.

parish (par-ish) *n.* part of a country which has its own church and priest. *a.* having to do with a parish. **parishioner** *n.* an inhabitant of a parish.

park *n.* a public recreation ground with gardens etc.; the private grounds round a large house; a place of great beauty specially preserved for visitors; a place where cars may be left for a period. *v.* leave a car for a time.

parliament (par-lia-ment) *n.* a body of people elected by voters, whose members meet to make laws. **parliamentary** *a.* having to do with parliament.

parole (par-ole) *n.* a kind of promise; the freeing of a prisoner before his sentence is completed, after his promise to be of good behaviour; the promise of a prisoner that, if allowed more freedom, he will not try to escape.

parrot (par-rot) *n.* a bird with a hooked bill and brightly coloured feathers; a person who repeats what others say without understanding it.

part *n.* a portion or division; a share in what is being done; a side in a quarrel; a section of a book, an instalment of a story; a necessary piece of machinery; one of the pieces sung or played which helps to make up the whole of a musical composition. *v.* separate. **part with** *v.* give up, give away. **parting** *n.* leaving; the line where the hair is parted.

particle (par-ti-cle) *n.* a tiny piece.

particular (par-tic-u-lar) *a.* special; not easy to please. *n.* detail.

partition (par-ti-tion) *n.* division into parts; a wall between two rooms. *v.* divide into parts by means of a partition.

partner (part-ner) *n.* a person who joins with others in some activity or business; a person who plays, dances etc. with another. *v.* be a partner to. **partnership** *n.* being a partner; a business run by partners.

party (par-ty) *n.* a number of persons working for the same cause; a group of people travelling or working together; a group meeting by invitation for pleasure or entertainment; a person who is concerned in some activity.

pass *v.* move to and beyond; give, hand over; succeed in an examination; give a judgment; send a ball to a player of the same side. *n.* success in an examination; a piece of paper giving permission to go somewhere; the act of passing to another player; a narrow path between high hills. **passbook** *n.* the book issued by a bank to a customer with particulars of the money he puts in and takes out. **passport** *n.* a document carried by a traveller in a foreign country. **password** *n.* a secret word known only to a few, which enables a person to be recognized as belonging to a particular group of people.

passage (pas-sage) *n.* voyage from one place to another; a going past or passing; a tunnel or corridor; an extract; the passing of a bill in Parliament. **passenger** *n.* a person who is taken on a journey by bus, boat, train, taxi etc.

passion (pas-sion) *n.* strong feeling of love, anger, hatred etc.; the suffering and death of Jesus. **passion-flower, passion-fruit** *n.* a climbing plant with a brilliant flower and fruit. **Passion Play** a play which deals with events in the life of Jesus. **Passion Week** the week before Palm Sunday.

past *a.* gone by. *n.* time gone by; the earlier days of a person's life. *adv.* after (of time); by (of passing, going etc.).

pasteurize (pas-teur-ize) *v.* heat liquids, especially milk, to a high temperature to kill any germs they may contain.

pastime (pas-time) *n.* anything which serves to make time pass more pleasantly.

pasture (pas-ture) *n.* a field of grass for the feeding of cattle; land of this kind. *v.* put cattle or sheep on a pasture.

pat *v.* strike lightly with the open hand or with a flat object. *n.* a tap with the open hand; a small piece of butter. *a.* just right; without stopping.

patch *n.* a piece of material used to mend a hole or strengthen a weak place; a piece of silk or plaster used to cover up an injured eye; a small differently coloured part of a surface; a small piece of ground, especially for growing plants. *v.* put a patch on. **patchwork** *n.* material made up of patches.

patent (pat-ent) *n.* a government grant giving a person the sole right to manufacture something he has invented; the invention protected by a patent. *v.* obtain a patent. *a.* protected by a patent.

path *n.* a narrow track made by animals or people walking; the way a thing moves. **pathless** *a.* with no paths.

pathetic (pa-thet-ic) *a.* sad.

patience (pa-tience) *n.* the ability to suffer pain, sadness etc. without complaining. *n.* a card game that can be played by one person; **patient** *n.* a person who is being treated by a doctor. *a.* having patience.

patriot (pa-tri-ot) *n.* a person who loves his country and is ready to defend it. **patriotic** *a.* loving or praising one's country. **patriotism** *n.* love of one's country.

patrol (pa-trol) *v.* go back and forth to keep watch. *n.* the act of patrolling; a group or person on patrol.

patron (pa-tron) *n.* a person who gives support to some person or cause. **patronage** *n.* encouragement by a patron. **patronize** *v.* help; give custom to; behave as if one is superior to another. **patron saint** a saint who is believed to protect a certain church or group.

pattern (pat-tern) *n.* a model or drawing to guide a person making something; a model on which to base one's life; a small sample; a design.

pauper (pau-per) *n.* a person who has no means of existence and has to rely on others for support.

pause *n.* a short stop; a sign in music to show that a note or rest is to be lengthened. *v.* make a short stop.

pave *v.* put stones on a road or path to make walking easier. **pavement** *n.* a paved path running along the side of a street.

paw *n.* the foot of an animal that has claws. *v.* beat the ground with the forefoot.

pawn *v.* place valuables in another person's care as a pledge for money borrowed. *n.* a piece in the game of chess. **pawnbroker** *n.* the person keeping a pawnshop. **pawnshop** *n.* a shop whose owner takes goods in pawn.

pay v. give money for goods; give back money; give visits, compliments, attention etc.; be to one's benefit. n. money received for work. **payment** n. paying.

pea n. the small seed of the pea plant used for food.

peace n. freedom from war or fighting; quiet, rest, calm.

peach n. a tree which bears round, juicy fruit with a stone-like seed; the fruit of the peach tree.

peacock (pea-cock) n. a large male bird with a splendid tail of coloured feathers which it spreads out like a fan.

peahen n. the female of the peacock.

pear n. a tree which has sweet juicy fruit, usually coloured green or yellow; the fruit of the pear tree.

pearl n. a hard, round silvery formation found in some oyster-shells. a. made of pearls. **pearl barley** grains of barley looking like small pearls.

peasant (peas-ant) n. a person who works on the land and is usually poor.

peat n. partly-decayed plants found on moors and bogs, used for fuel and for putting on the land.

pebble (peb-ble) n. a small stone which has been made round by the action of the sea, or a stream. **pebbly** a. full of pebbles.

peck v. strike with the beak intending to injure; pick up food by pecking. n. a blow or scar made by a beak; a measure of capacity (2 gallons) for dry goods.

peculiar (pe-cu-li-ar) a. belonging to, done by only one group or person; strange. **peculiarity** n. being strange; something odd or peculiar about a person or thing.

pedal (ped-al) n. part of a machine worked by the feet. a. having pedals. v. use a pedal or pedals.

pedlar (ped-lar) n. a person who goes from house to house selling small articles. **peddle** v. go from house to house selling.

peel n. the skin of fruit and of some vegetables. v. take off the peel; come off (of peel, wallpaper etc.). **peeler** n. an instrument for peeling. **peelings** n. peel that has been taken off.

peer v. look closely at. n. an equal; a member of the higher nobility most of whom sit in the House of Lords. **peeress** n. a woman peer; the wife of a peer. **peerless** a. having no equal.

peevish (peev-ish) a. easily irritated; inclined to be cross.

peg n. a pin of wood or other material driven into something to fasten parts together, or into the ground to support a tent. v. fix with pegs; mark out with pegs.

pellet (pel-let) n. a little ball the size of a pill, of food or medicine; a small bullet; a piece of small shot such as that used in airguns.

pelt v. throw things at; fall heavily (of rain etc.). n. the skin of an animal with or without the hair.

pen n. an instrument for writing; a small enclosure for domestic animals. v. write (usually a letter). **penfriend** n. a person, especially in another country with whom one keeps up a friendship through letters. **penholder** n. a holder in which the steel nib of a pen is placed. **penknife** n. a small pocket-knife made originally for making and mending pens made from feathers.

penal (pe-nal) a. having to do with punishment. **penalize** v. subject a person or a player in a game to a penalty. **penalty** n. punishment for doing wrong or for breaking rules.

pencil (pen-cil) n. a tube of wood containing a hard substance in the middle with which one can write. v. mark with a pencil.

pendulum (pen-du-lum) n. a piece of brass, stone or other material swinging freely by a rod, string, chain or rope from a fixed point.

penetrate (pen-e-trate) v. pierce into, make a way into; spread (of smells, ideas etc.). **penetrating** a. piercing. **penetration** n. the power to penetrate; a gaining of influence in the affairs of another country.

penguin (pen-guin) *n.* a seabird of the Antarctic whose wings are used for swimming and not for flying.

peninsula (pen-in-su-la) *n.* a piece of land almost surrounded by water. **peninsular** *a.* having to do with a peninsula.

penitence (pen-i-tence) *n.* sorrow for something done wrong, for sin. **penitent** *a.* sorry for things done wrong. **penitentiary** *n.* a prison in which the chief aim is to reform prisoners.

penny (pen-ny) *n.* a British bronze coin. There are now 100 pence in the pound; until 1971 there were 240.

pension (pen-sion) *n.* a regular payment made by the state or by a former employer to a person who is disabled, old, a widow etc. **pensionable** *a.* entitling one to draw a pension. **pensioner** *n.* a person receiving a pension.

people (peo-ple) *n.* men, women and children; those belonging to a nation, state or country. *v.* fill with people.

pepper (pep-per) *n.* a hot-tasting powder made from various plants and used for flavouring food; a plant which produces red or green seed-pods used for food. *v.* pelt (with), shower (with).

per cent from or out of each hundred – 10 per cent is one tenth or 10 out of each 100. **percentage** *n.* the number in each hundred; a certain number out of the whole.

perch *n.* the place where a bird rests, usually a stick or rod; a high seat. *v.* sit, rest.

perennial (per-en-nial) *n.* a plant that lasts for a long time. *a.* living through the winter; lasting a long time, rising again and again (an argument, dispute etc.).

perfect (per-fect) *a.* without a single fault; accurate; complete, absolute. **perfect** (per-fect) *v.* make perfect. **perfection** *n.* being or making perfect.

perforate (per-for-ate) *v.* make small holes in; make a line of holes in paper so that it can be torn easily.

perform (per-form) *v.* do; act, sing, do tricks etc. for an audience. **performance** *n.* action, the performing of a play etc. **performer** *n.* a person who performs or acts.

perfume (per-fume) *n.* scent; a prepared liquid that gives off an agreeable smell; a smell or scent. *v.* give a perfume to.

perhaps (per-haps) *adv.* it may be, possibly.

peril (per-il) *n.* danger; something that causes danger. **perilous** *a.* dangerous, full of risk.

period (pe-ri-od) *n.* a length of time; a full stop at the end of a sentence. *a.* having to do with a certain period of time (dress etc.). **periodic** *a.* coming at regular intervals. **periodical** *a.* periodic. *n.* a newspaper or magazine appearing at regular intervals.

periscope (pe-ri-scope) *n.* an instrument which contains mirrors so that one may look from behind a wall, from a trench or from under the sea at an object.

perish (per-ish) *v.* die; lose its quality. **perishable** *a.* perishing or going bad quickly.

permanent (per-ma-nent) *a.* intended to last for ever. **permanent wave** a way of treating the hair so that waves or curls are put in which last until they have grown out.

permit (per-mit) *v.* allow. **permit** (per-mit) *n.* a paper giving written permission to do something or go somewhere. **permission** *n.* consent.

perpetual (per-pet-u-al) *a.* continuing or lasting for ever; often repeated. **per-**

petuate v. keep from being forgotten. **in perpetuity** for ever.

perplex (per-plex) v. worry, confuse. **perplexity** n. being perplexed.

persecute (per-se-cute) v. annoy, oppress, treat cruelly. **persecution** n. the act or state of persecuting, being persecuted.

persevere (per-se-vere) v. keep on, continue to try. **perseverance** n. constant trying.

persist (per-sist) v. refuse to change ; last ; endure (of weather, conditions etc.). **persistence** n. continuation. **persistent** a. continuing.

personal (per-son-al) a. private ; in person, not through anybody else. a. of a person (appearance, courage etc.).

personality (per-son-al-i-ty) n. all that makes up a person's character ; a well-known person.

perspire (per-spire) v. give off a salty fluid through the pores of the skin, sweat. **perspiration** n. sweat.

persuade (per-suade) v. make a person do something by reasoning with him. **persuasion** n. the act of persuading. **persuasive** a. good at persuading others.

pest n. something that causes trouble and destruction. **pesticide** n. a substance which destroys pests in the home, the farm and the garden. **pestilence** n. a plague, a spreading disease.

pestle (pes-tle) n. an instrument used in a mortar for crushing substances.

pet n. an animal, bird etc. cared for and kept as a companion. v. fondle.

petal (pet-al) n. part of the flower which stands out from the centre like a coloured leaf.

petition (pe-ti-tion) n. a request, usually written and signed by a number of persons. v. draw up and present a petition.

petroleum (pe-trol-eum) n. oil found underground and refined to make petrol, paraffin and many other products. **petrol** n. refined petroleum, used to drive cars and other machines.

petticoat (pet-ti-coat) n. an underskirt worn by women and children.

petty (pet-ty) a. small, not important ; trivial. **petty cash** a fund set aside to make small payments. **petty officer** an officer in the navy who does not hold a commission.

pew n. a long wooden seat with a back, usually fixed to the floor of a church.

phantom (phan-tom) n. (pronounced *fantom*) a ghost, an image in a dream.

pharmacist (phar-ma-cist) n. (pronounced *farmacist*) a person licensed to mix drugs and prepare medicines. **pharmacy** n. a shop where medical preparations are sold.

pheasant (pheas-ant) n. (pronounced *fesant*) a long-tailed bird which is shot for sport and whose flesh is used for food.

phenomenon (phe-nom-e-non) n. (pronounced *fenomenon*) anything which is observed ; something or somebody remarkable or unusual. **phenomenal** a. remarkable, unusual.

philosophy (phi-los-o-phy) n. (pronounced *filosofy*) a system of thought, dealing with the nature and meaning of life, the world and the mind ; an attitude which helps a person to face misfortune, illness, danger and death. **philosopher** n. a student of philosophy ; a person whose life is guided by his personal philosophy.

phlegm n. (pronounced *flem*) a thick fluid that gathers in the nose and throat and is expelled by coughing ; slowness to act. **phlegmatic** a. not easily roused or put into a temper.

phone n. (pronounced *fone*) see **telephone**.

phosphorus (phos-phor-us) n. (pronounced *fosforus*) a yellowy substance that easily catches fire and shines faintly in the dark. **phosphorescent** a. giving light without burning.

photograph (pho-to-graph) n. (pronounced *fotograf*) or **photo** n. a picture produced by light passing into a camera through its lens on to light-sensitive film. v. take a photograph. **photographer** n. a person who takes photographs. **photographic** a. having to do with photographs. **photofinish** n. the finish of a race that is so close that the winner can only be decided by consulting a photograph.

phrase *n.* (pronounced *frase*) a group of words which form part of a sentence. *v.* put into words.

physical (phys-i-cal) *a.* (pronounced *fisical*) having to do with material things; having to do with the body. **physician** *n.* a doctor of medicine. **physic** *n.* medicine.

physics (phys-ics) *n.* (pronounced *fisics*) sciences that deal with matter and energy.

piano (pia-no) *n.* a musical instrument played by striking keys on a keyboard. **pianist** *n.* a person who plays a piano.

pick *v.* pluck, gather, pull; separate, tear apart; choose; use an instrument to do something. *n.* choice; a heavy tool with a handle and an iron head which has two pointed ends. **pick on** *v.* find fault with. **pick up** *v.* lift. **pick-up** *n.* the arm of a record player that goes over the record and produces the tune.

picket (pick-et) *n.* a small group of men or one man, on guard duty; a group of strikers standing outside the gates of a place of work to persuade other workers not to enter. *v.* place soldiers on guard or men at a factory gate.

pickle (pick-le) *n.* a mixture of vinegar, salt, water etc. that is used to preserve and flavour meat, fish and vegetables; food that is pickled. *v.* put things in pickle.

picnic (pic-nic) *n.* a pleasure trip on which food is taken to be eaten out of doors. *v.* go on such a trip.

picture (pic-ture) *n.* a drawing or painting; a beautiful object; what one sees on a screen. **picturesque** *a.* being like a picture. **pictorial** *a.* shown in pictures.

pie *n.* a baked dish consisting of meat or fruit covered with pastry.

piece *n.* a part of something; an example or instance of something; one article of a

set or collection; a particular length; a coin; a single composition or task. *v.* put together from pieces. **piecemeal** *adv.* bit by bit.

pier *n.* a structure built out into the sea to serve as a landing place for ships, or for pleasure; a pillar which helps to support a bridge.

pierce *v.* make a hole with a sharp instrument; sound sharply through; show through (darkness, fog etc.).

pig *n.* an animal bred on farms whose flesh is eaten as pork and bacon.

pigeon (pi-geon) *n.* a bird of the dove family.

pigment (pig-ment) *n.* colouring matter.

pike *n.* a large, slender, fierce fish which lives in fresh water; a weapon with a long shaft and a small metal head once used by infantrymen.

pile *n.* a number of things lying upon each other; a heavy timber pole, sometimes pointed at the lower end and driven into the ground; the raised hair-like surface on cloth or on a carpet. *v.* put into a pile. **atomic pile** an apparatus for producing atomic energy.

pilfer (pil-fer) *v.* steal, especially small quantities. **pilferer** *n.* a person who pilfers.

pilgrim (pil-grim) *n.* one who journeys, especially a long distance, to some sacred place. **pilgrimage** *n.* a journey made by pilgrims.

pill *n.* a small round ball of some medical substance, to be swallowed. **pillbox** *n.* small box for holding pills; a small fort with thick concrete walls.

pillar (pil-lar) *n.* an upright column of stone, wood, metal etc. used as a support or as a monument; a person who supports a cause; something shaped like a pillar. **pillar-box** *n.* an iron box in the shape of a pillar in which letters are posted.

pillow (pil-low) *n.* a bag filled with so

material on which one may rest the head; anything serving as a pillow. v. rest one's head. **pillowcase, pillowslip** n. the cotton, linen or nylon cover drawn over a pillow before use.

pilot (pi-lot) n. a person who takes a ship in and out of harbours or through channels; a person who controls an aeroplane. v. steer. a. experimental.

pimple (pim-ple) n. a small inflamed swelling or spot on the skin.

pin n. a small, slender, pointed piece of metal or wood used to fasten things together; any kind of device for fastening in which the main part is a pin; a wooden peg used for various purposes. v. fasten with a pin. **pincushion** n. a small cushion or pad in which pins are stuck ready to be used. **pinafore** n. a loose dress worn to protect the clothing when doing work, so called because it was pinned 'afore' (in front).

pincers (pin-cers) n. a tool for gripping things and taking nails out of wood.

pinch v. take firmly between the thumb and forefinger; hurt through being too tight. n. the act of pinching; that which can be taken up between the thumb and forefinger.

pine n. an evergreen tree which has small needle-shaped leaves and cones which carry its seeds. v. become thin through sorrow or anxiety; desire very much.

pineapple (pine-ap-ple) n. a large juicy fruit grown in the tropics, so called because the fruit bears some resemblance to the pine cone.

pink n. a light red colour; a sweet-smelling garden flower. v. punch cloth or leather with small holes for ornament; make high-pitched sounds (of a petrol engine). **pinking shears** scissors with notched edges specially made to cut cloth so that it will not fray.

pint n. one eighth of a gallon in liquid measure (1·75 pints — 1 litre).

pipe n. a hollow tube through which water, gas, steam etc. can flow; a tube of wood, clay etc., with a bowl at one end and a mouthpiece at the other, used for smoking; a musical instrument. v. take water, gas etc. through pipes; sing or talk in a thin, high voice; trim (a dress etc.). **piper** n. a person who plays a pipe.

piracy (pi-ra-cy) n. the capture of another vessel at sea by force; the operation of an illegal service (radio etc.). **pirate** n. a person who commits robbery on the sea, publishes matter with no legal right to do so.

pistol (pis-tol) n. a small gun held in the hand, a revolver, an automatic.

piston (pis-ton) n. a moveable cylinder made to fit inside a hollow tube or cylinder, which can be pushed up and down by steam or gas pressure to supply power to an engine.

pit n. a deep hole in the ground; a small scar left on the body as a result of some disease; the seats behind the stalls on the ground floor of a theatre; the place at which racing car drivers stop to refuel and get necessary repairs. v. make small holes in the skin; match (strength against).

pitch v. set up (tent etc.); throw; put music in a certain key; fall; move up and down; put the stumps into the ground (in cricket). n. a prepared ground on which a game is played; a place where a street trader puts his wares; the slope of a roof; a black substance like tar used to mend leaks in boats and fill cracks in pavements. **pitchfork** n. a large fork for pitching hay. **pitched battle** a battle fought in prepared positions.

pitcher (pitch-er) n. a large vessel with a handle and lip, used for holding liquids; the player in a baseball game who throws the ball to the batter.

pity (pi-ty) n. a feeling of sorrow for the sufferings of others; a reason for being sorry. v. feel sorrow for other people's sufferings. **pitiful** a. causing pity.

place n. a position, where a thing should be or is; a city, town, building etc.; a position on a surface, in a book etc.; rank, position among people; a position in a competition or race; duty. v. put; identify (a person).

plague n. an epidemic, the spread of disease; disaster caused by something other than disease. v. annoy.

plaid n. (rhymes with *had*) a long piece of cloth worn over the shoulders as part of the Scottish national dress; a piece of cloth with a design of coloured checks and squares.

plain a. easy to see, hear, understand; simple; out of uniform (of clothes); honest; not good-looking. n. an area of flat country.

plait v. twist lengths of hair, wool, straw, to make a kind of rope. n. hair, rope etc. that has been plaited.

plan n. a drawing showing the details and positions of the parts of a piece of land, a building or a machine; a scheme for doing things in the future. v. work out the details for a garden, house etc.; make arrangements for the future.

plane n. a tree with broad leaves and thin bark which falls off in large flakes; an aeroplane; a tool which has a sharp blade fitted into it, designed to smooth wood and metal; a flat surface. v. smooth with a plane.

planet (plan-et) n. one of the heavenly bodies that moves round the sun.

plank n. a long flat piece of timber used mostly for walking on and making floors.

plant n. a living thing that is not an animal and is smaller than a tree; machinery etc. v. put plants, trees etc. into the ground; found, set up or establish. **plantation** n. an area of land on which trees are planted; an estate on which cotton, sugar, tobacco etc. are grown. **planter** n. a person who grows crops on a plantation.

plaster (plas-ter) n. a soft mixture of lime, sand and water used for covering walls; a

cloth on which medicine has been spread, to lay on an injury or painful place. v. cover a wall with plaster; cover thickly (with mud, clay etc.). **plasterer** n. a workman who puts plaster on walls and ceilings.

plastic (plas-tic) a. easy to mould and make into shapes; made of plastic materials.

plate n. a shallow dish with edges slightly turned up, used for meals and other purposes; articles of gold and silver for use at meals and in churches; a thin flat sheet (of metal, gold etc.). v. cover with gold, silver etc. **plate glass** thick glass suitable for putting into shop windows.

plateau (pla-teau) n. an area of flat land high above sea level.

platform (plat-form) n. a raised floor in a hall for the use of public speakers; a raised area along the side of the tracks in a railway station.

platinum (plat-i-num) n. a hard, greyish white and very valuable metal used for making scientific apparatus and jewellery.

platoon (pla-toon) n. a body of soldiers of two or more sections, being part of a company and commanded by a lieutenant.

play v. take part in a game for pleasure; pretend to be or do; do, perform (jokes, tricks, etc.); perform in a drama or a play. n. games taken part in for pleasure; a drama for the stage; things done in a game. **player** n. a person who plays a game or who is in a drama. **playful** a. full of fun, always wanting to play. **playmate** n. a person with whom one plays.

plead v. put forward the case of a person in a court of justice; make an earnest appeal; make an excuse; use arguments for or against something. **plea** n. a statement, request, excuse.

please v. find something agreeable; like, wish, choose; a polite form of asking (meaning 'if you please.'). **pleasant** a. pleasing, agreeable, giving pleasure or enjoyment. **pleasure** n. a feeling of being happy.

pledge n. something given as a security that the giver will pay a debt or do what is required of him; a promise. v. put in pawn, give as a security; promise; drink the health of.

plenty (plen-ty) n. a large number or

quantity; as much or more than is needed. **plentiful** *a*. in plenty.

pliers (pli-ers) *n*. small pincers with long jaws for bending wire, holding small objects etc.

plight *n*. a sad or awkward situation or condition; a pledge or promise

plimsoll (plim-soll) *n*. a rubber-soled canvas shoe laced to fit the foot.

plod *v*. walk or work slowly but without pause or resting; make one's way slowly and with difficulty. **plodder** *n*. a person who works slowly but steadily and usually succeeds.

plot *n*. a secret plan to do or achieve something; the story or plan of a novel or play; a small piece of ground. *v*. plan secretly; make a plan or diagram; mark positions of points on a graph.

plough *n*. an agricultural implement for cutting and turning up the soil; a group of seven stars in the constellation of the Great Bear. *v*. turn up the soil with a plough; work at something slowly and with perseverance.

pluck *v*. pull out from its place of growth, as feathers, flowers etc.; take hold of a thing and pull. *n*. courage in face of difficulties. **plucky** *a*. having pluck or courage, needing pluck.

plug *n*. a piece of wood or other material used to stop up a hole; a device for making a connection with an electric supply. *v*. stop, fill up by putting in a plug; connect.

plum *n*. a tree bearing a soft sweet fruit with a smooth skin and a stone-like seed; the fruit of the plum. **plum pudding** boiled pudding containing dried fruits and spices, usually eaten at Christmas time.

plumage (plum-age) *n*. a bird's feathers.

plumber (plumb-er) *n*. a workman who puts in and repairs pipes etc. in connection with water supply and drainage, both inside and outside a building. **plumbing** *n*. the waterpipes, tanks and cisterns in a building.

plump *a*. well filled out, rather fat. *v*. fall heavily; drop suddenly (into a chair etc.)

plunder (plun-der) *v*. rob people by force, usually during war or riots. *n*. the goods taken in plundering.

plunge *v*. thrust something in; dive; go suddenly into something (an argument etc.). *n*. the act of plunging; a violent thrust. **take the plunge** do something difficult, disagreeable or risky.

plural (plu-ral) *n. & adj*. meaning more than one thing or person.

plus *prep*. added to; with the addition of *n*. the sign

pneumonia (pneu-mo-nia) *n*. (pronounced *numonia*) inflammation of the lung. **double pneumonia** inflammation of both lungs.

poach *v*. trespass and take game from another person's land; take something that belongs to another person; cook an egg by dropping it without the shell into boiling water.

pocket (pock-et) *n*. a small bag inserted into a garment for carrying things; a string bag at the corner of a billiard table. *a*. suitable for the pocket. *v*. put (something) into one's pocket; take something. **in pocket** having made a profit. **out of pocket** having made a loss. **pocket-money** *n*. a small allowance of money which one can spend as one pleases.

pod *n*. a long seed-vessel carried by plants like the pea and the bean

poem (po-em) *n*. a piece of writing in verse.

poet (po-et) *n*. a person who writes poems. **poetess** *n*. a woman poet. **poetic** *a*. having to do with poetry **poetry** *n*. poems, the writing of poems.

point *n*. the sharp end, as of a dagger, a pen, pencil, needle etc.; a piece of land jutting out into water; a dot; a position in time or space; a mark to indicate temperature, atmospheric pressure or water levels; a mark showing a score in games, competitions etc.; the use, the idea of anything; a quality (good and bad points). *v*. show, direct or be directed towards; fill in the spaces between bricks with new mortar. **pointer** *n*. anything that points; a dog trained to stand with its nose in the direction where game is to be found. **points** *n.* the moveable rails which enable a train to be moved from one track to another.

poison (pois-on) *n.* a substance which, if absorbed, may harm or destroy life. *v.* destroy or injure with poison. **poisoner** *n.* a person who kills by means of poison. **poisonous** *a.* containing poison; likely to injure, mentally, morally or in any other way.

poke *v.* thrust against or through something with the finger, a stick etc.; push, feel about (among rubbish, ashes etc.). *n.* the act of poking.

pole *n.* a long, rounded, slender piece of wood or metal made to stand erect; one of the two ends of the imaginary line drawn through the earth from north to south; one of the two ends of a magnet. **polar** *a.* having to do with the poles of the earth. **pole-vault** *n.* a leap over a high horizontal bar with the help of a long pole.

police (po-lice) *n.* an organized force whose work is to deal with crime, to maintain order and to see that laws are not broken. *v.* keep order in a place. **policeman, policewoman** *n.* a member of a police force.

policy (pol-i-cy) *n.* a plan of action; an agreement between an insurance company and a person or persons done in print and writing.

polio (pol-i-o) *n.* a shortened form of the word **poliomyelitis,** an infectious disease of the spinal cord which may cause paralysis.

polish (pol-ish) *v.* make shiny by rubbing. *n.* the surface obtained by polishing; good manners, polite behaviour.

polite (po-lite) *a.* showing good manners towards others in behaviour and speech. **politeness** *n.* being polite.

politics (pol-i-tics) *n.* the science or art of government; the conduct of a country's affairs. **political** *a.* having to do with politics. **politician** *n.* a person taking part in politics.

poll *n.* voting at an election. *v.* receive a certain number of votes.

pollen (pol-len) *n.* the fine powdery yellowish grains formed on flowers, which fertilize others and produce seed.

pollute (pol-lute) *v.* make dirty. **pollution** *n.* the act of polluting; the state of being polluted.

pond *n.* a body of water smaller than a lake, often artificially formed, used as a drinking place for cattle or for pleasure in a park or garden.

pony (po-ny) *n.* a small horse. **ponytail** *n.* a style of hairdressing in which the hair is tied at the back of the head and hangs loose.

pool *n.* a pond, a small body of standing water; a place to swim in; a still deep place in a stream or river; money staked by people on the results of races, football etc. *v.* put money together for everyone's use.

poor *a.* having little property or money; not good, deserving pity or help. **poorly** *adv.* not well done; ill.

pop *n.* a sharp, short noise. *v.* go or come quickly; make a sharp, short noise. *a. & n.* a shortened form of the word popular applied to certain pieces of art, music and those who do them.

pope *n.* the Bishop of Rome, head of the Roman Catholic Church.

popular (pop-u-lar) *a.* of the people; liked by the people.

porcelain (porce-lain) *n.* delicate china; pottery with a shiny surface.

porch *n.* a covered entrance leading to the door of a building.

pore *n.* a tiny opening in the skin of a person or animal; *v.* read or study with steady attention. **porous** *a.* having pores, allowing liquid to pass through.

pork *n.* the flesh of pigs used as food.

porridge (por-ridge) *n.* a breakfast dish made by boiling oatmeal in water and adding milk.

port *n.* a harbour; a town with a harbour; the left side of a ship or aircraft, facing forward; a sweet, dark red wine which originally came from Portugal. **porthole** *n.* a small hole or opening in the side of a ship which lets in light and air.

porter (por-ter) *n.* a person who carries luggage; a doorkeeper. **portable** *a.* that can be carried.

portion (por-tion) *n.* a part, a share.

portray (por-tray) *v.* make a picture, drawing or carving of something; describe in words; act as if on the stage. **portrayal** *n.* description. **portrait** *n.* a drawing, painting or photograph of a person or animal.

pose *v.* take or hold a position for an artist to draw or paint; pretend to be what one is not. *n.* a position taken up for a portrait; a pretence.

position (po-si-tion) *n.* a place; a way of holding the body; a rank, state.

positive (pos-i-tive) *a.* certain, very sure; helpful; showing light and shade as seen in the original, the opposite of a negative in photography.

possess (pos-sess) *v.* have, own, keep control, take control of a person. **possession** *n.* ownership, something possessed. **possessive** *a.* wanting to own or acquire.

possible (pos-si-ble) *a.* that can be done, that can happen. **possibility** *n.* being possible.

post *n.* a place where a person should be on duty; a place where soldiers are put; a position; the delivery of letters; an upright piece of wood used as a support, for displaying notices etc. *v.* put at a post; put letters into a pillar-box or take to a post office; put up a notice for all to see. **postage** *n.* payment for sending of letters etc. **postal** *a.* having to do with the Post Office. **poster** *n.* a notice displayed publicly. **postal order** a money order bought and cashed at a post office.

post- a prefix which means after or later

than. **postmortem** *n.* an examination of a body after death. **postpone** *v.* put off until another time. **postscript** *n.* a short message added to a letter after it has been signed (usually written PS).

pot *n.* a vessel of earthenware or metal, usually round and deep, used mostly in and around the house. *v.* put into a pot; shoot at, hit with a shot. **potherb** *n.* any herb whose leaves, roots etc. are used for cooking. **pothole** *n.* a hole in the road made by the wheels of vehicles or through subsidence; a deep hole or cave among rocks. **potter** *n.* a person who makes pots. **pottery** *n.* all kinds of pots.

potato (po-ta-to) *n.* a plant whose fleshy tuber is eaten as a vegetable.

pouch *n.* a small bag; a kind of bag in which a marsupial, such as a kangaroo, carries its young.

poultry (poul-try) *n.* birds, mainly chickens, ducks, geese and turkeys, reared on farms for food; the meat of poultry. **poulterer** *n.* a person who sells poultry for food.

pounce *v.* jump or swoop down suddenly.

pound *n.* 16 ounces in weight (2·2 pounds = 1 kilo); a hundred pence, expressed as £1; a place where stray animals are kept. *v.* strike heavily; crush.

pour *v.* send a liquid flowing in a stream out of a vessel; come flowing out or in; come dropping down (of rain).

poverty (pov-er-ty) *n.* being poor.

powder (pow-der) *n.* material that has been ground to dust and is used for many purposes. *v.* make into powder; cover with powder. **powder magazine** a place where gunpowder is stored.

power (pow-er) *n.* ability to do things, strength; force that can be used to do work; control; a person or persons having authority; a state which has great authority in the world. **powerful** *a.* having much power. **powerless** *a.* without power.

practical (prac-ti-cal) *a.* real, not just in the mind; clever at doing things; useful. **practically** *adv.* almost, very nearly.

practice (prac-tice) *n.* constant repetition of something in order to improve; something done regularly; some kinds of business (doctor, solicitor etc.); the doing of a thing which has been planned.

practise (prac-tise) *v.* do something repeatedly in order to become skilful; work in certain professions.

prairie (prai-rie) *n.* a wide area of treeless land on which grass grows.

praise *v.* say good things about. *n.* the act of praising; worship. **praiseworthy** *a.* worthy of being praised.

pram *n.* (short for **perambulator**) a small carriage in which a baby is wheeled.

prance *v.* move by springing on the hind legs as a horse does; dance and leap about.

prank *n.* mischievous trick.

pray *v.* make requests or give thanks to God; ask a person. **prayer** *n.* the act of praying. **prayerbook** *n.* a book containing prayers. **The Prayer Book** the book of prayers used in the Church of England.

preach *v.* put forward a religious teaching; advise, recommend, urge.

precede (pre-cede) *v.* go before. **preceding** *a.* coming before.

precious (pre-cious) *a.* very valuable; dear, much loved.

precipice (prec-i-pice) *n.* a cliff whose face overhangs the land below. **precipitous** *a.* high and overhanging like a precipice.

precise (pre-cise) *a.* exact; careful not to make mistakes. **precision** *n.* being ac-

curate. **precision tools** tools which measure small distances, quantities etc. very accurately.

predict (pre-dict) *v.* say what is going to happen in the future. **prediction** *n.* what is predicted.

prefabricate (pre-fab-ri-cate) *v.* make the parts of a building, ship or other construction separately, to be put together on the site. **prefab** *n.* (short for **prefabricated**) a prefabricated house.

prefer (pre-fer) *v.* like one thing or person rather than another. **preference** *n.* what is preferred.

prefix (pre-fix) *n.* a word or syllable placed in front of another word to alter its meaning.

prehistoric *a.* belonging to the days before recorded history.

premier (pre-mier) *n.* the prime minister or first in rank. **premiership** *n.* the office of premier.

prepare (pre-pare) *v.* get ready, make ready. **preparation** *n.* preparing, something prepared. **preparatory** *a.* in preparation, introductory.

prescribe (pre-scribe) *v.* order the use of. **prescription** *n.* what is prescribed, usually written on a small sheet to be presented to the chemist.

present (pre-sent) *a.* at the place agreed; not absent. *n.* a gift. **the present** now, this point in time. **presently** *adv.* soon.

present (pre-sent) *v.* give; put forward; introduce; perform (a play). **presentation** *n.* something presented; the ceremony or act of presenting.

preserve (pre-serve) *v.* save, keep from harm; keep from going bad; keep in good repair. *n.* jam; a place where animals, birds, insects, trees etc. are kept free from interference.

preside (pre-side) *v.* take charge of a meeting, a business, the work of an organization etc. **presidency** *n.* the office of president; the period of such an office.

president *n.* the person who presides over a government, a government department, a company etc. **presidential** *a.* having to do with a president.

press *v.* push; push with force; urge, demand. *n.* a machine for squeezing or pressing; a printing machine; the printing and newspaper business; reporters in this business.

pressure (pres-sure) *n.* a pressing of one thing on another; something which forces or compels people to do something. *v.* compel or force people to act in some way. **pressurized** *a.* made so that atmospheric pressure and temperature can be controlled.

pretend (pre-tend) *v.* make believe; try to make others believe things that are not true; claim to know, to be able to do etc. **pretence** *n.* an excuse; a claim to know, be able to do etc.

pretty (pret-ty) *a.* attractive, pleasing to the eye, but not beautiful. *adv.* fairly (good, bad, tall etc.).

prevent (pre-vent) *v.* stop something from happening; hinder. **prevention** *n.* the act or result of preventing. **preventive** *n.* something which prevents.

preview (pre-view) *n.* a view of a film, play, exhibition, goods on sale etc. before they are shown to the public.

previous (pre-vious) *a.* coming before or earlier; too quick (to speak, act etc.). **previously** *adv.* before.

prey *n.* a living being killed and eaten by another. *v.* hunt another animal for food. **prey on** (or upon) steal or plunder from; cause anxiety to (the mind).

price *n.* what something costs; value. *v.* ask or fix the price of. **priceless** *a.* having a value beyond all price.

prick *v.* puncture, make a hole in; cause pain by pricking. *n.* a small hole made by something sharp or pointed; pain caused by being pricked. **prickle** *n.* a small point sticking out (of a thistle, a hedgehog etc.). **prickly** *a.* having prickles.

pride *n.* a feeling of satisfaction at having done something well or having people's respect; a person, animal or thing one is proud of; too high an opinion of one's own importance. *v.* be proud of.

priest *n.* a clergyman, usually in the Roman Catholic Church or the Church of England; a minister of any religion, a person trained to perform religious acts or ceremonies.

primary (pri-ma-ry) *a.* first in rank of importance; first in time or order. **primary colours** (paints) red, yellow and blue from which all other colours can be made. **primary school** a school for very young children up to the age of 11.

prime *a.* chief; very good indeed. *v.* give a person all the facts so that he can make a judgment, act etc. **primer** *n.* a first textbook on any subject; the first coat of paint put on an unpainted surface. **Prime Minister** the head of the Cabinet or government of a country. **primate** an archbishop; one of the highest order of mammals, including the apes and man.

primitive (prim-i-tive) *a.* having to do with the earliest times; old-fashioned, not developed (of tools, weapons, civilizations etc.).

prince *n.* in Great Britain, the son or grandson of a king or queen; a ruler, especially of a small state; a male member of a royal family. **princess** *n.* in Great Britain the daughter or grand-daughter of a king or queen, or the wife of a prince.

principal (prin-ci-pal) *a.* most important. *n.* the head of a college.

print *v.* make a mark on paper, cloth etc. by pressing with inked type or coloured designs; make a photograph on paper from a negative. *n.* letters, designs etc. in printed form; marks left by the finger, the foot, the hand, an animal's paw etc.; printed cotton fabric. **printer** *a.* person who prints for a living.

prior (pri-or) *a.* at or of an earlier time; first (of engagements, claims). *n.* the head of a religious order; the next below an abbot in a monastery. **priority** *n.* the right to be considered before all others.

prison (pri-son) *n.* a building in which criminals and others condemned by the courts are locked up. **prisoner** *n.* a person kept in prison or in some other form of captivity.

private (pri-vate) *a.* having to do with one's own person or with a particular group; not to be entered by the public (of a room, a building etc.); secret; personal. *n.* a soldier who is not an officer. **privacy** *n.* being alone, the right to be alone.

privilege (priv-i-lege) *n.* the right possessed only by one person, by a member of a certain class or rank, the holder of a certain position etc.; a special favour. **privileged** *a.* having been granted privileges or a privilege.

prize *n.* the reward of victory in a contest; something worth struggling or sacrificing for. *a.* having won a prize (of an animal in a show etc.). **prizefight** *n.* a boxing match for money. **prize money** money got by the sale of something captured in battle; money won in a competition.

probable (pro-ba-ble) *a.* likely to happen or prove true. **probability** *n.* the state of being probable. **probably** *adv.* most likely to happen.

probation (pro-ba-tion) *n.* a period in which a person is tested for suitability before being given a post; a period in which offenders against the law are allowed to go free providing they commit no further offences.

problem (prob-lem) *n.* a difficult question to be answered or puzzle to be solved (in games, mathematics etc.); something in life which presents difficulties. *a.* offering problems.

proceed (pro-céed) *v.* move forward or onward; come forth; arise from some other condition. **proceeding** *n.* action or piece of conduct; a legal action. **proceeds** (pró-ceeds) *n.* profits.

process (pro-cess) *n.* actions which go on; a method of doing something; things which are done in order. *v.* treat something, especially food, in order to preserve it.

procession (proces-sion) *n.* a line or body of persons moving along in an orderly manner.

proclaim (pro-claim) *v.* make known to all. **proclamation** *n.* the act of being proclaimed; that which is proclaimed.

procure (pro-cure) *v.* obtain, get, especially with effort.

prodigal (prod-i-gal) *a.* wasteful; spending too much; generous (of nature).

produce (pro-dúce) *v.* make, grow, create; bring forward for others to see; cause; make a line longer; bring before the public. **produce** (pró-duce) *n.* that which is produced, especially on farms.

profession (pro-fes-sion) *n.* a kind of work which needs special education and training. **professional** *a.* having to do with a profession. *n.* a person who does something for a living (boxer, footballer, writer etc.). **professor** *n.* a university teacher who directs one branch of learning.

proficient (pro-fi-cient) *a.* skilled, expert at a particular thing. **proficiency** *n.* being proficient.

profile (pro-file) *n.* the outline or the side view of a face; a short outline of a person's life.

profit (pro-fit) *n.* advantage from some activity; money gained in business. *v.* bring or obtain some gain. **profitable** *a.* bringing profit.

profound (pro-found) *a.* deep; having great knowledge; needing a great deal of thought.

programme (pro-gramme) *n.* a list of what is to happen in a concert, a sports meeting, the names of the cast of a play etc.; a plan of what is to be done (in politics, industry etc.). **program** *n.* the facts that are put into a computer. *v.* put facts into a computer. **programmer** *n.* a person who supplies facts to a computer.

progress (pró-gress) *n.* forward movement. **progress** (pro-gréss) *v.* make progress.

prohibit (pro-hib-it) *v.* forbid; state that a thing must not be done. **prohibition** *n.* an order forbidding a thing. **prohibitive** *a.* likely to prevent the use or purchase of.

project (pro-ject) *v.* plan; throw an outline or a picture on a screen; throw a missile into space; stand out beyond the surface (a cliff, a spike etc.). **project** (pró-ject) *n.* a plan. **projectile** *n.* a missile thrown or shot. **projector** *n.* a machine that projects a picture.

prolong (pro-long) *v.* make longer in space (a line) or in time (a visit, a speech etc.). **prolongation** *n.* being prolonged, made longer.

promenade (prom-e-nade) *n.* a place where one can walk, especially in public and for pleasure; such a walk or ride. *v.* go up and down a promenade.

prominent (prom-i-nent) *a.* standing out, projecting, easily seen; well-known, important, distinguished. **prominence** *n.* being prominent, that which is prominent.

promise (prom-ise) *n.* an undertaking to do, to give etc. something; that which one promises to do or give etc. *v.* make a promise.

promontory (prom-on-to-ry) *n.* a cliff or high point of land standing out from the coastline.

promote (pro-mote) *v.* raise somebody to a higher rank or position; organize the sale of something, advertise a play, book etc. **promotion** *n.* a raising in rank; the act of promoting; something promoted.

prompt *a.* without delay, on time. *v.* be the reason for doing something; remind an actor of his words when he forgets them. **prompter** *n.* a person who prompts actors in a play. **promptitude** *n.* being prompt.

pronoun (pro-noun) *n.* a word used instead of a noun (he, his, she, hers, me etc.).

pronounce (pro-nounce) *v.* make the sounds of words; declare, give as an opinion. **pronunciation** *n.* the way in which a word is pronounced or in which a language is spoken.

proof *n.* facts which show that a thing is true; a first copy of something printed, to make sure that it is correct and satisfactory. *a.* giving safety or protection against.

prop *n.* a stick or pole used to prevent things from falling; any other kind of support; a person who supports another in some way. *v.* support; keep in position.

propagate (prop-a-gate) *v.* increase the numbers (plants, animals, diseases etc.);

spread widely (of news, knowledge etc.). **propaganda** *n.* teachings, news spread far and wide; false, misleading information.

propel (pro-pel) *v.* drive forward. **propeller** *n.* a shaft with curved blades that whirl round to drive a boat or an aeroplane. **propulsion** *n.* a method of propelling (by jet, engine, rocket etc.).

proper (prop-er) *a.* as it should be; as they should be. **proper noun** the name of a person or a place.

property (pro-per-ty) *n.* everything which is owned, possessions; what a thing does, how it may be recognized; a piece of furniture or decoration on a stage; anything handled by an actor.

prophecy (proph-e-cy) *n.* a statement as to what is going to happen. **prophesy** *v.* say what is going to happen. **prophet** *n.* a person who prophesies or teaches.

proportion (pro-por-tion) *n.* the relation of one thing to another in size, quantity, length, breadth etc.; share or part.

proposal *n.* something proposed. **proposition** *n.* a plan or scheme to be considered or adopted.

propose (pro-pose) *v.* put forward plans or ideas, usually for others to consider and decide on; ask a person to marry one; suggest a person for an office in a company, organization, etc.

proprietor (pro-pri-e-tor) *n.* a person who owns a business, hotel etc. **proprietress** *n.* a woman proprietor.

prosecute (pros-e-cute) *v.* carry on, continue to do something; bring a person to trial in court; carry on a legal case. **prosecution** *n.* prosecuting; being prosecuted.

prospect (pros-pect) *n.* a view over land or sea etc.; something looked forward to. *v.* search (for gold, precious metals etc.). **prospective** *a.* possible, likely. **prospectus**

---

n. a printed account giving details of a business, a school, a book etc.

prosper (pros-per) *v.* be successful, do well. **prosperous** *a.* successful, prospering, flourishing. **prosperity** *a.* being successful; prosperous.

protect (pro-tect) *v.* keep from harm or danger. **protection** *n.* protecting; being protected. **protective** *a.* that protects. *n.* something that protects. **protector** *n.* a person or thing that protects.

protest (pro-tést) *v.* speak against, object to something. **protest** (pró-test) *n.* a statement protesting against something. **Protestant** *n.* a member of a Christian church which is not Roman Catholic.

prototype (pro-to-type) *n.* the original or the model, the first of a series of things from which others will be copied.

proud *a.* showing a reasonable pride; showing too much pride, having too high an opinion of oneself or what one can do; splendid.

proverb (pro-verb) *n.* a short saying, often well known, giving words of advice, stating an important truth in very few words.

provide (pro-vide) *v.* furnish, supply; prepare beforehand; state that something is necessary (usually in a contract or an agreement).

providence (pro-vi-dence) *n.* the way God's care over His creatures is shown. **provident** *a.* careful to provide for future needs. **providential** *a.* as though done by providence.

province (prov-ince) *n.* a large division of a country; a branch of learning; a department of business. **the provinces** all parts of the country which are outside the capital. **provincial** *a.* having to do with a province; typical of the provinces as contrasted with the capital of a country (speech, manners etc.).

provision (pro-vi-sion) *n.* preparation for future needs; the part of a legal document, an agreement etc., which says what must happen under certain circumstances (see **provide**). *v.* supply with

food, stores etc. **provisions** *n.* food and stores especially for a journey, a garrison etc.

provoke (pro-voke) *v.* stir up, arouse, call forth (laughter, rioting etc.); cause to do something; make angry. **provocation** *n.* provoking, being provoked.

prowl *v.* go about in search of prey, plunder, or whatever may be found. **prowler** *n.* an animal or a person who prowls.

prudent (pru-dent) *a.* careful, thinking before acting. **prudence** *n.* being prudent; careful thought before action.

pry *v.* peer, peep or enquire with great curiosity; find something out by prying or enquiring.

psychology (psy-chol-o-gy) *n.* (pronounced *sykology*) the study of the mind and how it works. **psychologist** *n.* an expert in psychology.

public (pub-lic) *n.* the people who make up the state, the nation, the community. *a.* having to do with the people. **public house** or **pub** a house where alcoholic drinks are sold and consumed on the premises. **publican** *n.* a keeper of a public house; a tax-collector (in Roman times and in the Bible). **publication** *n.* publishing; making or made known to the public. **publicity** *n.* being known and recognized by all; the means to give a person or thing publicity. **publish** *v.* make known to the public; print a book or periodical. **publisher** *n.* a person or firm which publishes books, magazines etc.

puddle (pud-dle) *n.* a small pool of water, especially dirty water, as in a road after rain has fallen.

puff *n.* a short quick blast of wind or breath; a soft pad for putting powder on the face; a piece of pastry filled with jam, cream etc. *v.* make puffs; swell, make to swell. **puffy** *a.* swollen.

pull *v.* use force to draw or haul in a certain direction. *n.* the action of pulling; a draw at a pipe, a cigarette or a long drink.

pulley (pul-ley) *n.* a wheel with the rim

hollowed out so that ropes or chains can run over it.

pulp *n.* the soft, fleshy part of fruit; material such as rags or wood, torn up, crushed and mixed with liquid as in the making of paper. *v.* make into pulp; become like pulp.

pulpit (pul-pit) *n.* a raised platform in a church enclosed by a wooden frame from where a clergyman delivers his sermon.

pulse *n.* the regular throbbing of the arteries caused by the pumping of the blood by the heart; any regular throb. *v.* throb, beat.

pump *n.* a machine for forcing liquids or gases out of something or through pipes; a light shoe used for dancing. *v.* force liquids etc. through pipes.

punch *n.* a tool for piercing or stamping materials or for making holes; a blow, usually with the fist; a drink made with wine or spirits mixed with hot water, sugar, lemons, spices etc. *v.* strike hard with the fist; work with a punch.

punctual (punc-tu-al) *a.* arriving or doing a thing at the fixed time, not late.

punctuate (punc-tu-ate) *v.* put all the stops, commas, question marks etc. into a piece of writing; interrupt. **punctuation** *n.* putting in all the stops, commas etc.

puncture (punc-ture) *n.* a small hole made by pricking with a stone or a pointed instrument, often in the tyre of a car or bicycle. *v.* make a puncture.

punish (pun-ish) *v.* subject a person or living being to some penalty, pain, loss, imprisonment etc. for some offence. **punishment** *n.* punishing; being punished.

puny (pu-ny) *a.* very small, very weak.

pupil (pu-pil) *n.* a person who is learning under the instruction of a teacher; the dark opening in the centre of the eye.

puppet (pup-pet) *n.* a doll which moves either on strings or is worked by the hand thrust inside it. **puppeteer** *n.* a person who gives puppet-shows.

purchase (pur-chase) *v.* buy. *n.* something bought; buying; a firm grip for holding or raising something.

pure *a.* not mixed with anything else; clean, without evil; distinct and clear (of notes); simple, nothing but, unmixed (imagination, nonsense etc.). **purify** *v.* make pure. **purity** *n.* being pure.

purpose (pur-pose) *n.* an aim, what one

means to do. **purposely, on purpose** *adv.* as a result of purpose or aim, and not by chance.

purr *v.* make a low continuous murmuring sound as a cat does. *n.* the sound of purring.

purse *n.* a small bag, pouch or case for carrying money *v.* draw the lips together into tiny wrinkles.

pursue (pur-sue) *v.* follow, intending to overtake, capture, kill etc.; work at, spend one's time doing something. **pursuit** *n.* the act of pursuing; the way one spends one's time.

push *v.* use force to move something away; press (buttons, bells etc.); press oneself forward. *n.* the act of pushing.

put *v.* move something into a place or a position; mark (a word, a cross).

putty (put-ty) *n.* a paste made of whiting and linseed oil and used for fixing panes of glass, stopping up holes in woodwork etc.

puzzle (puz-zle) *n.* something difficult to understand; a kind of game to be worked out. *v.* be perplexed about something; think hard about something.

pyjamas (py-jam-as) *n.* a jacket and trousers worn for sleeping in at night.

pyramid (pyr-a-mid) *n.* an object with a base of three or more sides and sloping surfaces which meet at a point; one of the great stone structures built by the ancient Egyptians as royal tombs.

Q

quack *n.* the cry of a duck; a person who pretends to possess knowledge or qualifications which he does not possess. *v.* make the cry of a duck. *a.* something given or sold by a quack.

quadrangle (quad-ran-gle) *n.* a square or oblong space, usually in a school or college, surrounded by buildings; a figure with four sides.

quadruple (quad-ru-ple) *a.* four times or by four times. *n.* a number four times that of another. **quadruplet** *n.* one of four children born to one mother at the same time.

quaint *a.* strange or odd, but in an interesting and pleasing way; not familiar, old-fashioned.

quake *v.* tremble, shake (of the earth and sometimes of persons) *n.* an earthquake.

qualify (qual-i-fy) *v.* be well suited for something, often a post or occupation; obtain certificates etc. giving a person the authority to take up a certain profession. **qualification** *n.* the certificate or the training that allows a person to take up a profession.

quality (qual-i-ty) *n.* a certain degree of goodness; a feature (hardness, height, intelligence etc.) that distinguishes a certain person or thing from others.

quantity (quan-ti-ty) *n.* size, weight, amount, number.

quarantine (quar-an-tine) *n.* a period, originally of forty days, during which a person or animal is kept away from all others to prevent the spread of disease. *v.* put and keep in quarantine.

quarrel (quar-rel) *n.* a disagreement, an angry dispute. *v.* take part in a quarrel.

quarry (quar-ry) *n.* an open space in the ground from which stone is dug; an animal, a bird or a person who is pursued or hunted. *v.* take stone from a quarry.

quart *n.* a measurement of liquids; two pints; a quarter of a gallon; 1·136 litres.

quarter (quar-ter) *n.* one of four equal parts; a direction, a district; a place to live in (in the plural); mercy granted to an enemy. *v.* divide into quarters. **quarterly** *a.* happening once every three months. *n.* a magazine which is published every three months. **quartet** *n.* a group, or a piece of music for a group of four singers or four players.

quay *n.* a man-made landing-place where ships can be loaded and unloaded.

queen *n.* a female ruler; the wife of a king; a girl chosen to represent a group or a society; a bee, wasp or ant which produces eggs; a piece in the game of chess; a card next in importance to the king in the pack.

queer *a.* strange, odd, peculiar; causing suspicion; not well, faint.

quell *v.* put down, subdue, suppress (a rebellion or rising).

quench *v.* put out (fire); satisfy (thirst); put an end to (hope); cool in water (of red-hot iron).

query (que-ry) *n.* a question. *v.* express a doubt about, question the truth of something.

quest *n.* a search.

question (ques-tion) *n.* a word or sentence that requires an answer; something to be discussed, to be decided. *v.* doubt, query something; ask a question or questions.

queue *n.* a line of people or vehicles waiting their turn. *v.* form, get into a queue.

quick *a.* fast moving; able to do things in a short time; intelligent; lively; prompt; **quicken** *v.* make or become quicker. **quickly** *adv.* in a quick manner.

quiet (qui-et) *a.* silent, still; restful; free from trouble. *n.* freedom from noise or disturbance. **quieten** *v.* make or become quiet.

quill *n.* the large or tail feather of a bird; the same feather once used as a pen; the spine of a porcupine.

quilt *n.* a thick cover for a bed made by stitching two thicknesses of material with soft warm padding between them. *v.* make a quilt.

quintuplet (quin-tu-plet) *n.* one of five children born to one mother at the same time.

quit *v.* leave, go away from; stop (work, grumbling etc.).

quite *adv.* entirely, altogether, completely; fairly (good, tall etc.); more or less; truly.

quiver (quiv-er) *v.* tremble or make tremble. *n.* the case in which an archer carries his arrows.

quiz *v.* ask questions as a test of knowledge. *n.* a test of knowledge, often done as a game or in a broadcast. **quizmaster** *n.* one who asks questions in a quiz.

quoit *n.* a metal ring used in the game of quoits, thrown from a distance at a peg in the ground; a rubber ring used in the game of deck quoits.

quota (quo-ta) *n.* a limited number, share, amount; a limited number of goods or of people allowed to enter or immigrate (of a country).

quote *v.* repeat in speech or in writing the words of another; name a price which a person will charge. *n.* a punctuation mark placed before and after something quoted. **quotation** *n.* something quoted; a price quoted.

R

rabbi (rab-bi) *n.* a teacher of the Jewish law; the principal officer of a Jewish synagogue.

rabbit (rab-bit) *n.* a small, long-eared animal which burrows in the ground; the flesh of the rabbit used as food.

rabble (rab-ble) *n.* a disorderly crowd, a mob; a scornful way of referring to a crowd or to the lowest class of people.

rabies (ra-bies) *n.* an infectious disease of the brain which affects animals, especially dogs, and which can be passed on to people through being bitten.

race *n.* a contest of speed; a group of persons, a tribe or a nation believed to have the same ancestors; one of the main natural divisions of living beings. *v.* compete in speed with another person; make something go fast; train animals or birds to compete in races. **racer** *n.* any animal or thing that races. **racial** *a.* having to do with races or people. **racing** *a.* having to do with races or speed.

rack *n.* a framework or a stand specially made to hold things; a medieval instrument of torture designed to stretch the limbs of those who were placed on it.

racket (rack-et) *n.* a loud, confused noise; a dishonest way of getting money; a light bat having a network of cord stretched on an oval frame used in playing tennis, badminton and some other games (sometimes spelt **racquet**)

radar (ra-dar) *n.* a device by which the position of an object can be found by measuring the time in which the echo of a radio wave returns to its source and the direction from which it comes (short for Ra(dio) d(etecting) a(nd) r(anging).

radiant (ra-diant) *a.* shining, sending out light; looking joyful and delighted.

radiate (ra-di-ate) *v.* send out rays or lines like rays from a centre; spread out in rays or as if in rays. **radiation** *n.* radiating, something radiated. **radiator** *n.* an apparatus for radiating heat.

radio (ra-di-o) *n.* communication by wireless telegraphy; broadcasting; a wireless device for receiving radio broadcasts. **radiogram** *n.* a gramophone and radio receiver combined.

radish (rad-ish) *n.* a plant grown in gardens for its red root which is eaten with salad.

radium (ra-dium) *n.* a metal which sends out rays capable of penetrating solid matter, and which is used in the treatment of certain diseases.

radius (ra-dius) *n.* the distance from the centre to the circumference of a circle; an area within a fixed distance of a certain point.

raffia (raf-fia) *n.* fibre from the leaf-stalks of a palm-tree growing in Madagascar, used for making matting, baskets, hats and other articles, and for tying plants and flowers.

raffle (raf-fle) *n.* a method of raising money by selling tickets and choosing the prize-winning numbers by lot. *v.* dispose of by raffle.

raft *n.* a floating platform made of various materials, such as tree-trunks, rubber, planks, empty barrels etc. tied together and used as a substitute for a boat.

rafter (raft-er) *n.* one of the sloping beams or timbers which hold up the outer covering of a roof.

rag *n.* a piece of cloth torn from a larger piece; old, torn clothing.

rage *n.* fury, violent anger; something about which people are enthusiastic or which is in fashion. *v.* act or speak with great anger, furiously; move with violence (storms etc.).

raid *n.* a sudden attack by robbers, police etc.; a sudden attack on or by an enemy force. *v.* make a raid, take part in a raid.

rail *n.* a bar of wood or metal making part of a fence; a steel bar fastened to the ground to help provide a track on which vehicles may run; the railway, the railway system; a bar of wood or metal put into a certain place and having a certain use (for towels, pictures etc.). **railing** *n.* a barrier made of rails with posts to support them. **railway** *n.* a track on which trains run; all the engines that run on it, buildings, stations etc. that serve it and the people who manage it.

rain *n.* water in drops falling from the clouds to the earth; a fall of rain; anything falling like rain (arrows, blows etc.). *v.* send down, fall. **rainbow** *n.* a large coloured arch in the sky seen opposite the sun during a rainstorm. **rainfall** *n.* the amount of rain falling in one area during a fixed period. **rainproof** *a.* able to keep out rain.

raise *v.* lift up, move to a higher position; set up (a monument etc.); make appear (laughter); make louder; bring up (a question); make, grow, produce; get (money, funds etc.).

raisin (rai-sin) *n.* a dried grape used in cookery.

rake *n.* a tool with a long handle and teeth for gathering hay, grass or leaves together and for breaking the surface of the ground. *v.* gather together with a rake; search thoroughly (among rubbish etc.).

rally (ral-ly) *v.* bring or come together ready for action; begin to recover, gain strength. *n.* the return of the ball several times by both sides before a point is scored (in tennis); a large gathering to bring about new efforts; a competition between car drivers in which strict rules are followed to test performance.

ram *n.* a male sheep. *v.* drive or force by heavy blows; pack tight; run into or strike (of ships etc.).

ramble (ram-ble) *v.* walk about in a leisurely manner; take a long walk for pleasure; grow in many directions with long shoots; talk of various things without keeping to one subject. *n.* a leisurely walk.

ramp *n.* a sloping walk or passageway; a sloping way from one level to another for cars, wheelchairs etc. to avoid steps.

ranch *n.* a large farm, especially in North America or Australia, for raising cattle, sheep or horses. **rancher** *n.* a person who owns or works a ranch.

rancid (ran-cid) *a.* having an unpleasant stale smell or taste; having gone bad (of fat or butter).

random (ran-dom) *a.* done, made, happening etc. without any aim or purpose. **at random** done, made, dropped etc. anyhow or anywhere.

range *v.* set in order in a row or rows; go through or over (country, forests etc.); extend in two directions; vary within certain limits (wages, prices etc.). *n.* a row or line; a piece of ground with targets for shooting; the distance to which a bullet or shell may be fired; the extent between two limits; a stretch of land for grazing; a large stove for cooking, having an oven and points for heating various articles at the same time.

rank *n.* a row; a number of soldiers, police etc. standing or marching side by side; a position in a scale, grade or standing (of officers etc.). *v.* arrange in order. *a.* growing too fast (weeds); smelling or tasting bad.

ransack (ran-sack) *v.* search thoroughly; plunder, rob.

ransom (ran-som) *n.* a sum of money paid to free a prisoner or to recover goods which have been stolen or taken. *v.* pay the price demanded for release or recovery.

rap *v.* strike with a quick blow. *n.* a quick, smart blow; the sound of such a blow.

rapid (rap-id) *a.* quick, speedy; descending steeply (of a slope). **rapids** *n.* that part of a river which flows swiftly over a steep slope in the bed. **rapidly** *adv.* quickly, speedily.

rapture (rap-ture) *n.* great joy, great delight. **rapturous** *a.* with great delight.

rare *a.* unusual, uncommon, not often found, seen, felt, experienced etc.; thin (of the air). **rarity** *n.* something uncommon.

rascal (ras-cal) *n.* a dishonest person; a mischievous child, fond of playing tricks.

rash *a.* with too much haste and not enough thought. *n.* a breaking out of tiny red spots on the skin.

rasher (rash-er) *n.* a thin slice of ham or bacon for frying.

raspberry (rasp-berry) *n.* a small red berry with many seeds that grows on a bush, used for making jam and pies.

rat *n.* a long-tailed rodent resembling but much larger than a mouse.

rate *n.* a measured speed, height, weight, quantity, temperature or price; a tax on land and buildings raised by a parish, town or county; class, grade (first-rate etc.). *v.* set a value on (chances, property etc.). **ratepayer** *n.* a person who owns or rents property and has to pay rates on it.

rather (rath-er) *adv.* more gladly, more willingly; to a certain extent.

ratify (rat-i-fy) *v.* make an agreement or contract legal by signing it or by some other action.

ration (ra-tion) *n.* a fixed allowance given for a period, usually of food; the allowance of food given to a member of the armed forces. *v.* limit the issue of food, petrol, water etc.

rattle (rat-tle) *v.* give out a number of short, sharp sounds; make something rattle; talk quickly. *n.* a series of short, sharp sounds; a baby's toy that produces a rattling sound.

ravage (rav-age) *v.* destroy or damage greatly; rob, plunder and destroy.

rave *v.* talk wildly, excitedly or angrily; talk or write with foolish enthusiasm. **raving** *a.* talking wildly.

ravel (rav-el) *v.* separate (a rope, a piece of cloth etc.) into threads.

raven (ra-ven) *n.* a large black bird resembling a crow. *a.* black and glossy.

ravine (ra-vine) *n.* a long, deep, narrow valley.

raw *a.* uncooked; not prepared or manufactured (of wool, cotton etc.); damp, cold (of the climate); not trained; sore, not healed.

ray *n.* a beam of light, heat or energy; one of the many lines coming from a central point; a large fish with a flat body.

rayon (ray-on) *n.* a silk-like material made artificially and used for making clothing.

razor (ra-zor) *n.* a sharp-edged tool used for shaving the hair from the face and body.

re- a prefix meaning again, added to many words the meaning of which can often be guessed as in **reappear, rearrange**.

reach *v.* stretch out the hand for and take; go to and arrive at a place; extend as far as. *n.* the distance to which the hand will stretch; the distance within which one may take or capture (a person or thing); part of a river or a canal between two bends. **reach out, reach for** *v.* stretch out the hand for.

read *v.* look at and understand the meaning of something written or printed; understand the meaning of (a riddle, a person's thoughts etc.); study a subject; indicate, show (of the barometer, the thermometer etc.). **reader** *n.* a person who reads; a lecturer in a university; a book from which one may practise reading.

reading (read-ing) *n.* the action of one

who reads; a way of understanding something; a figure on a dial; an entertainment which consists of reading; one of the stages in putting a bill through Parliament.

ready (read-y) *a.* completely prepared, in a fit condition; quick in seeing, speaking, replying, writing etc.; within reach, in a fit condition to be used; likely to do something at any time; prepared beforehand (ready-made, ready-cooked etc.). **readily** *adv.* promptly, quickly; willingly. **readiness** *n.* in a prepared state (for use, to do etc.).

real (re-al) *a.* true, not imagined; genuine, not imitation. **reality** *n.* the state of being real. **in reality** in fact, actually.

realize (re-al-ize) *v.* understand clearly; make something come true; obtain (a profit) through selling or work.

realm *n.* a kingdom, the state of Great Britain (used in terms such as Defence of, the State of etc.); a region.

ream *n.* a standard quantity among those who sell paper, formerly 480 sheets, now usually 500 sheets.

reap *v.* cut and take in a harvest of grain; obtain as a result or a reward.

rear *n.* the back part of anything. *a.* at the back, having to do with the back. *v.* raise and care for a young person or a young animal; raise to an upright position; rise on the hind legs.

reason (rea-son) *n.* the cause of a belief or an event; the power to understand; good sense, a knowledge of what is right. *v.* use one's reason, think clearly; argue, use sensible arguments. **reasonable** *a.* fair, acting according to reason.

reassure (re-as-sure) *v.* give a person confidence, remove doubts.

rebel (ré-bel) *n.* one who rises in arms against a ruler. *a.* having to do with a rebel or rebels. **rebel** (re-bél) *v.* rise in arms, resist. **rebellion** *n.* rebelling.

recapitulate (re-ca-pit-u-late) *v.* go over

or repeat the main points of a plan, discussion or report (sometimes shortened to **recap**). **recapitulation** *n.* the repeating of the main points of an argument.

recede (re-cede) *v.* go back, appear to go back, slope back (the chin, the hair line, the forehead etc.).

receive (re-ceive) *v.* get, accept; admit (into an organization etc.); entertain, welcome. **receiver** *n.* a person who receives (stolen goods etc.); an apparatus for receiving broadcast programmes. **The Official Receiver** the official appointed to take charge of the property of a person or a firm which is bankrupt.

recent (re-cent) *a.* having happened, being done or made not long ago. **recently** *adv.* only a short time ago.

reception (re-cep-tion) *n.* receiving, being received; a way of receiving or being received; the receiving of guests, the quality of radio or television signals received. **receptive** *a.* able to receive ideas quickly; **receptionist** *n.* a person employed to receive guests in a hotel, patients in a surgery or callers.

recess (re-cess) *n.* a short time when work or business is stopped; a space in the wall of a room that is set back; an inner part, kept secret or not easily reached.

recipe (rec-i-pe) *n.* (pronounced *ressipy*) a set of directions telling how something, especially a cooked dish, is prepared.

recite (re-cite) *v.* repeat the words from memory; give a list or an account. **recital** *n.* an account; a musical performance. **recitation** *n.* the act of reciting; what is recited.

reckless (reck-less) *a.* not caring what happens or will happen.

reckon (reck-on) *v.* calculate the number or amount; consider somebody or something to be, have etc.

recognize (rec-og-nize) *v.* be able to know again; admit something to be true;

agree about something. **recognition** *n.* recognizing, being recognized.

recoil (re-coil) *v.* draw back, rebound, come back; *n.* the rebound of the weapon on firing (of a gun).

recollect (rec-ol-lect) *v.* remember. **recollection** *n.* the act of remembering; what is remembered.

recommend (rec-om-mend) *v.* speak well of; put forward as worthy; advise a person to do something. **recommendation** *n.* recommending, being recommended; a statement, often written, in favour of a person, often spoken, in favour of a thing (medicine, soap, goods in general).

recompense (rec-om-pense) *v.* repay, reward. *n.* a reward or payment for having done something.

reconcile (rec-on-cile) *v.* become friends after a quarrel; be satisfied with after a disappointment. **reconciliation** *n.* being reconciled (after quarrels, arguments etc.).

reconnoitre (rec-on-noi-tre) *v.* inspect or survey the position of an enemy to estimate his strength. **reconnaissance** *n.* the act of reconnoitring.

record (ré-cord) *n.* an account in writing, or taken in any other way, to be preserved; things known about the past history of a person or thing; a disc, a magnetic tape, a film etc. on which sound or pictures have been made; the best, highest, largest etc. so far recorded. **record** (re-córd) *v.* keep for reference; make a gramophone record or tape recording; mark on a scale. **recorder** *n.* an apparatus that records sounds; a musical instrument similar to a flute. **recording** *n.* a piece of music, a speech etc. recorded on magnetic tape or on a disc, to be played back when required.

recover (re-cov-er) *v.* get again or regain something lost; become well again; regain a state or position once held. **recovery** *n.* recovering; being recovered.

recreation (rec-re-a-tion) *n.* refreshment of body and mind by some agreeable pastime. **recreation ground** an open piece of land on which games can be played.

recruit (re-cruit) *n.* a new member of a society; a recently enlisted member of the forces. *v.* obtain new members; get back (health, strength etc.).

rectangle (rec-tan-gle) *n.* a four-sided

figure with four right angles.

rectify (rec-ti-fy) *v.* put right, take out mistakes.

rector (rec-tor) *n.* a Church of England clergyman in charge of a parish; a person in charge of certain universities and other institutions.

recuperate (re-cu-per-ate) *v.* recover (health, strength, losses etc.). **recuperation** *n.* recovery of health or fortunes.

recur (re-cur) *v.* happen again; come again to the mind.

red *n.* the colour of blood. *a.* having the colour of blood. **redden** *v.* make red.

redeem (re-deem) *v.* get back by payment; set free by paying a ransom; fulfil (promises etc.); take one's own goods out of pawn by paying money; compensate, make up for.

reduce (re-duce) *v.* make smaller in size, amount, extent or number; change to a different form or condition. **reduction** *n.* reducing, being reduced.

redundant (re-dun-dant) *a.* no longer needed (of workpeople, old machinery etc.). **redundancy** *n.* being redundant.

reed *n.* the straight stalk, usually hollow, of various tall grasses growing in marshy places; a piece of cane or metal put into the mouthpiece of musical instruments such as the oboe, clarinet and bassoon, which helps to produce the sound.

reef *n.* a narrow ledge of rock or sand lying near the surface of the water; part of a sail that can be rolled up and tied to reduce the area exposed to the wind.

reek *n.* a strong unpleasant smell. *v.* smell strongly and unpleasantly.

reel *n.* a roller or cylinder on which to wind something; a gay Scottish dance. *v.* rock or sway under a blow or shock; walk unsteadily; seem to rock or sway (before the eyes).

refer (re-fer) *v.* send, pass to, hand to;

direct the attention to; turn to for information; speak about. **referee** *n.* a person to whom questions are referred; a person who controls certain games and matches such as football, boxing, hockey etc.

reference (ref-er-ence) *n.* the act of referring; a person to whom one may refer for details about another person's character; a written statement concerning a person's character; a note telling where certain facts may be found (usually in books).

refine (re-fine) *v.* purify. **refined** *a.* purified; well-mannered, cultured. **refinement** *n.* good manners, speech and taste. **refinery** *n.* a building where raw products are refined.

reflect (re-flect) *v.* cast back (light, heat, sound etc.); think carefully. **reflection** *n.* anything reflected; thought about some matter; blame. **reflector** *n.* something that reflects (light etc.); a small disc fixed on the back of vehicles for reflecting light at night.

reform (re-form) *n.* improvement, putting right what is wrong. *v.* improve, make or become better

refrain (re-frain) *v.* keep oneself from doing something. *n.* a chorus, repeated at the end of each verse of a song.

refresh (re-fresh) *v.* give new strength by taking food, drink or rest. **refreshment** *n.* that which refreshes.

refrigerate (re-frig-er-ate) *v.* preserve by freezing. **refrigeration** *n.* the preservation of food by freezing. **refrigerator** *n.* a box, cabinet or small room in which food is kept cold to preserve it.

refuge (ref-uge) *n.* shelter or protection from danger etc.; a place or means of refuge; a low platform in the middle of a street on which people may take refuge from traffic while crossing. **refugee** *n.* a person who has taken refuge in another place, especially a foreign country.

refund (re-fund) *v.* give back or repay money. *n.* money given back.

refuse (re-fúse) *v.* be unwilling to do something. **refusal** *n.* the act of refusing. **refuse** (ré-fuse) *n.* that which is thrown away as worthless. **refuse dump** a place where household refuse is thrown after being collected.

regard (re-gard) *v.* look on a person or thing with a particular feeling; consider; pay attention to. *n.* a look, a gaze; thought, attention; respect.

regatta (re-gat-ta) *n.* a meeting at which races of yachts, rowing boats and other vessels are held.

regent (re-gent) *n.* a person who rules a country at a time when its monarch is too young, too old or too ill.

regiment (reg-i-ment) *n.* an army unit consisting of two or more battalions, and commanded by a colonel; a large number (beggars, vagabonds etc.). *v.* organize, put under strict discipline. **regimental** *a.* having to do with a regiment.

region (re-gion) *n.* a part of the earth's surface; part of the body. **regional** *a.* having to do with a region or regions.

register (reg-is-ter) *n.* a list of names; the range of a voice or a musical instrument; a device for recording numbers or measurements. *v.* cause to be recorded; show on the dial of an instrument, or on the human face; pay a fee to send a letter by special post. **registrar** *n.* an official who keeps records of births, marriages and deaths; a doctor in a hospital training to be a specialist. **registration** *n.* recording, sending by registered post. **registry** *n.* a place where registers are kept. **register office** (usually called **registry office**) a place where births, marriages and deaths are recorded and where marriages can take place.

regret (re-gret) *v.* feel sorry. *n.* a feeling of sorrow. **regrets** *n.* feelings of sorrow for what has been lost or done.

egular (reg-u-lar) *a.* even, well-arranged; happening at fixed times. *n.* a professional soldier. **regularity** *a.* being regular.

egulate (reg-u-late) *v.* control, direct according to a rule or method; control by mechanical means; adjust, put in order. **regulation** *n.* a rule or order *a.* according to rule or order.

ehabilitate (re-ha-bil-i-tate) *v.* restore to a good condition; give special treatment to a person to enable him to work and live normally.

ehearse (re-hearse) *v.* practise. **rehearsal** rehearsing (music, drama, etc. for public performance).

eign *n.* a period in which a ruler is in office. *v.* be in office as a monarch.

ein *n.* a long narrow strap fastened to the bridle by which the movements of a horse or other animal are controlled. *v.* control with reins. *n.* control (of government etc.).

eindeer (rein-deer) *n.* a kind of deer with branched antlers found in arctic regions, kept for transport and for its milk, meat and hide.

einforce (re-in-force) *v.* strengthen with some added piece of material; make stronger with more men, materials, ships etc. **reinforcements** *n.* men, ships, materials etc. to increase the strength of an army, fleet or air force.

einstate (re-in-state) *v.* put back into a former position or state; give a person back his former position.

eject (re-jéct) *v.* throw away as being useless; refuse to accept. **reject** (ré-ject) *n.* something rejected. **rejection** *n.* being rejected, rejecting.

ejoice (re-joice) *v.* be glad. **rejoicing** *n.* great joy, merrymaking.

elate (re-late) *v.* tell; think of at the same time; have connection with another fact or event.

relation (re-la-tion) *n.* connection; the telling about something; a person in the same family.

relative (rel-a-tive) *n.* a person connected with another by blood or marriage; *a.* of two or more things considered in relation to each other.

relax (re-lax) *v.* become less firm, make less firm or tight; make less strict; use less effort and energy. **relaxation** *n.* relaxing, being relaxed; recreation; something which relaxes.

relay (re-lay) *n.* a set of men, animals etc. taking turns; a team race in which one member takes up the race from another. *v.* pass on a message or a broadcast programme by relays.

release (re-lease) *v.* set free; let go; allow news to be published. *n.* releasing, being released (prisoners, news etc.).

relent (re-lent) *v.* become less severe. **relentless** *a.* strict, severe, without pity.

relic (rel-ic) *n.* something which has survived from the past and is valued; the remains of a saint or martyr kept after death.

relief (re-lief) *n.* the lessening or removal of pain or distress; something bringing relief; reinforcements of troops sent to help those besieged in a town or fort; a design or figure that stands up from the surface from which it has been cut. **relieve** *v.* give or bring relief.

religion (re-li-gion) *n.* the belief in a god who controls the affairs of men; one of the many systems of worshipping such a god (Christianity, Islam etc.). **religious** *a.* believing in and worshipping God; having to do with religion.

relish (re-lish) *n.* something used to give flavour to a dish; pleasure in something. *v.* find pleasure in.

rely (re-ly) *v.* depend. **reliable** *a.* that may be relied or depended on.

remain (re-main) *v.* stay, be left after others have gone or been taken. **remains** *n.* what is left; ruins (of buildings etc.); a dead body, a corpse. **remainder** *n.* persons or things left over.

remark (re-mark) *v.* say. *n.* something said. **remarkable** *a.* unusual, extraordinary.

remedy (rem-e-dy) *n.* a cure. *v.* cure, put right. **remedial** *a.* intended to furnish a remedy (exercise etc.).

remember (re-mem-ber) *v.* call to mind things which have happened in the past;

send or give greetings to. **remembrance** *n.* remembering; being remembered.

remind (re-mind) *v.* cause a person to remember something. **reminder** *n.* something sent, written, said etc., intended to remind.

remit (re-mit) *v.* excuse punishment or payment of a debt; send money in payment. **remission** *n.* pardon of sins; freeing from debt or punishment. **remittance** *n.* money sent in payment.

remnant (rem-nant) *n.* a part or a number remaining; an odd piece of cloth or material which has not been sold.

remote (re-mote) *a.* far away; long ago; faint (of ideas, possibility etc.).

remove (re-move) *v.* take off, take away; put an end to, get rid of; dismiss; move a house, place of business etc. from one place to another. **removal** *n.* the act of removing. **remover** *n.* a person who moves furniture etc. when people move house or business; something that removes (scratches, stains etc.).

renew (re-new) *v.* do a thing again; make new or as good as new; replenish, replace with the same kind of thing. **renewal** *n.* being renewed.

renovate (ren-o-vate) *v.* restore to good condition.

renown (re-nown) *n.* fame. **renowned** *a.* famous.

rent *n.* payment made regularly for the use of a building or other property; a tear or open place in cloth or other material. *v.* pay or charge rent.

repair (re-pair) *v.* put into working order again; put right a wrong or wrongs. *n.* repairing, being repaired; a state or condition (good, bad, excellent etc.).

repeat (re-peat) *v.* do or say again; say what has been learnt or what has been said by others. *a.* other, similar (performance etc.). **repeated** *a.* said or done again and again.

repel (re-pel) *v.* drive or thrust back; make one feel dislike or disgust. **repellent** *n.* something which repels (insects etc.).

repent (re-pent) *v.* be sorry for something said or done. **repentance** *n.* regret.

replenish (re-plen-ish) *v.* fill up again.

reply (re-ply) *v.* answer. *n.* an answer.

report (re-port) *v.* give an account; present oneself (for duty, interview etc.); make a complaint. *n.* a statement, an account of some event; an account of a pupil's progress in school; a noise as from an explosion. **reporter** *n.* a person employed by a newspaper to report events of interest.

repose (re-pose) *v.* rest, sleep, lie quietly. *n.* rest, sleep. **repository** *n.* a place where things may be stored.

represent (rep-re-sent) *v.* stand for, be a symbol of; pretend to be what one is not; speak or act for others (in parliament, on municipal councils etc.). **representative** *n.* a person who represents a group of people or a firm, to sell its products.

reprieve (re-prieve) *v.* put off or delay the punishment of a person. *n.* the postponement of a punishment; the remission of the death penalty.

reprimand (rep-ri-mand) *v.* reprove a person for a fault or misdeed. *n.* a reproof, especially by one's superior officer.

reproach (re-proach) *v.* blame or find fault with a person. *n.* blame; a matter for blame.

reproduce (re-pro-duce) *v.* make a copy of something seen or heard; increase through breeding, by means of seeds or in any other way. **reproduction** *n.* reproducing, something reproduced (e.g. jewellery, pictures).

reptile (rep-tile) *n.* a cold-blooded animal such as a lizard, crocodile or snake, that creeps or crawls.

republic (re-pub-lic) *n.* a country whose governors are elected by the people and which has a president instead of a monarch.

repulse (re-pulse) *v.* beat off, drive back, repel; reject, refuse to accept. *n.* repulsing, being repulsed. **repulsive** *a.* causing a feeling of disgust.

reputation (rep-u-ta-tion) *n.* the opinion of people about a person, a group of persons or things.

request (re-quest) *n.* the act of asking for something; the thing asked for. *v.* ask, make a request.

require (re-quire) *v.* need, desire, order, command. **requirement** *n.* something demanded. **requisite** *n.* something that is necessary (for an occupation, a hobby etc.).

rescue (res-cue) *v.* deliver from imprisonment, violence, danger etc. *n.* the act of rescuing or being rescued. **rescuer** *n.* a person who rescues or has rescued.

resemble (re-sem-ble) *v.* be like. **resemblance** *n.* likeness.

resent (re-sent) *v.* feel angry at. **resentful** *a.* feeling or showing anger. **resentment** *n.* a feeling of anger, that one has been injured etc.

reserve (re-serve) *v.* keep back or save for future use; keep for a special purpose; book or pay beforehand for something (rooms, seats etc.). *n.* something that has been reserved; a place kept apart for special use (nature reserve); a lack of warmth or friendliness in a person. **reserves** *n.* military forces held back for use when needed. **reservation** *n.* the act of reserving; what is reserved. **reservoir** *n.* a place, either natural or made by man, where water is stored for use in the home and in industry.

reside (re-side) *v.* live, dwell, have one's home. **residence** *n.* the place where one resides. **resident** *n.* a person living in a certain place. **residential** *a.* consisting mainly of houses, flats etc.

resign (re-sign) *v.* give up an office or a claim; accept willingly. **resignation** *n.* resigning; being resigned.

resin (res-in) *n.* a sticky sap that flows from certain trees when cut, used in making varnish, lacquer and other substances.

resist (re-sist) *v.* strive against, oppose; be proof against; be undamaged by; withstand, not give in to. **resistance** *n.*

resisting; the force that resists. **resistant** capable of resisting (damp, rain, disease etc.).

resolve (re-solve) *v.* choose to do; settle on; decide. **resolution** *n.* determination, the act of resolving.

resort (re-sort) *v.* turn to for help or use; go often to a place. *n.* resource; something, somebody resorted to; some place visited by people (for holidays, health etc.).

resource (re-source) *n.* wealth, supplies of anything at hand when needed; pastimes resorted to so as to keep the mind occupied; qualities needed to meet difficulties; an action resorted to when all else has failed.

respect (re-spect) *n.* high regard and admiration; a detail, a particular. *v.* think highly of. **respectable** *a.* worthy of respect; of some importance. **respectful** *a.* showing respect. **respects** *n.* greetings.

respirator (res-pi-ra-tor) *n.* an apparatus through which a person can breathe when the air is rare as in high altitudes, or polluted.

respond (re-spond) *v.* answer; do something in answer. **response** *n.* answer.

responsible (re-spon-si-ble) *a.* expected as a duty to do a thing or service; reliable, trustworthy, capable; (a post) needing a responsible person. **responsibility** *n.* being responsible; some thing for which one is responsible. **responsive** *a.* answering quickly to (affection, instruction etc.).

rest *n.* freedom from work or movement; sleep; a device which gives support; a sign in music marking an interval of silence. *v.* be still, not moving; support or be supported by. **restful** *a.* quiet, peaceful. **restless** *a.* never quiet, unable to rest.

restaurant (res-tau-rant) *n.* a place where meals are served to customers.

restore (re-store) *v.* give back; repair,

make as it was before; bring back to one's former state. **restoration** *n.* restoring; being restored. **restorative** *n.* capable of restoring; something which may restore.

restrain (re-strain) *v.* hold back from action; keep under control. **restraint** *n.* restraining; being restrained.

restrict (re-strict) *v.* keep within limits, not going to extremes. **restriction** *n.* a limitation; that which keeps something within limits.

result (re-sult) *v.* happen because of something that has happened before; bring about, cause. *n.* that which results; which is produced by a cause; something found by calculation or study.

resurrect (res-ur-rect) *v.* raise from the dead; bring back (old ways, songs, sayings, arguments etc.). **resurrection** *n.* bringing back. **Resurrection** *n.* the rising again of Jesus Christ after his burial.

retail (re-tail) *n.* the sale of goods from a shop to the public in small quantities. **retailer** *n.* a person who sells by retail.

retain (re-tain) *v.* keep possession of, hold; keep in mind; hire by paying a fee. **retainer** *n.* a servant of a person of high rank. **retention** *n.* retaining, being retained. **retentive** *a.* having the power to retain.

retire (re-tire) *v.* withdraw; go to a place apart; go to bed; go back (of an armed force); give up work. **retired** *a.* having retired. **retirement** *n.* the state of having retired. **retiring** *a.* shy, reserved.

retreat (re-treat) *v.* move back in face of an enemy. *n.* the signal for retreating; a place where one can be alone.

retrieve (re-trieve) *v.* get into one's possession again; rescue; find and fetch killed or wounded game (of a dog). **retriever** *n.* a dog used for retrieving killed and wounded game.

return (re-turn) *v.* go or come back to a place; take, give, pay, carry, put or send back; elect a person to a seat in Parliament. *n.* going or coming back; a report or statement. **returns** *n.* money obtained from business deals or sales.

reveal (re-veal) *v.* make known; show, display. **revelation** *n.* revealing, making known; something made known.

revenge (re-venge) *v.* do harm or injury to another in return for injury done to you. *n.* the harm or injury done.

revenue (rev-e-nue) *n.* money coming in; all the money the government receives in taxes and by other means. **Inland Revenue** money received through taxation. **revenue officer** a customs officer who checks goods brought into a country in order to collect the due tax.

revere (re-vere) *v.* regard with great respect; treat as being sacred. **reverence** *n.* a feeling of great respect. **Reverend** the title of a clergyman.

reverse (re-verse) *a.* opposite to (in order etc.). *v.* turn the other way; do the opposite; make to go the opposite way. *n.* the opposite; a defeat, a misfortune.

review (re-view) *v.* go over again; inspect troops etc.; think over what has passed; report on a book or a play. *n.* such a report; a periodical which contains articles on literature, the arts, events of the day etc.; a military or naval inspection.

revise (re-vise) *v.* read again carefully, think about again. **revision** *n.* revising; being revised.

revive (re-vive) *v.* make or become conscious or active again; put into use or come into use again. **revival** *n.* being revived; reviving.

revoke (re-voke) *v.* take back or withdraw. **revocation** *n.* the act of withdrawing, revoking.

revolt (re-volt) *v.* rise in rebellion; turn away in disgust. *n.* the act of rebelling. **revolting** *a.* disgusting.

revolution (rev-o-lu-tion) *n.* the complete overthrow of a government; a complete change in the ways of doing things; the act of going round.

revolve (re-volve) *v.* go round in a circle; think over (a problem). **revolver** *n.* a pistol which has a revolving chamber carrying the cartridges, enabling it to be fired a number of times before reloading.

reward (re-ward) *n.* that which is given for some service or work of special value. *v.* give a reward.

rheumatism (rheu-ma-tism) *n.* (pronounced *rumatism*) a disease which affects the joints and the muscles. **rheumatic** *a.* having to do with rheumatism.

rhinoceros (rhi-noc-er-os) *n.* a large, heavily-built animal with a grey skin and one or two horns on its snout, found in Africa and Asia.

rhododendron (rho-do-den-dron) *n.* a large evergreen shrub bearing pink, purple or white flowers.

rhubarb (rhu-barb) *n.* a garden plant with large green leaves and thick, juicy stalks, that may be stewed or made into pies.

rhyme *n.* the agreement in the ends of lines of verse, or words (such as fill and kill, beam and team); a poem with rhymes in it. *v.* be in rhyme, end with the same sound; make verses with rhymes.

rhythm (rhy-thm) *n.* a regular beat in music, speech, dancing or movement; the way in which certain events follow each other. **rhythmical** *a.* in rhythm.

rib *n.* one of the curved bones that run from the backbone to the front of the body over the chest, protecting the heart and lungs; the rib of an animal with the meat on it; something which is like a rib in shape; a raised line in cloth.

ribbon (rib-bon) *n.* a band of silk or other cloth used for decoration; a piece of ribbon used for some special purpose (a medal or decoration etc.); a long thin piece of material; a strip.

rice *n.* the seeds or grain of a grass that grows in warm climates.

rich *a.* wealthy, having much money or property; valuable, costly, expensive; fertile, having many natural resources; containing much butter, fat, sugar, eggs etc. **riches** *n.* wealth. **richly** *a.* expensively, thoroughly.

rid *v.* clear, make free of. **riddance** *n.* being delivered or free of. **get rid of** free oneself of.

riddle (rid-dle) *n.* a question designed to puzzle others; something which is dif-ficult to solve or answer; a sieve for stones or cinders. *v.* shake a riddle to pass things through it; fill with holes.

ride *v.* be carried by (a horse etc.) or in (a cart, train etc.). *n.* the time when one rides, a journey. **rider** *n.* a person who rides.

ridge *n.* a long, narrow chain of hills or raised area; a raised strip where sloping surfaces meet.

ridicule (rid-i-cule) *n.* words or actions intended to make fun of something or somebody. *v.* make fun of, make look ridiculous. **ridiculous** *a.* absurd, laughable.

rifle (ri-fle) *v.* search (a room etc.) in order to rob. *n.* a gun with a long barrel, fired from the shoulder. **rifle range** a place where people may practise shooting with a rifle.

rig *v.* fit out a ship with masts, sails etc.; put together (a shelter, scaffolding etc.). **rigging** *n.* the ropes which support the masts and sails of a ship. **rig out with** supply all that is necessary for school, certain sports, work etc.

right *a.* good, according to law; accurate; the best; neither acute nor obtuse (of an angle); straight; correct; as things should be. *n.* the right side; that which is good; a just claim. *adv.* well (feel, look right etc.). **righteous** *a.* doing what is right. **rightful** *a.* just, according to law.

rigid (rig-id) *a.* stiff, firm, not yielding or bending; strict, not changing from things said, ordered etc.

rigour (rig-our) *n.* strictness, harshness, sternness. **rigorous** stern, severe (discipline); harsh (climate).

rim *n.* an outer edge, border or margin; a framework of a wheel between tyre and spokes.

rind *n.* the thick skin or covering of certain fruits (bacon, cheese etc.).

ring *v.* give out a clear musical sound;

surround, make a circle or ellipse etc. round; put a ring on (a finger, a bird's leg etc.); make something ring. *n.* a loud clear sound; a circular band often made of gold or silver, to wear on the finger; any circular band (for machinery etc.); a circle; a group of people; an enclosure for a circus or for some sport.

rink *n.* a sheet of ice prepared for skating, or a smooth floor prepared for roller-skating.

rinse *v.* dip in water to get rid of dirt, soap etc. *n.* a cleaning of things through rinsing; something in which hair is rinsed in order to alter its colour.

riot (ri-ot) *n.* disturbance of the peace by a group of disorderly people; a large amount of sound, colour etc. *v.* make a riot.

rip *v.* tear, pull, cut apart. *n.* a torn place. **ripsaw** *n.* a saw used to saw wood along the grain.

ripe *a.* ready for reaping or gathering; fully developed in body and mind; ready for things to happen (plucking, development, building) or for doing things (mischief). **ripen** *v.* become ripe.

ripple (rip-ple) *n.* a small movement or the sound of a small movement on the surface of water; laughter or voices gently rising and falling. *v.* rise and fall gently.

rise *v.* get up, stand up; appear above the horizon; come to life after being dead, get up after having slept; increase, come to a higher position; slope upwards; rebel; start (of a river, a quarrel); become more lively (of the wind etc.). *n.* a slope; a coming (to power, influence etc.); a coming up (of the sun etc.); an increase.

risk *n.* chance of danger, injury or loss. *v.* take the risk of injury, danger or loss. **risky** *a.* full of risk.

rite *n.* a ceremony, especially an important religious ceremony.

rival (ri-val) *n.* one who wants the same thing as another, or to do something better than another. *v.* be as good as, try to be as good as. **rivalry** *n.* being rivals.

river (riv-er) *n.* a large stream of water flowing into the sea or into a lake; a large stream; a great flow.

rivet (riv-et) *n.* a metal pin or bolt used for fastening metal plates or pieces together. *v.* drive in rivets; fasten with rivets; direct and keep (one's attention) on a thing.

road *n.* an open way specially prepared to carry traffic; a way to a place or to a certain state.

roam *v.* wander about with no fixed purpose, aim or direction.

roar *n.* a loud, deep noise, as of a lion or thunder, or of a person in pain or anger. *v.* make such sounds.

roast *v.* bake in an oven; cook over or in front of a fire. *n.* a piece of meat prepared for roasting, or one already roasted.

rob *v.* steal from others or take things from others by force. **robber** *n.* a person who robs. **robbery** *n.* robbing; having robbed.

robe *n.* a long loose garment worn by men or women, especially kings, queens, judges, mayors etc. *v.* put a robe or robes on.

robin (rob-in) *n.* a small bird having a red or reddish breast.

robot (rob-ot) *n.* a machine made to act and do certain things as if it were a person; a person who acts like a machine (through fatigue, drugs etc.).

rock *n.* a large stone standing on land or jutting from the sea; a hard sweet made with various flavours; stone. *v.* move to and fro.

rocket (rock-et) *n.* a tube-shaped device filled with material that burns very fast so that the gases push it into the air.

rod *n.* a thin stick, wand or staff with various uses (punishment, hanging curtains, fishing, as part of a machine etc.).

rodent (ro-dent) *n.* the order of mammals known especially for their long sharp teeth, used for gnawing, nibbling and biting; mice, rats, squirrels, beavers, rabbits etc.

rogue *n.* a scoundrel, rascal, a dishonest person; a person who is fond of playing tricks.

roll *v.* move by turning over and over; move between two surfaces; move or advance in a stream or with a rolling motion; flatten by rolling something on it; make a long low sound; move from side to side. *n.* something that is rolled (cloth, bread etc.); a rolling movement; a long low sound; a list of names. **roller** *n.* a cylinder used to roll things or a machine containing such rollers.

romance (ro-mance) *n.* a story of adventure or love, quite unlike what happens in real life; something unreal, attractive, picturesque. **romantic** *a.* having to do with romance.

romp *v.* play or frolic in a noisy manner. *n.* a frolic. **romper, romper-suit** *n.* a garment for a child, loose-fitting, in which it can move easily.

roof *n.* the top covering of a building, a tent or a vehicle. *v.* put a roof on. **roofing** *n.* material used to make roofs.

rook *n.* a large black bird like a crow; a castle in the game of chess. *v.* make money by cheating others. **rookery** *n.* a place, usually a number of high trees where rooks live and breed.

room *n.* a portion of space within a building, separated from others by walls or partitions; space (to move, do things etc.); opportunity (for progress, improvement). **room-mate** *n.* a person who lives in the same room as another, sharing costs. **roomy** *a.* having plenty of space or room.

roost *n.* a pole or branch on which birds may sleep or rest. *v.* rest, sleep (of birds).

root *n.* that part of a plant or tree that is under the ground and provides its nourishment; that part of a hair, tooth or nail which resembles a root in its position or use; the source or essence of a matter. *v.* make roots when put into the ground; stand still with fear, terror etc. (be rooted to the spot); turn up, search.

rope *n.* a strong, thick cord, usually of twisted strands of material. *v.* tie or bind with a rope or ropes; lasso (cattle).

rosary (ro-sa-ry) *n.* a series of prayers used in the Roman Catholic Church; a string of beads used to count these prayers when they are being recited.

rose *n.* a bush which has prickles on its stems and bears a sweet-smelling flower; the flower of the rose tree. **rosy** *a.* having the colour of red roses; bright, cheerful (outlook, prospects). **rosette** *n.* a small bunch of ribbons resembling a rose, used as an ornament or badge.

rot *v.* decay, become soft or weak due to decay; make a thing decay. *n.* decay.

rotate (ro-tate) *v.* move or make move round a central point; follow in a regular way (of crops). **rotation** *n.* going round, following in a set order.

rouge *n.* a red powder used for colouring the cheeks.

rough *a.* uneven, not smooth; neither calm nor quiet; disorderly, violent; not easy, having had or being given harsh treatment; badly finished, not complete. *n.* a person who is rowdy, impolite and violent. *v.* make rough. **roughly** *adv.* in a rough manner; about (of space or time — miles, weeks etc.).

round *a.* like a ball or a circle in shape. *n.* a regular series of visits (of the doctor, postman etc.); a single part of a match; a song for two or more groups, each singing the same melody but beginning at a different time. *adv.* changing direction (round the corner, the buildings etc.); on all sides; in a circle. *v.* make or become round, go round. **rounders** *n.* a game for two teams played with a bat and ball in which players run round a prepared course and back to the starting point.

roundabout (round-a-bout) *a.* using a longer way round. *n.* a circular platform with wooden horses on which children ride, and which goes round and round; a merry-go-round; a place where roads join, where traffic, instead of going across, moves round a circular or oval space.

rouse *v.* bring out of sleep, wake up;

become or make more active, angry or enthusiastic.

rout *n.* complete defeat and flight. *v.* put an enemy to flight. *n.* a noisy, disorderly crowd.

route *n.* a way or road taken or planned. **routine** *n.* a regular way of doing things.

rove *v.* wander about, roam. **rover** *n.* a person who wanders.

row *n.* (rhymes with *so*) a number of people or things in a line. *v.* make a boat move by pulling on oars. **row** *n.* (rhymes with *now*) a noisy dispute or quarrel; a commotion or uproar. **rowdy** *a.* rough and noisy.

royal (roy-al) *a.* having to do with a king or queen; splendid. **royalty** *n.* royal position or persons; payment of money to those who have written books or music. **royalist** *n.* a supporter of King Charles I in the English Civil War; a person who is in favour of a state having a monarch.

rub *v.* move something backwards and forwards on something else; remove something such as dirt or a pencil mark (**rub off, rub out**). *n.* the act of rubbing.

rubber (rub-ber) *n.* an elastic material made from the juice that comes from certain trees when the bark is cut; a piece of rubber specially made for erasing pencil marks; three games between the same persons in whist or bridge.

rubbish (rub-bish) *n.* waste material; litter thrown away as being of no use; nonsense.

rucksack (ruck-sack) *n.* a kind of knapsack carried on the back by hikers.

rudder (rud-der) *n.* the plate of wood or metal fixed to the stern of a boat for the purpose of steering; a similar device fixed to an aeroplane to enable it to move right or left.

ruddy (rud-dy) *a.* having a red face, often a sign of good health; reddish in colour.

rude *a.* impolite, rough in manner; not well finished, rough (of a manufactured article).

rue *v.* repent. *n.* a small evergreen herb with a strong scent and bitter-tasting leaves.

ruffian (ruf-fian) *n.* a violent, lawless man, a rough brute.

ruffle (ruf-fle) *v.* destroy the smoothness of something; gather cloth together to make tiny folds. *n.* a strip of cloth, lace etc. drawn together at one edge and used as a trimming on a dress. **ruffled** *a.* annoyed.

rug *n.* a small, usually thick carpet used as a floor covering; a large thick piece of woollen cloth or blanket used as a covering.

rugged (rug-ged) *a.* roughly broken, rocky, uneven; wrinkled, furrowed; severe, hard (of the life one lives); sturdy, strong and honest but with rough manners.

ruin (ru-in) *n.* destruction, complete downfall; being decayed, destroyed. *v.* cause the destruction of. **ruins** *n.* remains (of buildings etc.). **ruinous** *a.* in ruins; causing ruin.

rule *n.* a law or custom generally followed, which tells people how to behave; a piece of wood or metal with a straight edge used for measuring and drawing straight lines. *v.* govern; decide; make a line or lines with a rule. **ruler** *n.* a person who rules; a rule for making straight lines etc. **ruling** *n.* a decision.

rumble (rum-ble) *v.* make a deep, heavy continuous sound. *n.* a rumbling sound.

rummage (rum-mage) *v.* search through a place by turning things over and moving them about. *v.* various odds and ends.

rumour (ru-mour) *n.* gossip; things talked about which may or may not be true. *v.* report by rumour.

run *v.* move more quickly than walking, so that for an instant both feet are off the ground at the same time; stand as a candidate for election; go, move (of trains etc.); flow; work, be in good or bad order; transport by car, ship etc.; cause to run, flow or move; come back again and again (of things in the mind); move or cause to move into another state (dry, into difficulties etc.); manage, organize; extend or make in a certain direction (with along, to etc.). *n.* the act of running or moving; a trip or journey; an enclosed space; a single score made by batsmen running from one wicket to the one

opposite; a number of notes sung or played in order; a number of happenings.
runaway *n.* a person, animal etc. running away. **runway** *n.* a prepared surface along which an aeroplane can take off and land.
rung *n.* one of the crosspieces forming the steps of a ladder.

runner (run-ner) *n.* a person or animal that runs; a smuggler or smuggling vessel; a long piece of cloth placed on a sideboard; a long stem that grows from a plant and takes root.
rural (ru-ral) *a.* having to do with the country and not the town.
rush *v.* go fast, cause to go fast; come or pass rapidly; attack and capture quickly; hurry. *n.* the act of rushing; great activity; a sudden demand (in shops, trade etc.); the stem of a plant which grows on marshy ground. **rush hours** the times when most people fill the trains and buses on their way to and from work.
rust *n.* a red or orange-coloured coating which forms on iron when exposed to the air and the damp; a disease of plants in which the leaves and stems become spotted and turn a reddish colour. *v.* become covered with rust; decay because of rust. **rustless** *a.* that does not rust. **rusty** *a.* covered with rust; suffering through lack of use or neglect (of something one has once learned).
rustic (rus-tic) *a.* having to do with the countryside; simple, homely, made of roughly worked branches. *n.* a countryman with country accent and manners.
rustle (rus-tle) *v.* make a number of soft, light sounds as of leaves, silk or papers rubbing together; steal cattle or horses. *n.* the sound made when something rustles. **rustler** *n.* a stealer of cattle or horses.
rut *n.* a furrow or track in the ground made by the wheels of vehicles; a way of life that has not changed for a long time. *v.* make ruts in the ground.
ruthless (ruth-less) *a.* without any pity or mercy.
rye *n.* a plant or grass whose grain is used for making flour, and as food for cattle.

S

Sabbath (Sab-bath) *n.* the day of rest and worship (Saturday for Jews, Sunday for Christians).
sabotage (sab-o-tage) *n.* the deliberate damaging of machinery by discontented workers; interference with a country's production by resistance workers or enemy agents during war time. *v.* commit acts of sabotage.
sabre (sa-bre) *n.* a heavy one-edged sword with a curved blade, used by cavalry.

saccharin (sac-cha-rin) *n.* a substance made from coal-tar which is about 400 times as sweet as sugar and is used as a sugar substitute.
sack *n.* a large oblong bag made of coarse cloth or paper, used for carrying goods such as coal, cement, flour, potatoes etc. *v.* discharge from employment; plunder or loot a town, village etc. in time of war.
sacred (sac-red) *a.* having to do with God or religion; solemn (of promises etc.). **sacrament** *n.* a solemn religious ceremony such as baptism, marriage and holy communion.
sacrifice (sac-ri-fice) *v.* offer a life or something of value to a god; give up something liked for a special purpose. *n.* something sacrificed.
sad *a.* sorrowful, mournful, causing sorrow. **sadden** *v.* make sad. **sadness** *n.* the state of being sad.
saddle (sad-dle) *n.* a seat for a rider on a horse or other animal, or on a bicycle. *v.* put a saddle on. **be saddled with** bear great responsibility. **saddler** *n.* one who makes saddles and harness.
safari (sa-fa-ri) *n.* an expedition lasting several days for hunting or taking photographs of wild life.
safe *a.* free from danger, unhurt; secure, not causing harm. *n.* a steel or iron box,

strongly made for the keeping of valuables, papers, jewels etc. **safety** *n.* being safe; a safe place.

saga (sa-ga) *n.* an old story about the deeds of gods and heroes, especially of the Danes and Northmen; the story of a family told in a series of books.

sail *n.* a canvas sheet spread out to catch the wind and make a boat move through the water; a device with four arms fixed on the side of a windmill to catch the wind; a voyage or excursion in a boat. *v.* move forward over water; set off on a sea voyage; control a boat or ship. **sailor** *n.* a person who sails alone or with others; a member of a ship's crew.

saint *n.* a person declared by the church to be worthy of worship through the holiness of his life.

sake *n.* reason; good. **for my, your sake etc.** for my, your good or welfare; because of the regard in which I, you etc. are held.

salad (sal-ad) *n.* a dish of uncooked green plants or other vegetables served cold with meat, eggs, cheese etc. **salad dressing** a mixture of oil, vinegar, cream etc. to be eaten with salad. **fruit salad** a mixture of fruits, cut up and eaten cold.

salary (sal-a-ry) *n.* a fixed payment, usually monthly, for work done.

sale *n.* the exchange of money for goods; the offering of goods at prices that are lower than the usual ones; the selling of goods by auction. **salesman, saleswoman** *n.* people employed to sell goods either in or out of a shop.

salient (sa-lient) *a.* prominent, most important.

saliva (sa-li-va) *n.* the liquid which is always present in the mouth, keeping it moist and helping to digest food.

sallow (sal-low) *a.* (of the human skin) pale yellow, unhealthy-looking.

saloon (sa-loon) *n.* a room in a hotel or a ship in which people may meet together to dine; a room set apart for a special purpose (billiards etc.). **saloon car** a motor car with a solid roof, seating four or more persons.

salt *n.* a white substance obtained by mining or from sea water and used to flavour and preserve foods; a chemical which contains an acid and a mineral; an old sailor. *v.* put salt on. *a.* containing salt. **salty** *a.* containing salt; having a taste of salt.

salute (sa-lute). *n.* a greeting between officers and men of the forces which consists in raising the right hand to the forehead and bringing it down to the side again; a firing of guns to show respect and honour to a country or a person. *v.* greet in one of these ways.

salvage (sal-vage) *v.* save property from loss in a fire or some other disaster. *n.* the property saved; waste material saved for use again, sometimes in another form; payment given to those who have saved property.

salvation (sal-va-tion) *n.* saving, having been saved, especially from sin or its results; that which saves somebody.

same *a.* not another; no different. *adv.* in a similar way (of feeling, thinking etc.).

sample (sam-ple) *n.* one of a number of things intended to show what the rest are like. *v.* try, take a sample of.

sanction (sanc-tion) *n.* permission to do something; the action of one or more states towards another, usually through stopping trade with it, to force it to fulfil some duty.

sanctuary (sanc-tu-a-ry) *n.* a holy place, especially in a church, where people were formerly able to take refuge from arrest; a country to which people of other countries go for refuge; the refuge given by a church, a country, another person etc.

sand *n.* a large number of tiny fragments of rock as seen on the seashore. *v.* rub with sand to smooth or polish. **sands** *n.* large areas of sand on the seashore and occasionally, of the desert. **sandpaper** *n.* tough paper with sand glued to it, used for smoothing rough surfaces.

sandal (san-dal) *n.* a kind of shoe consisting of a sole with thongs or straps to fasten it to the foot.

sandwich (sand-wich) *n.* two or more slices of bread with meat, eggs, lettuce, tomato etc. between them. *v.* place between two things.

sane *a.* healthy in mind, not mad. **sanity** *n.* being sane, soundness of mind.

sanguine (san-guine) *a.* hopeful, cheerful.

sanitary (san-i-ta-ry) *a.* having to do with health or conditions such as cleanliness, which make for health; favourable to health. **sanitation** *n.* measures, especially drainage, taken to protect health.

sap *n.* the liquid in a plant which takes food to all its parts. *v.* drain away the strength. **sapling** *n.* a young tree.

sarcasm (sar-casm) *n.* harsh and hurtful remarks, taunts. **sarcastic** *a.* using sarcasm.

sardine (sar-dine) *n.* a small fish which is caught and preserved in olive oil or tomato sauce.

sari (sa-ri) *n.* a long piece of cotton or silk forming the outer garment of Hindu women, one end of which is worn over the head or shoulder.

sash *n.* a long band of cloth or silk worn over the shoulder as part of a uniform, or round the waist for decoration; a framework in which panes of glass are set and which can be made to move up and down as part of a window. **sashcord** *n.* the cord which moves on a pulley and raises or lowers the sash.

satchel (satch-el) *n.* a leather, plastic or canvas bag with a shoulder-strap used for carrying schoolbooks.

satellite (sat-el-lite) *n.* a small body or a moon which moves round a planet; a country which is dominated and politically controlled by another more powerful one; a man-made device, usually containing scientific instruments, put into orbit round the earth.

satin (sat-in) *n.* a material of silk or rayon, smooth and shiny on one side, used mainly for ribbons and dresses.

satire (sat-ire) *n.* a kind of writing or speaking which shows up the evil or foolishness in people by mocking or casting ridicule on them. **satirical** *a.* mocking. **satirist** *n.* a writer who uses satire as his method of attack.

satisfaction (sat-is-fac-tion) *n.* being contented; something that makes one contented. **satisfactory** *a.* giving satisfaction or pleasure. **satisfy** *v.* give contentment or satisfaction.

saturate (sat-u-rate) *v.* make or become wet; make one substance take in the greatest possible amount of another.

sauce *n.* a preparation, usually liquid, which can be eaten with food to give it an added flavour. **sauceboat** *n.* a vessel in which sauce is served at table. **saucer** *n.* a small, round shallow dish to hold a cup. **saucepan** *n.* a small pan used for boiling or stewing. **saucy** *a.* impertinent, impudent.

sauna (sau-na) *n.* a kind of steam bath originally used by the people of Finland.

saunter (saun-ter) *v.* stroll, walk in a leisurely way.

sausage (sau-sage) *n.* chopped up meat mixed with seasoning, and sometimes with bread, packed into a special skin. **sausage-meat** *n.* chopped up meat used for making sausages. **sausage roll** cooked sausage with a covering of pastry.

savage (sav-age) *a.* wild, rugged (of country); fierce, wild (of people, beasts etc.). *n.* a primitive, uncivilized person. *v.* be attacked, trampled on; severely bitten etc. **savagery** *n.* being savage, savage behaviour.

save *v.* rescue from loss, danger, injury or death; put aside for use at a later time; avoid wasting things, time etc. *prep.* except. **saviour** *n.* a person who rescues another. **The Saviour** Jesus Christ.

savour (sa-vour) *n.* taste, flavour. *v.* taste and enjoy; seem to have present in it (of remarks etc.). **savoury** *a.* tasting or smelling good, with a salty and not a sweet taste.

saw *n.* a tool for cutting, with a thin metal blade containing a row of sharp teeth; an old or wise saying. *v.* use a saw; move backwards and forwards with a sawing motion. **sawdust** *n.* tiny fragments of wood which fall off when sawing. **sawmill** *n.* a mill where wood is cut by mechanically operated saws. **sawyer** *n.* a person employed to saw wood.

saxophone (sax-o-phone) *n.* a musical wind instrument made of brass, with keys on which the fingers are pressed to select the notes.

say *v.* utter words; give an opinion; advise or command; repeat (one's prayers etc.). *n.* an opinion. **saying** *n.* a well-known remark or proverb.

scab *n.* the crust which forms over a sore when it is healing; a disease of plants; a person who refuses to join others who are striking (slang).

scabbard (scab-bard) *n.* the case into which the blade of a sword or dagger is put for safety.

scaffold (scaf-fold) *n.* a kind of frame carrying a platform, put up against walls for builders and painters to work on; a platform on which executions took place. **scaffolding** *n.* the framework of a scaffold.

scald *v.* hurt through burning with hot liquid or steam; clean by the use of boiling water or steam. *n.* a burn caused by hot liquid or steam.

scale *n.* one of the thin, flat, hard plates that cover the skin of certain fishes and reptiles; small flakes of skin that come loose and fall off; marks at regular distances on certain measuring instruments the proportion between the small measurements on a map or diagram and the real distances; the size or extent notes going up or down in order (in music); one of the pans of a balance or weighing machine. *v.* scrape scales from drop off in scales; climb a wall, a hill, a cliff etc.

scallop (scal-lop) *n.* a kind of shellfish which has grooves on its shell; a curved edging put on cloth for ornament.

scalp *n.* the skin and hair of the head. *v.* take the scalp of an enemy (as in the case of American Indians long ago).

scalpel (scal-pel) *n.* a small, light knife used by surgeons when performing operations.

scamp *n.* a worthless rascal; a mischievous person. *v.* do work carelessly.

scan *v.* look very carefully at something look quickly over something; go over a surface with a beam of light in order to transmit a picture in television.

scandal (scan-dal) *n.* disgraceful behaviour; the offence caused by such behaviour; careless or harmful gossip often not founded. **scandalous** *a.* shocking (of behaviour, stories etc.).

scant *a.* very little. **scanty** *a.* scant in amount or quantity, small in size.

scapegoat (scape-goat) *n.* one who is made to take the blame for the misdeed of others.

scar *n.* a mark remaining after a wound or damage. *v.* make a scar or scars on.

scarce *a.* not enough for the need or the demand; rarely seen or met with. **scarcity** *n.* smallness of supply. **scarcely** *adv.* not quite, hardly.

scare *v.* make afraid, frighten; drive away *n.* a sudden fright. **scarecrow** *n.* an object dressed in clothes, set up to imitate the figure of a man and used to scare away birds.

carf *n.* a long strip of material worn round the neck or over the head for warmth or decoration.

catter (scat-ter) *v.* send or throw in many directions; go in many directions. **scattered** *a.* set apart from each other.

cavenger (scav-en-ger) *n.* a creature that feeds on the remains of animals, birds or insects.

cene *n.* the place where something happened; something which happens; an outbreak of anger in front of others; a view spread out before the eye; part of a play; a division of one of its acts. **scenery** *n.* the appearance of a place or landscape; the hangings, painted woodwork etc. on the stage which acts as background to a play.

cent *n.* smell; the smell left behind by animals, which can be followed by certain dogs; the way towards a discovery (of detectives etc.). *v.* give a scent to.

ceptre (scep-tre) *n.* a rod or wand held in the hand as a symbol of power by a king or ruler.

chedule (sched-ule) *n.* a list or statement giving the time allowed for each part of a process, a journey etc. *v.* make plans for certain dates and times.

cheme *n.* a plan, either secret or not secret for doing something. *v.* make a plan of this kind.

chnorkel (schnor-kel – also **snorkel**) *n.* a device on a submarine which takes in and expels air so that the submarine can remain under water for long periods; a tube which enables a person swimming under water to breathe and thus remain under the surface for long periods.

cholar (schol-ar) *n.* a learned person; a student or pupil; a student who because of merit is granted money to enable him to go on with his studies. **scholarship** *n.* learning or knowledge; a regular sum of money granted to enable a person to continue his studies.

chool *n.* a place in which children are

given education; a period in which teaching is given; all the students or pupils attending a school; a department of a college or university; a large number of fish, whales etc. swimming and feeding together. *v.* teach or train. **schoolfellow, schoolmate** *n.* a pupil who goes to the same school at the same time as another. **schooling** *n.* education; teaching.

science (sci-ence) *n.* knowledge obtained by examining and seeing how things work. **science fiction** stories dealing with real or imagined discoveries in science, especially in space travel. **scientific** *a.* having to do with science. **scientist** *n.* an expert in any of the branches of science.

scissors (scis-sors) *n.* a cutting instrument consisting of two blades joined at a point so that they can be brought together for cutting.

scoff *v.* mock, jeer, ridicule. *n.* an expression of ridicule, scoffing.

scold *v.* find fault with, blame angrily. **scolding** *n.* a severe reprimand, the condemnation of a person for something done.

scoop *n.* a small, deep shovel with a short handle for ladling flour, sugar etc.; the large bucket at the end of a mechanical shovel used to pick up earth etc. *v.* use a scoop; make a hole.

scooter (scoo-ter) *n.* a child's toy steered by a handlebar, with two small wheels and a platform between them for the feet; a motor bicycle with small wheels, a motor-scooter.

scope *n.* the opportunity to act or work freely; power, limits in which one may work.

scorch *v.* mark by burning; become marked by heat, the sun etc.

score *n.* a record of points made by competitors in a game; a copy of the music showing all the vocal and instrumental parts; twenty. *a.* twenty in number. *v.* keep a record of points gained, especially in cricket; mark with cuts, lines or scratches; make a score for an orchestra or group of instrumentalists. **scorer** *n.* a person who keeps the score in a game; a person who scores points or goals.

scorn *n.* contempt, a feeling that something is not worthy of respect. *v.* look down on or feel that somebody or something is unworthy. **scornful** *a.* showing scorn.

scoundrel (scoun-drel) *n.* a villain, a wicked person.

scour *v.* clean dirt, grease or rust off by rubbing; look everywhere to find a thing or person.

scout *n.* a soldier, a warship or an aeroplane sent out to reconnoitre or discover the enemy's position and movements; a member of a road patrol belonging to an organization whose work is to help motorists. *v.* act as a scout. **boy scout** a member of the organization for boys founded by Baden Powell in 1908. **scoutmaster** *n.* an officer who leads a troop of boy scouts.

scowl *v.* frown, look angry and bad-tempered. *n.* a frown.

scramble (scram-ble) *v.* make one's way in a hurry by using hands and feet, over rough ground; struggle with others to get things; cook eggs in a pan by mixing them with butter, milk etc. *n.* a struggle to get something.

scrap *n.* bits of paper, things no longer wanted; food left over after meals. *v.* throw away as useless, set aside to be broken up. **scrapbook** *n.* a book in which photographs, newspaper cuttings etc. are pasted.

scrape *v.* make clean by drawing a sharp instrument over a surface; hurt or damage by scraping; rub across something; put together by effort or with difficulty (money etc.). *n.* a scraping sound; something scraped (on the leg, furniture etc.); a difficult situation.

scratch *v.* mark by rubbing or making lines with something sharp or rough; hurt oneself through being scratched; scrape with claws, fingernails or anything else; use nails or claws for digging as poultry and birds do; remove a name from a list. *n.* a mark or sound produced by scratching.

scrawl *v.* write carelessly or poorly. *n.* careless or poor writing.

scream *v.* utter a loud, sharp cry; *n.* a loud, sharp cry.

screech *v.* make a harsh, shrill cry or noise as parrots and certain other birds do. *n.* a harsh, shrill cry.

screen *n.* anything that can be used to protect or hide; white or silver material stretched on a frame on which slides or films can be projected; the cinema; a sieve through which stones, grain or sand can be sieved. *v.* hide, shelter; show on a screen, make a film of.

screw *n.* a metal peg or nail with a groove in the head and a spiral ridge called a thread which can be driven into wood with a screwdriver; the propeller of a ship or an aeroplane. *v.* fasten with screws; twist, alter the shape, force. **screwdriver** *n.* a tool fitting into the head of a screw to drive it in or take it out by turning.

scribble (scrib-ble) *v.* scrawl, write badly and carelessly. *n.* untidy, careless writing or drawing.

script *n.* handwriting, printing in imitation of handwriting; the text of a play given to the cast for rehearsal. **scriptures** *n.* the sacred books of various religions. **The Holy Scriptures** the Bible. **script-writer** *n.* a person who writes scripts for radio television etc.

scroll *n.* a roll of paper or parchment especially one on which there is writing.

scrub *v.* rub hard with a brush, using soap and water. *n.* land covered with low trees and shrubs.

scruff *n.* the back of the neck.

scrutiny (scru-ti-ny) *n.* very close and detailed examination; a re-count of votes after an election. **scrutineer** *n.* a person who sees that election papers are properly counted. **scrutinize** *v.* examine in great detail.

scuffle (scuf-fle) *n.* a confused struggle or fight. *v.* take part in a scuffle; struggle with others in a scrambling, confused manner.

scullery (scul-le-ry) *n.* a small room where the dirty work of the kitchen such as washing up the dishes, is done.

sculpture (sculp-ture) *n.* the art of forming figures in wood, stone, marble granite, clay, plastics etc.; a single piece of such work. *v.* make sculptures, decorate in sculpture.

scum *n.* a layer of froth or unwanted matter which settles on the top of liquids worthless, or seemingly worthless people. v. remove scum from the surface of a liquid.

scurry (scur-ry) v. go or move quickly and in haste. n. a scurrying rush; the flitting passage of snow, leaves, birds etc.

scuttle (scut-tle) v. scurry away; make holes in the bottom or sides of a ship to sink it. n. a box or any kind of container for holding coal, usually placed in a corner of the hearth.

scythe n. a tool with a curved blade fastened to a handle, for mowing grass etc. v. cut down with a scythe.

sea n. the salt waters that cover nearly three-quarters of the earth's surface, each part having its own name; the salt water of the earth in general; the state of the sea (high, stormy etc.); a large quantity or number (faces, mud etc.). **seasick** a. sick from the motion of the sea.

seal n. a furry marine mammal with flippers, mainly found in the cold waters in both the northern and southern hemispheres; a piece of metal on which there is a design which can be stamped on wax; the piece of wax or other material with the design stamped on it as proof that a document is genuine. v. put a seal on; close tightly so that the seal has to be broken before opening. **sealed orders** instructions given to an officer which must not be opened until a given time or at a given place. **sealing-wax** n. wax used for sealing letters or documents.

seam n. a line where two pieces of material are sewn together; a layer of coal or other mineral between layers of different rock. **seamstress** (or **sempstress**) n. a woman who earns her living by sewing.

search v. look carefully in order to find. n. the act of searching. **searchlight** n. a powerful light which can throw a beam in any direction.

season (sea-son) n. one of the four divisions of the year — spring, summer, autumn and winter; the time of the year when something is at its best or is done. v. flavour food by adding spices or other substances. **seasoning** n. substances added to food to give it an appetizing flavour. **in season** ripe, ready for use.

seat n. something used for sitting on; the part of a chair etc. on which one sits; the part of the body or of a garment on which one sits; a large house, particularly one in the country; a place where something is carried on (learning, government etc.). v. have seats for. **seat oneself, be seated** sit down.

secede (se-cede) v. withdraw from an alliance or an association. **secession** n. the act of seceding.

second (sec-ond) n. one of the sixty parts of a minute; one who helps a boxer or wrestler between rounds; one who supports a person fighting a duel. a. next after the first in order, place, time, rank etc.; like one which has gone before. v. speak in a meeting in support of a motion. **secondary** a. coming after the first in time, order, importance etc. **second-hand** a. used, not new.

secret (se-cret) n. something not to be told to any other person; a reason not generally known. a. kept from all others; quiet, not well known (of places, collections, hoards etc.). **secrecy** n. being secret; able to keep secrets. **secrete** v. put in a secret place. **secretive** a. in the habit of keeping secrets, not revealing one's thoughts.

secretary (sec-re-tary) n. a person who deals with correspondence, keeps records etc. for a business, person or organization; a high official of an organization or a government. **secretarial** a. having to do with secretaries. **secretariat** n. the group of people who keep records, perform the duties of secretaries; the office or department in which they work.

section (sec-tion) n. a part cut off; one of the parts into which something may be divided; one of the parts which, put together, make a whole; a division or part of a body of people (soldiers, police etc.). **sectional** a. composed of sections.

sector (sec-tor) n. part of a circle cut off by two lines drawn from the centre to the circumference; one of the sections of a fighting front in battle.

secure (se-cure) a. free from fear, safe; fastened, not likely to fall, be moved etc.;

sure, certain. v. make secure or fast; get something.

security (se-cur-i-t̄y) n. freedom from fear or danger; something of value handed over as a guarantee that a debt will be paid or some other obligation carried out.

sedative (sed-a-tive) n. a medicine which calms or soothes. **sedation** n. being under the influence of a sedative.

sedition (se-di-tion) n. words, writings or actions intended to cause discontent or rebellion against a government. **seditious** n. of the nature of sedition.

see v. have the use of, have the power of sight; notice, observe; understand; have experience or knowledge; visit, be visited; accompany; find out; make sure, attend to; ensure (that something is done).

seed n. that part of a plant from which another plant will grow. v. remove seed from; produce seed. **seedling** n. a young plant grown from seed.

seek v. look for, ask for.

seem v. appear to.

seep v. leak slowly. **seepage** n. that which leaks out.

see-saw n. a children's game played on a plank, also called a see-saw, balanced at the middle so that the ends rise and fall.

segment (seg-ment) n. a part cut off from a circle by a straight line; a part into which something divides naturally (as of an orange etc.).

segregate (seg-re-gate) v. set apart from the main body. **segregation** n. being segregated, removed from the rest.

seize v. take hold of suddenly; grasp with the mind; take possession of. **seizure** n. seizing; being seized; a sudden attack of some illness.

seldom (sel-dom) adv. not often.

select (se-lect) v. choose in preference to another. **selection** n. choosing; things chosen. **selector** n. a person who chooses.

selfish (sel-fish) a. thinking more of oneself than of others.

sell v. exchange for money; keep things to be sold; be sold.

semaphore (sem-a-phore) n. a means of signalling by holding flags in both hands, different letters of the alphabet being shown by the positions in which the flags are held.

semi- (sem-i-) a prefix meaning half, as semicircle, semiconscious, semiskilled. **semicolon** (;) a punctuation mark indicating a rather greater separation between the parts of a sentence than that shown by a comma.

senate (sen-ate) n. the most important law-making body in ancient Rome; one of the legislative bodies, usually the smaller one, known as the Upper House, which makes laws in some countries, as in the United States, France and Italy; the ruling body in some universities. **senator** n. a member of the senate of a country.

send v. cause or order to go or be carried.

senior (se-nior) a. older in years; of higher rank; the elder of two persons in a family bearing the same name, usually abbreviated to snr.

sensation (sen-sa-tion) n. feeling; a state of excitement felt by a large number of people. **sensational** a. causing a sensation, giving news in a way which causes a sensation.

sense n. one of the five powers of sight, hearing, touch, taste or smell by which we are conscious of ourselves· and all around us; feeling, being conscious of; meaning (of sentences, poems, remarks etc.). **sensible** a. showing good sense, conscious of. **senseless** a. foolish, unconscious.

sensitive (sen-si-tive) a. quick to feel or be conscious of things; easily hurt or offended.

sentence (sen-tence) n. a group of words which make a statement or ask a question; a decision by a judge or magistrate on the punishment to be given to an offender. v. give punishment.

sentiment (sen-ti-ment) n. a feeling; all one feels about a person, or a subject. **sentimental** a. affecting the feelings, easily moved, showing sentiment or tender feeling.

sentry (sen-try) n. a soldier stationed at a place to keep guard.

separate (sép-a-rate) *a.* not joined together. **separate** (sep-a-ráte) *v.* make or become separate. **separation** *n.* separating; being separate. **separator** *n.* a machine used for separating cream from milk.

septic (sep-tic) *a.* caused by infection from disease germs.

sequel (se-quel) *n.* an event which follows another; a novel which continues the story of a previous novel. **sequence** *n.* something which follows on.

serenade (ser-e-nade) *n.* the performance of a piece of music especially a love song in the open air at night; a composition in music. *v.* perform a serenade.

serene (se-rene) *a.* calm, clear; peaceful, happy. **serenity** *n.* being serene.

sergeant (ser-geant) *n.* a non-commissioned officer in the army ranking above a corporal; a police officer ranking between a constable and an inspector. **sergeant-major** *n.* an officer ranking above a sergeant; a non-commissioned officer of the highest rank.

series (ser-ies) *n.* a number of events happening after each other and all having to do with each other; a set of articles issued at the same time. **serial** *n.* anything published or broadcast in instalments at regular intervals.

serious (se-ri-ous) *a.* of solemn character or appearance; bringing possible danger; earnest.

sermon (ser-mon) *n.* an address or speech given from a pulpit in a church on a religious subject; a serious talk.

serpent (ser-pent) *n.* a snake; a sly, crafty person.

serum (se-rum) *n.* the thin liquid part of the blood; liquid taken from that part of the blood of an animal which has had a certain disease and which, when injected into a human being, may prevent him from getting it.

serve *v.* do work for wages; do duty; wait on at mealtimes or generally; fulfil a need; spend time; in tennis, start play by striking the ball over the net. **servant** *n.* one who serves in any way. **servile** *a.* behaving like a slave or servant; having no spirit of independence. **servitude** *n.* slavery, being forced to work for others.

service (serv-ice) *n.* being a servant; a department of government (postal, transport etc.); help; plates, dishes etc. for use at table; a religious ceremony; the act of serving in tennis; the keeping of a machine or apparatus in working order. **serviceable** *a.* giving good service.

session (ses-sion) *n.* the meeting of a court, of Parliament or a conference; a university term.

set *v.* go down (of sun, moon and stars); put something into a certain state or condition; cause somebody to do a thing; put something in a place where it will grow, work or do what is wanted; fit music to words; become firm or solid. *n.* a number of things grouped together; an apparatus for receiving radio or television programmes.

settle (set-tle) *v.* go and live in another place; come to rest on; become or make calm; sink or cause to sink; decide on, make an agreement; pay; put in order. **settler** *n.* a person who has settled in a new land to develop it. **settlement** (set-tle-ment) *n.* the settling of a debt, quarrel etc.; a group of people settled in a new colony.

several (sev-e-ral) *a.* more than two or three but not many.

severe (se-vere) *a.* violent (of illnesses, storms etc.); strict, stern; plain, without decoration. **severity** *n.* being severe.

sew *v.* (rhymes with *so*) fasten cloth, leather etc. by making stitches with needle and thread;

sewer (sew-er) *n.* an underground drain made of wide pipes which carries waste away from houses and factories. **sewage** *n.* waste material from houses etc. which flows through the sewers. **sewage farm** a place where sewage is treated with chemicals and made into fertilizer.

sex *n.* being male or female. **sexual** *a.* having to do with sex.

sexton (sex-ton) *n.* a man who is charged with taking care of a church, its contents, the graveyards, ringing the bell, grave-digging etc.

shabby (shab-by) *a.* very much worn; dressed in shabby clothes; unfair, mean (of conduct, treatment etc.).

shack *n.* a small, roughly-built house.

shackle (shack-le) *n.* a ring of iron for fastening the wrist or ankle, usually connected by a chain to the floor or a wall. *v.* put shackles on; stop a person doing or thinking freely.

shade *n.* partial darkness caused by cutting off the direct rays of light; a different degree of colour; something to shield or partly cover. *v.* cut off the direct rays of light from; darken (on a drawing etc.). **shading** *n.* shadow put on a drawing to give light and shade. **shady** *a.* giving shade from the sun.

shadow (shad-ow) *n.* an area of shade; the shape thrown on the ground, a wall etc. by cutting off the rays of light; the slightest trace (of doubt, a smile etc.). *v.* darken by shadows; follow a person to watch his movements.

shaft *n.* a long pole or rod forming the main part of a spear, lance or arrow; a ray or beam; the handle of an axe, hammer or other tool of the same kind; one of the bars of wood between which a horse is harnessed to pull a cart; a long narrow space, usually vertical, to contain a lift in a building or the cage in which miners descend into the mine.

shaggy (shag-gy) *a.* rough and coarse.

shake *v.* move quickly up and down or from side to side; become or make weaker. *n.* shaking, being shaken; a glass of milk with flavour added and shaken. **shaky** *a.* weak, unreliable, unsafe.

shallow (shal-low) *a.* not deep.

sham *v.* pretend to be. *n.* a pretence. *a.* pretended, not real.

shambles (sham-bles) *n.* a place of slaughter; a place of confusion.

shame *n.* the feeling one has after doing something foolish or dishonourable; something to be sorry about. *v.* cause others to feel shame; make a person do something through shame. **shameful** *a.* bringing shame, worthy of shame.

shampoo (sham-poo) *v.* wash the hair or clean upholstery and carpets with a special preparation. *n.* the act of shampooing; the preparation used.

shanty (shan-ty) *n.* a small, roughly-made hut or cabin; a song sung by sailors in rhythm with their work.

shape *n.* form, as seen by the eye; arrangement, fitness. *v.* give a shape to. **shapely** *a.* of a pleasing shape.

share *n.* a part. *v.* divide; join with others in using or doing.

shark *n.* a fish that lives in oceans and which ranges in size from 30 centimetres to 13·5 metres.

sharp *a.* with a keen edge for cutting or piercing; having a point or angle; shrill, piercing; quickly seeing, hearing, understanding etc.; severe, harsh; quick (walk, run etc.); prompt. *adv.* promptly, suddenly.

shatter (shat-ter) *v.* suddenly break in pieces; weaken, destroy.

shave *v.* cut hair off the face, head etc.

with a razor; come very near to touching. *n.* a narrow miss. **shaving** *n.* a very thin slice of wood shaved off a larger piece with a plane or a chisel.

shawl *n.* a piece of material worn chiefly by women as a covering for the shoulders or head.

she *pron.* a female person; a female animal; the way of referring to a ship, even though it may have the name of a male (e.g. Lion, Prince Edward etc.).

sheaf *n.* a bundle of corn, bound up after reaping; a large bunch of flowers; a bundle of papers laid on top of one another and tied together.

shear *v.* remove by cutting with a sharp instrument. **shears** *n.* a tool for shearing consisting of two blades riveted together.

sheath *n.* a case or covering for a sword, dagger etc. **sheathe** *v.* put into a sheath.

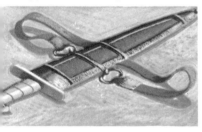

shed *v.* let fall; take off (clothing etc.); spread (light etc.). *n.* a building used for storing things, keeping animals etc.

sheep *n.* a short, stocky domestic animal which eats grass and is reared for its wool and meat.

sheer *a.* very thin, almost transparent; complete (joy, lunacy, folly etc.); very steep.

sheet *n.* a large rectangular piece of cloth used for covering a bed; a covering; a thin piece of material (glass, plywood etc.).

sheik *n.* (pronounced *shake*) an Arab chief or head. **sheikdom** *n.* the territory ruled by a sheik.

shelf *n.* a thin slab of wood, stone or other material standing out from a wall and used for holding things; a ledge standing out from a vertical face of rock. **shelve** *v.* put on a shelf; put aside for a time.

shell *n.* the hard covering of eggs, nuts, some seeds and certain animals; the

outer framework of a building, ship etc.; a metal case filled with explosive, fired from a gun. *v.* take something out of a shell; fire shells (at a position etc.). **shellfish** *n.* animals living in water and having shells, such as mussels, oysters, lobsters, crabs and shrimps.

shelter (shel-ter) *n.* something that gives refuge from rain, danger etc.; protection. *v.* be a shelter for, give shelter to; take shelter.

shepherd (shep-herd) *n.* a person who looks after sheep. *v.* look after and guide people.

sheriff (sher-iff) *n.* the chief officer for carrying out the law in a county of the United States of America. **High Sheriff** (in England) an officer of the Crown who carries out certain duties in some counties and cities.

sherry (sher-ry) *n.* a wine first produced in southern Spain but now a name given to wines made elsewhere in imitation of Spanish sherry.

shield *n.* a piece of defensive armour carried on the arm and used to protect a soldier in battle; a picture of a shield on a coat of arms; a kind of screen to give protection from gunfire, wind, dust etc. *v.* protect.

shift *v.* move from one place or position to another. *n.* a group of workmen who work the same hours. **shiftless** *a.* lazy, not willing to work. **shifty** *a.* deceitful, not to be trusted.

shilling (shil-ling) *n.* a British coin once worth twelve pence, equal to five pence today.

shimmer (shim-mer) *v.* shine with a soft, continually moving light. *n.* a soft, faint light.

shin *n.* the front part of the leg below the knee as far as the ankle. *v.* climb quickly.

shine *v.* give out or reflect light; do a thing well, do well at a subject; make shine. *n.* brightness, polish. **shiny** *a.* having a shine.

shingle (shin-gle) *n.* a thin oblong piece of wood used like a tile for covering roofs and sometimes walls; small pebbles on the seashore made round in shape by the action of water. *v.* put shingles on a roof or wall. **shingles** *n.* a disease in which inflamed spots appear on the skin, most often round the waist.

ship *n.* a vessel, larger than a boat, that

sails the seas. *v.* send in a ship; take members, or become a member of a ship's crew. **shipshape** *a.* in good order. **shipwreck** *n.* destruction of a ship by storm, collision, striking rocks etc. **shipwright** *n.* a person who builds and repairs ships. **shipment** *n.* goods sent by ship. **shipyard** *n.* a place where ships are built or repaired.

shirk *v.* avoid doing work or duty.

shirt *n.* a loose-fitting garment with buttons down the front, a collar and long or short sleeves.

shiver (shiv-er) *v.* shake or tremble with cold, fear, excitement etc. *n.* a trembling movement.

shoal *n.* a sandbank, a place where water is shallow; a large number of fish swimming together.

shock *n.* a sudden and violent blow or collision; the effect of an electric current passing through the body; the effect of some injury or bad news on a person; a number of sheaves of corn put together in a field to dry, supporting each other so that the rain will run off them. *v.* cause shock, suffer shock.

shoe *v.* put a shoe or shoes on. *n.* an outer covering for the foot; a curved band of iron nailed to the hoof of a horse. **shoehorn** *n.* a shaped piece of horn or metal used to make a shoe slip on to the foot more easily. **shoetree** *n.* a device of metal or wood put into shoes when they are not being worn to help keep them in shape.

shoot *v.* aim and fire from a gun, a bow etc.; hit, wound or kill by shooting; send out quickly (flames etc.); grow quickly; cause sharp darting pains in some part of the body; pass through or over quickly; take photographs or make films. *n.* a new and young growth on a plant.

shop *n.* a building in which goods are sold; a place where machines and other goods are made and repaired. *v.* go to shops to buy things. **shopkeeper** *n.* a person who carries on business in a shop. **shoplifting** *v.* stealing goods from shops. **shopsoiled** *a.* damaged through being handled or left too long in a shop window. **shop-steward** *n.* an official of a trade union who represents workers in a factory.

shore *n.* the land along the side of the sea, a lake or a river.

short *a.* not long in time or space; easily falling to crumbs as pastry does when it contains fat. *adv.* suddenly. **shortage** *n.* not having enough. **shorten** *v.* make shorter. **shorthand** *n.* a way of writing rapidly, using simple strokes instead of letters. **short of** not having enough of. **short-sighted** *a.* unable to see distant objects clearly.

shot *n.* the noise made when a gun is fired; an attempt to hit by shooting; a number of small pellets of lead contained in the cartridge of a sporting gun; a person who shoots (well or badly); a heavy metal ball used in a throwing competition.

shoulder (shoul-der) *n.* that part of the body where the arm (in man) or foreleg (e.g. in a sheep) is joined. *v.* take on the shoulder; take responsibility or do work; push through a crowd.

shout *v.* call or cry out loudly. *n.* a loud cry.

shove *v.* push (something); push rudely and roughly. *n.* a good strong push.

shovel (shov-el) *n.* a tool resembling a spade with a blade like a scoop, used for moving earth, snow, coal etc. *v.* use a shovel.

show *v.* display, allow to be seen; guide, conduct, point out; make others understand, prove; be visible. *n.* the act of showing; a display, a collection of things displayed. **showcase** *n.* a case with a glass top or front in which things of interest are displayed. **showman** *n.* a man who organizes public shows such as circuses.

shower (show-er) *n.* a short fall of rain, hail or snow; a large number, coming at the same time; a shower-bath. *v.* send or give in large numbers (letters, favours etc.)

shrapnel (shrap-nel) *n.* a hollow shell or bomb containing an explosive charge and bullets which can be made to scatter in all directions at a given time after firing.

shred *n.* a piece, especially a narrow strip cut or torn off; the smallest bit. *v.* tear apart, to shreds.

shriek *v.* scream. *n.* a scream.

shrill *a.* high-pitched and piercing.

shrimp *n.* a small, long-tailed shell-fish used for food.

shrine *n.* a building devoted to something or somebody highly respected, or to a saint.

shrink *v.* become or make less or smaller through heat, cold or moisture; move back (through fear, unwillingness etc.).

shrivel (shriv-el) *v.* become wrinkled and dried up through heat, cold, dryness or old age.

shrub *n.* a bush or small tree with many stems growing up from the ground. **shrubbery** *n.* a garden or part of a garden where shrubs are cultivated.

shrug *v.* raise and lower the shoulders to show that one doubts, does not care etc. *n.* such a movement.

shudder (shud-der) *v.* tremble, as from horror, fear or cold. *n.* a trembling of the body.

shuffle (shuf-fle) *v.* walk, dragging the feet; do things in a clumsy way; mix playing cards in a pack to alter their positions; avoid doing what one should. *n.* a shuffling movement or walk.

shun *v.* keep away from a place or person; avoid.

shunt *v.* move a train from one railway track to another.

shut *v.* close (doors etc.); become closed, remain closed; cease business; hurt or pinch by shutting; keep in, keep out. **shutter** *n.* a removable cover for a window.

shuttle (shut-tle) *n.* a boat-shaped piece of wood which takes thread from one side of a loom to another, weaving between the threads. **shuttle-cock** *n.* a piece of cork with feathers in it, struck with a racket to and fro in badminton.

shy *a.* timid, uncomfortable when others are present; easily frightened away. *v.* start or turn away as in sudden fear.

sick *a.* not well in body or mind; sick in the stomach. *n.* those who are ill. **sick bay** part of a ship reserved for those who are ill. **sicken** *v.* be in the early stage of an illness; make one feel sick. **sickly** *a.* weak, liable to become ill.

side *n.* one of the surfaces of an object; one of the surfaces not including top or bottom, front or back (of a house etc.); either of the two surfaces of paper, cloth, leather, plastic etc.; either the right or left part of a human body or that of an animal; part of an area or a thing (a street etc.); one of two groups opposed to each other; descent through one parent, mother or father. *v.* take the part of in a quarrel. **sideways** *adv.* towards the side, with one side turned towards the viewer. **siding** *n.* a short railway track lying at the side of a main line.

siege *n.* the process of surrounding and capturing a fortified place by cutting off supplies, bombarding, attacking etc.

sieve *n.* a utensil, the bottom of which is perforated or made of wire net, used to separate fine particles of matter from coarse ones, or liquids from solids. *v.* pass through a sieve.

sift *v.* pass through a sieve. **sifter** *n.* a small kitchen utensil like a sieve.

sigh *v.* let out one's breath audibly as from sorrow or relief; long for. *n.* the act or sound of sighing.

sight *n.* the power to see; something well worth seeing; seeing, being seen; the distance one can see; something that looks odd or ugly; a device on a gun, a compass etc. which guides the eye. v. see something; get sight of.

sign n. a mark or figure used instead of the word or words it represents; words or pictures painted on a board to give information to people; something that shows the existence of another thing; a movement made instead of speaking. v. write one's name; show by a sign. **signatory** n. a person who has signed or has joined in signing a document. **signature** n. a person's name.

signal (sig-nal) n. a movement or a device used to give an order or some information; something which causes action. v. make a signal.

signify (sig-ni-fy) v. make known by speech, signs or action; be a sign of, mean. **significance** n. meaning, importance of something. **significant** a. important, having a special meaning.

silence (si-lence) n. absence of noise, sound or speech. v. make silent. **silencer** n. a device fitted to the exhaust pipe of a petrol engine or on a gun to reduce the noise. **silent** a. saying nothing, making no noise.

silhouette (sil-hou-ette) n. a picture in black or an object seen in outline with the light behind it. v. be shown in silhouette.

silk n. material manufactured from the fine shiny thread made by silkworms. **silkworm** n. a kind of caterpillar which spins the fine thread of silk to make its cocoon. **silky** a. smooth, soft like silk.

silly (sil-ly) a. foolish, stupid.

silver (sil-ver) n. a shiny white metal used for making ornaments, coins, mirrors and utensils for the dining table; coins once made of silver but now of metal resembling silver. **silversmith** n. a person who makes articles of silver. **silverware** n. articles, especially for use on the table, made of silver. **silver wedding** the 25th wedding anniversary. **silvery** a. like silver.

similar (sim-i-lar) a. having a likeness or resemblance. **similarity** n. likeness.

simmer (sim-mer) v. keep a liquid very hot, just at boiling point.

simple (sim-ple) a. easy to understand, do or use; unlearned, ignorant; plain, with no decoration or luxury; with nothing added or altered. **simply** adv. in a simple manner, only, completely. **simpleton** n. a foolish person. **simplicity** n. being simple. **simplify** v. make easier or more understandable.

sin n. wrong-doing, any serious offence; a mistake, something that is not sensible. v. do wrong, commit a sin. **sinful** a. wicked.

since prep. between a particular past time and the present; ago, before now.

sincere (sin-cere) a. honest, not deceitful. **sincerely** adv. in a sincere way. **sincerity** n. being sincere.

sinew (sin-ew) n. a cord or tendon which fastens the muscles to the bones. **sinewy** a. strong.

sing v. make music with the voice, with or without words; make a humming sound as of a kettle. **singer** n. a person who sings, especially in public. **singsong** n. an informal gathering of friends who sing together.

singe v. burn the ends of hair; make brown or black by burning. n. a slight burn.

single (sin-gle) a. one only; not married; only to be used by one person. n. a single run in cricket; a game (of tennis etc.) between two people; a one-way ticket for a train, bus etc.

singlet (sin-glet) n. a vest, a garment worn under a shirt.

singular (sin-gu-lar) n. one person or thing. a. strange, outstanding.

sink v. go down under the water or in a liquid; go down, cause to go down in sound, in strength, in value etc. n. a basin of stone, porcelain, etc. with a pipe to drain away the water. **sinker** n. a small lead weight fastened to a fishing line to keep it under water.

sip v. drink a little at a time. n. a very small quantity drunk at a time.

sir n. a respectful form of address used to a man; the title of a knight or baronet.

sister (sis-ter) n. the daughter of the same parents as another person; a senior nurse in a hospital; a nun in the Catholic Church. **sister-in-law** n. the wife of one's brother or the sister of one's husband or wife.

sit *v.* rest on the lower part of the body; perch; remain on eggs until they hatch; hold a meeting of parliament, a committee etc.; make sit.

site *n.* a place on which anything has been or is situated; a place where a building is to be erected. *v.* erect a building somewhere.

situation (sit-u-a-tion) *n.* condition; place where a town, building etc. is; employment. **situated** *a.* in a certain place or condition.

size *n.* the largeness or smallness of a thing; measurements of clothing, shoes etc.; a sticky substance mainly used with a brush to close up the pores or holes in paper, plaster etc. to make painting easier. *v.* apply size.

skate *n.* a metal blade which can be fixed to the sole of a shoe or boot making it possible to glide on icy surfaces; a large sea fish used as a food. *v.* go on skates. **roller-skate** *n.* a skate which has four small wheels instead of a blade and which is used on smooth surfaces. *v.* go on roller-skates.

skeleton (skel-e-ton) *n.* the bones of a human being or other animal fitted together as they would be in life; the framework of any kind of construction; the main parts of a plan, a map, scheme etc. which remains to be finished. **skeleton key** a key which will open many different locks.

sketch *n.* a rough drawing; a short description; the outline of a plan. *v.* make a sketch or sketches.

ski *n.* one of a pair of long, slender pieces of hard wood, metal or plastic which can be fitted to a shoe and used for gliding over snow. *v.* travel on or use skis.

skid *n.* the slipping movement of the wheels of a car or other vehicle, especially when driven too fast over a slippery surface. *v.* make such a slipping movement.

skiff *n.* a small boat, light enough to be sailed or rowed by one person.

skill *n.* the ability to do something well. **skilful** *a.* having skill. **skilled** *a.* trained; having skill and experience.

skim *v.* remove scum, cream, grease etc. from the surface of a liquid; move quickly and lightly over; read a thing very quickly.

skin *n.* the outer covering of the body of a human being, animal, vegetable or fruit; the solid layer which forms on milk when it cools. *v.* take off the skin.

skip *v.* spring, jump or leap lightly; jump using a skipping-rope; pass over without reading.

skipper (skip-per) *n.* the captain of a small ship or boat; the captain of a football or cricket team.

skirmish (skir-mish) *n.* a short, sharp fight between small bodies of men or two fleets. *v.* take part in a skirmish.

skirt *n.* a garment, the lower part of a dress or coat that hangs from the waist. *v.* pass along the edge or side of.

skittle (skit-tle) *n.* a game in which a ball is rolled along an alley to knock down a number of bottle-shaped pieces of wood; one of the pieces of wood used in the game. *v.* get members of a cricket team out one after the other.

skull *n.* the bony framework of the head which encloses the brain.

skunk *n.* a small, striped North American mammal with a bushy tail which when attacked puts out an evil-smelling fluid.

sky *n.* the space we see above us, containing the sun, moon, stars and clouds. **skyline** *n.* the outline of hills, buildings etc. seen against the sky.

slack *a.* loose, not tight; careless, not attending to work; not active or having much work to do. *v.* be careless or lazy. *n.* that part of a rope which hangs freely or loosely; coal dust. **slacken** v. become or make slack. **slacker** n. a person who is lazy, who slacks.

slake v. satisfy one's thirst; add water to quicklime making slaked lime.

slam v. shut or shut noisily; dash or knock with force. n. the noise made when something is slammed.

slander (slan-der) n. an untrue statement that injures another person's good name or reputation. v. utter slander about another person.

slang n. certain words and phrases used in conversation but not used in good speech or writing. v. use vulgar language to another person.

slant v. slope; present news so that it supports only one side or one point of view. n. a slope.

slap v. strike with the open hand or something flat; put something down with a loud, quick noise; put paint on carelessly. n. a quick blow with the hand or something flat.

slash v. make long slits or cuts; strike with sharp strokes; slit a garment for decoration. n. a long cut or wound.

slate n. a fine-grained blue-grey rock that can be split into large flakes and is used for covering roofs; a sheet of slate in a wooden frame used for writing. v. cover a roof with slate.

slaughter (slaugh-ter) v. kill animals or people. n. killing (in battle, on the roads, of animals etc.).

slave n. a person who is owned by another person and made to work for no wages. v. work very hard. **slavery** n. the state of being a slave or having slaves. a slave to in the power of (drink, gambling etc.).

slay v. kill, usually in battle.

sledge n. a low platform on runners of steel made to slide on snow or ice; a large hammer used by a blacksmith. v. ride on a sledge.

sleep v. rest both body and mind, closing the eyes and becoming unconscious; provide room for sleeping. n. the state of being asleep. **sleepless** a. without sleep. **sleepy** a. needing sleep.

sleeper (sleep-er) n. a person who sleeps (heavily or lightly); a heavy beam of wood or sometimes of concrete on which railway lines are laid; a train on which there are bunks for sleeping.

sleet n. snow, hail and rain falling together. v. fall as sleet.

sleeve n. that part of a dress or coat that covers the arm; an envelope for a gramophone record.

slender (slen-der) a. long and narrow; slim; poor, slight.

slice n. a thin, broad, flat piece cut from something such as a loaf, a ham etc.; a utensil with a broad, flat blade used for cooking. v. cut into slices.

slick a. smooth, skilful, smart and speedy at doing something. n. a patch of oil discharged on water by a ship.

slide v. move smoothly on a slippery surface; move quietly. n. the act of sliding; the slope down which one may slide; a colour photograph which can be projected on a screen; a small piece of glass on which things are placed to be examined through a microscope.

slight a. small in amount; slim, slender. v. treat rudely, neglect. n. an example of rude or neglectful treatment. **slightly** adv. a little.

slim a. slender, small, not very good (of hopes, chances etc.); slender (of things and persons). v. do things to make one slim.

slime n. thin, soft, sticky mud; the sticky substance left behind by snails. **slimy** a. like slime; covered with slime.

sling n. a band of material put round an object to lift it; a piece of leather joined to cords and used for throwing stones. *v.* throw with a sling; suspend so that a thing hangs or is lifted (the arm, a hammock etc.).

slink *v.* go away quietly as if in fear, cowardice or shame.

slip *v.* slide accidentally and lose one's balance; move quietly and quickly; escape (from the grasp or grip); put on or off quickly (of clothing). *n.* the act of slipping; making mistakes; a loose cover or a garment; a small piece of paper; a small twig cut from a plant to be put in soil to take root; a fielder in cricket. **slipknot** *n.* a knot tied so that it slips along the string round which it is tied. **slipstream** *n.* the stream of air forced back by the propeller or jet engine of an aeroplane. **slipper** *n.* a light shoe which can be easily slipped on for wear in the house. **slippery** *a.* smooth, easy to slide on.

slit *n.* a straight narrow cut or opening. *v.* make a slit or narrow opening; be slit or cut along its length.

slog *v.* hit hard as in boxing, cricket etc.; keep on, work hard and long. **slogger** *n.* a person who hits hard; a person who works hard and long, with great determination.

slogan (slo-gan) *n.* an easily remembered cry or phrase used by a party or a group, or to advertise something.

sloop *n.* a small sailing vessel with one mast; a small warship used in the Second World War for submarine escort duty.

slop *v.* splash; spill over the edge of a vessel; make something spill; make a mess with some liquid (e.g. paint). **sloppy** *a.* wet, full of puddles; carelessly done. **slops** *n.* waste water and liquid used in the home.

slope *n.* a slanting position; a tract of land which rises or falls. *v.* be in a slanting position; have a slant (handwriting, poles in the ground etc.).

slot *n.* a narrow opening designed to receive narrow objects, especially coins. **slot-machine** *n.* a machine with a slot into which one puts coins in order to obtain goods, play games of chance etc.

sloth *n.* laziness, idleness; a South American mammal that lives in the branches of trees, eats leaves and fruits and moves very slowly.

slouch *v.* sit, stand or walk in a lazy way, with drooping head or bent shoulders. *n.*

a slouching way of bearing oneself or walking.

slough *n.* a swamp or marsh. *v.* cast off, especially of a snake which sloughs its skin again and again.

sloven (slov-en) *n.* a person who is untidy, dirty and careless about his dress, appearance, work and habits. **slovenly** *a.* of or like a sloven.

slow *a.* taking a long time, not quick; not acting or learning quickly; showing a time earlier than the correct time (of watches and clocks). *v.* go slower. **slowly** *adv.* at a slow speed.

sludge *n.* thick mud; thick dirty oil or grease; sewage from houses and factories.

slug *n.* a slow-moving creature that looks like a snail but has no shell and which destroys young garden plants; a small pellet for firing from a gun. **sluggish** *a.* slow moving, not very active. **sluggard** *n.* a lazy, slow-moving person.

sluice *n.* a channel for conducting water to places where it is needed and for regulating water levels. *v.* wash with a stream of water.

slum *n.* a dirty street, dwelling or part of a city inhabited by the poorest people crowded together.

slumber (slum-ber) *v.* sleep quietly, peacefully and comfortably. *n.* a sleep which may be peaceful or troubled.

slump *v.* fall or drop heavily; drop suddenly and steeply (of trade, prices etc.). *n.* a sudden fall or drop.

slur *v.* pronounce words indistinctly; join two notes in music, passing without a break from one to the next. *n.* a remark intended to damage another person's reputation or character.

slush *n.* soft snow, which is partly melted.

sly *a.* cunning, doing things secretly; deceitful.

smack *n.* a slap with the open hand; a blow (with a cricket-bat etc.); a small boat, especially one used for fishing. *v.* give a blow with the open hand. **smacking** *n.* blows with the palm of the hand. **smack one's lips** part the lips with a smacking sound; show pleasure at the prospect of food or anything good.

small *a.* little, not large; unimportant. **small change** coins of silver and copper of small value. **smallholding** *n.* a piece of land on which vegetables etc. are grown for the market. **smallpox** *n.* a disease which spreads from one person to another, often leaving lasting scars on the face and body.

smart *a.* bright, clean, well-dressed; clever, having a good brain; in the latest fashion; severe (of blows, scolding etc.). *v.* feel or cause a sharp pain. **smarten** *v.* make or become smart.

smash *v.* break or be broken suddenly and with violence; collide; break through. *n.* a violent breaking; a collision, especially between vehicles such as cars, trains etc.

smear *v.* spread dirt, ink, oil etc. over something; spread over (with ointment, lotion etc.). *n.* a dirty or greasy mark made by smearing.

smell *v.* be aware of by means of the nose; possess the sense of smell; give out a smell. *n.* something one is aware of through smelling; the act of smelling.

smelt *v.* separate metal from its ore by melting it. *n.* a small fish valued for its flesh as food.

smile *n.* a look of pleasure, happiness or amusement on the face. *v.* give a smile to express happiness or any other feeling (sarcasm, boredom etc.).

smirk *n.* a silly, disagreeable smile. *v.* smile in a silly disagreeable way.

smith *n.* a person who works in iron or other metals — gold, silver, tin etc. (see **blacksmith**).

smock *n.* a loose garment worn over other clothes for protection. **smocking** *n.* embroidery stitches used to gather cloth into a pattern.

smoke *n.* the cloud, often grey, brown or black, given off when something burns. *v.* give off smoke; draw the smoke from burning tobacco or other substances into the mouth and let it out again; dry and preserve meat, fish etc. by the use of smoke from wood fires. **smoker** *n.* a person who smokes tobacco; a compartment of a train for the use of those who smoke. **smokestack** *n.* a tall chimney which lets out smoke from a furnace or factory. **smoky** *a.* giving out smoke; full of smoke.

smooth *a.* not rough to the touch, having a surface like glass or silk; free from lumps when beaten; with no bumping or shaking (of a road, a crossing in a boat etc.). *v.* make smooth; get rid of difficulties.

smother (smoth-er) *v.* kill by depriving of air necessary to life; put out a fire by keeping air from it; cover (with mud etc.); hold back necessary etc.

smoulder (smoul-der) *v.* burn or smoke slowly without flame; remain undetected (of the feelings — hate, envy etc.).

smudge *n.* a dirty mark or smear. *v.* make a dirty mark or smear; become smeared.

smug *a.* very satisfied with what one is or does.

smuggle (smug-gle) *v.* carry goods illegally in or out of a country without paying customs duties; take things or people to places against the rules (arms, keys etc.). **smuggler** *n.* a person who smuggles goods into or out of a country.

snack *n.* a light meal eaten quickly. **snack bar** a counter where snacks may be bought and eaten.

snag *n.* something (a branch, a rock etc.) sticking up out of the ground or the bed of a river; a difficulty that has not been expected.

snail *n.* a small animal with a soft body and a shell that lives in water and on land.

snake *n.* a serpent; a long crawling reptile which may be poisonous. **snake-charmer** *n.* a person who can control the movements of snakes through music.

snap *v.* seize or try to seize with the teeth; break, open or close with a sudden sharp sound; take a quick photograph. *n.* the sound of something being broken or closed.

snare *n.* a trap with a noose used for catching animals and birds; anything intended to catch or trap a person unawares. *v.* catch in a snare; be taken unawares.

snarl *v.* show the teeth and growl; speak roughly and harshly. *n.* the action or sound of snarling.

snatch *v.* make a sudden effort to seize something with the hand; get something quickly when the chance occurs. *n.* the act of snatching; a bit or fragment of something (a song, rhyme etc.).

sneak *v.* go quietly in a sly manner; tell about the wrongdoings of others to the teacher or a superior; steal. *n.* a cowardly person; a person who sneaks.

sneer *v.* smile or curl the lip in a manner which shows scorn; say scornful words. *n.* the act of sneering.

sneeze *v.* send out air suddenly through the nose and mouth as when one has a cold. *n.* the act of sneezing.

sniff *v.* draw air through the nose in short breaths. *v.* the act of sniffing (often to smell something).

snigger (snig-ger) *n.* a sly, half-suppressed laugh, often at something which is improper. *v.* give such a laugh.

snip *v.* cut with scissors or shears in small quick strokes. *n.* a cut or slit made by snipping; a small piece snipped off.

snipe *v.* fire shots from a hiding-place. *n.* a bird with a long bill that lives in the marshes. **sniper** *n.* a person who fires shots from a hiding-place.

snob *n.* one who imitates and seeks the friendship of those of wealth or high rank in society and despises those whom he thinks are less important than he is. **snobbery** *n.* snobbishness; being snobbish. **snobbish** *a.* of a snob or like a snob.

snoop *v.* prowl around enquiring in a

mean, sly manner into other people's business. **snooper** *n.* a person who snoops, often to give information to enemies or superiors.

snore *v.* breathe noisily with harsh sounds while asleep. *n.* the sound of snoring.

snort *v.* force the breath violently through the nose in excitement or anger; express or say something in this way, with anger, fury etc. *n.* the act of snorting.

snout *n.* the long nose and sometimes the jaws of an animal that stand out from the face.

snow *n.* small white flakes of frozen water which fall slowly to the ground in winter. *v.* come down from the sky, dropping as snow. **snowball** *n.* a ball of snow made by rolling snow until it grows large, or rolling it in the hands for throwing. **snowdrift** *n.* snow blown by the wind into a large heap. **snowflake** *n.* one of the tiny flakes made up of small crystals of snow. **snowplough** *n.* a machine driven by a motor for pushing snow away from roads and railways. **snowy** *a. & adv.* bringing snow; covered with snow; the colour of snow.

snub *v.* treat with scorn; give slights to. *n.* behaviour full of scorn or slights. *a.* short and turned up at the tip (of the nose etc.).

snuff *v.* sniff (mainly of animals); put out a candle by removing the burnt end of the wick. *n.* a powdered tobacco taken into the nose by sniffing.

snuffle (snuf-fle) *v.* breathe with sniffing sounds as if one has a cold in the head. *n.* the act of snuffling.

snug *a.* warm, comfortable, away from the cold and the wind; fitting closely and comfortably. **snuggle** *v.* get close so as to be warm and comfortable.

soak *v.* become or make wet through; take up liquid as blotting paper does; put something in liquid to make it very wet;

go through (clothes, roofs etc.) as liquid does.

soap *n.* a substance made from fat or oil and used for washing. *v.* rub with soap; put soap on. **soapsuds** *n.* the foam or froth made through rubbing soap with water. **soapy** *a.* with soap; like soap.

soar *v.* fly high in the air; hover in the air without movement of the wings; go high (of hopes, prices etc.).

sob *v.* weep, drawing in the breath sharply. *n.* the action of sobbing; the sound of sobbing.

sober (so-ber) *a.* quiet, thoughtful, solemn in manner and speech; not drunk, not in the habit of drinking beer, wine etc. **sobriety** *n.* being sober. **sober down** *v.* become quiet after having been noisy.

soccer (soc-cer) *n.* a name widely used for association football.

sociable (so-cia-ble) *a.* liking the company of other people, having a friendly nature and disposition.

social *a.* having to do with friendship and companionship; having to do with the daily life of people as a whole, living in communities; of human society, its ranks and classes; having to do with the problems of the poor, those who are ill, the aged, children etc. **socialism** *n.* the belief that all the main industries and wealth of a country should be under the control of its people. **socialist** *n.* a person who holds this belief.

society *n.* a body of individuals living as members of a community; companionship, company; an organization of persons formed for a special purpose. *a.* having to do with people of high rank, fashion etc.

sock *n.* a short stocking which does not reach to the knee; a loose sole worn inside a shoe to make it fit better.

socket (sock-et) *n.* a hollow specially made so that another thing may fit into it.

sod *n.* a piece of grass taken from the earth with its roots attached.

soda (so-da) *n.* a substance used in the making of soap, glass and other materials, and for washing and cleaning. **sodium bicarbonate** a substance used in baking and as a medicine. **soda fountain** a counter at which sodas, ice-cream etc. are served; a container from which soda water is drawn by taps. **soda-siphon** *n.* a bottle filled with water and carbon-dioxide which forces out soda-water when a valve is opened. **soda-water** *n.* water into which a gas (carbon dioxide) has been added to make it bubble.

sodden (sod-den) *a.* wet through, soaked through; heavy through not being cooked long enough.

sofa (so-fa) *n.* a long upholstered seat with back and arms.

soft *a.* easily altering in shape when pressed; not loud (of speech, music etc.); not cold or fierce (of breezes etc.); free from impurities and good for washing (of water); not containing alcohol (of drinks). **soften** *v.* make or become soft.

soggy (sog-gy) *a.* soaked, thoroughly wet; damp and heavy with water; heavy (of bread and cakes).

soil *n.* earth, dirt, ground, especially the soft workable top layer of earth on which plants and trees are grown; a particular kind of earth (sandy, clay etc.). *v.* make dirty or foul; stain; become foul or stained.

solace (sol-ace) *n.* something that gives comfort in trouble. *v.* comfort, console or cheer a person.

solar (so-lar) *a.* having to do with the sun; proceeding from the sun (heat, energy etc.).

solder (sol-der) *n.* metal which can be easily melted and applied with a hot iron to join the surfaces of harder metals together. *v.* use solder. **soldering-iron** *n.* a tool used for soldering.

soldier (sol-dier) *n.* one who serves in an army for pay; an army commander. *v.* act or serve as a soldier. **soldier on** v. keep on working in spite of opposition or difficulties.

ole n. a flat fish with a hook-like snout that swims in the sea; the under part of the foot; the bottom part of a boot or shoe. a. the only, the single (survivor, heir etc.).

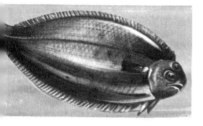

olemn (sol-emn) a. grave, sober, serious in speech, voice, tone, face etc.; serious in intention; carried out with serious ceremony. **solemnity** n. seriousness, ceremony.

olicitor (so-lic-i-tor) n. a member of the legal profession who advises people on questions of law and prepares documents dealing with legal matters.

olid (sol-id) a. not hollow, having the interior completely filled up; not liquid or gas; strong, firm (of buildings etc.); firm, that can be relied on; sound (of reasons, arguments); n. a solid substance or body, not hollow, not liquid or gas. **solidify** v. become solid.

oliloquy (so-lil-o-quy) n. the act of talking to oneself. **soliloquize** v. talk to oneself.

olitary (sol-i-tar-y) a. quite alone, having no friends or companions; lonely, secluded (of places); single, being the only one or ones (occasion, exception etc.). **solitude** n. the state of being alone; absence of human life; a lonely place.

olo (so-lo) n. a musical composition intended only for one singer or instrumentalist; any performance such as a dance, a flight, done by one person; a game of cards. **soloist** n. a person who performs a solo, chiefly in music.

oluble (sol-u-ble) a. capable of being dissolved in another substance; capable of being solved (a crime etc.).

olution (so-lu-tion) n. the answer or the way of finding an answer to a problem or mystery; dissolving or the result of dissolving something in a liquid. **solve** v. reach a solution; find the answer to a problem or a mystery.

some a. a number of, a quantity of; certain; about; approximately. **somebody** pron. a person. **somehow** adv. by some method. **something** pron. some article, event, happening etc. **sometime** adv. at some time. **sometimes** adv. on some occasions; now and then. **somewhat** adv. rather. **somewhere** adv. in or at some place.

son n. the male child of a parent. **son-in-law** n. the husband of one's daughter.

song n. the act of singing; a short composition with words and music; the tuneful sounds produced by certain birds.

sonnet n. a poem of 14 lines which rhyme according to a definite scheme.

soon adv. within a short time of the present or after a certain event; in the near future; promptly. **sooner** adv. earlier; rather. **as soon as** at the time when.

soot n. black powder formed when something burns, which rises in small particles and clings to the sides of the chimney or pipe conveying the smoke.

soothe v. make quiet or calm; make a pain less; calm the feelings; give a sense of comfort.

soprano (so-pra-no) n. the highest singing voice in women or boys; the part for such a voice; a singer who sings soprano. a. having to do with soprano (song, part etc.).

sorcerer (sor-cer-er) n. a man who is supposed to practise magic through contact with evil spirits. **sorcery** n. evil acts done by a sorcerer.

sordid (sor-did) a. dirty, filthy, mean, dishonest.

sore a. tender and painful; suffering from wounds or bruises; suffering in the mind. n. a sore spot or place on the body. **sorely** adv. severely.

sorrow (sor-row) n. sadness, grief caused by loss, disappointment etc. n. a disappointment, misfortune etc.

sorry a. feeling sorrow or regret, wretched, pitiful.

sort n. a group of things which are in some way alike. v. separate into groups of things which resemble each other. **out of**

sorts not in a normal state of health, rather ill.

soul *n.* the spiritual part of man distinct from the body; a person, a human being; the inspiration or life (of a party etc.); high spirits, courage, energy; the spirit of a dead person.

sound *n.* something that can be heard. *a.* healthy, in good condition; sensible; thorough. *v.* produce sound from; give forth sound; test by striking, test the depth of the sea.

soup *n.* a liquid made by boiling meat, fish or vegetables in water, and adding seasoning and sometimes milk.

sour *a.* having a sharp taste, the opposite of sweet; made acid or having fermented; bad-tempered and peevish. *v.* turn something sour.

source *n.* the place where a river or stream rises; an origin, the place from which anything rises; a book, a statement or a person supplying information.

souse *v.* plunge into water or throw water on; be soaked or drenched; steep in pickling liquid for preservation; be soaking.

south *n.* the direction in which the right arm points when one faces the sunrise. *adv.* to, at, from etc. the south. **south-east** *n., a. & adv.* halfway between south and east. **south-west** *n., a. & adv.* halfway between south and west. **southerly** *adv.* in or from the south. **southern** *a.* having to do with the south.

souvenir (sou-ve-nir) *n.* something given or kept for remembrance.

sovereign (sov-er-ign) *n.* the ruler of a country; a king, queen or emperor; a British gold coin no longer in circulation. *a.* having supreme power, self-governing; never-failing, having great efficiency (as a remedy).

soviet (so-vi-et) *n.* in Russia, a council of workers; a higher council, part of the Russian machinery of government. **Soviet Union** the Union of Soviet Socialist Republics ruled by a council called the Supreme Soviet.

sow *v.* (rhymes with *grow*) scatter or plant seed over or on the ground to make it grow; strew or sprinkle with anything; spread abroad (distrust, hatred etc.).

sow *n.* (rhymes with *now*) an adult female pig; the adult female of certain other animals.

soya, soya bean *n.* a plant and its seed, the seed used as a valuable food for human beings and animals.

space *n.* that in which all things exist and move; the distance between things; a place in which there are no people or things; a period of time. *v.* divide into spaces, set some distance apart. **space capsule** *n.* a container for instruments or astronauts launched into space and capable of being recovered on return. **spacecraft** *n.* a vehicle capable of travelling in space. **spacious** *a.* containing much space (a house, street, playing-field etc.).

spade *n.* a tool for digging with a broad iron blade and a long handle; one of the four suits in a pack of cards.

spaghetti (spa-ghet-ti) *n.* a food eaten mainly in Italy, made from wheat and sold in the form of long string-like pieces.

span *n.* the distance between the tip of the thumb and the tip of the little finger when the hand is extended; the distance between the supports of a bridge; the full extent of anything (memory etc.). *v.* extend over a space (a bridge etc.); make something to extend over space.

spangle (span-gle) *n.* a small piece of glittering material; *v.* sprinkle or glitter with spangles.

spank *v.* hit with the open hand, usually as a punishment for a child. *n.* a blow with the open hand; a smart slap or smack.

spanner (span-ner) *n.* a tool for gripping or turning the head of a bolt, a screw or a nut.

spare *v.* refrain from harming, punishing or destroying somebody or something; find money, time, thought etc. for something. *a.* more than one needs at any particular time; thin, lean (of persons).

spark *n.* a tiny glowing particle thrown off by burning wood or by one hard body such as steel, striking another; the least little bit (of interest, pity, humour etc.).

sparking-plug n. a device in the cylinder of a petrol engine which creates the electric spark to set it in motion.

sparkle v. shine, give out flashes of light.

sparrow (spar-row) n. a small, brownish-grey bird common in Great Britain and in many other parts of the world.

spasm n. the sudden abnormal contraction of a muscle; a sudden short attack; any sudden burst of activity, anger, energy etc. **spasmodic** a. taking place irregularly.

spastic (spas-tic) a. disabled because of faulty links between the brain and parts of the human body, bringing about spasmodic movements. n. a person suffering in this way.

spate n. a heavy downpour of rain; a flood; a sudden burst of activity in business etc.

spatter (spat-ter) v. scatter or dash in small drops or particles. n. the act of spattering; the splash or spot of something spattered.

spawn n. the eggs of fish and certain water animals; the material from which mushrooms and other fungi grow. v. lay or produce in great numbers.

speak v. use language, talk in conversation; talk to an audience. **speaker** n. a device which is part of a radio or television set, or which can be attached, to magnify the sound; a person who speaks or makes speeches. **The Speaker** the officer who acts as chairman in the British House of Commons, the House of Representatives in the United States or some other similar assembly.

spear n. a weapon for thrusting or throwing consisting of a long wooden handle on to which is fixed a sharp head of iron or steel. v. pierce with a spear.

special (spec-ial) a. particular, not common; different from what is ordinary or usual; having to do with a particular

person. **specialist** n. one who specializes. **speciality** n. something one does unusually well. **specialize** v. be an expert in some activity. **specially** adv. particulary.

species n. a group of individuals having features which distinguish them from other groups, as the human species; a sort of (crime etc.).

specific (spe-cif-ic) a. exact, precise. **specification** n. an account in detail of the materials to be used and the work to be done. **specify** v. mention or set out, giving all details.

specimen (spec-i-men) n. one thing taken as an example, to represent others like it; a typical animal, mineral, plant etc.

speck n. a small spot of a different colour from its background; a very little bit or particle. **speckle** n. one or many marks or spots on a background. v. make or show such marks.

spectacle (spec-ta-cle) n. a great show or display in public or in a theatre, circus etc.; a sight worth remembering; something seen as unworthy, sad, ridiculous. **spectacles** n. two glass lenses fixed in a frame resting on the nose, designed to assist a person to see better. **spectacular** a. making a spectacle. **spectator** n. a person who looks on at some activity.

spectre (spec-tre) n. a ghost, phantom, some object causing terror or dread.

spectrum (spec-trum) n. a band of colours formed when a beam of light passes through a piece of glass of a certain shape.

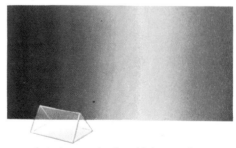

speculate (spec-u-late) v. think or meditate on something; buy and sell goods, shares in businesses, companies etc. to make profits. **speculation** n. the act of speculating. **speculator** n. a person whose activity is to speculate.

speech *n.* the manner of speaking; the power to speak; that which is spoken, a remark or declaration; what an actor says at one time during an act of a play. **speechless** *a.* unable for some reason to speak.

speed *n.* swiftness in moving, travelling or doing things; the rate of speed measured in kilometres etc.; *v.* move along quickly; drive a car faster than is allowed. **speedometer** *n.* a device attached to a motor vehicle to measure speed. **speedway** *n.* a racing track for motor vehicles. **speedy** *a.* quick.

spell *v.* name or write the letters of a word in their proper order. *n.* a form of words supposed to have magic power; a period of time. **spellbound** *a.* as if bound by a spell, enchanted, fascinated. **speller** *n.* a person who spells. **spelling** *n.* the way a word or words are spelt.

spend *v.* pay out money in return for goods; pass (time); use up (energy). **spendthrift** *n.* one who spends his money etc. wastefully.

sphere *n.* a solid body which appears to be round from whatever point it is seen; the surroundings in which a person works, the company he keeps.

sphinx *n.* a stone statue in Egypt with a lion's body and man's head; a monster in Greek mythology who asked passers-by a riddle and killed all those who could not answer it.

spice *n.* a substance, usually part of a plant or tree (ginger, nutmeg, cinnamon etc.) used to flavour food; something that gives interest, a suggestion (of humour etc.).

spider (spi-der) *n.* a small creature with eight legs that lives on insects.

spike *n.* a sharp, pointed piece of metal; an ear of grain such as barley; a number of small flowers growing on one stem. **spiked** *a.* having spikes.

spill *v.* allow liquid to run or fall from a container; fall from a horse, bicycle, carriage etc. *n.* a spilling of liquid etc.; a throw from a horse, vehicle etc.; a small piece of wood or paper used for lighting candles, fires, pipes of tobacco etc.

spin *v.* make cotton, wool or other material into threads so that it can be woven; make a web (of a spider); tell a story; make a thing go round and round; move quickly; go round quickly. *n.* a spinning movement; a short ride (on a bicycle etc.). **spindle** *n.* a long rod on which thread is wound as it is spun. **spin-drier** *n.* an electrical machine that dries clothes after washing by spinning them in an enclosed space. **spinning wheel** an old-fashioned, simple machine with a wheel and pedal for spinning cotton or wool into threads.

spinach (spin-ach) *n.* a garden plant with green leaves which is eaten as a vegetable.

spine *n.* the backbone; a stiff, pointed thorn; a sharp point growing from the coat of an animal such as a hedgehog; the part of a book's cover that holds the front and back together. **spinal column** a number of small bones in man and some animals through which runs the spinal cord containing the most important nerves of the body.

spinster (spin-ster) *n.* a woman who has not married.

spiral (spi-ral) *n.* something which starts at a central point and moves from it in a long curve, winding round itself. *a.* going upwards, onwards or in any other direction in circles.

spire *n.* a tall structure rising gradually to a point, usually built on the top of church towers.

spirit (spir-it) *n.* that part of a human being thought of as separate from the body; the soul; a ghost or spectre; a state of mind, a way of thinking or feeling. *v.* take away in secret. **spirited** *a.* full of spirit and energy, lively. **spirit level** an instrument with a glass tube containing spirit, used to test whether a surface is level or not. **spirits** *n.* drinks which contain a larger proportion of alcohol than beer and wine. **spiritual** *a*. having to do with the soul and the spirit; having to do with the church. *n*. a religious song sung originally by negroes in the United States. **spiritualism** *n*. the belief that one may receive messages from and communicate with the spirits of people who have died.

spit *n*. a rod or bar on which meat is cooked over a fire; the liquid which forms in the mouth and which helps to digest food, spittle or saliva; a long narrow point of land extending into a sea or a lake. *v*. send out from the mouth; send out with a spitting noise (of engines etc.); fall in scattered drops as of rain, hail or snow.

spite *n*. a desire to harm others or cause damage; a single instance of such desire. *v*. hurt another person because of spite. **spiteful** *a*. showing spite. **in spite of** in defiance of.

splash *v*. spatter, wet or soil by dashing drops of a liquid on to something or somebody; make one's way with splashing. *n*. the act, sight or sound of splashing; the mark left by a splash; a patch of colour.

splendid (splen-did) *a*. magnificent, gorgeous, excellent. **splendour** *n*. brilliant or magnificent appearance; glory.

splice *v*. join two ends of rope, string etc. together; join two pieces of wood so that they overlap. *n*. the join made in rope, string or wood etc. by splicing; the part of the handle of a cricket bat that fits into the blade.

splint *n*. a thin strip of wood or other material used to keep a broken bone in position.

splinter (splin-ter) *n*. a small piece of wood, metal etc. with sharp angles, broken off a larger piece; a fragment of metal thrown off by the explosion of a bomb or shell. *v*. split or break into splinters; be broken into splinters.

split *v*. break or cause to break into two or more parts; pull or knock apart; divide (a group etc.); divide between two or more persons. *n*. a crack or break. the act of splitting. **the splits** the feat of sinking to the floor, extending the legs at right angles to the body, only done by trained acrobats and dancers.

splutter (splut-ter) *v*. make a sound as if spitting; talk quickly and in an excited way so that the words are not clearly heard. *n*. spluttering; rapid talk not easily understood.

spoil *v*. damage, make of less value; injure a person's character by unwise treatment (children etc.); become bad through keeping too long. *n*. things that have been stolen or taken by force.

spoke *n*. one of the bars of wood or metal which connect the hub of a wheel with its rim; a rung of a ladder.

spokesman (spokes-man) *n*. a person who is chosen to speak for others.

sponge *n*. an animal that lives in the sea; the framework or skeleton of this animal, made up of elastic material full of holes and used for washing and cleaning; a piece of rubber or plastic material made for this purpose. *v*. get goods from a person or live at his expense. **sponge cake** a very light sweet cake made with flour and eggs. **sponger** *n*. a person who sponges on others.

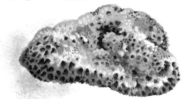

sponsor (spon-sor) *n*. a person who makes himself responsible for another; an advertiser who pays for a radio or television programme in return for the advertisement of his goods. *v*. act as sponsor for another person or for a radio or television programme.

spontaneous (spon-ta-neous) *a*. done without thinking beforehand or being urged by other persons.

spook *n*. a ghost, a spectre. **spooky** *a*. making a person feel uncomfortable or afraid, suggesting ghosts or spirits.

spool *n.* a reel on which thread, wire, photographic film, typewriter ribbon, magnetic tape etc. is wound.

spoon *n.* a utensil consisting of a shallow bowl and a handle used in the kitchen and for eating. *v.* take up with a spoon. **spoonful** *n.* as much as a spoon will hold.

sport *n.* an activity carried on for exercise, usually including much movement of the body; fun, mirth; a person who shows good humour in face of difficulties or if he loses a game. *v.* show proudly (a medal, a tie etc.). **sports** *n.* a meeting for athletic contests.

spot *n.* a small mark or stain on cloth or on the skin; a place, a locality; a spotlight in a theatre. *v.* become marked with spots; recognize (usually from a distance among others). **spotless** *a.* very clean; with no spots. **spotlight** *n.* a projector which throws a circle of light on to a particular place or person. **spotty** *a.* with many spots.

spout *n.* a pipe or tube through which a liquid is poured; a continuous stream of liquid discharged as if from a spout either upwards or falling from a height. *v.* come out, send out with great force.

sion (of fashion, disease etc.) over an area; a food preparation which is made to be spread on bread etc.

sprig *n.* a small twig, shoot or branch.

spring *v.* jump suddenly; come into being grow. *n.* a leap, jump or bound; a spurting of water from the earth, flowing away or standing as a pool; the first season of the year between winter and summer when everything begins to spring or grow; a piece of metal which, when pulled, returns quickly to its original shape; the ability to spring.

sprinkle (sprin-kle) *v.* scatter in small drops or particles. **sprinkler** *n.* a device for sprinkling. **sprinkling** *n.* a very small amount sprinkled on.

sprint *v.* make a short, quick run at full speed; cover a distance by sprinting. *n.* a short run at full speed; a race over a short distance.

sprout *v.* begin to grow, shoot forth *n.* a small shoot of a plant which has just appeared. **Brussels sprouts** green buds which grow on the stem of a cabbage plant and are eaten as vegetables.

spry *a.* active, nimble.

spur *n.* a pointed device attached to the heel of a horseman's boot to urge the horse on; anything that makes a person work harder or be more active; the hard spike on the leg of a cock. *v.* urge on.

sprain *v.* injure or twist a joint. *n.* an injury caused by spraining.

sprawl *v.* sit or lie with arms and legs stretched out in a careless way. *n.* the act of sprawling, a sprawling position.

spray *n.* water or other liquid broken up into very small drops falling or blown through the air; liquid prepared for certain purposes to be applied as a spray; the apparatus used for spraying. *v.* scatter liquid in small drops.

spread *v.* stretch out, unfold; lay on, cover a larger space; extend or become extended over a wide area; take time by spreading (payments etc.). *n.* the expan-

spurt *v.* squirt or gush out in a stream or jet. *n.* a sudden forcible gush of water or liquid, of steam, gas etc.; a great increase of effort over a short space of time.

sputnik (sput-nik) *n.* an artificial satellite put into space, especially the first Russian satellite.

spy *n.* a person who keeps secret watch on the actions of others; one employed by a government to get secret information about the military or other affairs of other countries or organizations. *v.* watch in secret; catch sight of.

squabble (squab-ble) *v.* quarrel noisily. *n.* a noisy quarrel about something trivial or unimportant.

squad *n.* a small number of people working together; a small number of soldiers, usually ten, plus a sergeant and a corporal; the smallest military unit. **squadron** *n.* a unit of cavalry, warships or aircraft fighting together.

squalid (squal-id) *a.* foul, dirty, needing care and cleanliness, filthy; wretched; degrading and unworthy. **squalor** *n.* filth and misery.

squall *n.* a sudden strong wind which quickly dies away; a sudden cry, especially of a baby. *v.* blow in a squall; utter in a screaming tone.

squander (squan-der) *v.* spend money, time, energy etc. wastefully and to very little purpose.

square *n.* a flat shape with four equal sides and four right angles; an open space in a town with streets and buildings all round it; the result when a number is multiplied by itself; an instrument for drawing and measuring right angles. *a.* shaped like a square; fair, honest, complete, satisfying; having to do with a number multiplied by itself. *v.* make square, give a square shape to; multiply a number by itself; settle (a debt etc.).

squash *v.* crush; put down (a revolt). *n.* a large number of people in a small space; a game played with a rubber ball on a small court; a drink based on a fruit juice, often mixed with water.

squat *v.* sit on one's heels; settle on land or in an empty house without permission. *a.* short and thick. **squatter** *n.* a person who enters and settles in property without the permission of its owner.

squeak *n.* a short, sharp, high-pitched cry; a sharp high-pitched sound. *v.* utter or produce a squeak or squeaks.

squeal *n.* a shrill, high-pitched cry, louder than a squeak, often indicating pain, fear etc. *v.* utter or produce squeals.

squeamish (squeam-ish) *a.* easily made sick; easily shocked or disgusted; very particular.

squeeze *v.* press things together; press to extract something; press oneself against others. *n.* the act of squeezing; a close embrace; a narrow escape. **squeezer** *n.* a device for squeezing.

squelch *v.* make a splashing or sucking sound. *n.* a squelching sound.

squib *n.* a small firework that can be thrown by hand.

squint *v.* have eyes which look in different directions; look with the eyes half closed. *n.* a crossing of the eyes.

squire *n.* a man who owns most of the land in a certain district; in the Middle Ages, a young man who attended a knight and who would himself one day be a knight.

squirm *v.* twist the body; wriggle; feel uncomfortable; feel embarrassed as a result of a reprimand or unfortunate remark.

squirrel (squir-rel) *n.* a small rodent, with grey or red fur and a bushy tail, which lives among trees and eats nuts.

squirt *v.* force out liquid in a jet from a narrow opening; come out in a jet-like stream. *n.* the act of squirting; a small quantity of liquid squirted.

stab *v.* pierce or wound with a sharp knife or other instrument. *n.* the act of stabbing; a wound made by stabbing; a feeling like a stab.

stable (sta-ble) *n.* a building in which horses are sheltered and fed; a collection of animals (for racing etc.). *v.* put horses into a building to rest and feed. **stabling** *n.* stables etc. for horses.

stack *n.* a large heap or pile of hay, straw etc.; a single chimney for carrying smoke out of a building or a ship; a great quantity or number. *v.* pile or arrange in a stack.

stadium (sta-dium) *n.* a large open space with seats all round it, arranged in tiers.

staff *n.* a stick, pole or rod used for walking, climbing or as a weapon; a pole used to support a flag; a number of assistants working together under a manager, headmaster etc.; the five parallel lines on which notes of music are written, sometimes called a stave.

stag *n.* an adult male deer.

stage *n.* the platform in a theatre on which the actors perform; everything having to do with the theatre; a platform raised from the floor (for speakers etc.); a part of a journey, a single step in a process or growth. *v.* put something — a play etc. on the stage. **stagecoach** *n.* a coach drawn by horses which used regularly to carry passengers from place to place before the days of railways. **stagestruck** *a.* eager to go on the stage, to become an actor or actress.

stagger (stag-ger) *v.* walk, move or stand unsteadily; make or become helpless with shock, amazement; arrange things, especially lunch hours so that they do not come together. *n.* the act of staggering.

stagnant (stag-nant) *a.* not running or flowing (of water etc.). **stagnate** *v.* become foul through standing too long; be inactive, sluggish or dull.

stain *v.* make dirty marks or marks of a different colour; make wood etc. a different colour with specially prepared liquid. *n.* the liquid used for staining; a patch of colour or a dirty mark; an imperfection in a person's character. **stainless** *a.* (of knives, forks, garden tools etc.) that will not stain or become rusty.

stair *n.* one of a number of steps leading up or down; a series or flight of steps **staircase, stairway** *n.* a flight of stairs leading from one level to another.

stake *n.* a post driven into the ground to support or hold something; a post to which a person was bound who was to be burnt to death; a personal interest in something; money laid down for a bet or wager. *v.* support with a stake; put money on the result of a game, a race etc. **at stake** at risk.

stale *a.* no longer fresh; having lost interest and novelty (a stale joke); having lost freshness or vigour through too much practice or hard work.

stalk *n.* that part of a plant which supports a leaf, flower or fruit. *v.* walk with slow, stiff strides; move quietly in pursuit of something.

stall *n.* a place in a stable for one horse or cow; a small shop with an open front, a table on which goods are placed for sale a number of fixed seats in a church for the choir. *v.* (of an engine) stop suddenly and unexpectedly; make an engine stop in this way. **the stalls** the seats in a theatre nearest the stage.

stallion (stal-lion) *n.* a full-grown male horse from which foals are bred.

stalwart (stal-wart) *a.* tall, strong and well-built; brave, valiant, firm, reliable enthusiastic. *n.* a strong, brave person, a steady and reliable supporter in a cause.

stamen (sta-men) *n.* that part of a flower often in the centre, which bears the pollen.

stammer (stam-mer) *v.* speak with sudden stops and pauses, or repeating parts of words; hesitate in speech because of embarrassment etc. *n.* the act of stammering.

stamp *v.* put down the foot with force; put a mark on something with a stamp; put a postage stamp on a letter. *n.* the act of stamping; a device with a design or words cut into it which is used for printing; a piece of printed paper made to be stuck on letters as a sign that the postage on them has been paid.

stand v. keep in an upright position on the feet; rise to one's feet; remain (an offer etc.); be in a certain position; put in a certain place; be in a certain place; bear (pain, noise etc.). n. a piece of furniture made to hold things; a stall, a place where things are exhibited; a structure from which people may watch sports and matches.

standard (stan-dard) n. a flag, banner or other object raised on a pole to rally an army, to indicate loyalty to a ruler etc.; a pole on which something may be placed; a measure or level by which weights, lengths, sizes or values may be compared. a. most widely recognized and used.

stanza (stan-za) n. a group of lines forming part of a poem.

staple (sta-ple) n. a piece of metal shaped like the letter U with two points; a small strip of metal which, when pressed over papers with a special stapling machine, fastens them together. a. the chief (product, food etc.). v. fasten papers together with a stapling machine.

star n. one of the bodies (not a planet) that may be seen in the sky at night; a figure with 5 or 6 points; a leading actor or performer. v. take the chief part in a performance or film. **starfish** n. a marine animal having the shape of a five-pointed star. **starry** a. lit by stars; shining.

starch n. a solid white substance with no taste obtained from wheat, potatoes etc.; starch prepared for stiffening linen and for use in industry. v. use starch to stiffen garments.

stare v. look for a time with the eyes wide open; gaze. n. a staring gaze.

start v. begin to move, go, set out; come suddenly into activity; set something in motion. n. a beginning; the amount of time or the distance by which one starts in front of the rest; a sudden movement as if surprised or startled.

startle (start-le) v. give a shock, a surprise, make a person start suddenly.

starve v. be hungry, suffer through not having (food, love, care etc.); make others starve through refusing food etc. **starvation** n. the condition of being starved.

state n. the condition in which a person or thing is; all the people under one government. a. having to do with the state (railways etc.); having to do with ceremony (reception etc.). v. express in words. **stately** a. majestic; magnificent. **statement** n. something stated. **statesman** n. a person who takes an important part in managing the affairs of a state.

static (stat-ic) a. not changing, at rest. **static electricity** electricity in the atmosphere which interferes with the sending or receiving of wireless signals.

station (sta-tion) n. a position in which one remains; a building used for a particular purpose; a place where railway trains stop. v. put at a certain place. **stationary** a. remaining in the same place.

stationer (sta-tion-er) n. a person who sells writing paper, pens and other writing materials. **stationery** n. all kinds of writing materials. **The Stationery Office** the government department which publishes and distributes government books, papers and pamphlets.

statistics (sta-tis-tics) n. the science which deals with the collection and use of numerical facts; the facts themselves.

statue (stat-ue) n. the figure of a person or animal represented in stone, wood, bronze, plastic or any other material. **statuary** n. statues. **statuette** n. a small statue.

statute (stat-ute) n. a law made by a person or a body such as parliament having the power to make laws: **statute law** law made by acts of parliament etc.

staunch a. loyal, trustworthy; strong, substantial. v. stop the flow of a liquid, especially blood from a wound.

stave v. break, smash (stave in); avoid

(stave off). *n.* the five lines on which notes of music are written (see **staff**).

stay *v.* remain in a place, situation, company etc.; stop (hunger etc.). *n.* the length of time one remains; the stopping of an action at law.

steady (stead-y) *a.* firm, not likely to fall, fixed securely; not changing speed or direction; free from excitement; *v.* make steady, become steady. **steadily** *adv.* in a firm or steady manner.

steak *n.* a thick tender slice of meat (usually beef) or of fish, for grilling or frying.

steal *v.* take something belonging to another; move, come or go very quietly and secretly; pass by (of years etc.)

steam *n.* the vapour into which water turns when it boils; surplus energy. *v.* rise and pass off in the form of steam; move by steam power; cook by means of steam over boiling water. **steam power** the power by which machines are run through producing steam in a boiler.

steel *n.* iron which has been hardened by heat and mixed with small quantities of other substances; something made of steel, as a knife-sharpener. *a.* made of steel.

steep *a.* having a sharp slope. *v.* soak in water or other liquid, for softening, cleansing etc.

steeple (steep-le) *n.* the tower of a church which has a spire rising from its roof. **steeplechase** *n.* a race across country on foot or on horseback in which many obstacles (hedges, fences etc.) are met.

steer *v.* guide a car, a boat, a ship etc. in the required direction. *n.* an almost fully grown male calf raised for beef.

stem *n.* the main part of a tree or plant above ground; the stalk which supports a leaf, flower or fruit; the long, slender part of a tobacco-pipe or a wineglass; the upright timber at the forward end of a ship or boat to which the side timbers or metal plates are joined.

stench *n.* a very disagreeable smell.

step *v.* move by lifting up the foot and putting it down again in a new position. *n.* the movement of one foot made by stepping; the sound made by somebody walking; a movement of the feet in time with others in marching or dancing; a very short distance; a move towards some purpose; a level place for the foot when going up or down. **stepladder** *n.* a folding ladder with steps fitted into its frame. **stepping-stone** *n.* a stone on which one may step when crossing a stream.

step- a prefix indicating a relative through the remarriage of a widowed parent. **stepfather** *n.* the husband of one's widowed mother. **stepmother** *n.* the wife of one's widowed father. **stepbrother, stepsister** *n.* the child of an earlier marriage of one's stepfather or stepmother. **stepdaughter, stepson** *n.* the child of an earlier marriage of one's husband or wife.

stereo (ste-re-o) or **stereophonic** *a.* having to do with sound reproduced through two speakers from a radio or gramophone. *n.* the radio or gramophone producing the sound.

stern *a.* strict, severe; of a very serious character. *n.* the back part of a ship or boat.

stethoscope (steth-o-scope) *n.* an instrument used by doctors to listen to a patient's breathing and the beating of the heart.

stew *v.* cook by boiling slowly in a closed vessel. *n.* a preparation of meat, fish etc. cooked by stewing.

steward (stew-ard) *n.* one who manages the property and money matters of another person; a man who arranges for the comfort of passengers on a ship or aircraft; a man who organizes a dance, a race meeting or any other public function. *v.* act as a steward; manage. **stewardess** *n.* a woman steward.

stick *n.* a piece of wood broken off a tree or shrub; a piece of wood cut and trimmed for walking or any other purpose; something shaped like a stick. *v.* pierce or puncture with a pointed instrument; join, be joined with; put something into a certain position; become fixed, come to a stop. **sticky** *a.* that sticks.

stiff *a.* not easily bent; not easy to ,do; blowing strongly. **stiffen** *v.* make or become stiff.

stifle (sti-fle) *v.* make unable to breathe properly; keep back (facts) repress (a yawn etc.).

stile *n.* a series of steps to enable people to get over a gate or fence.

still *adv.* quiet, not moving; at or up to this time; even, yet. *a.* remaining in place or at rest, free from noise, calm, hushed, with no waves.

stilt *n.* one of two poles, each of which has a support for the foot some distance above the ground.

stimulate (stim-u-late) *v.* excite, rouse, bring about action or effort. **stimulant** *n.* a drink or food that makes people more active. **stimulus** *n.* something that stimulates, quickens action, feeling, thought etc.

sting *n.* the sharp pointed organ of an insect or animal which injects poison into the body; the pain or injury caused by a sting. *v.* prick or wound with a sting; give or feel a sting or a sharp pain.

stink *v.* have a bad smell. *n.* a strong offensive smell, a stench.

stir *v.* move or make move; move round and round as with a stick or a spoon; excite (anger, pity, etc.); rouse from inactivity. *n.* a state of general excitement, a commotion.

stirrup (stir-rup) *n.* a foot-rest which hangs down from the saddle of a horse.

stitch *n.* one complete movement of a needle, pulling a thread between two holes made in cloth; various movements of the needle in knitting, crochet and other kinds of work with thread; a sharp pain in the side often caused by running.

stock *n.* goods for sale; goods stored; liquid in which meat and vegetables have been stewed, used to make soup etc. *v.* keep for sale.

stocking (stock-ing) *n.* a covering of wool, cotton, nylon or silk for the foot and leg.

stoke *v.* put fuel on a fire, especially for an engine or a furnace. **stokehold** *n.* the place where a ship's furnaces are stoked **stoker** *n.* a man who attends to the fire of an engine or a furnace.

stole *n.* (of the church) a narrow strip of silk or other material worn by a priest over the shoulders and which hangs down in front; a collar of fur or other material worn over the shoulders by women.

stomach (stom-ach) *n.* the pouch in the body in which food is digested.

stone *n.* the substance of which rocks are made; a piece of this substance; the rather large and hard seed inside plums, peaches, cherries and some other fruit. *v.* throw stones at. **stony** *a.* having many stones; without feeling or expression; merciless; hard like stone.

stool *n.* a seat with no back; a short low support for the feet.

stoop *v.* bend the body forwards and downwards; behave badly, unwisely or selfishly. *n.* a position in which the head and shoulders are held forward.

stop *v.* make an end of movement; cease from, leave off; fill up a hole or opening; prevent something happening or being done. *n.* a halt after movement; a place at which public vehicles, cars, buses, trains, etc. stop; a punctuation mark, a full stop; something that stops anything from moving. **stoppage** *n.* the condition of being stopped or obstructed. **stopper** *n.* an object which closes a hole, especially in a bottle. **stop-watch** *n.* a watch used to time races etc., that can be started and stopped when needed to measure the time taken.

store *v.* supply or stock something kept until needed; keep for future use; put things into a warehouse. *n.* a place where things are kept for use later. **storage** *n.* the act of storing; a place where something is stored; the price charged for storing.

stork *n.* a wading bird with long neck, legs and bill.

storm *n.* a disturbance of the air, with strong wind, rain, hail, snow, thunder, lightning or dust; a violent and sudden attack; a violent outburst. *v.* shout in anger; capture by storm. **stormy** *a.* accompanied by storms; accompanied by outbursts of temper etc.

story (sto-ry) *n.* an account, either fiction or truth, about an event or a series of events.

stout *a.* not fat, but of solid build; strong, stalwart; strong in construction, not likely to wear out quickly. *n.* a strong, dark beer, heavier than ale.

stove *n.* a kind of box made of metal or brick in which a fire can be lit and from which heat can be obtained for heating or cooking.

stow *v.* pack into something (a ship, a trunk, a cupboard etc.). **stowaway** *n.* a person who has hidden himself on a ship or aircraft in order to make a journey without paying the fare.

straddle (strad-dle) *v.* stand or sit across something with the legs wide apart.

straggle (strag-gle) *v.* go, come or spread out in a scattered irregular way; fall behind or stray from the rest of those on a walk. **straggler** *n.* one who straggles.

straight *a.* going one way without turns or bends; level, flat, horizontal; honest, honourable, upright in one's dealings; free from wrongdoing. *adv.* in good order; directly. *n.* the straight part, especially of a racecourse. **straighten** *v.* make straight or tidy. **straightforward** *a.* honest; easy to understand or do.

strain *v.* stretch tightly; exert to the limit; weaken or injure by straining; pass liquid through a sieve or cloth. *n.* the state of being strained; something that strains; a

test of someone's nerve, courage etc.; music; a breed (of animals, plants etc.).

strait *n.* a narrow passage of water connecting two large bodies of water; a position of difficulty, stress or need. **strait-jacket** *n.* a stiff garment designed to prevent a lunatic from struggling or harming himself.

strand *n.* each of the strings or yarns which are twisted together to make a rope or cord; a string (of beads, pearls etc.). **stranded** *a.* driven ashore, left in a helpless position, often in a strange place.

strange *a.* unusual; not used to, out of one's usual surroundings; not known, met or seen before. **stranger** *n.* a person whom one does not know, a newcomer in a place or locality.

strangle (stran-gle) *v.* kill by squeezing the throat and preventing breathing; prevent something continuing (trade, business etc.). **stranglehold** *n.* anything that prevents the development or life of a person or group. **strangulation** *n.* being strangled.

strap *n.* a narrow strip of leather or other material for holding, lifting, pulling etc. *v.* attach by a strap; beat with a strap.

strategy (strat-e-gy) *n.* the art of planning a military campaign or managing any important business affair. **strategic** *a.* having to do with strategy.

stratosphere (strat-o-sphere) *n.* the layer of thinner air which surrounds the earth, lying above the atmosphere.

straw *n.* the stalks of wheat, barley and other kinds of cereal after the grain has been taken off; a single stalk of straw; a narrow, hollow paper tube. **strawberry** *n.* a plant that grows close to the ground and produces red fruit which is delicious to eat.

stray *v.* turn away from the right path, get lost. *a.* having become lost, found apart from others. *n.* any wandering, homeless or friendless creature.

streak *n.* a long narrow mark, smear or band of colour. *v.* mark with a streak or streaks; move quickly. **streaky** *a.* having streaks.

stream *n.* a body of flowing water, a river or brook; a flow of water, liquid, gas, people, words etc. *v.* run, flow, wave or blow; send forth in a stream; move in a stream (of living things). **streamer** *n.* a long narrow flag, strip of paper, anything that will wave in the wind. **streamlined** *a.* having a shape that offers least resistance to the air so that a streamlined aeroplane or car can travel at greater speed.

street *n.* a public way through a town or village with houses or shops on one or both sides; the people (living) in a street.

strength *n.* the state of being strong; something that makes strong; the power to resist force, wear etc. **strengthen** *v.* make stronger.

strenuous (stren-u-ous) *a.* full of force and energy; very active.

stress *n.* strain, pressure, pull etc. exerted on one thing by another, or pressure on a person; emphasis on a thing, a word or part of a word when speaking. *v.* lay emphasis on.

stretch *v.* draw out, reach out; make longer; extend; draw tight; become stretched. *n.* the act of stretching; an extent or period of time. **stretcher** *n.* a framework usually of two poles with canvas between them for carrying sick or injured persons.

strew *v.* let fall in small pieces over a surface, scatter or be scattered far and wide.

strict *a.* stern, requiring obedience; absolute, complete (secrecy, confidence); exact (account etc.).

stride *v.* walk with long steps; walk with vigour or haste; pass over by one stride. *n.* the distance covered by taking one step.

strife *n.* conflict, quarrelling, fighting.

strike *v.* hit, deliver a blow or thrust; produce (sparks etc.) by hitting or rubbing; occur, come to the mind; move in a certain direction; take down, lower (camp etc.); come upon or find; take root, put into soil to take root; refuse to work in order to get better pay or conditions, shorter hours etc. *n.* the act of striking. **striker** *n.* a person who strikes. **striking** *a.* that strikes; causing great interest.

string *n.* a piece of cord thinner than a rope for tying parcels etc.; a piece of cord stretched tightly for some purpose (music etc.); a number of objects such as beads or pearls threaded on a string; a line of people or objects. *v.* put a string or strings on; put objects on a string. **string band** a band made up of stringed instruments. **string beans** a kind of bean, the pods having stringy parts down the side. **stringy** *a.* like string, having tough fibres.

strip *v.* take off clothes, covers etc.; rob, plunder, take away from; clear out or empty. *n.* a narrow piece (land, cloth etc.). **strip cartoon** a number of pictures following each other and telling a story. **strip lighting** lighting by long strips of glass tube instead of bulbs.

stripe *n.* a broad or narrow line or band of a different colour from the background; a badge shaped like a V on the jacket sleeve of a British soldier or police officer. **striped** *a.* marked with stripes.

strive *v.* struggle, try hard, exert oneself towards an end; struggle in opposition to another force.

stroke *n.* the act of striking; a blow; a mark made by one movement of a pen or brush; one of a number of regular movements or sounds; a sudden attack of illness of the brain. *v.* pass the hand gently over something.

stroll *n.* a quiet, slow walk usually for pleasure. *v.* take a stroll.

strong *a.* having great strength of body or some part of the body; having great power of mind, will etc.; great in numbers and power; not easily yielding or giving way; forceful, vigorous (wind); containing much alcohol (of drinks); having much flavouring in it; affecting the taste, smell, sight etc. a great deal.

strop *n.* a leather strap for sharpening a razor.

structure (struc-ture) *n.* anything that is built; the way in which a thing is formed, put together, built etc.

struggle (strug-gle) *v.* fight, work hard, make efforts. *n.* a fight, usually a small one not involving many people.

stub *n.* the remains of a pencil, a cigarette, a cigar etc. *v.* strike (one's toe); put out. **stubble** *n.* the stumps of grain after the harvest has been gathered.

stubborn (stub-born) *a.* obstinate, not yielding; hard, tough, stiff, hard to move.

stud *n.* a small button or fastener that can be passed through two holes to bring together two pieces of material; a large-headed nail for driving into a door, a shield etc. as an ornament. *v.* scatter on a surface.

studio (stu-di-o) *n.* the workroom of an artist, painter or sculptor; a room specially equipped for broadcasting radio or television programmes, or where films are made for the cinema.

study (stud-y) *v.* spend time and energy in learning things, especially from books; examine carefully. *n.* the act of studying; a room used for study; a composition or exercise done as a practice or to give practice to others. **student** *n.* one who studies in a school or university or who strives to learn.

stuff *n.* the material out of which something is made; any sort of material. *v.* pack tightly into something; pack flavouring (herbs, breadcrumbs, sausage meat etc.) into a bird before cooking; fill the inside of a dead bird, animal, reptile etc. to preserve its natural form for exhibition. **stuffing** *n.* material used to stuff things, either for cooking or other purposes. **stuffy** *a.* (of a building) badly ventilated; (of a person) old-fashioned, easily shocked.

stumble (stum-ble) *v.* strike the foot against something; walk unsteadily; discover a thing by accident.

stump *n.* the lower end of a plant or tree left when the main part has been cut off; the part of anything left when the rest has been broken or cut; each of the upright sticks in cricket which make up the wickets. *v.* put a batsman out when he is not standing in the crease by touching the stumps with the ball. **stumpy** *a.* short and thick.

stunt *v.* check the growth of. *n.* a performance showing skill or strength; something spectacular done to attract attention.

stupid (stu-pid) *a.* foolish, dull in mind. **stupidity** *n.* being stupid.

stupor (stu-por) *n.* the state of near unconsciousness through drink, drugs or any other cause. **stupefaction** *n.* being stupefied. **stupefy** *v.* make almost unconscious.

sturdy (stur-dy) *a.* strongly formed or built; firm, loyal.

stutter (stut-ter) *v.* stammer. **stutterer** *n.* a person who stammers.

sty *n.* a small building for pigs to live in; an inflamed spot on the edge of the eyelid (sometimes spelt stye).

style *n.* a way of speaking, writing or doing a thing; a fashion. *v.* design (dresses, cars etc.). **stylish** *a.* fashionable; in the latest style.

subdivide (sub-di-vide) *v.* divide a part of something into smaller parts.

subdue (sub-due) *v.* defeat, overcome; make quiet (noise, cries etc.).

subject (súb-ject) *n.* something talked about, thought about, studied, written about etc.; one who is under the rule of the sovereign; being likely to have (diseases, attacks of faintness, rage etc.); depending on. **subject** (sub-jéct) subdue; bring under control.

subjugate (sub-ju-gate) *v.* subdue, conquer. **subjugation** *n.* conquering; conquest.

sublet (sub-let) *v.* let part of a building or house of which one is already a tenant.

sublime (sub-lime) *a.* grand, perfect in thought, language, achievement etc.

submarine (sub-ma-rine) *a.* under the sea. *n.* a ship which is equipped to be navigated under water.

submerge (sub-merge) *v.* sink out of sight; plunge below the surface; be or remain under water.

submit (sub-mit) *v.* surrender; put oneself under the control of; put forward, offer (solution, suggestion etc.). **submission** *n.* the act of submitting.

subnormal (sub-nor-mal) *a.* below the normal; lacking in some power or other, mostly of the mind.

subscribe (sub-scribe) *v.* give money with many other people towards some object; agree to take and pay for something regularly; give consent to something being done. **subscriber** *n.* a person who subscribes. **subscription** *n.* subscribing, money subscribed.

subsequent (sub-se-quent) *a.* coming later or after (an event, a section etc.).

subside (sub-side) *v.* sink to a lower level; quieten down. **subsidence** *n.* a sinking (often of the ground or the surface of a road).

subsidy (sub-si-dy) *n.* money granted by a government or public body towards some object. **subsidize** *v.* give money as a subsidy.

subsist (sub-sist) *v.* exist, continue in existence or alive. **subsistence** *n.* the means of existing, or being kept alive.

substance (sub-stance) *n.* matter; a kind of matter; the main thing talked about or studied; property, wealth.

substantial (sub-stan-tial) *a.* strong, large; wealthy, having great influence; having to do with the importance of something (agreement etc.).

substitute (sub-sti-tute) *n.* a person or thing acting in the place of another. *v.* take the place of, act as a substitute.

subterranean (sub-ter-ra-nean) *a.* being, acting below the surface of the earth.

subtitle (sub-ti-tle) *n.* a second title for a book or play, usually in the nature of an explanation; words in English projected on a foreign language film to help viewers to understand what is being said.

subtract (sub-tract) *v.* take away. **subtraction** *n.* the act of subtracting.

suburb (sub-urb) *n.* a district, usually mainly of houses, lying immediately outside a city or town. **suburban** *a.* having to do with a suburb (housing, transport etc.).

subversive (sub-ver-sive) *a.* intended to cause the downfall of a government or other powerful body by spreading rumours, making people distrust it etc. **subversion** *n.* subversive conduct. **subvert** *v.* try to destroy some superior power in this way.

subway (sub-way) *n.* an underground passage taking people from one place to another, especially under streets.

succeed (suc-ceed) *v.* have the desired result; do what one intended to do; take the place of another because of family descent, election or in any other way. **success** *n.* the act or result of succeeding; a thing or person having succeeded.

succession (suc-ces-sion) *n.* the way one thing comes after another; the right of succeeding to a title, an estate, wealth etc.

succumb (suc-cumb) *v.* yield, give way to superior force; die.

such *a. pron.* of the same kind, extent, character etc.; so big, good, bad, much etc.

suck *v.* draw into the mouth by the action of the lips and the tongue; draw (in, up etc.) in other ways; put into the mouth and roll with the tongue; draw in by suction. **sucker** *n.* an organ in some animals by which they can attach themselves to a surface; a new root of a plant. **suction** *n.* removal of air, gas, or a liquid so that things are sucked into the vacuum; attaching by sucking.

sudden (sud-den) *a.* quick, coming without warning. **suddenly** *adv.* in a sudden manner.

suds *n.* soapy water, foam, lather remaining after washing.

sue *v.* make a claim against another person in a court of law; ask for (a truce, peace).

suede *n.* (pronounced *swade*) soft leather, finished on the flesh side with a smooth, soft surface.

suet (su-et) *n.* hard fat taken from round the kidneys of sheep and cattle and used for the making of pastry etc.

suffer (suf-fer) *v.* feel or undergo pain, injury, distress or loss. **suffering** *n.* pain, injury, loss, anything unpleasant that can cause one to suffer.

suffice (suf-fice) *v.* be enough, satisfy. **sufficient** *a.* enough.

suffocate (suf-fo-cate) *v.* cause difficulty in breathing; kill through depriving somebody or something of air; feel discomfort through lack of fresh air.

suffrage (suf-frage) *n.* the right to vote in elections. **suffragette** *n.* a woman who, in the early years of the twentieth century, worked for women's suffrage.

sugar (sug-ar) *n.* a sweet substance extracted from the sugar cane and sugar beet and used to sweeten drinks and foods. *v.* sweeten or coat with sugar.

suggest (sug-gest) *v.* bring a plan or idea before a person's mind to be thought about or acted on; propose to a person something as being possible.

suggestion (sug-ges-tion) *n.* the act of suggesting; being suggested; something suggested or that suggests.

suicide (su-i-cide) *n.* the intentional killing of oneself; a person who kills himself intentionally; the intentional destruction of one's own prospects or future. **suicidal**

a. leading to suicide; rash, foolish, likely to be very harmful to oneself.

suit *n.* a set of garments or armour, intended to be worn together; a case in a law court; one of the four sets of cards — hearts, diamonds, spades or clubs. *v.* look well with; be agreeable to. **suitable** *a.* such as would suit, be right for the purpose.

suite *n.* (pronounced *sweet*) a company of followers attending on another person; a set of rooms in a hotel; a number of articles of furniture which go together in one room.

sulk *v.* show by one's face and manner that one is in a bad temper. **sulky** *a.* bad tempered.

sullen (sul-len) *a.* bad-tempered, sulky; of a sulky disposition; dismal, gloomy (of sounds, the weather etc.).

sulphur (sul-phur) *n.* a light yellow substance that burns with a blue flame and has a strong smell, used for making matches, gunpowder, medicine and rubber.

sultry (sul-try) *a.* hot and damp (of the weather).

sum *n.* the total obtained by adding numbers or amounts together; an amount of money. **sum up** *v.* say briefly; make a judgment on.

summary (sum-ma-ry) *n.* a short account giving the main points only. **summarize** *v.* make a summary.

summer (sum-mer) *n.* the second and warmest season of the year between spring and autumn.

summit (sum-mit) *n.* the highest point; the top; the highest point of one's hopes, fortunes etc.; a meeting between heads of state.

summon (sum-mon) *v.* call for the presence of; rouse, gather up, call into action. **summons** *n.* an order to appear, a command to do something.

sun *n.* the star from which the earth and all

the other planets receive light and heat; the sun's light and heat; any star which has satellites. **sunbeam** *n.* a ray of sunlight. **sunburn** *n.* a place where the skin has been burnt or made brown by the sun. **sundial** *n.* a device for telling the time from observing a shadow thrown by the sun. **sunlight** *n.* the light given off by the sun. **sunny** *a.* having much sunlight; cheerful. **sunrise** *n.* the rising of the sun in the morning. **sunset** *n.* the going down of the sun in the evening.

sundae (sun-dae) *n.* a portion of ice-cream with fruit or syrup poured over it, often with cream, chopped up nuts etc. on top.

sundry (sun-dry) *a.* various. **sundries** *n.* various small things or items.

superb (su-perb) *a.* wonderful, magnificent.

superficial (sup-er-fi-cial) *a.* being near the surface, not deep (wounds etc.); faint, slight (resemblance); not thorough or detailed (knowledge, examination).

superfluous (su-per-flu-ous) *a.* more than is wanted; being left over.

superhuman (su-per-hu-man) *a.* above or beyond what is human; having more than human power.

superimpose (su-per-im-pose) *v.* put one thing on top of another.

superintend (su-per-in-tend) *v.* oversee, direct, supervise. **superintendent** *n.* a person who superintends; a manager.

superior (su-per-i-or) *a.* higher in rank; better; greater in numbers; better than other things or people. **superiority** *n.* being better.

superman (su-per-man) *n.* a man who has more than human powers such as cunning, will power, brain power etc.

supermarket (su-per-mar-ket) *n.* a large store which sells all kinds of goods and where people can serve themselves.

superstition (su-per-sti-tion) *n.* the belief in magic, witchcraft; the fear of what is unknown or mysterious. **superstitious** *a.* having to do with superstition; full of superstition (of a person).

supervise (su-per-vise) *v.* watch and direct work that is being done. **supervision** *n.* supervising. **supervisor** *n.* one who supervises.

supper (sup-per) *n.* the evening meal, the last of the day.

supplant (sup-plant) *v.* take the place of another thing or person.

supple (sup-ple) *a.* bending easily without breaking; moving easily; responding to ideas quickly.

supplement (sup-ple-ment) *n.* something added later to a book; an extra addition to a newspaper or journal. *v.* add to something. **supplementary** *a.* additional.

supply (sup-ply) *v.* provide with what is needed. *n.* the act of supplying; what is supplied (food, goods etc., often referred to as supplies).

support (sup-port) *v.* bear or hold up; maintain, provide for; help, strengthen. *n.* that which supports (things, people in need etc.).

suppose (sup-pose) *v.* take something to be true whether it is or not; be expected to do something.

suppress (sup-press) *v.* put an end to; keep back something from being known or seen, especially news. **suppression** *n.* being suppressed; keeping back. **suppressor** *n.* a device fitted to a motor or electrical device to stop intereference with radio or television reception.

sure *a.* certain; without any doubt of something; confident; reliable, to be depended on. **surely** *adv.* certainly.

surf *n.* the white foam seen when the waves break on the shore or on the rocks. **surfboard** *n.* a board used for the sport of riding the surf.

surface (sur-face) *n.* the outer face or outside of an object; the top of a liquid; the outward appearance as distinguished from what a thing or person is really like. *v.* give a surface to; come to the surface.

surge *n.* a forward movement. *v.* move forward; rise.

surgeon (sur-geon) *n.* a doctor who is qualified to perform operations. **surgery** *n.* the practice of treating disease and injuries by operations; the room in which people wait before they consult the doctor. **surgical** *a.* having to do with surgery.

surname (sur-name) *n.* the name which a

person has in common with the other members of his family.

surpass (sur-pass) *v.* be greater than; do better than.

surplice (sur-plice) *n.* a loose-fitting white gown with wide sleeves worn over a cassock by clergymen and members of church choirs.

surplus (sur-plus) *n.* the amount remaining after all needs have been met.

surprise (sur-prise) *v.* come upon, discover suddenly; astonish; attack without warning. *n.* the feeling of being surprised. *a.* sudden, unexpected. **surprising** *a.* causing surprise.

surrender (sur-rend-er) *v.* give oneself or one's party up (to an enemy etc.); give up hope. *n.* the act of surrendering.

surround (sur-round) *v.* be all round; shut in all round. *n.* the part of the floor left uncovered between the walls and the carpet. **surroundings** *n.* everything that is or was around.

survey (sur-vey) *v.* take a general view of; measure and find the extent of land; examine the condition of a house or a building. *n.* a statement giving the results of surveying land, a house etc. **surveyor** *n.* a person whose work is to survey land or buildings.

survive (sur-vive) *v.* live longer than others; remain alive after an event has killed others. **survivor** *n.* a person who has survived.

suspect (sus-péct) *v.* guess, imagine; have a feeling that a person is guilty. **suspect** (sús-pect) *n.* a person who is suspected of something. **suspicion** *n.* suspecting. **suspicious** *a.* showing or causing suspicion.

suspend (sus-pend) *v.* hang, remain in the air or in a liquid; stop (payment, trading, hostilities etc.); bar or prevent a person carrying on his usual activities for a limited time. **suspender** *n.* an elastic band or strap for keeping up socks or stockings. **suspension** *n.* suspending, being suspended. **suspension bridge** a bridge, the roadway of which is suspended from cables hanging between great towers of steel or other building materials.

suspense (sus-pense) *n.* uncertainty about something; not being sure.

sustain (sus-tain) *v.* hold up; keep from falling; keep (a person, the mind etc.) in

good spirits after some misfortune; suffer, undergo (injuries).

swab *n.* a large mop used on board ship for cleaning decks; a piece of sponge, cotton wool etc. for cleaning the mouth of a patient or taking a specimen from the throat etc.; the material collected by a swab.

swagger (swag-ger) *v.* walk or talk in an insolent, proud and overbearing manner. *n.* the act of swaggering.

swallow (swal-low) *v.* let something go down the throat to the stomach; make disappear. *n.* a small bird that migrates to warm countries in winter and comes back to Britain every summer.

swamp *n.* an area of soft, wet, marshy ground. *v.* flood or drench with water; be plunged into or overwhelmed with (work etc.).

swan *n.* a large graceful swimming bird with a long, slender neck, usually white in colour.

swarm *v.* (of birds or insects) move together in a great number; (of bees) move round the queen when migrating to form a new hive or colony; appear to move in large numbers. *n.* a large number of bees, insects etc, moving together.

swarthy (swarth-y) *a.* having a dark-coloured skin and complexion.

swathe *v.* wrap tightly round and round.

sway *v.* move unsteadily from side to side; control, direct. *n.* control; direction of a powerful person.

swear *v.* declare solemnly before God that what one says is true; make a solemn promise; use bad language.

sweat *v.* give up moisture through the skin. *n.* moisture given out in this way. **sweater** *n.* a kind of knitted jersey, usually of thick wool, worn by athletes, or by other people for warmth or casual wear.

sweep *v.* move dust or dirt away with a brush or broom; push away, clear away as if with a brush; pass over; move over or along lightly; extend; *n.* the act of sweeping or clearing away; a person whose work is to sweep chimneys.

sweet *a.* tasting like sugar; pleasing. *n.* sugar, boiled and with other things added, eaten as a luxury; a sweet dish or pudding. **sweeten** *v.* make sweet. **sweetheart** *n.* a person who is loved by another of the opposite sex.

swell *v.* increase in size, amount etc. *n.* a rise in the level of water; the rise and fall of the waves. **swelling** *n.* a swollen place, especially on the body.

swelter (swel-ter) *v.* suffer from great heat, perspire.

swerve *v.* suddenly change direction.

swift *a.* quick, speedy. *n.* a small bird very much like a swallow.

swill *n.* kitchen refuse given to pigs. *v.* wash by flooding with water.

swim *v.* move along in water by movements of the arms and legs or (of fishes) of the fins and tail; cross by swimming; move on the surface of a liquid; seem to be swimming or moving (before the eyes). *n.* the act of swimming; a time when one swims. **swimmer** *n.* a person who swims.

swindle (swin-dle) *v.* cheat a person of his money. *n.* a process, a piece of swindling, the act of swindling. **swindler** *n.* a person who swindles.

swine *n.* a pig; a coarse, disgusting person.

swing *v.* make something move to and fro; turn or make something turn; move with a circular movement or to and fro. *n.* a swinging movement; a seat hanging from above by ropes or chains so that one may sit in it and swing; a strong rhythm in music or poetry.

swirl *v.* move with a whirling motion.

swish *v.* move or set moving swiftly through the air with a hissing sound. *n.* a swishing movement or sound.

switch *n.* a device on the railway lines to direct trains on to another track; a device to put an electric light, a cooker etc. off and on; a supple, easily bending branch of a tree used as a stick. *v.* turn electric current on and off; move a train from one line to another change (conversation etc.). **switchback** *n.* a mountain road having many sharp bends; a zigzag arrangement on railways for climbing steep slopes; a construction on a fairground for giving rides which go up and down.

swoon *n.* a fainting fit. *v.* have a fainting fit.

swoop *v.* come down with a swift rush. *n.* a swift movement downwards or towards.

sword *n.* a weapon that consists of a long steel blade fixed to a hilt or handle.

syllable (syl-la-ble) *n.* a part of a word which may be split from other parts.

syllabus (syl-la-bus) *n.* the plan or outline of a course of studies.

symbol (sym-bol) *n.* a sign, mark or object which represents something else, as the cross in Christianity and the various mathematical signs.

sympathy (sym-pa-thy) *n.* a feeling of friendliness and agreement existing between people. **sympathetic** *a.* showing or feeling sympathy. **sympathize** *v.* feel sympathy for.

symphony (sym-pho-ny) *n.* a long, elaborate musical composition consisting of three or more movements, played by a large orchestra.

symptom (symp-tom) *n.* a sign or indication of something (illness, madness, unrest etc.).

synagogue (syn-a-gogue) *n.* a building used by Jews as a place of worship.

syncopate (syn-co-pate) *v.* change the rhythm of music, placing the accent on beats which are not normally accented. **syncopation** *n.* the act of syncopating; a tune which has been syncopated.

syndicate (syn-di-cate) *n.* a number of firms in commerce which combine to do business or supply goods.

synopsis (syn-op-sis) *n.* the brief outline of a book, a play etc.

syringe (syr-inge) *n.* a device which draws in liquid and forces it out again in a stream, used for spraying and injecting liquids into the body.

syrup (sy-rup) *n.* a thick, sweet, sticky liquid made by boiling sugar in water.

system (sys-tem) *n.* a number of parts making a whole or working together; a set of ideas or principles; a plan or method. **systematic** *a.* based on a system; showing method, arranged in regular order.

T

tab *n.* a small loop fastened on a garment for hanging; a label.

table (ta-ble) *n.* a piece of furniture consisting of a flat top, usually on four legs; a table for some special use (dining, feeding birds etc.); a list in which facts are arranged in an orderly manner.

tableau (tab-leau) *n.* (pronounced *tablo*) a grouping of persons to represent a scene or a picture, with no words or actions.

tablet (tab-let) *n.* a writing pad containing many sheets of paper fastened together along the top; a flat piece of wood, stone or metal on which words have been written; a cake of soap; a small flat pellet of medicine.

tack *n.* a small nail with a large head for fastening down carpets etc.; a long stitch for fastening pieces of cloth together until they can be properly sewn. *v.* fasten with tacks; sew with tacking stitches; sail in a zigzag direction to make the best use of the wind.

tackle (tack-le) *n.* ropes and pulleys needed for lifting heavy weights, for raising or lowering the sails of ships etc.; equipment needed for a special purpose; the act of stopping an opponent in football, rugby etc. *v.* deal with a problem; set to work on a task.

tact *n.* great skill and understanding in dealing with people; ability to handle difficult situations without giving offence. **tactful** *a.* having or showing tact. **tactless** *a.* lacking or not showing tact.

tadpole (tad-pole) the young of a frog or toad.

taffeta (taf-fe-ta) *n.* a shiny, stiff silk or rayon cloth, often used for lining dresses.

tag *n.* a piece of card, paper or other tough material used to mark or label something; the binding of metal, plastic or other hard material at the end of a shoelace, string, cord etc.; a game in which one child chases and tries to touch another. *v.*

fasten on; follow on at the end of a part of people; touch as in the game of tag.

tail *n.* the moveable part which grows a the back or end of the body of an animal something resembling a tail; the side of coin opposite to that which carries the portrait of a monarch, a president etc. *v.* move or follow in a line. **tail-light** *n.* the light at the rear end of a car or othe vehicle.

take *v.* hold with arms, teeth, hands c with an instrument; capture; possess steal; borrow; use up (time); accept i exchange find out (temperature, read ings etc.); receive into the body; carry accompany; occupy (a seat, pew); un dergo (an examination); enjoy (a bath, trip); write down (notes); consider (person to be); perform (a walk); requir (persistence, courage). *n.* what has beer taken (in admission, in a shop etc.).

talc *n.* a soft, smooth mineral that can be split into thin plates or ground into a ver fine powder. **talcum powder** a very fin white powder made from talc which i perfumed and used on the body.

tale *n.* a story, a rumour, a report.

talent (tal-ent) *n.* a special natural ability to do a thing well. **talented** *a.* having talent.

talk *v.* speak, say things; be able to speak give information; discuss matters; make somebody do a thing or be in a certair state through talking to him. *n.* a conversation; a lecture or address; a rumour

tall *a.* of more than average height (o persons); high (of objects); hard to believe (of stories).

tallow (tal-low) *n.* hard fat or suet, usually from animals, used in the making o candles, soap etc.

tally (tal-ly) *n.* a ticket or label. *v.* match agree with other amounts or facts.

talon (tal-on) *n.* a claw, especially that o a bird of prey, an eagle, a hawk etc.

tambourine (tam-bou-rine) *n.* a small drum consisting of a circular wooden frame with skin stretched over it, and in the frame small metal plates which give a jingling sound when it is shaken.

tame *a.* accustomed to living with human beings (of animals); dull, not interesting. *v.* make tame, fit to live with human beings. **tamer** *n.* a person who tames wild animals.

tamper (tam-per) *v.* interfere, meddle (with).

tan *a.* yellowish brown. *v.* make an animal's skin or hide into leather; become brown through having been burnt by the sun. *n.* the brown colour one becomes through being burnt by the sun. **tanner** *n.* a person who tans hides.

tandem (tan-dem) *n.* a bicycle made for two persons to ride on, one behind the other. *a.* one behind the other.

tang *n.* a sharp flavour; a smell which is easily recognized (the sea, coffee etc.).

tangent (tan-gent) *n.* a straight line touching but not cutting a curve or a circle; a sudden change from one subject to another in conversation etc.

tangerine (tanger-rine) *n.* a small, loose-skinned variety of orange.

tangle (tan-gle) *n.* an amount of string or hair twisted together and difficult to undo; a confusion (of traffic, in a person's business etc.). *v.* make a tangle.

tango (tan-go) *n.* a South American dance with a strong rhythm; the music for this dance.

tank *n.* a large container for carrying liquid or gas; an armoured fighting vehicle first used in the war of 1914—18. **tanker** *n.* a ship which carries petroleum; a heavy lorry which carries petroleum.

tankard (tank-ard) *n.* a large drinking mug, usually for beer, with a handle and sometimes a hinged lid.

tantalize (tan-ta-lize) *v.* torment by making a person hope for things he can never get.

tap *n.* a device for controlling the flow of liquid from a pipe; a quick, light blow. *v.* make a hole to let liquid come out; get information by secret means (a phone, radio signals etc.). *v.* give a tap to.

tape *n.* material in narrow strips for tying up parcels, for use in making garments, and other purposes. **magnetic tape** tape specially prepared to record sound. *v.* fasten or bind with tape; record sounds on magnetic tape. **tape measure** *n.* a length of tape with marks on it indicating measurements. **tape recorder** a machine into which tapes can be inserted for recording sounds.

taper (tap-er) *v.* become or make smaller at one end. *n.* a long, very thin candle.

tapestry (tap-es-try) *n.* cloth in which threads are woven by hand to make a design or picture.

tar *n.* a black substance made from coal, thick and very sticky when hot and hard when cold. *v.* put tar on. **tarmac** *n.* a mixture of tar and small stones, used to surface roads and runways for aeroplanes. **tarpaulin** *n.* thick canvas treated with tar to make it waterproof.

tarantula (ta-ran-tu-la) *n.* the name given to large poisonous spiders found in southern Europe and America.

tardy (tar-dy) *a.* moving slowly; late or behind time.

target (tar-get) *n.* any object used for aiming at with rifles, arrows etc.; anything aimed at other than by throwing or firing (a charity appeal etc.).

tariff (tar-iff) *n.* a list of goods and services supplied by a hotel, a list of taxes levied on imported goods.

tarnish (tar-nish) *v.* lose colour or brightness (of metals); cause to tarnish; be spoilt (a person's reputation) *n.* a loss of colour or brightness.

tarry (tar-ry) *v.* stay for a time in one place.

tart *n.* a small piece of pastry shaped like a saucer, its centre filled with fruit, jam etc. *a.* sour in taste.

tartan (tar-tan) *n.* woollen cloth with stripes of different colours crossing at right angles; cloth with a tartan pattern, not necessarily of wool.

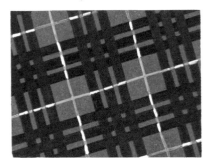

tartar (tar-tar) *n.* a hard, chalky substance deposited on the teeth.

task *n.* a piece of work, a duty to be done. *v.* strain, overwork. **task force** a force under one commander, organized for carrying out a special operation or mission.

tassel (tas-sel) *n.* an ornament consisting of a bunch of thin cords or threads tied at one end to make a knob or ball.

taste *n.* the sense by which the flavour of something is known when it is taken into the mouth; the kind or amount of flavour that substances give when taken into the mouth; a small quantity of, put into the mouth; a liking for; the sense or knowledge of what is good in certain things or actions. *v.* be conscious of the taste of something; know, experience something (travel, music etc.). **tasteless** *a.* showing little taste, having no taste.

tatter (tat-ter) *n.* a rag, a piece torn off. **tattered** *a.* ragged.

tattoo (tat-too) *n.* a signal on a drum to call soldiers or sailors to retire to their quarters; coloured designs marked on the skin. *v.* prick the skin and make coloured designs on it.

taunt *n.* an insulting remark intended to hurt a person's feelings. *v.* insult in a scornful way.

taut *a.* tightly drawn, stretched, not slack.

tavern (tav-ern) *n.* a public house, an inn, a place where food and drink can be bought and consumed.

tax *n.* money paid by the people of a country towards the cost of its government, defence, health services, education etc.; a strain (on strength etc.); a burden some duty. *v.* lay a tax or burden on, make great demands on. **taxation** *n.* the act of taxing; the level of taxes, the money raised by taxes.

taxi (ta-xi) *n.* a car which one may hire to be driven from place to place (short for taxicab) *v.* move over the surface of the ground or water as an aeroplane does except when taking off or landing.

tea *n.* the dried leaves of an evergreen plant grown in Asia; the drink made by pouring boiling water on the leaves; a regular time when tea is drunk. **teatime** *n.* the time when tea often with cakes or biscuits, is regularly served.

teach *v.* give instruction. **teacher** *n.* a person who teaches or instructs. **teaching** *n.* the work of a teacher; that which is taught.

team *n.* a number of persons playing on the same side in a match; a number of persons doing something together; two or more horses or oxen drawing a cart, a plough etc. **team up** *v.* work together with others on some project. **teamwork** *n.* the combined effort of a team working well together.

tear *v.* (rhymes with *fair*) pull apart or in pieces by force; become torn; rush at great speed. *n.* a place where something has been torn, a rent.

tear *n.* (rhymes with *ear*) a drop of salty water that comes from the eyes when one weeps and sometimes laughs.

tease *v.* make fun of another person, sometimes causing annoyance; worry or annoy another person by continual interference. *n.* a person who teases others.

technical (tech-ni-cal) *a.* having to do with great skill in some industry (engineering, weaving, printing etc.). **technician** *n.* a person expert in the methods of a particular art or industry. **technique** *n.* skill, or method of doing things expertly. **technology** *n.* that branch of knowledge dealing with science and engineering, applied to industry.

tedious (te-di-ous) *a.* boring, making one weary or tired.

teem *v.* abound, contain in large numbers; be present in large numbers.

teens *n.* the period in one's life between the ages of 12 and 20.

teetotal (tee-to-tal) *a*. not drinking or agreeing with the drinking of liquids containing alcohol. **teetotaller** *n*. a person who is teetotal.

tele- a prefix meaning distant, which refers specially to sight and sound. **telegram** *n*. a communication sent by telegraph. **telegraph** *n*. a system of communication by the use of electric current along wires or by wireless. **telephone** *n*. communication with persons a long way off through an apparatus that transmits speech. *v*. use a telephone to communicate. **teleprinter** *n*. an instrument that prints messages as they come in over long distances. **telescope** *n*. an instrument with lenses that makes distant objects appear much nearer. **television** *n*. still or moving pictures transmitted over great distances.

tell *v*. give information about something; relate a story or experience; order a person to do something; distinguish between things; reveal secrets. **teller** *n*. one who tells; a person who counts votes in a meeting or in parliament. **telltale** *n*. a person who tells another person's secrets.

temper (tem-per) *n*. the state of one's mind; a state of mind shown by outbursts of anger. **temperament** *n*. the way a person thinks, feels and acts.

temperance (tem-per-ance) *n*. self-control, being moderate in all things such as eating, drinking, smoking etc.; avoiding the use of all intoxicating drinks. **temperance hotel** a hotel in which no alcoholic drinks are served. **temperate** *a*. behaving with moderation or temperance; not too hot, not too cold (of the weather or climate).

temperature (tem-per-a-ture) *n*. heat and cold as measured in degrees on a thermometer.

tempest (tem-pest) *n*. a violent storm, often with rain, hail or wind. **tempestuous** *a*. violent, stormy (of wind, weather or a person's nature).

temple (tem-ple) *n*. a building used for the worship of a god; the flat part of the

head between the ear and the forehead.

temporary (tem-po-ra-ry) *a*. lasting or intended to last only a short time.

tempt *v*. attempt to persuade a person to do evil; appeal, seem very good (to buy, eat etc.); attract a person to do something. **temptation** *n*. being tempted; something that tempts.

tenant (ten-ant) *n*. a person who pays rent for the use of a building or of land. **tenement** *n*. a house or a portion of a house rented by a tenant as a separate dwelling.

tender (ten-der) *a*. not hard, easy to chew; easily broken, soft, delicate; very young; kind, soft-hearted, easily hurt. *n*. an estimate of the amount of work to be done and its cost. *v*. offer, submit or put in such an estimate.

tendon (ten-don) *n*. the thick cord that joins a muscle to a bone in the bodies of human beings and animals.

tendril (ten-dril) *n*. a thread-like part of a plant that reaches out and twists round anything that can give the plant support.

tennis (ten-nis) *n*. a game played on a tennis court by two or four players in which they hit a ball forwards and backwards over a net with a racket.

tenor (ten-or) *n*. the third part, next to the lowest (or bass) in four-part harmony; music written for this part; a person who sings this part or within this range; the general meaning of a speech; the general course of one's life.

tense *a*. tightly drawn or stretched; in a strained state of the nerves; (of a time) when feelings run high and one is excited. *n*. that part of a verb which shows past, present or future. **tension** *n*. being tense or strained.

tent *n.* a moveable shelter of skins, coarse cloth or specially treated canvas supported by poles and held in place by ropes fastened with pegs.

tentacle (ten-ta-cle) *n.* a slender flexible boneless growth on some animals which acts as a feeler, a limb and a means of catching prey.

tepid (tep-id) *a.* moderately warm.

term *n.* a fixed period of time; the parts into which the year of a school, college etc. is divided; words expressing clear meanings in science etc. **terms** *n.* something agreed to between people; relations (good or bad) between people.

terminal (ter-mi-nal) *a.* taking place at the end of each term. *n.* the end of a railway or an air line; a place where electric points are joined. **terminate** *v.* end (an agreement, a period of work, a contract etc.). **terminus** *n.* the station at the end of a railway line, bus line etc.

terrace (ter-race) *n.* a flat piece of ground rising like a step, or with a steep slope above the lower part; a row of houses all joined together. *v.* form land into terraces for ornament or agriculture.

terrible (ter-ri-ble) *a.* causing terror; causing discomfort. **terrific** *a.* terrible, making one afraid. **terrify** *v.* fill with fear or horror. **terror** *n.* great fear.

terrier (ter-ri-er) *n.* a small active dog, once used to hunt burrowing animals such as rabbits or foxes but now mostly as a pet.

territory (ter-ri-to-ry) *n.* any area of land; an area of land occupied by a particular race or ruled by one ruler; the land occupied by a particular group of animals, birds etc.

terse *a.* brief in speech; going straight to the most important point.

test *n.* a trial for quality, speed etc.; an examination in a school or college or carried out by a doctor. **test match** one of a series of matches played at agreed times between the best teams of the cricket-playing nations.

testament (tes-ta-ment) *n.* a written statement saying what a person wishes to be done with his property after his death (see **will**); one of the two main divisions of the Bible, the Old and New Testaments.

testify (tes-ti-fy) *v.* give evidence in favour or against a person; declare some fact or other. **testimonial** *n.* a statement made in writing by one person to testify to the abilities or good qualities of another person. **testimony** *n.* a statement declaring that something is true.

tether (teth-er) *n.* a rope, chain etc. by which an animal is fastened to prevent it moving too far from a point. *v.* fasten by a tether.

text *n.* the printed part of a book, not including illustrations; a short sentence or phrase, usually out of the Bible, on which a preacher bases his sermon. **textbook** *n.* a book which gives instruction in a subject.

textile (tex-tile) *a.* having to do with the making of cloth or any material that is woven; woven (fabrics). **textiles** *n.* all kinds of woven fabrics.

than *conj.* a word used in comparison of states, actions etc.

thank *v.* say that one is grateful. **thanks** *n.* expressions saying one is grateful. **thank you** a polite expression. **thankful** *a.* grateful, expressing thanks. **thankless** *a.* showing no thanks or gratitude; bringing no reward.

that *a.* a word which points out. *pron.* a word pointing out a definite thing (not this, that); a word referring to a word used before. *conj.* a word which joins two sentences or phrases.

thatch *n.* a covering of straw, heather or other material over the roof of a house. *v.* cover a roof with such materials.

thaw *v.* (of the weather) become warm enough to melt ice and snow. *n.* a time when the ice and snow melt.

theatre (thea-tre) *n.* a place, either in a specially designed building or in the open air where plays are performed and entertainments given; a room where lectures are given; a room in which operations are performed; a place where important things happen or have happened (operations in war). **theatrical** *a.* having to do with the theatre.

theft *n.* the act of stealing; an instance of stealing.

their *a.* of them (the possessive form of the pronoun they). **theirs** *pron.* something belonging to them.

them *pron.* a word referring to things, animals or people already known. **themselves** *pron.* them, the ones already mentioned.

theology (the-ol-o-gy) *n.* the learning which deals with God and His relations with the world, and with religion.

theory (the-o-ry) *n.* the general principles in the study of any subject; a belief put forward to explain something.

therapy (ther-a-py) *n.* a kind of medical treatment (water, herbal, occupational etc.). **therapeutic** *a.* having to do with healing.

there *adv.* in, to or at a certain place; used with is, was etc. (there is, was was). **thereafter** *adv.* after that. **therefore** *adv.* because of that, as a result of that.

thermo- a prefix concerning temperature or heat. **thermometer** *n.* an instrument that measures temperature. **thermonuclear** *a.* capable of producing very high temperatures through nuclear energy. **thermos flask** a flask which will keep hot things hot and cold things cold for several hours. **thermostat** *n.* a device which will keep the temperature of a room, water-tank or oven even and unchanging.

these *a. & pron.* nearer to the speaker than others; persons or things nearer than others.

they *pron.* the plural of he, she and it; a word referring to more than one person, animal or thing.

thick *a.* some distance from side to side, from front to back, from top to bottom; having parts which are very close together (hair, fur, bristles); partly solid (mud, soup); husky, hoarse, not clear. *n.* the most crowded and active part (of the fight). **thicken** *n.* make thicker. **thicket** *n.*

a place where bushes are thick. **thickness** *n.* being thick.

thief *n.* a person who steals. **thieve** *v.* steal.

thigh *n.* the part of the leg between the hip and the knee in man.

thimble (thim-ble) *n.* a small cap, usually of metal, worn on the tip of the finger when sewing, to push the needle.

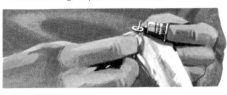

thin *a.* the opposite of thick; having edges or surfaces close together; not fat, carrying little spare flesh; not thickly packed (hair, grass); not thick, easily flowing (of liquids); not strong (voice). *v.* make or become thin.

thing *n.* an object which exists; an action one performs; clothing, equipment, especially when going out, for work, sports etc.; a subject one writes, talks about etc.

think *v.* form an idea in the mind; have an opinion about something; turn over in the mind, meditate about things; have an idea; consider something as being in a certain state etc.

thirst *n.* the feeling caused when one needs to drink; a painful sensation of dryness in the mouth; a strong desire for something (knowledge etc.). **thirsty** *a.* having a thirst.

this *adj. & pron.* a word which points out, meaning (the one) nearer to us or (the one) just mentioned.

thistle (this-tle) *n.* a wild plant with prickly leaves and purple flowers, the emblem of Scotland.

thong *n.* a narrow strip of hide or leather used to fasten things, or as the lash of a whip.

thorn *n.* a spine or prickle on a plant; one of certain trees which bear thorns. **thorny** *a.* bearing thorns; difficult to solve, causing trouble or annoyance.

thorough (thor-ough) *a.* complete; carried out in every detail. **thoroughbred** *n.* an animal of pure blood whose parents were of the same strain, not mixed with any others. **thoroughfare** *n.* a main road; a passage or way through.

those *a. & pron.* plural of that; (persons or things) farther away from the speaker than others.

though *conj.* in spite of the fact that; even if; as though; as if.

thought *n.* the act of thinking, meditation; care given to something; idea; expectation (of something happening). **thoughtful** *a.* showing thought or care. **thoughtless** *a.* showing no thought or care.

thrash *v.* beat soundly to punish; defeat completely in a match or contest; move with violence (as a fish does when hooked).

thread *n.* a very thin length of cotton, wool, silk, linen etc.; a line of thought or argument; the spiral ridge that runs round a screw helping it to grip. *v.* put thread through the eye of a needle, through beads etc.; make a way through a number of people. **threadbare** *a.* worn thin so that the threads of the cloth are plainly visible.

threat *n.* a spoken or written intention to do harm to another; a sign of future trouble (a strike, war etc.). **threaten** *v.* utter threats; warn of future trouble.

thresh *v.* separate the grain from the stalk of corn by beating it either by hand or with a machine.

threshold (thresh-old) *n.* the piece of horizontal wood lying across the bottom of a doorway; the opening, the beginning (of a new age, of discoveries etc.); the point where something begins to show (pain, etc.).

thrift *n.* care in the use of money and goods; the avoidance of waste, economy. **thrifty** *a.* economical, avoiding extravagance or waste.

thrill *n.* a sudden feeling of keen excitement. *v.* cause a thrill; feel a thrill. **thriller** *n.* a novel, play or film in which mystery and excitement are the main features.

thrive *v.* grow strong and healthy; prosper, become richer; flourish.

throat *n.* the front part of the neck; the passage through which food and air pass from the mouth to the stomach and lungs.

throb *v.* beat rapidly and with force as the heart does when a person is excited. *n.* a strong vibration as of an engine.

throne *n.* the chair on which a king, queen or other ruler sits during ceremonies; the office of a sovereign. **the Throne** the royal authority of the king or queen.

throttle *v.* hold tightly by the throat to stop a person breathing; control the flow of petrol, steam etc. to an engine by opening or closing a valve. *n.* the valve which controls the flow of fuel to an engine.

through *prep.* in at one end, side or surface and out at the other; past; between or among; during the whole period of (the night etc.); by means of (perseverance, fear). *adv.* all the way, the whole distance; from end to end (reading). **throughout** *adv.* completely; everywhere; in every part of.

throw *v.* hurl, make a thing go through the air either by a quick movement of the arm or by a machine; put on (a garment) quickly; make a rider fall to the ground. *n.* the act of throwing.

thrush *n.* a bird, common in Britain, which sings sweetly; a disease, mainly affecting children, in which small whitish spots appear in the mouth.

thrust *v.* push hard, drive with force; push one's way; stab or pierce with a sword. *n.* the act of thrusting; a stab at something.

thud *n.* a sudden dull sound as of a heavy blow or fall. *v.* beat or strike with a dull sound.

thumb *n.* the short thick inner finger of the human hand, next to the first or index finger; the place for the thumb in a glove. *v.* turn over with the thumb, often quickly, without reading everything.

thump *v.* strike or beat with the fist or

something heavy. *n.* a blow with something thick and heavy, producing a dull sound.

thunder (thun-der) *n.* the loud noise that comes with a flash of lightning due to a discharge of electricity in the air; a noise that sounds like thunder. *v.* make thunder; make a noise like thunder; shout with a loud voice, attack a person or persons in loud tones. **thunderstorm** *n.* a storm in which there is thunder and lightning.

thus *adv.* in this way; in the way just indicated.

tick *n.* a light sharp clicking like that made by a clock; a tiny mark put at the end of an exercise and against figures and names when they are checked; a small bloodsucking insect that buries itself in the skin of certain animals; the cloth case of a mattress, pillow etc. containing hair, feathers etc. *v.* make a ticking sound; make a tick in writing.

ticket (tick-et) *n.* a small piece of paper or card showing that one has paid the fare on a bus, train etc., or been given admission to a theatre, cinema or other public building; a label attached to goods to show their price. *v.* mark with a ticket.

tickle (tick-le) *v.* touch or stroke with the fingers to create a tingling feeling on the skin; please, delight somebody. *n.* a tickling feeling. **ticklish** *a.* easily made to laugh and squirm when tickled; puzzling, difficult, needing careful thought (of a problem).

tide *n.* the regular rise and fall of the sea on the coasts; the rise and fall of one's luck, fortunes, people's opinions etc. **tidal** *a.* having to do with the tides. **tidal wave** a large, destructive wave produced by an earthquake or some great disturbance of the forces of nature.

tidings (ti-dings) *n.* news, information, intelligence.

tidy (ti-dy) *a.* in good order; having orderly habits. *v.* make tidy, put in good order.

tie *v.* fasten by means of rope etc.; make the same score as another in a game. *n.* something that ties (friendship, family ties etc.); a band worn round the neck under a collar, and tied in front; something that prevents one from doing all one would like to do; a result in which

two teams or competitors finish equal; a curved line joining two notes of music that are to be played or sung without a break.

tier *n.* (rhymes with *fear*) one of a number of rows of seats rising one above the other so that spectators can see well.

tiff *n.* a slight quarrel; a fit of bad temper or humour.

tiger (ti-ger) *n.* a large fierce animal of the cat family living in Asia. **tigress** *n.* a female tiger.

tight *a.* fastened, close-fitting; stretched; firm, difficult to undo; closely-packed, full. **tighten** *v.* make or become tighter. **tights** *n.* a close-fitting garment covering the body from the waist downwards, and the legs.

tile *n.* a thin slab or plate of baked clay used for covering roofs, lining walls, paving etc. *v.* put tiles in place.

till *prep. & conj.* up to the time of. *n.* a drawer in a shop in which money is kept. *v.* cultivate land. **tiller** *n.* a person who tills the soil; a lever fitted to the top side of a rudder for steering a boat.

timber (tim-ber) *n.* wood ready for use in building; trees which are growing to provide timber; the large pieces of timber already built into houses, ships etc.

time *n.* the passing of seconds, minutes, hours, days, months, years etc.; a measured period of time; a point or moment in time; an occasion, a repeated happening; a word which indicates multiplication; a way in which one feels or has felt (a good time etc.); a way of measuring time (summertime); a measurement of time in music. *v.* measure the time taken to do something; fix a time for. **time bomb** a bomb set to explode at a certain time. **time-table** *n.* a list showing on what day and at what time certain things are to happen.

timid (tim-id) *a.* easily alarmed, shy, quick to take fright. **timidity** *n.* the state of being timid.

tin *n.* a shiny white metal which looks like silver, used in plating other metals, especially in the making of cans for preserving food. **tin foil** very thin sheets of tin used in wrapping tobacco, sweets or for use in cookery.

tinder (tin-der) *n.* soft material that easily catches fire from a spark. **tinderbox** *n.* a box containing flint, steel and tinder, used for making fire.

tinge *v.* give a slight touch of colour to; add a slight amount of (pleasure, envy etc.). *n.*-a slight amount or degree.

tingle (tin-gle) *v.* have a feeling of slight stings or prickly pains from cold, a sting or a blow. *n.* a tingling feeling.

tinker (tin-ker) *n.* a person who journeys from place to place mending kettles, pots and pans. *v.* try to mend; play with something that is not working properly.

tinkle (tin-kle) *v.* make a number of short ringing sounds. *n.* a short ringing sound.

tinsel (tin-sel) *n.* cheap material made of metal cut out in thin strips to give a sparkling effect.

tint *n.* a pale colour; a dye for the hair. *v.* give a pale colour to, colour lightly; apply a tint to the hair.

tiny (ti-ny) *a.* very small, minute.

tip *n.* the thin pointed end of; a small piece added to the end of something (a walking stick, billiard cue etc.); a small present of money given in return for service; a useful piece of information. *v.* make something slant, set it on one end, turn it upside down; empty out of a vessel; strike with a sharp light blow; give a tip or tips to (a waiter etc.); warn of some coming danger or crisis. **tip-off** *n.* a piece of secret information, a warning. **tip-toe** *a.* on the tips of the toes. *v.* walk in this way.

tire *v.* make weary; exhaust the patience of a person; become weary or fatigued. **tired** *a.* exhausted, weary in body and mind; bored. **tireless** *a.* untiring, never tired. **tiresome** *a.* boring (of a person, speech etc.); annoying.

tissue (tis-sue) *n.* part of the material of which an animal or plant is made; a very light woven fabric; a paper handkerchief; a number, a mass (of lies, rumours etc.). **tissue paper** very thin paper used for wrapping delicate articles.

title (ti-tle) *n.* the name of a book, play, picture, piece of music etc.; a special name to show one's occupation, rank etc (Mr, Dr, Sir, Lord); the right to possess o to succeed to money or property; the championship in some sport.

toad *n.* an animal that looks like a frog and which lives mainly on land. **toadstool** *n.* an umbrella-shaped fungus looking like a mushroom, which can be poisonous.

toast *v.* make brown and crisp by heating in front of a fire or under a grill; make a speech and drink to the health or in honour of. *n.* bread in slices made brown and crisp by toasting on both sides.

tobacco (to-bac-co) *n.* a plant with large leaves which are dried and used for smoking; the leaves so prepared. **tobacconist** *n.* a person who sells tobacco for smoking, pipes, cigarettes, snuff etc.

toboggan (to-bog-gan) *n.* a long narrow light sledge curved upwards and backwards at the front, used originally for transport over snow but now mainly for sport. *v.* use a toboggan or take part in sport using a toboggan.

today (to-day) *n.* this present day. *adv.* on this present day; at the present time, in these days.

toe *n.* one of the five divisions of the front part of the foot; that part of the sock, stocking or boot that covers the toes. *v.* put a toe on (a sock etc.); kick with the toe.

toffee (tof-fee) *n.* a sweet made with sugar or treacle boiled with butter, sometimes with nuts etc. **toffee-apple** *n.* an apple coated with toffee, held on a small stick.

together (to-geth-er) *adv.* in each other's company; with each other (of things); at the same time; without interruption (hours, days); taking part in the same activity or action.

toil *n.* hard and continuous work needing labour and effort. *v.* work, move or travel with difficulty, weariness or pain.

toilet (toil-et) *n.* the act or process of dressing including bathing, arranging the hair etc.; the articles used for this purpose; a lavatory, bathroom, dressing-room etc.

token (to-ken) *n.* a sign, symbol, something representing some fact, feeling etc. (of mourning, consent); something used instead of money; something not done seriously but as a gesture (resistance etc.).

tolerate (tol-er-ate) *v.* endure without resisting or speaking; endure or resist the action of a drug, poison etc. **tolerant** *a.* disposed to tolerate actions etc. of others. **tolerance** *n.* the act or power to tolerate.

toll *n.* the payment required to pass over a road, bridge etc.; payment taken; sacrifice; tax. *v.* cause a large bell to ring slowly and regularly for summoning people to church or for announcing a death.

tomahawk (tom-a-hawk) *n.* a light axe used by the North American Indians as a weapon and tool.

tomato (to-ma-to) *n.* a soft red or yellow fruit with a juicy centre and many seeds, eaten with meat and in salads; the plant bearing the tomato.

tomb *n.* a place dug out of the earth or cut out of a rock, into which a dead body is put. **tombstone** *n.* a stone raised as a memorial over a grave or tomb, which usually bears an inscription.

tomboy (tom-boy) *n.* a girl who likes to play rough, noisy games.

tomorrow (to-mor-row) *n.* the day after this day. *adv.* on the day after this day.

ton *n.* a measure of weight equal, in Great Britain, to 2,240 pounds (about 1,016 kilos); also **tonne** *n.* the metric ton equal to 1,000 kilos.

tone *n.* a sound; the spirit, character of a group of people; the amount of light or shade in a colour; the interval between certain notes of music. *v.* give a certain sound or colour to a thing; give health and vigour to a person. **tonic** *n.* a medicine that gives strength; the keynote of a musical scale.

tongs *n.* a tool consisting of two arms hinged at a point and used for seizing, holding or lifting things.

tongue *n.* in man and many other animals, an organ in the mouth which can move, and which is the chief means of taste, and in man alone, of speech; a language; an animal's tongue used as food; something like a tongue (of a shoe, of flame etc.).

tonight (to-night) *n.* the night after this day. *adv.* on the night after this day.

tonsil (ton-sil) *n.* one of the two oval masses of tissue at the back of the throat. **tonsillitis** *n.* inflammation of the tonsil or tonsils.

too *adv.* in addition, also, as well; beyond what is desired (high, dear, cheap etc.) or allowed.

tool *n.* an instrument held in the hand in order to do certain work; a machine which does the work of a tool; a person who is used by another person for his own benefit. *v.* to work with a tool for ornament (on leather, metal etc.).

toot *n.* a short sharp sound as from a whistle or a horn. *v.* give such a sound.

tooth *n.* one of the hard white structures attached to the upper and lower jaws, used for chewing and biting food; a hard spike sticking out in a rake, comb, saw etc.

top *n.* the highest point or summit; the upper part or surface; the part which is higher than another (of the street); the part of a plant above the ground (turnip, carrot etc.); a toy with a pointed tip on which it can be made to spin. *v.* reach the top; go over the top; put a top on; take the top off. *a.* at the top; higher than others (shelf); foremost, principal (place).

topic (top-ic) *n.* something talked about, a subject for discussion or of a speech. **topical** *a.* having to do with the topics of the day.

topple (top-ple) *v.* fall forwards through having too heavy a top; turn upside down, make something topple.

topsy-turvy (top-sy-tur-vy) *a.* with the

top where the bottom should be; upside-down; in complete confusion.

torch *n.* a light made with wood soaked in oil or tallow to make it burn brightly; an electric light which can be carried in the hand. **torchlight** *n.* the light of torches.

torment (tor-ment) *v.* give great physical or mental suffering to; worry, annoy, pester. *n.* a state of great agony, suffering or misery; a source of pain, agony or misery.

tornado (tor-na-do) *n.* a violent whirl-wind in which winds rush round a centre carrying homes and everything else before them.

torpedo (tor-pe-do) *n.* a large metal shell shaped like a cigar which after being fired will propel itself towards a target. *v.* attack, damage or destroy with one or more torpedoes.

torpid (tor-pid) *a.* inactive, sluggish, dull, slow. **torpor** *n.* sluggish inactivity, slowness.

torrent (tor-rent) *n.* a river or stream rushing violently downhill; a violent downpour of rain; an overwhelming flow (of lava, of abuse, of laughter etc.).

torrid (tor-rid) *a.* (of the climate) very hot.

tortoise (tor-toise) *n.* a four-legged reptile which has a hard shell on its back. Some live on land, others swim in water

torture (tor-ture) *v.* cause severe physical or mental suffering. *n.* the act of causing such suffering; the suffering caused; the cause of such suffering.

toss *v.* throw up into the air; move up and down or from side to side; throw from one person to another. *n.* a tossing movement, the act of tossing.

tot *n.* a very small child; a small portion of drink. *v.* add up.

total (to-tal) *a.* complete (success, failure etc.). *n.* the total amount or number; the whole. *v.* find the total, add up; amount to, reach a total of.

totem (to-tem) *n.* an object in nature, often an animal, considered as an emblem of a family or a related group of people, made by American Indians and set up on a totem pole for all to see.

totter (tot-ter) *v.* walk with unsteady steps, swaying and rocking; sway and rock as if about to fall.

touch *v.* bring a part of the body into contact with another object so as to be able to feel it; be in contact (of objects); strike or press lightly; cause feelings of sorrow, sadness, pity, gratitude etc. *n.* one of the five senses; a stroke of a brush or pencil to finish a picture; the final stage of making a plan or doing a task; a small amount; a slight attack (cold, rheumatism etc.). **touchy** *a.* quickly and easily offended. **in touch** in communication. **touchdown** *n.* the act of a player in rugby football touching the ball to the ground behind the opponent's goal.

tough *a.* not easily cut or broken; strong, hard-wearing; difficult, unpleasant (of problems or tasks); severe; violent; disorderly. **toughen** *v.* make tough, become tough

tour *n.* a journey beginning and ending at home, visiting many places in succession; a period of duty at one place (chiefly military); a round of inspection. *v.* travel from place to place. **tourism** *n.* organized touring. **tourist** *n.* a person making a tour, especially for pleasure. **tourist agency** a business company which arranges tours.

tournament (tour-na-ment) *n.* a trial of skill in a game in which competitors play a series of contests; in the Middle Ages, a contest between armed knights on horseback.

tourniquet (tour-ni-quet) *n.* a device

usually made with a bandage for stopping the flow of blood from an artery by tightening and twisting round the affected limb.

tout *n.* a person who harasses and worries people to buy things, sells information about racehorses etc. *v.* worry people to get business, votes etc.; sell information, obtain information etc. for purposes of betting.

tow *v.* drag or pull by means of a rope or chain. *v.* the act of towing, the state of being towed; broken fibres of material used for making rope, for cleaning oily machinery etc. **towrope** *n.* the rope used for towing.

towards (to-wards) *prep.* in the direction of; concerning, about (a person, enemy etc.); as a help to (raising money, getting well etc.).

towel (tow-el) *n.* a cloth for wiping or drying something wet. *v.* rub well with a rough towel. **towelling** *n.* material out of which towels are made.

towel-rail *n.* a rail over which a towel is placed.

tower (tow-er) *n.* a very high building either standing alone or as part of a collection of buildings; such a structure used as a fortress or prison. *v.* be higher than; rise up. **tower over** *v.* surpass in ability, strength etc. another or others. **tower of strength** a person who helps or supports another.

town *n.* an area, inhabited and larger than a village but smaller and less important than a city; the people living in a town.

toxic (tox-ic) *a.* caused by a poison, poisonous. **toxin** *n.* a poison, especially one caused by bacteria growing in plants or animals.

toy *n.* a child's plaything. *a.* made as a toy; very small (of a dog). *v.* play with; handle something fondly.

trace *v.* make a plan, diagram or map; copy by drawing over transparent paper; print in a curved, broken manner as if with difficulty; follow (footprints, marks etc.). *n.* a mark showing that somebody or something has been at a place or that something has happened there; a very small amount left behind. **tracer** *n.* (bullet or shell) a missile which when fired leaves a line of flame or smoke behind it. **tracing** *n.* a drawing made by the process of tracing, with tracing paper.

track *n.* a mark or marks left by a vehicle, a human being or an animal; a rough roadway made by the passing of many feet or wheels; the rails, sleepers etc. on which a railway runs; a course laid out for running or racing. *v.* follow tracks. *a.* having to do with a track (track events in sport). **tracker** *n.* a person who follows the tracks of wild animals.

tract *n.* a stretch of land; a group of organs in the body (nerves, digestive organs etc.); a pamphlet, usually on religion, printed and distributed in large numbers.

traction (trac-tion) *n.* the act of drawing or pulling; the power to pull loads. **traction engine** a heavy steam engine on wheels, once used for rolling the surfaces of roads and for pulling heavy loads. **tractor** *n.* a powerful motor vehicle used for doing work, mainly on farms.

trade *n.* buying, selling and exchanging goods between individual people and countries; a way of making a living; people in certain businesses (the trade); *v.* carry on trade; exchange things. **trade in** give up an article plus a certain amount of money in exchange for another one of the same kind. **trademark** *n.* a symbol shown on goods to distinguish one maker's goods from those of another. **tradesman** *n.* a person who keeps a shop or delivers goods.

tradition (tra-di-tion) *n.* the handing down of customs, beliefs, legends etc. from one generation to another; beliefs etc. handed down by tradition. **traditional** *a.* in agreement with tradition; handed down by tradition.

traffic (traf-fic) *n.* the coming and going of persons, vehicles, ships etc. along an agreed way of travel; the business done by a railway, an airline etc.; trading (liquor, drugs etc.). *v.* trade; carry on trade.

tragedy (trag-e-dy) *n.* a play with an unhappy ending; an unhappy event, possibly ending in death or disaster. **tragic** *a.* having to do with tragedy.

trail *n.* a stream of dust, smoke, people etc. behind something moving; a line, mark or scent left by an animal or a person; a path or track worn across a wild region. *v.* drag or be dragged along; set something trailing or floating after itself as it moves (dust etc.); grow along the ground and over walls etc. (of plants). **trailer** *n.* a vehicle trailed along behind another; a few short extracts from a film shown in order to advertise it in advance.

train *n.* a set of carriages or wagons connected to a locomotive; a number of persons, vehicles etc. travelling together; a series (of events); part of a long dress that trails on the ground. *v.* teach; bring up (a child or an animal); make grow in the required direction; aim (a gun). **trainer** *n.* a person who trains people or animals; an aeroplane used for training pilots. **training** *n.* fitness, physical or mental, achieved by instruction and constant practice.

traitor (trai-tor) *n.* a person who betrays his friend, his group of people, his organization or his country.

tram *n.* an electric car running along a street; **tramcar** *n.* a tram specially made to carry people as passengers. **tramlines** *n.* the lines on which trams run.

tramp *v.* tread or walk heavily; go on foot. *n.* the act of tramping; the sound of a heavy tread; a person who goes from place to place doing odd jobs and having no regular work.

trample (tram-ple) *v.* tread heavily, destroying or damaging as one goes; tread harshly, show no consideration for (feelings etc.).

tranquil (tran-quil) *a.* quiet, calm. **tranquillity** *n.* the state of being tranquil; calmness.

trans- a prefix meaning across or from one to another, which is used with many words. **transaction** *n.* business taking place between people. **transcribe** *v.* copy writing. **transcription** *n.* copying, sometimes from shorthand notes. **transfer** (trans-fér) *v.* change jobs or property. **transfer** (tráns-fer) *n.* an example of transferring. **transfix** *v.* pierce through. **transform** *v.* change into another shape or kind. **transfusion** *n.* taking blood from one person and injecting it into another. **transgress** *v.* break a law or a commandment. **transgression** *n.* the act of transgressing. **transistor** *n.* a device which replaces the valve in radio sets, hearing aids and other equipment of the same kind. **transit** *n.* taking or being taken from one place to another. **transition** *n.* a change from one condition to another. **translate** *v.* put into another language. **transmit** *v.* send, allow to pass through (a message etc.). **transparent** *a.* capable of being seen through. **transplant** *v.* plant in another place. **transport** (trans-pórt) *v.* carry to another place. **transport** (tráns-port) *n.* the means of carrying to other places.

trap *n.* a device for catching animals; a trick or plan to deceive people; a small carriage pulled by a pony. **trapdoor** *n.* a door in the floor, a ceiling or a roof, which can be lifted up.

trapeze (tra-peze) *n.* a swing consisting of a short horizontal bar attached to the ends of two suspended ropes, used for gymnastic exercises and in circuses.

rash *n.* anything worthless or useless; foolish talk, nonsense.

ravel (trav-el) *v.* go from place to place, make a journey for pleasure or on business. *n.* the act of travelling, especially to and from distant places.

raverse (trav-erse) *v.* pass across, over or through. *n.* the act of passing.

ray *n.* a flat, shallow piece of wood, plastic or metal with raised edges used for carrying things; a tray and what is in or on it.

reacherous (treach-er-ous) *a.* disloyal to a friend, deceitful; not firm or secure (of paths etc.). **treachery** *n.* betrayal of trust, disloyalty.

reacle (trea-cle) *n.* a dark, sticky, sweet liquid obtained in the refining of sugar.

read *v.* step, walk; trample, crush. *n.* the sound of walking; part of a stair on which the foot is placed; the part of a tyre which is in contact with the ground. **treadle** *n.* a lever worked by the foot to make a machine move. **treadmill** *n.* a device consisting of a wheel which moves round and often supplies power through a person or animal walking on its steps or treads.

reason (trea-son) *n.* the betrayal by a person of his country.

reasure (treas-ure) *n.* valuables (gold, silver, jewels etc.); something which is greatly valued. *v.* value highly; put away or keep in store for future use. **treasurer** *n.* the person who looks after the money of a company or a society. **The Treasury** the department of government which looks after the finances of the country. **treasury** *n.* a book containing valuable information or literary extracts.

reat *v.* behave towards; consider; give medical aid to; pay for food, drink etc. for a person; deal with a subject in speech or writing. *n.* anything that gives pleasure or enjoyment. **treatment** *n.* the way of treating or being treated. **treatise** *n.* a book or something written treating of some particular subject. **treaty** *n.* an agreement made between nations.

reble (tre-ble) *a.* highest part in music, soprano; three times as much. *n.* a person who sings or plays the highest part in music. *v.* make or become three times as much or as many.

tree *n.* a large perennial plant with a thick stem or trunk, and branches from which grow twigs and leaves; a piece of wood for a special purpose as holding up a roof or keeping a shoe in shape. **treeless** *a.* with no trees.

trek *n.* a long journey made by ox-wagon (in South Africa); a journey, especially a difficult one. *v.* travel by ox-wagon (in South Africa); make a long, difficult journey.

trellis (trel-lis) *n.* a frame made of light pieces of wood crossing each other. *v.* train or support (a plant etc.) on a trellis.

tremble (trem-ble) *v.* shake from a feeling of fright, cold etc.; (of things) shake lightly; (of the voice) shake. *n.* the act of trembling; a fit of trembling.

tremendous (tre-men-dous) *a.* very great, dreadful, awful.

trench *n.* a ditch, usually dug by man for protection, drainage etc. **trenches** *n.* the front line of battle in the first World War.

trend *n.* the general course of events; fashion.

trespass (tres-pass) *v.* go on another person's land without permission; take up other people's time. *n.* the entry on other people's land etc.; an offence, sin or wrong.

trestle (tres-tle) *n.* a frame consisting of a horizontal bar on two pairs of spreading legs. **trestle bridge** a bridge resting on a framework made in trestle fashion.

trial (tri-al) *n.* a thing or an experience that annoys or tests; an attempt to do something; the examination of a person before a court of law to determine innocence or guilt. *a.* having to do with a trial, done by way of trial, to test a thing.

triangle (tri-an-gle) *n.* a flat figure with three sides and with three angles; a musical instrument made from a tri-angular steel rod which produces a light, ringing sound. **triangular** a. in the shape of a triangle.

tribe n. a group of the same race, with the same language and customs. **tribal** a. having to do with a tribe or tribes.

tribunal (tri-bun-al) n. a group of people acting as judges in order to hear appeals against such things as high rents, unjust prison sentences etc.

tribute (trib-ute) n. a payment demanded regularly by a ruler or a conqueror from those he rules or has conquered; something done or said to show respect or to honour another person. **tributary** a. (of a state) paying tribute to a more powerful one. n. a small stream flowing into a larger one.

trick n. something done to deceive; a mischievous act; a clever act, a feat of skill; one round of a card game. v. deceive. **trickery** n. the practice of deceiving, doing tricks. **tricky** a. likely to deceive; needing skill.

trickle (trick-le) v. flow or fall in drops or in a small stream. n. a thin flow or stream; a quantity of anything (money etc.) received in small amounts.

tricycle (tri-cy-cle) n. a cycle with three wheels, one in front and the other two behind, one on each side.

trifle (tri-fle) n. something of little importance or value; a small sum of money; a dish consisting of sponge cake soaked in wine, covered with cream, custard, jam etc. v. not treat seriously; amuse oneself, play with; waste time.

trigger (trig-ger) n. a lever on a rifle, gun or pistol by which it is fired. **trigger off** v. start something, start a chain of events.

trigonometry (trig-o-nom-e-try) n. that branch of mathematics that deals with the relations between the sides and angles of triangles.

trill n. a sound made by the voice or a instrument which shakes between tw notes. v. (of birds, the human voice etc. make such a sound.

trim a. tidy, neat. v. make neat; remove b clipping etc.; deck with ornaments, de corate. n. proper condition or order. **trim ming** n. things used for decoration.

trinity (tri-ni-ty) n. a group of three Trinity (in Christianity) Three Persons i one God-Father, Son and Holy Ghost.

trinket (trin-ket) n. a small jewel or orna ment, usually of little value.

trio (tri-o) n. a group of three persons c things; a musical composition to b played or sung by a group of three.

trip v. step lightly or nimbly; stumble make somebody stumble; cause a perso to make a mistake or say something h had not intended to say. n. a journey fo pleasure or business; a sudden stumble slip, mistake or error.

triple (tri-ple) a. made up of three parts three times as great. v. make three times as great. n. an amount etc. three times a great. **triplet** n. one of three children bor to the same mother at the same time **triplicate** a. of which three are alike. n one of three things which are alike.

tripod n. a stool with three legs; a three legged support for a camera.

triumph (tri-umph) n. victory; the rejoic ing at the winning of a victory. v. win victory. **triumphant** a. rejoicing at having triumphed.

trivial (triv-i-al) a. not important; or dinary.

trolley (trol-ley) n. a small cart with two or four wheels which is pushed by hand a small table for use in the home which runs on tiny wheels, one on the end o each leg; the wheel of a tramcar or bu which connects it to an overhead electri cable. **trolleybus** n. a bus, not running or rails, which takes power from an overhead cable.

trombone (trom-bonè) *n.* a large wind instrument consisting of a curved brass tube widening into a bell, which produces notes by sliding one part of the tube in and out of the other.

troop *n.* a company of cavalry; a company of boy scouts; a group of children, people, animals etc. on the move. *v.* gather in a company; come or go together. **trooper** *n.* a soldier in a cavalry regiment. **trooping the colour** the ceremony of carrying the flag or colours before troops.

trophy (tro-phy) *n.* something kept in memory of a victory or success, in war, hunting or sport etc.; a prize.

tropic (tro-pic) *n.* a line of latitude just over $23\frac{1}{2}$ degrees south of the equator (tropic of Capricorn) or just over $23\frac{1}{2}$ degrees north of the equator (tropic of Cancer). **tropical** *a.* having to do with the tropics, coming from the tropics. **the tropics** that part of the world lying between these two lines.

trot *n.* a pace faster than a walk but slower than a run. *v.* go, ride, lead a horse etc. at a trot.

trouble (trou-ble) *v.* bring about worry, anxiety, discomfort; take pains, face inconvenience, to do something. *n.* worry, anxiety; something causing work, discomfort, inconvenience; disturbance, unrest; illness (heart, kidney etc.). **troublesome** *a.* causing trouble; difficult.

trough *n.* (pronounced *troff*) a long open box out of which animals feed; a hollow between waves; an area of low pressure in the atmosphere.

trousers (trou-sers) *n.* an outer garment covering the lower part of the body and each leg separately.

trousseau (trou-sseau) *n.* (pronounced *trooso*) a set of clothes, linen etc. which a bride brings with her at marriage.

trout *n.* a freshwater fish which is caught by rod and line for sport and for food.

trowel (trow-el) *n.* a tool with a flat blade for applying cement, plaster etc.; a tool with a curved blade used in the garden.

truant (tru-ant) *n.* a girl or boy who stays away from school without the consent or knowledge of his teacher or parents. **truancy** *n.* playing truant.

truce *n.* a short pause in fighting by agreement on both sides; the agreement making this truce.

truck *n.* a small barrow on two wheels used by a railway porter; an open railway carriage used for carrying heavy goods.

trudge *v.* walk wearily (along or over).

true *a.* not lying or fiction; loyal, faithful; exact, accurate; rightful (king, heir etc.). *n.* the exact or right position. **truly** *adv.* truthfully, sincerely, really.

trumpet (trum-pet) *n.* any of a family of musical instruments of brass consisting of a tube curved round upon itself. *v.* make known everywhere; make a sound like that of a trumpet (of elephants).

trunk *n.* the main stem of a tree; the body of a person or animal without the head or limbs; a large box for holding clothes and other articles; an elephant's nose or snout. **trunks** *n.* short garments stretching from hip to thigh and worn for running, swimming etc. **trunk call** a telephone call to a distant place. **trunk road** a main road used chiefly by long-distance traffic.

truss *n.* a bundle, a pack (hay, straw etc.); a cluster of flowers growing on one stalk. *v.* tie up, bind, fasten; fasten with skewers (fowls made ready for cooking).

trust *n.* faith, belief in the goodness, justice etc. of somebody; responsibility put on a person; a large commercial concern made up of many companies. *v.* have faith, believe in; hope. **trustworthy** *a.* worthy of being trusted. **trusty** *a.* an old-fashioned way of saying trustworthy. *n.* a convict who has been given special privileges because of being trusted.

try *v.* attempt to do something; test for a result; bring a case into a court of law. *n.* an attempt; a score of three points in Rugby football, earned by putting the ball down behind the opponent's touchline. **trying** *a.* annoying, irritating. **try on** test a garment on one's person for size. **try out** use or experiment with a thing to test it.

tub *n.* a broad, round, wooden open vessel used for holding rainwater, or for washing clothes etc.; a vessel for bathing in, a bathtub; as much as a tub holds.

tube *n.* a hollow cylinder of metal, glass, rubber etc. for holding or taking liquids from one place to another; a small metal container with a screw top for holding things that can be squeezed out, such as paint, toothpaste, mustard etc.; an underground railway. **tubing** *n.* material of rubber or plastic which can be cut into tubes for various purposes.

tuber (tu-ber) *n.* a thick underground stem or shoot from which new plants will grow.

tuberculosis (tu-ber-cu-lo-sis) *n.* an infectious disease which may affect any part of the body, but which mostly affects the lungs.

tuck *n.* a fold in material, stitched down, either to make the material shorter or for ornament. *v.* thrust into some small place (a pocket etc.); fold in, draw up in folds; make tucks.

tuft *n.* a bunch of feathers, hairs, grass, flowers, leaves etc. held at the base.

tug *v.* pull with force; drag, haul; tow (a vessel). *n.* the act of tugging; a hard pull; a small boat used to tug other boats. **tug-of-war** *n.* a contest in which two teams pull against each other on a rope.

tuition (tu-i-tion) *n.* teaching in some subject.

tulip (tu-lip) *n.* a bell-shaped plant which grows on a tall stem from a bulb and flowers in spring.

tumble (tum-ble) *v.* fall; roll about; perform acrobatic tricks; move or toss about, putting things in disorder; make fall. *n.* the act of tumbling, a fall. **tumbler** *n.* a flat-bottomed drinking-glass with no stem; an acrobat.

tumour (tu-mour) *n.* a diseased growth or swelling in some part of the body.

tumult (tu-mult) *n.* the uproar or disturb-ance made by a crowd; a confused state of mind. **tumultuous** *a.* noisy; in a tumult.

tuna (tu-na) *n.* a large fish from the ocean whose flesh is used for food.

tune *n.* a series of notes following each other and forming a melody; agreement in pitch or harmony. *v.* put the strings of a musical instrument in tune; adjust the various parts of a machine or engine. **tuner** *n.* a person who tunes musical instruments.

tunic (tu-nic) *n.* a coat or jacket worn as a part of a military uniform; a loose sleeveless dress worn by a girl or woman, gathered at the waist by a belt.

tunnel (tun-nel) *n.* an underground passage. *v.* make an underground passage.

turban (tur-ban) *n.* a man's headdress made by winding a length of cloth round the head; a similar headdress worn as a hat by women.

turbulent (tur-bu-lent) *a.* violent, tumultuous. **turbulence** *n.* being turbulent.

tureen (tu-reen) *n.* a large deep dish with a cover for holding soup, vegetables etc. at table.

turf *n.* the covering of grass with its matted roots on a field, lawn etc. *v.* lay turf on land. **the turf** a racecourse; the pastime, occupation etc. of racing horses. **turf accountant** a person who has an office for taking bets on horseracing.

turkey (tur-key) *n.* a large domesticated bird; the flesh of the turkey.

turmoil (tur-moil) *n.* disturbance, trouble, confusion.

turn *v.* face a different way; go round; change in condition; move round; make go. *n.* the action of turning; a change of direction or in condition; a chance to do something; one short performance on the stage. **turnstile** *n.* a gate with bars at the top which turn and let a person through, once admission has been paid.

turnip (tur-nip) *n.* a plant with a thick fleshy root which is eaten as a vegetable and given as food to cattle.

urpentine (tur-pen-tine) *n.* an oily substance which comes from cone-bearing trees and which is used for mixing paints, removing stains etc.

urquoise (tur-quoise) *n.* a greenish-blue precious stone; the colour of the turquoise.

urtle (tur-tle) *n.* a large marine reptile whose soft body is protected by a shell like that of a tortoise.

usk *n.* a long pointed tooth, grown as one of a pair on elephants, walruses, wild boar etc.

ussle (tus-sle) *v.* struggle. *n.* a short period when one struggles or wrestles.

utor (tu-tor) *n.* a person who instructs another in some branch of learning. *v.* teach another person privately.

weed *n.* a coarse woollen cloth often woven with threads of different colours, either by hand in Scotland or by machine elsewhere. *a.* (of articles) made from this cloth. tweeds *n.* a suit of clothes made of tweed.

weezers (tweez-ers) *n.* very small pincers or tongs for picking up small objects, pulling out hairs etc.

wig *n.* a small shoot from the branch or stem of a tree.

wilight (twi-light) *n.* the light in the sky just before the sun rises and just after it sets.

win *n.* one of two children or animals born to the same mother at the same time; one of a set of two articles.

wine *n.* string or cord. *v.* wind or twist (of plants); form by twisting.

winge *n.* a sudden sharp pain; a sudden unexpected feeling (sadness, regret etc.).

winkle (twin-kle) *v.* shine with quick, flickering gleams of light as a star does; be bright with amusement or pleasure (of a person). *n.* a twinkling light; a sparkle in the eyes.

wirl *v.* turn or make turn round and round; spin, whirl.

wist *v.* turn or wind a number of strands, threads etc., one around the other; turn one end or part of some thing off or on; move, making a spiral shape (smoke); turn, curve (a road etc.); change position, move restlessly. *n.* a sudden jerk; something made by twisting; the direction given to a ball.

twitch *v.* give a sudden sharp jerk or movement (of the face etc.). *n.* a sudden quick jerk or pull. twitch-grass *n.* a kind of coarse grass that grows as a weed in gardens.

twitter (twit-ter) *v.* chirp. *n.* the sound of birds chirping; the sound of excited voices.

two-way *a.* having traffic going in two directions in one street. two-way street a street of this kind. two-way stretch elastic material which stretches both ways. two-way switch an arrangement by which electric current can be switched on or off at two points.

tycoon (ty-coon) *n.* a businessman having great wealth and power.

type *n.* a kind or sort; blocks of metal with letters on them used for printing; a kind or size of printing. *v.* use a typewriter. typewriter *n.* a machine on which, by pressing keys, one can print letters on paper. typist *n.* a person who is employed to type.

typhoid (ty-phoid) *n.* an infectious, often fatal fever causing inflammation of the intestines and often due to eating and drinking impure food and drink.

typhoon (ty-phoon) *n.* a violent storm or hurricane with fierce winds, occurring mostly in India and the western Pacific.

typical *a.* serving as a type or example of others of the same kind.

tyrant (ty-rant) *n.* a king or ruler especially one who has obtained absolute power by force or who uses his power oppressively or unjustly. tyrannical *a.* of or like a tyrant. tyranny *n.* the cruel or unjust use of power.

tyre *n.* a band of metal or rubber fitted on to the rim of a wheel to make a good running surface.

U

ugly (ug-ly) *a.* not pleasing in looks; disagreeable, threatening danger or difficulty.

ukulele (u-ku-le-le) *n.* a small musical instrument with four strings resembling a guitar, much used in Hawaii.

ulcer (ul-cer) *n.* an open sore either on the outside or inside of the body which discharges poisonous matter. **ulcerated** *a.* having formed an ulcer or ulcers.

ultimate (ul-ti-mate) *a.* the last, the final; the one beyond which it is impossible to go. **ultimatum** *n.* a list of demands sent by one party to another with notice that if they are not met within a fixed time measures will follow to enforce them; a statement of conditions.

ultra- (ul-tra-) a prefix meaning going beyond what is normal. **ultramarine** *a.* of a brilliant pure blue colour. *n.* a pigment of this colour. **ultraviolet** *a.* beyond the violet; belonging to that part of the spectrum which the eye cannot see, and the rays of which are used in treating skin diseases.

umbrella (um-brel-la) *n.* a covering of nylon, cotton, silk or plastic over a folding frame fixed on a handle and used as a shelter from the rain.

umpire (um-pire) *n.* a person who acts as judge in a game (especially cricket or tennis) or in a dispute. *v.* act as judge in a game or dispute.

un- a prefix meaning either the opposite of (unhappy, unkind) or the reverse of the action (**unbutton, unlock, unroll**).

unanimous (u-nan-i-mous) *a.* of one mind; in complete agreement; showing complete agreement (a vote).

uncanny (un-can-ny) *a.* mysterious, arousing superstitious feelings; strange.

uncle (un-cle) *n.* the brother of one's mother or father; the husband of one's aunt.

uncouth (un-couth) *a.* awkward, clumsy; strange, rough in manners, ungraceful in appearance or form.

under (un-der) *prep.* beneath; lower in rank, age, height, depth etc. than; below in price, value; below the surface of being acted on in some way (repair review, consideration etc.).

under- (un-der-) a prefix meaning either placed under in position (underground or rank (undersecretary) or not as much large etc. as is needed (underpaid, under production).

undercarriage (un-der-car-riage) *n.* the landing gear of an aircraft.

undercover (un-der-cov-er) *a.* working o done out of sight of the public; secret.

undergo (un-der-go) *v.* experience, pass through (hardship etc.).

underhand (un-der-hand) *a.* secret crafty and dishonourable (of actions) with the hand held below the shoulder with the racket held below the wrist (in cricket and tennis).

undermine (un-der-mine) *v.* injure c weaken (a person's power, influence etc.) by underhand means; dig under the foundations either to bring buildings down or blow them up (as in warfare).

underneath (un-der-neath) *prep.* under beneath.

underrate (un-der-rate) *v.* place too low a value or estimate on (especially on a person, a team etc.).

undersell (un-der-sell) *v.* sell goods at a lower price than one's competitors; sell for less than the real value.

understand (un-der-stand) *v.* know the meaning of; get to know, learn or hear view or accept with sympathy (another person's actions etc.); believe. **understanding** *a.* agreement; an agreement about something; power to grasp with the mind, intelligence; sympathy with others; seeing things from other people's point of view.

understudy (un-der-stud-y) *n.* an actor who takes the place of another who is unable to appear. *v.* study another person's part in a play in case he may not be able to appear.

undertake (un-der-take) *v.* agree to do something, promise. **undertaker** *n.* a person whose business is to prepare the dead for burial and to take charge of funerals. **undertaking** *n.* a piece of work, a task; a promise, pledge or guarantee something one has undertaken to do.

uniform (u-ni-form) *a.* of the same form character, size, colour etc. *n.* a dress worn by all members of an organization (police, traffic wardens, the army, navy, air force etc.).

unify v. form into one, unite; make uniform.

union (u-nion) n. joining; things, states, religious groups or societies joined and made one; being joined in marriage, in beliefs or in some other way. **unite** v. become one, join together (of states, groups etc.). **unity** n. becoming or being united; being in sympathy with each other, agreeing.

universe (u-ni-verse) n. the earth, the planets, the stars, space; all of matter and energy; mankind in general. **universal** a. involving all, affecting all (language, peace etc.).

university (u-ni-ver-si-ty) n. a place of higher education which grants degrees and where students carry on research in various subjects; the members of a university.

unless (un-less) conj. except on condition that; if not.

until (un-til) conj. up to the time that or when.

up adv. to, towards; to a point that is higher; out of bed; to a more advanced position (move); to an equal point (catch); to an adult state (bring); to an end (finish); completely (eat, drink); more loudly (speak); to as far as (the present); as many as (a number).

uphold (up-hold) v. support; keep up (old ways); maintain (a position, a belief); confirm (a sentence of a court etc.).

upholster (up-hol-ster) v. provide stools, armchairs, sofas etc. with springs, cushions and covering.

upkeep n. the process of keeping something in good order, repair, good condition, especially a building or establishment; the cost of upkeep including repairs etc.

upon (up-on) prep. on.

upper (up-per) a. higher in place or position; higher in rank; facing upward. n. the upper part of a boot as distinguished from the sole. **uppercut** n. a swinging blow directed upwards, usually towards an opponent's chin. **uppermost** a. the highest in place, rank, order, power.

upright (up-right) a. erect, vertical, not inclined or leaning over; righteous, honest, just. n. one of the upright parts of a construction (goalpost etc.).

uprising (up-ris-ing) n. a revolt or rebellion.

uproar (up-roar) n. a violent and noisy disturbance; a confused noise.

uproot (up-root) v. tear up by the roots; remove completely; remove people from the place where they have been living.

upset (up-set) v. overturn, knock or tip over; put into confusion; disturb physically or mentally; cause trouble. n. a disturbance, a slight illness.

upside-down (up-side-down) adv. with the upper part or side underneath; in confusion, complete disorder.

upstairs (up-stairs) adv. to or on a higher floor. a. having to do with an upper floor. n. an upper floor.

upstream (up-stream) adv. towards or in the higher part of a stream or river; against the current.

up-to-date (up-to-date) a. extending to the present time; keeping up with the latest in fashion, news, ideas etc.

upward (up-ward) a. ascending; moving towards a higher level (thrust etc.). adv. towards a higher level.

urban (ur-ban) a. having to do with cities or towns.

urchin (ur-chin) *n*. a small boy, especially one who is mischievous; a ragged, shabbily dressed child.

urge *v*. try to persuade a person; drive, push or force along (a horse). *n*. something that urges or pushes. **urgent** *a*. needing immediate attention; expressed with great force (appeals).

urine (u-rine) *n*. waste liquid from the body which collects in the bladder and is discharged.

urn *n*. a vase, usually having its own stem and base; a small vase in which the ashes of a dead person may be placed; a metal container, often with its own heating apparatus, from which tea or coffee may be served hot.

use (pronounced *yooz*) *v*. employ for some purpose; consume (a stove, a petrol engine). **used** *a*. second-hand. **used to** accustomed to; having been for a long time in the habit of.

use *n*. (pronounced *yoos*) the act of using or being used; a way of being employed or used; purpose (of worrying, hard work etc.); value (of articles); the power to use (eyes, limbs etc.). **useful** *a*. of use. **useless** *a*. having no use.

usher (ush-er) *n*. one who shows persons to their seats in a church, theatre etc.; an attendant who keeps order in a law court. *v*. act as an usher, take people to their places; be the beginning of (a new age etc.). **usherette** *n*. a female attendant acting as an usher in a theatre, cinema etc.

usual (u-su-al) *a*. such as generally happens; in common use. **usually** *adv*. in the ordinary way; habitually.

usurp (u-surp) *v*. take and hold without right a position, an office, power etc. belonging to another. **usurpation** *n*. the act of usurping, the wrongful seizure and occupation of a throne.

utensil (u-ten-sil) *n*. any tool or instrument used in the house, especially in the kitchen.

utility (u-til-i-ty) *n*. usefulness; something useful to the public, usually supplied by a governing body (gas, electricity, drainage etc.). **utilize** *v*. put to use, make profitable use of.

utmost (ut-most) *a*. of the greatest amount, quantity etc.; the best of one's power; the farthest (extreme, ends).

utter (ut-ter) *v*. give forth sounds or words, state opinions; make known publicly; put false money into circulation. *a*. complete, total. **utterance** *n*. the act of uttering; something uttered. **utterly** *adv*. completely.

V

vacant (va-cant) *a*. empty, having no contents, not occupied; not taken up with work etc.; not occupied with thoughts; (of an estate) having no claimant. **vacancy** *n*. the state of being vacant; a vacant post. **vacate** *v*. give up the occupation of. give up a post or position.

vacation (va-ca-tion) *n*. that part of the year when schools, universities, law courts etc. are closed.

vaccinate (vac-ci-nate) *v*. protect the body from certain diseases, especially smallpox, by injecting vaccine into it. **vaccine** *n*. a substance from the blood of a cow prepared for injection into the human body. **vaccination** *n*. the practice of vaccinating; being vaccinated.

vacuum (vac-u-um) *n*. a space from which all air has been removed. **vacuum cleaner** a cleaner which, by sucking air, picks up dust and dirt. **vacuum flask** a flask with a vacuum jacket which prevents a change in temperature of the contents.

vagabond (vag-a-bond) *n*. one who is without a fixed place to live, and wanders from place to place; a worthless person.

vague *a*. not clear or distinct; not definite in meaning.

vain *n*. without real value or result; useless; having too high an opinion of one's looks, abilities etc. **in vain** without result, to no purpose; without the respect deserved.

vale *n.* a word used mainly in poetry for a valley.

valentine (val-en-tine) *n.* a letter or card sent to one's sweetheart or to a friend on St Valentine's Day, February 14.

valet (val-et) *n.* a manservant who is his master's personal attendant, looking after his clothing and seeing to his needs.

valiant (val-i-ant) *a.* brave, courageous (of persons); showing great bravery (of deeds). **valour** *n.* bravery, boldness in facing danger.

valid (val-id) *a.* sound; just, well-founded (reason, objection etc.); binding in law.

valley (val-ley) *n.* a stretch of low land, usually with an outlet between hills or mountains; a low region drained by a great river system.

value (val-ue) *n.* worth or importance in money or in any other way. *v.* estimate what something is worth; how important it is. **valuable** *a.* having value or great use or importance. *n.* something of value, especially an article. **valuation** *n.* the fixing of the value of a thing; the value a thing is fixed at, or is declared to be worth.

valve *n.* a device for controlling the flow of liquid, air or gas through tubes or pipes, as in a car or cycle tyre; a structure in a blood vessel which allows the blood to flow in one direction only; a device in certain wind instruments (trumpets, cornets, horns etc.) which, when certain keys are pressed, alters the length of the tubes and changes the pitch of notes.

vandal (van-dal) *n.* a person who wilfully destroys or damages property and works of art. **vandalism** *n.* wanton damage to property, works of art etc.

vane *n.* a device with a pointer fixed on top of a spire or building to show the direction of the wind; a device fixed on a windmill to turn the sails into the wind;

the blade of a propeller or other flat surface acted on by the wind or weather.

vanish (van-ish) *v.* disappear from sight, become invisible; cease to exist (of hopes, fears etc.).

vanity (van-i-ty) *n.* too much pride in one's appearance or in the things one can do; something vain or worthless.

vapour (va-pour) *n.* the gas into which some substances are changed when they are heated — steam in the case of water; mist in the atmosphere. **vapour bath** an enclosed space or apparatus for containing vapour, used as a bath.

varnish (var-nish) *n.* a transparent liquid that can be painted on to wood, metal etc., to give a shiny surface; a coating of varnish. *v.* apply varnish with a brush or by other means. **varnish paint** paint with the varnish in it.

vary (va-ry) *v.* change or alter in form, appearance, substance etc.; become or cause to be different. **variation** *n.* varying, being varied; in music, a melody repeated, changing its forms. **variegated** *a.* marked with patches or spots of different colours. **variety** *n.* a number of different things or kinds; a kind of entertainment consisting of singing, dancing, acrobatics etc. given by performers appearing either singly or in small groups; change in surroundings, occupations, pleasures etc. **various** *a.* many, several; differing one from another.

vase *n.* a vessel, generally higher than it is wide, made of glass, earthenware, porcelain etc. used mainly for ornament or for holding cut flowers.

vaseline (vas-e-line) *n.* a trade name for a yellowish greasy substance made from petroleum used mainly as an ointment and in medical preparations.

vast *a.* immense; of very great size, area, quantity (plain, army, sum etc.); very great in degree, quantity etc. (haste, importance etc.).

vat *n.* a large tank or container for liquids.

vault *n.* a large room or cellar; an arched construction, part of the roof of a building or a sewer; a burial chamber; a strong room for storing valuables. *v.* to construct or cover with a vault; take a single leap or spring. **vaulting-horse** *n.* an apparatus used in gymnastics for vaulting.

veal *n.* the flesh of the calf used as food.

vegetable (veg-e-ta-ble) *n.* a plant, especially one whose fruits, seeds, roots, tubers etc. are used for food; the edible part of such plants as served at table. *a.* derived from plants (oil, fibre etc.). **vegetarian** *n.* a person who does not eat meat, confining his diet wholly or almost wholly to vegetable products. **vegetate** *v.* live as a plant does, doing little, thinking little. **vegetation** *n.* plants, trees, bushes.

vehicle (ve-hi-cle) *n.* anything used to carry people or things, usually on wheels; a means of conveying (as air does sound or wire does electricity); a means of expressing ideas, thoughts or feelings (language, poetry etc.).

veil *n.* a piece of transparent material used as part of a headdress, especially by women; a piece of material worn to cover the face; something that covers or hides (smoke etc.); something pretended (friendship). *v.* hide (fear, disgust etc.). **take the veil** accept the life and make the vows of a nun.

vein *n.* one of the blood-vessels that carries blood to the heart from various parts of the body; a vein-like marking on a leaf and in some kinds of stone, marble, wood etc.; a crack in a rock in which mineral deposits and ores are found.

velocity (ve-loc-i-ty) *n.* speed, rate of speed; a measured rate of speed.

velvet (vel-vet) *n.* a fabric of silk, silk and cotton, cotton etc. which has a short raised pile, making it feel soft to the touch. **velvety** *a.* smooth and soft, feeling like velvet.

veneer (ve-neer) *n.* a thin layer of better quality wood laid over cheaper wood in the making of furniture etc.; a pleasing appearance concealing a person's true character. *v.* put on a veneer.

venerable (ven-er-a-ble) *a.* worthy of respect or reverence because of a person's high character or the dignity of the office he holds.

vengeance (ven-geance) *n.* the infliction of an injury or suffering on others in return for a wrong done. **vengeful** *a.* desiring or seeking vengeance or revenge.

venison (ven-i-son) *n.* the flesh of the deer used as food.

ventilate (ven-ti-late) *v.* provide a room, a mine etc. with fresh air; make air circulate; open a question for discussion; make an argument or an opinion known. **ventilation** *n.* ventilating; being ventilated; any means of ventilating.

ventriloquist (ven-tril-o-quist) *n.* a person who produces sounds so that they seem to come from another person or place.

venture (ven-ture) *v.* take a risk; be so bold as to do a thing; put forward (an opinion). *n.* a risky or daring enterprise. **venturesome** *a.* willing to take risks.

verandah (ve-ran-dah) *n.* an open space with roof and floor extending on one side or round the sides of a house, sports pavilion etc.

verb *n.* a word which says what somebody or something does; a being or doing word.

verbal (ver-bal) *a.* having to do with

words, especially spoken words; expressed in speech (message etc.).

verdict (ver-dict) *n.* the decision or answer of a jury about a matter submitted to their judgment; an opinion given, often after much thought and examination.

verge *n.* a narrow strip of grass by the side of a road or a path; a limit beyond which something happens (tears, exhaustion etc.).

verger (ver-ger) *n.* a church official who looks after the interior of the church and acts as an attendant; an official who carries a staff before a bishop or dean in a church.

verify (ver-i-fy) *v.* prove something to be true by examining evidence etc.; test whether or not something is true by examination. **verification** *n.* the act of verifying; finding or testing the truth of something.

vermin (ver-min) *n.* animals or insects which are harmful, objectionable, or which bring disease, such as foxes, mice and fleas. **verminous** *a.* caused by vermin; infested with vermin.

versatile (ver-sa-tile) *a.* clever at many different things and able to turn easily from one to another.

verse *n.* poetry; a form of writing in lines, each line being part of a pattern of accented syllables etc. and sometimes rhyming; a poem or a small section of a poem; a certain kind of line in verse; one of the numbered parts of a chapter in the Bible. **versify** *v.* tell in verse; turn into verse; compose verses.

version (ver-sion) *n.* an account of some matter from the point of view of one person; a translation into another language; a particular form of telling or translation (the Authorised and Revised Versions of the Bible etc.).

vertebra (ver-te-bra) *n.* one of the small bones or segments which make up the backbone. **vertebrae** *n.* a number of these segments. **vertebrate** *a.* (of animals) having a backbone or spinal column.

vertical (ver-ti-cal) *a.* upright; at right angles to the earth's surface.

very (ve-ry) *adv.* extremely, exceedingly. *a.* mere (thought etc.); actual (thing).

vessel (ves-sel) *n.* a hollow article such as a cup, bowl, pot, pan or bottle made to hold things; a ship.

vest *n.* a short undergarment worn next to the body. *v.* furnish or supply (with power or authority).

vestibule (vest-i-bule) *n.* a small hall between the outer door and the rooms of a house or building; the porch of a church.

vestige (ves-tige) *n.* a mark, trace or sign of something not now existing; a slight amount of something (truth etc.).

vestry (ves-try) *n.* a small room attached to a church where the robes are kept, and which the minister sometimes uses as a study or private room.

veteran (vet-e-ran) *n.* a former soldier, sailor or airman, especially one who has seen active service; one who has seen long service in any office; a very old motor vehicle, specially valuable because of its age.

veterinary (vet-er-i-na-ry) *a.* having to do with the diseases of animals, especially domesticated ones. **veterinary surgeon** (or **vet.**) one who treats the ailments of domestic animals.

veto (ve-to) *n.* the right to forbid or reject something. *v.* prevent the passing of laws, resolutions in meetings etc. by using this power.

vex *v.* irritate, annoy, make angry; torment, worry. **vexation** *n.* something that worries or annoys one. **vexed question** a question which needs much consideration.

via (vi-a) *prep.* by way of, by a route that passes through (usually followed by a place name); by means of .

viaduct (vi-a-duct) *n.* a bridge, in olden times with many arches, today often of steel girders etc.; which carries a road or railway over a valley, a road, a built-up area etc.

vibrate (vi-brate) *v.* move quickly backwards and forwards like the strings of a guitar when they are plucked; quiver or tremble. **vibration** *n.* the act of vibrating, the motion of a string etc. when plucked; a single vibration (measured at so many to the second).

vicar (vic-ar) *n.* in the Church of England, a clergyman acting as the priest of a parish. **vicarage** *n.* the house in which a vicar lives.

vice *n.* any kind of wrong-doing; any kind of bad habit; a device with two jaws which can be brought together by a screw to grip and hold a piece of work in position. **vicious** *a.* spiteful, evil, with evil intention; having an ugly disposition (of people and animals).

vice- a prefix denoting a substitute, deputy or the next in rank (vice-admiral, vice-chairman etc.).

vicinity (vi-cin-i-ty) *n.* the region near a place; the neighbourhood; nearness to (an action etc.).

victim (vic-tim) *n.* a person or animal suffering from misfortune or any kind of evil; a person or animal hurt or sacrificed (war, bad housing, crime etc.). **victimize** *v.* make a victim of; punish unfairly; swindle or cheat (the poor, the elderly etc.).

victor (vic-tor) *n.* one who has defeated an opponent; a conqueror; a winner in any contest. **victory** *n.* success in a battle or any contest. **victorious** *a.* having won a victory.

victual (vict-ual) *v.* (pronounced *vittle*) supply or store with food or provisions; take in provisions. **victuals** *n.* provisions, food and drink. **licensed victualler** a public-house keeper who is licensed to sell spirits, beer etc.

video (vid-e-o) *a.* having to do with television or the reception of television pictures. **videotape** *n.* magnetic tape which records sight and sound, used for recording and storing television programmes or films.

view *n.* sight, seeing; that which is seen; a scene; an opinion about something; an aim, intention or purpose. *v.* see, look over (land, houses etc. before buying); consider, have an opinion about; watch a television programme. **viewer** *n.* one who watches a television programme; one who is appointed to inspect or examine a viewfinder *n.* a device attached to a camera which enables one to see what will be in the picture taken. **viewpoint** *n.* the particular situation from which one has formed certain opinions.

vigil (vig-il) *n.* keeping awake to keep watch for any purpose; a period of watchful attention during the day or night. **vigilant** *a.* watchful, alert to danger etc.

vigour (vig-our) *n.* strength, energy of body or mind; force, activity with which things are done (pursuit, attack etc.) **vigorous** *a.* full of vigour; strong and active; powerful.

viking (vi-king) *n.* one of the sea-robbers from Norway and Denmark who raided the coasts of Europe and Britain over a thousand years ago.

vile *a.* evil, wicked; offensive, disgusting (smells etc.); foul (language); wretched (weather); poor, wretched (slavery).

villa (vil-la) *n.* a house, usually in the suburbs of a town; a country residence; an ancient Roman farmhouse which had its own estate and produced most of the things needed for those who lived there

village (vil-lage) *n.* a place smaller than a town with a main street, a few shops, one or two inns and a church. *a.* having to do with a village (life, industry etc.). **villager** *n.* a person living in a village.

villain (vil-lain) *n.* a wicked man, a scoundrel; a character in a play who is the source of evil in its plot or story **villainous** *a.* having the character of a villain; wicked.

vindictive (vin-dic-tive) *a.* revengeful, wanting to take revenge.

vine *n.* a climbing plant which supports itself by means of tendrils; the common kind of vine grown in Europe which produces grapes. **vineyard** *n.* a piece of ground on which grapevines are grown. **vinegar** *n.* an acid liquid made from wine etc. used for preserving and flavouring in the preparation of foods. **vintage** *n.* the grape harvest.

violate (vi-o-late) *v.* break rules, laws, promises, instructions etc.; disturb rudely (peace, privacy); pass by force and without right (a frontier); behave badly in a sacred place (altars, churches etc.).

violent (vi-o-lent) *a.* acting with force; having to do with force (measures, death); extreme (heat, pain etc.); furious (haste). **violence** *n.* rough force; injurious action; a violent act.

violin (vi-o-lin) *n.* a musical instrument with four strings, held under the chin and played with a bow. **viola** *n.* a violin of a rather larger size which plays lower notes. **violoncello** (or **cello**) *n.* a bass violin played with a bow and held between the player's knees. **violinist, violoncellist, cellist** *n.* musicians who play these instruments.

virgin (vir-gin) *n.* an unmarried girl; a maiden. **The Virgin Mary** the mother of Jesus Christ.

virile (vir-ile) *a.* manly, vigorous, showing strength, vigour, spirit and forcefulness.

virtual (vir-tu-al) *a.* being a certain person or thing though not named as such (a virtual king, ruler, master etc.).

virtue (vir-tue) *n.* goodness, excellence; any good quality of a person or thing. **virtuous** *n.* possessing virtue, upright and righteous (of persons).

visa (vi-sa) *n.* the stamp on a passport made by an official of a foreign country giving the holder of the passport permission to visit it.

viscount (vis-count) *n.* a nobleman next below an earl or count and next above a baron.

vision (vi-sion) *n.* the power to see; the act of seeing; the power to imagine, to perceive the problems etc. that lie ahead; an image of what is not present — of the past or future; something seen; a scene or a person of more than ordinary beauty. **visible** *a.* that can be seen. **visionary** *a.* as seen in a vision; unreal, imaginary. *n.* one who sees visions; one who has ideas which cannot work. **visual** *a.* having to do with seeing. **visual aids** devices such as films, photographs etc. which help the student.

visit (vis-it) *v.* go to see a person because of friendship, duty, business etc.; make a stay; come or go to a place. *n.* the act of visiting; a stay at a place or with a person. **visitor** *n.* one who visits or makes a visit.

vital (vi-tal) *a.* necessary to life; having life; having energy, enthusiasm etc. (personality); having to do with the truth or importance of a thing (error, problems). **vitality** *n.* physical strength, vigour, power to endure. **vital organs** the brain, heart, lungs, stomach etc. which are essential to life.

vitamin (vit-a-min) *n.* one of the substances in food which is necessary if a person is to live and be in good health, though not in itself supplying energy.

vivid *a.* very bright and clear (colour, light, objects etc.); full of life (personality); strong, distinct (recollection).

vivisect (viv-i-sect) *n.* operate on the living bodies of animals for purposes of experiment. **vivisection** *n.* the practice of vivisecting.

vocabulary (vo-cab-u-la-ry) *n.* a list of words in a book; the words of a language; a book containing a list of words; the words known to a person.

vocal (vo-cal) *a.* having to do with the voice; intended for singing as music. **vocal cords** parts of the larynx which vibrate as air passes through them, and produce the voice. **vocalist** *n.* a singer.

vocation (vo-ca-tion) *n.* an occupation or trade; the work one feels compelled to do; a special ability for something. **vocational** *a.* having to do with a vocation (training, guidance, schools etc.).

vogue *n.* fashion (of a particular time); **in vogue** in fashion, accepted by all or by large sections of the public.

voice *n.* the sounds uttered by human beings when speaking, shouting, singing etc.; the quality of such sounds (good, deep, melodious etc.); the power to speak or sing. *v.* give an opinion; express (discontent, disappointment etc.); put into words.

volcano (vol-ca-no) *n.* an opening in the earth's crust, usually at the top of a mountain, through which molten lava is flung into the air. **volcanic** *a.* having to do with a volcano (eruption); discharged from a volcano (rock, mud etc.).

volley (vol-ley) *n.* a number of shells, bullets, arrows etc. discharged in the same direction at once; in tennis, the return of a ball before it has touched the ground; in cricket, a full toss, not touching the ground. *v.* be discharged together, of guns, arrows etc.; return a tennis ball before it has touched the ground.

volt *n.* a unit of electrical force. **voltage** *n.* electrical force measured in volts.

volume (vol-ume) *n.* a book; a book which is one of a set or series; the amount of space occupied by a substance; a large amount (smoke, abuse etc.); sound (of a radio etc.).

voluntary (vol-un-ta-ry) *a.* done without being told or commanded; given of one's free will. *n.* a piece of music, especially organ music performed before or during a ceremony.

volunteer (vol-un-teer) *n.* a person who does something willingly and without being told; a person who enlists in the armed forces without being conscripted. *v.* offer one's services for some purpose; enlist of one's own free will.

vomit (vom-it) *v.* bring back the contents of the stomach through the mouth; send out large quantities (smoke etc.).

vote *n.* the expression of a person's wish either by showing his hand or by the use of the ballot; the right to such an expression; the decision reached through voting. *v.* express a wish by a vote; determine something by a vote; propose. **voter** *n.* a person who votes or has voted.

voucher (vouch-er) *n.* a ticket or document showing that money has been paid and received; a ticket used in place of money (gift, luncheon etc.).

vow *n.* a solemn promise (marriage, secrecy etc.). *v.* make a vow; pledge oneself to do, make, give etc.

vowel (vow-el) *n.* one of the letters a, e, i, o, u, and sometimes y, spoken through

the open mouth without interference from the tongue, teeth or lips.

voyage (voy-age) *n.* a journey by water, especially to a distant place. *v.* make a voyage, travel by sea or water. **voyager** *n.* a person who makes a voyage · or voyages.

vulgar (vul-gar) *a.* coarse, ill-mannered. **vulgarity** *n.* vulgar behaviour; a vulgar act or speech.

vulture (vul-ture) *n.* a large bird of prey whose head and neck are almost bare of feathers, and which feeds on the flesh of dead animals.

W

wad *n.* a small mass of soft material used for stuffing, padding or packing; a bundle or roll of banknotes.

wade *v.* walk through a substance such as water or snow, that hinders movement; go through (water, a task etc.) with difficulty. **wader** *n.* a bird, such as a stork or crane, that wades. **waders** *n.* high waterproof boots used for wading.

wafer (wa-fer) *n.* a thin, crisp biscuit, usually eaten with ice cream; a thin disc of bread used in Holy Communion in Church; a small thin piece of sticky paper, used for fastening larger pieces together.

waffle (waf-fle) *n.* (pronounced *woffel*) a small cake made of batter cooked on a special kind of iron made of two parts hinged together.

waft *v.* carry lightly through the air or over the water; *n.* the sound or smell of something wafted.

wag *v.* move or make move from side to side. *n.* a merry person, full of wit and fond of playing jokes.

wage *n.* that which is paid for work or services at the end of each day or each week. *v.* carry on (war).

wager (wa-ger) *n.* a bet; the act of betting. *v.* bet on the result of a match, race etc.

wagon or **waggon** (wag-gon) *n.* a four-wheeled vehicle for carrying heavy goods; a railway truck.

waif *n.* a person, especially a child, without home or friends. **waifs and strays** homeless children; cats and dogs wandering about the streets without owners.

wail *v.* cry or weep in a loud shrill voice; make a wailing sound (the wind etc.). *n.* a loud, mournful cry.

waist *n.* the middle part of the human body between the ribs and the hips; that part of a garment that goes round the waist. **waistcoat** *n.* a close-fitting sleeveless garment that buttons in front, designed to be worn under a jacket.

wait *v.* stay or remain until something expected happens; be ready; delay, postpone. *n.* a time spent in waiting. **waiter** *n.* a man who waits at table in a restaurant or hotel. **wait on** *v.* serve, look after, attend to at meals. **waitress** *n.* a woman who waits at table.

wake *v.* stop sleeping; stop another person sleeping. *n.* the watch over a dead person before burial; the track left by a ship as it moves through the water. **wakeful** *a.* not able to sleep.

walk *v.* travel on foot making steps in turn so that there is always one foot on the ground; make somebody or something walk; pass over on foot. *n.* a path or road along which one walks; a journey on foot; a way of walking. **walkie-talkie** *n.* a two-way radio telephone light enough to be carried about by one person.

wall *n.* an upright structure of stone, brick, concrete etc. forming the side of a building or a room, or marking off one piece of land from another; something reminding one of a wall (of water, fire etc.). *v.* surround with a wall; shut up within walls; fill up (a doorway etc.) with a wall. **wall bars** a gymnasium apparatus consisting of wooden bars attached to a wall

and used for doing exercises. **wall-flower** *n.* a plant with brown, red, yellow or orange flowers. **wallpaper** *n.* paper used for covering the walls of a room as a decoration.

wallet (wal-let) *n.* a small, book-like folding case which holds money, papers etc. in the pocket; a bag for holding food, clothing, toilet articles etc. as for use on a journey.

wallow (wal-low) *v.* roll about, usually in water, mud, dust etc. as pigs do.

walnut (wal-nut) *n.* a nut with a hard shell, eaten especially at Christmas; the wood of the walnut tree, used in making furniture.

walrus *n.* a large sea animal with flippers, tusks and a very thick skin.

waltz *n.* a dance in which couples move round and round; the music in three-time for such a dance. *v.* make a person waltz; dance in the step of the waltz.

wan *a.* pale, looking ill, sad and anxious; suggesting illness (of the look, the smile etc.).

wand *n.* a slender stick, carried supposedly by a magician or a fairy, in order to work magic; a rod carried by an usher, a steward etc. in processions as a symbol of power.

wander (wan-der) *v.* go from place to place without any set purpose; stray from the path; let the thoughts go their own way. **wanderer** *n.* one who wanders. **wanderings** *n.* travels.

wane *v.* grow less and less in size, strength, importance, power, daylight etc.

want *v.* require, need; be without; desire, wish for. *n.* the absence of something wanted, a necessity; great poverty.

wanton (wan-ton) *a.* done out of hate, spite or for no known cause (damage etc.).

war *n.* fighting between two or more countries; a struggle against some evil (want, famine etc.). **war cry** a cry shouted in battle; a slogan used by a group in a contest or a campaign. **warhead** *n.* the explosive head of a shell, a torpedo or a rocket-fired missile. **warlike** ready for war, in the mood to make war. **warpaint** *n.* paint put on the body and face by certain primitive tribes when they go to war. **warrior** *n.* a soldier, a fighter, a man engaged or experienced in war. **on the warpath** angry; seeking to make war or to pick a quarrel.

warble (war-ble) *v.* sing with trilling notes. *n.* the act of warbling; the song of a bird.

ward *n.* a person left in the care of another (after the death of parents etc.); a division of a city or area of local government; a separate room in a prison or hospital, usually for a particular class of patient (children, emergency etc.). **ward off** *v.* avoid, keep away (a blow, a disaster etc.). **warden** *n.* a person who has authority to watch over or care for a place, a thing or some proceeding (church, air raid, traffic etc.). **warder** *n.* a person who acts as a guard in a prison.

wardrobe (ward-robe) *n.* a cupboard with books and shelves for holding clothes; the clothes one owns; the stock of clothes etc. of a theatrical company.

ware *n.* different kinds of goods; articles for sale; kinds of pottery (Delft etc.). **warehouse** *n.* a building in which goods for sale are stored. **warehouseman** *n.* a man in charge of a warehouse; a person who owns a warehouse for the storing of other people's merchandise.

warm *a.* having a certain amount of heat; not cold; keeping heat in (warm clothes); sincere, enthusiastic (welcome, reception); close, intimate (friends); lively (argument, debate). *v.* make or become warm; grow kindly towards someone. **warm up** *v.* prepare for a game or sporting event by doing exercises beforehand.

warn *v.* give notice to a person of some danger or of something that is going to happen. **warning** *n.* the act of warning; something that warns.

warp *v.* become bent or twisted; bend or turn from the true direction. *n.* a bend or twist in something as in wood that has dried unevenly; the threads in a loom over and under which the crossthreads (weft or woof) are passed.

warrant (war-rant) *n.* a right, an authority for doing something; a document giving a person a certain right (search etc.). *v.* give a person the right to do a thing; guarantee the delivery, quantity, quality etc. of something bought.

warren (war-ren) *n.* a place where rabbits breed and live.

wart *n.* a small, hard growth on the skin.

wary (wa-ry) *a.* watchful, remaining on one's guard; on the alert, careful, cautious.

wash *v.* clean by using water or other liquids; flow over and against (the waves); remove by washing (dirt, stains); carry away by water (overboard). *n.* articles, the number or quantity of articles washed; a thin layer of colour applied with a brush; the movement of water. **washbasin** *n.* a large bowl or basin for washing the face and hands. **washer** *n.* a machine for washing clothes or dishes; a small flat ring put between a nut and bolt to tighten a joint.

wasp *n.* a flying insect with a black and yellow striped body and a sting in its tail

waste *a.* thrown away because not wanted; not used (energy, matter etc.); in a state of emptiness and ruin (land); *n.* things thrown away, not wanted; empty deserted land, desert; useless spending of money or energy; gradual decay and destruction. *v.* spend, throw away, use badly, squander (money, effort, words); destroy, ravage (a country); lose weight and strength; use more of than is necessary. **wasteful** *a.* causing waste; using more than is needed. **wastepipe** *n.* a pipe for taking away water etc. or for conveying waste liquid from sinks and baths in houses and other buildings.

watch *v.* look, observe; be careful, remain aware of; keep awake to observe or protect. *n.* the act of watching; a period of duty watching; a small timepiece or clock worn on a chain or on the wrist. **watch committee** a committee of a local government body which has supervision over police services etc. **watchman** *n.* a man employed to guard a building, especially during the night. **watchword** *n.* a word, a short phrase or a rallying cry of a party etc.; a slogan.

water (wat-er) *n.* a colourless liquid that forms rain, fills rivers, seas, lakes etc., which when pure has no taste or smell. *v.* sprinkle, moisten or drench with water (a street, a garden); supply animals with drinking water; add water to other liquids (milk etc.). *a.* powered by water (mill). **watercolour** *n.* paint made by mixing with water. **water-level** *n.* the height of the water in a reservoir, pond etc. **waterlogged** *a.* overflowing with water. **waterpower** *n.* power to drive machinery by the use of water. **waterproof** *a.* not letting water through. **watershed** *n.* high land on each side of which rivers and streams flow. **watertight** *a.* fastened so that water cannot leak through. **waterway** *n.* a stream, river, canal etc. on which boats and ships can travel. **watery** *a.* containing too much water; running with water.

wattle (wat-tle) *n.* sticks and twigs woven together to make fences, walls etc.; the flesh hanging down from the chin or throat of a turkey or a chicken; a shrub with yellow flowers growing mainly in Australia.

wave *v.* move gently to and fro; make something move in this way; give a signal by waving something; curve up and down or in and out; make a person's hair wave. *n.* a long moving ridge of water; something resembling a wave which rises and falls (heat etc.); the kind of vibration by which electric energy, sound etc. are spread. **wavy** *a.* in waves, resembling waves.

wax *n.* a substance of plant or animal origin, used for making candles and polishes. *v.* rub, smear, stiffen, polish etc. with wax; grow larger (anger, discontent); grow in size (of the moon) between new moon and full moon. **waxen** *a.* made of wax; like wax. **waxwork** *n.* figures, ornaments etc. made of wax.

way *n.* a path, road, street; a route; a method of doing something; a distance (long, short etc.); space for passing or advancing; a habit or custom; a manner of living or behaving; a mode or fashion; a direction. **waylay** *v.* attack on the road;

wayside *n.* the side of the road. *a.* situated by the side of the road (inn etc.).

we *pron.* you and I; I with one or more others.

weak *a.* not strong, easy to break; not good or efficient; feeble, infirm; not having enough of a certain substance in it (tea, coffee etc.). **weaken** *v.* become or make weak. **weakling** *n.* a weak or feeble creature. **weakness** *n.* the state of being weak; a fault (in construction, character etc.).

wealth *n.* a great amount; a great number (things, money, property etc.); **wealthy** *a.* having wealth, rich.

weapon (weap-on) *n.* any instrument used in attack or defence – a sword, rifle, cannon etc.; a means of getting one's own way (tears, sarcasm etc.).

wear *v.* have on the body as covering, for use or ornament (coat, disguise etc.); make less useful by wearing; last well when one wears something; pass on gradually (the day etc.). *n.* gradual damage through wearing; clothing or other articles for wearing; use (of an article); style of dress for a particular time or activity (evening, sports etc.). **wearable** *a.* that may be worn, fit to wear. **wear and tear** gradual damage to articles by ordinary use.

weary (wea-ry) *a.* tired by labour, strain etc.; causing tiredness (journey). *v.* make weary, become weary. **wearisome** *a.* causing weariness; tiresome, boring, dull.

weasel (wea-sel) *n.* a small animal with a long slender body and red-brown fur which feeds on rats, mice, birds' eggs etc.

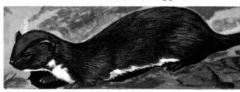

weather (weath-er) *n.* the state of the atmosphere, its heat, coldness, wetness, amount of wind etc. *v.* expose to the weather to make something ready for use; last when exposed to the weather; come safely through a storm, danger etc. **weathercock** *n.* a device, often shaped like a cock, put on top of a building to show the direction of the wind. **weather-proof** *a.* able to stand up to all kinds of weather. *v.* make (a garment) proof against bad weather.

weave *v.* make threads into cloth by crossing them over and under each other; wind in and out or through (crowds, traffic etc.). *n.* the kind of weaving in cloth (plain, fancy etc.). **weaver** *n.* a person who weaves cloth.

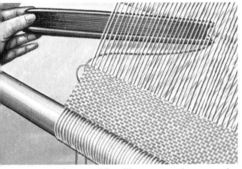

web *n.* a thin silken network woven by spiders and other small creatures; the skin joining the toes of ducks and other birds that swim. **webbing** *n.* strong, woven material of various widths, used for upholstery, binding the edges of carpets etc.

wed *v.* marry, take for husband or wife. **wedding** *n.* the act or ceremony of marrying.

wedge *n.* an angled piece of wood or metal; used to split wood or rock by being hammered to widen an opening; anything in the shape of a wedge (pie, cake, cheese). *v.* force in as one does a wedge; thrust (oneself) in between.

weed *n.* a wild, unwanted plant growing in a garden; a useless plant, especially one that grows strongly and quickly. *v.* take out weeds from cultivated land; get rid of what is not wanted or undesirable. **weeds** *n.* the black clothes and veil once worn by a widow. **weedy** *a.* having many weeds; thin and weakly (of a person or animal).

week *n.* a period of seven days beginning with Sunday; seven days after a named day. **weekday** *n.* any day of the week except Sunday; the part of the week when people go to work. **weekend** *n.* the time from finishing work at the end of the week, usually Friday, to starting again usually Monday morning. **weekly** *adv.* once a week; lasting a week.

weep *v.* show grief by tears or crying; discharge water or liquid as from a sore; the stem of a plant etc.

weigh *v.* measure how heavy a thing is; bring down through something being heavy (tree weighed down by fruit etc.); make sad by trouble, care, oppression etc.; show a certain weight. **weigh-in** *n.* the checking of a person's weight on entering a competition (wrestling, boxing, a horse-race etc.). **weight** *n.* the amount a thing weighs; the force with which something is thrust down towards the earth; importance (opinions, matters); a piece of metal used on a balance or scale for measuring how much something weighs; a heavy load or burden. *v.* load with things to make heavier.

weir *n.* a barrier wall or dam put across a river to control its flow or direct it for running a mill, for supplying water to gardens, fields etc.; a fence or network put into a stream or river to catch fish.

weird *a.* strange, odd; mysterious, ghost-like (sounds, shapes etc.).

welcome (wel-come) *n.* a word of kindly greeting; a joyful reception (of a person, thing, news etc.). *v.* greet or receive with pleasure. *a.* gladly received; agreeable; permitted with pleasure (to come, go, use etc.).

weld *v.* join together pieces of metal by heat, hammering, pressure etc.; make more firm (friendship). **welder** *n.* a person employed to weld metal.

welfare (wel-fare) *n.* being healthy in body and mind. **welfare state** a state in which the responsibility for the welfare of its people is in the hands of the government, (health, housing, working conditions etc.). **welfare work** work devoted to helping people.

well *adv.* in the right, satisfactory or de-sired way; excellently; in good health; easily, clearly (see, hear); intimately (knowing persons or things); thoroughly; a word used with other words whose meaning can be guessed.

well *n.* a hole or shaft in the ground usually lined with brick or stone from which water is obtained; a hole drilled into the earth for obtaining petroleum or other valuable liquid products; a vessel (ink); a deep enclosed space as in a staircase, often extending from roof to basement.

wellingtons (wel-ling-tons) *n.* high waterproof boots made of rubber reaching up to the knees.

west *n.* the direction in which the sun sets. *a.* towards the west; from the west (wind). **westbound** *a.* travelling towards the west. **westerly** *a.* towards the west. **western** *a.* in, of or from the west. *n.* a book or film dealing with life in the west of the United States, particularly during the wars with the Indians. **westward** *a.* moving, facing or situated towards the west.

wet *a.* covered or soaked entirely or in part with water or some other liquid; moist, damp, not hardened or dry; rainy, having a rainy climate. *n.* that which makes wet, especially rain. *v.* make wet. **wet rot** a decaying of timber through being alter-nately wet and dry.

whack *n.* a smart, hard blow. *v.* strike a smart, hard blow. **whacked** *a.* a common expression for being exhausted, tired out with hard work. **whacking** *n.* a beating.

whale *n.* a large sea animal with a fish-like body hunted for its oil and meat. One variety, the blue whale, is the largest mammal on earth.

wharf *n.* a structure built on the shore of, or projecting out into a harbour, river etc. so that vessels can be moored alongside it for loading, unloading etc. **wharfage** *n.* the storage or payment for the storage of goods at a wharf or for the use of a wharf.

what *pron.* a word which asks a question (name, actions, things etc.); a word which exclaims (nonsense, a pity); a word relating to a thing or action. *adv.* to what extent (does it matter?); as much as (what you like; what I can). **whatever** *pron.* anything that; no matter what.

wheat *n.* grain from which white and brown flour is made and which is used for making bread, cakes etc. **wheaten** *a.* made from wheat.

wheel *n.* a circular object or disc made to turn on its centre or on an axle; a circular frame used for steering a vehicle or ship. *v.* push or pull a wheeled vehicle; turn in a curve or circle; change direction (right or left) when marching. **wheelbarrow** *n.* a small cart with one wheel which is pulled or pushed by hand. **wheelbase** *n.* the distance between the front and rear wheels of a vehicle. **wheelchair** *n.* a chair mounted on large wheels and used by invalids.

wheeze *v.* breathe with difficulty with a whistling sound. *n.* the sound made when one breathes in this way; a bright idea, a cunning trick.

whelk *n.* a small sea animal with a spiral shell like a snail, some varieties of which are used as food in Europe.

when *adv.* a questioning word concerning time. *conj.* at the time that. **whenever** *conj.* at whatever time; at any time when.

where *adv.* in what place, at what place; to or from what place? from what source?; **whereabouts** *n.* the place where a person or thing is. **wherever** *conj.* in at or to whatever place. **wherewithal** *n.* the things, supplies or money needed to do a certain thing.

whether (wheth-er) *conj.* a word which presents two things or actions of which one is to be chosen. **whether or no** in whatever circumstances.

whey *n.* the liquid part of sour milk after the curds have been separated to make cheese.

which *pron.* what one? (of two or more); a word referring to something mentioned before (which I saw, which came etc.). *adv.* what one of a certain number al-ready mentioned (which book); from, to, behind, opposite, above, below a certain thing (the horse on which I rode etc.).

whichever *pron.* any one of a number; no matter which.

whiff *n.* a slight puff of wind, air, scent, vapour, smoke; a single taking of smoke into the lungs when smoking.

while *n.* a space of time (for a while); *conj.* during the time that, throughout the time that, as long as; **while away** cause time to pass easily or in some pleasant manner.

whim *n.* a sudden desire, often for something strange.

whimper (whim-per) *v.* cry with low, frightened, broken sounds. *n.* a whimpering cry or sound.

whine *v.* utter a long, complaining cry or sound as from discomfort, uneasiness or unhappiness. *n.* a whining sound or voice, a peevish complaint.

whip *n.* a stick on which a cord or lash has been fastened, used for urging on a horse or for punishing; the member of a political party who is responsible for seeing that other members vote; an order given by a political party; a dish made with egg white and cream, whipped to a froth and flavoured either with flavouring or with fruit pulp. *v.* strike with a whip or with something slender and flexible, with sharp, repeated strokes; drive out with strokes or lashes; bring in members of parliament to vote; beat egg-whites, cream, etc. to make them stiff; take, move or be moved quickly.

whippet (whip-pet) *n.* small dog of an English breed, probably part greyhound, part terrier, used in racing and catching rabbits.

whirl *v.* turn round or spin quickly; go off, travel rapidly; send, drive or carry in a circular or curving course. *v.* a whirling movement; a rapid succession of events tending to confuse. **in a whirl** confused

by some action or by so many things happening at once. **whirligig** *n.* something that whirls or goes round quickly.

whirlpool *n.* water that goes round and round, sucking floating objects down when they reach the middle. **whirlwind** *n.* a violent wind that whirls round and round.

whirr or **whir** *v.* go, fly, dart etc. quickly with a buzzing sound. *n.* the act or sound of whirring.

whisk *n.* a small brush for removing dust from clothes; a small implement made with loops of wire held together in a handle, for beating or whipping eggs, cream etc.; a quick, sweeping movement (of the tail etc.). *v.* move with a rapid sweeping stroke; move quickly through the air; whip (eggs, cream etc.) with a whisk or beating implement; take away, snatch quickly.

whiskers (whis-kers) *n.* hair growing on the sides of a man's face; the hairs on the face which are shaved off each morning; the long stiff hairs that grow about the mouth of a cat, mouse, rat and some other animals.

whisky (whis-ky) *n.* a strong alcoholic drink made from grain, especially barley, rye and oats; a drink of whisky.

whisper (whis-per) *v.* speak with soft, low sounds, using only the breath and with no voice; talk secretly, privately; make a soft, rustling sound (of trees, the breeze etc.). *n.* the voice of one who whispers; something said in a whisper; a soft, rustling sound as of leaves in the wind.

whist *n.* a card game played by four

players, two against two, with a pack of 52 cards.

whistle (whis-tle) *n.* a sound produced by forcing air through a small space, by the mouth, a pipe etc.; a device for producing such sounds as by a small pipe, the breath, steam etc. *v.* make the sound of a whistle; make a tune by whistling; pass quickly with a whistling sound; call or signal by whistling.

white *a.* the colour of pure snow reflecting nearly all the colours of sunlight; pale in complexion, having a light skin. *n.* the part of the egg between the yolk and the shell; the white part of the eyeball. **whiten** *v.* make white. **white-collar** *a.* belonging or having to do with people who work, not on manual jobs but in offices, the professions etc. **white feather** a symbol of cowardice. **white flag** a symbol of surrender. **whitewash** *n.* a mixture of materials in water used for whitening walls etc. *v.* put on whitewash.

whither (whith-er) an old word now replaced by where. *adv.* to what place, point, end etc.

whiz *v.* make a humming or hissing sound as of something moving through the air. *n.* the sound of a whizzing object; a swift movement producing such a sound.

who *pron.* what person?; a person referred to before (the man who etc.). **whom, to whom, from whom, with whom** to, from with a certain person already mentioned. **whose** *pron.* belonging to a person or thing already mentioned.

whole *a.* uninjured, undamaged, unbroken; complete, having everything that should be there (pack, set, day, troop etc.). *n.* the entire quantity, extent, number, period etc. **wholemeal** *n.* wheat prepared with the complete grain including bran. **wholesale** sold in large quantities, usually for sale again to the public. **wholesome** *a.* good for the health, pure, sound. **wholly** *adv.* entirely.

whoop *n.* a loud cry or shout, as made by children and warriors. *v.* utter a loud cry or shout as a call, or in excitement; cry as an owl does. **whooping cough** a coughing disease of children in which they gasp, giving whooping sounds.

why *adv.* for what? for what cause, reason, for what purpose?

wick *n.* a length of thread running through the middle of a candle; a strip of material in an oil lamp by which the oil is drawn up to be burnt.

wicked (wick-ed) *a.* evil, bad, sinful. **wickedness** *n.* wicked conduct; the state of being wicked; a wicked act or thing.

wicker (wick-er) *n.* twigs or canes woven together, usually to make fences, furniture and baskets. *a.* made of wicker, covered with wicker. **wickerwork** *n.* work consisting of weaving twigs etc. articles made of wicker.

wicket (wick-et) *n.* a small opening often closed by a sliding pane of glass at which tickets are sold or business is done; in cricket, either of the two sets of sticks, each consisting of three stumps with two bails on top, in front of which the batsman stands; the stretch of grass between the wickets; the person who is batting (when his wicket falls, he is out). **wicket-gate** *n.* a small door or gate, usually made in or as part of a larger one. **wicket-keeper** *n.* the player who stands behind the wicket to stop balls, catch batsmen out etc.

wide *a.* broad from side to side, not narrow; open to the full extent; bringing in many subjects, cases etc.; full, with much room (clothing); far from what was aimed at (in cricket, archery etc.). *adv.* fully (awake); far away from the mark. *n.* a bowled ball that passes outside the batsman's reach.

widespread *a.* spread over or occupying a large space or area. **width** *n.* the extent from side to side, the wideness; a piece of a certain width (of cloth, timber etc.).

widow (wid-ow) *n.* a woman whose husband has died and who has not married again. **widower** *n.* a man whose wife has died and who has not married again.

wield v. hold and exercise (power, authority, influence); manage, use, handle a weapon, tool or instrument.

wife n. a married woman whose husband is still living.

wig n. a covering of hair for the head, worn to hide baldness, for disguise, working in the theatre etc.

wigwam (wig-wam) n. an American Indian hut or tent made with poles, on the top of which bark, mats and skins are laid.

wild a. not tame (of animals); not cultivated (of plants); deserted, not cultivated, uninhabited, waste (of land); frantic, crazy, mad; violently excited, unruly, lawless; disorderly. n. an uncultivated desolate and uninhabited region. **wilderness** n. a wild, deserted expanse of land or water. **wildly** adv. in a confused way (talk etc.).

will v. a word which shows something which is to happen in the future (will come, will go etc.); leave property and money by writing on paper or having written down one's wishes as to what shall be done with it. n. a statement written by a person concerning the future of his property after his death; determination; the power to affect or alter one's own actions or those of others; a wish or desire. **wilful** a. obstinate, determined to have one's own way; intentional (murder, damage). **willing** a. ready to do what is asked or needed.

willow (wil-low) n. a tree or the wood of a tree with tough branches which bend easily, the wood used for making cricket bats and the twigs for making baskets.

wilt v. lose strength, become weak; droop and wither, as a fading flower does.

wily (wi-ly) a. cunning, sly, artful.

win v. succeed by striving and effort; gain a victory, be first in a race; achieve by chance. n. the act of winning a contest.

winner n. the person or animal that wins.

wince v. shrink, start as in pain or from a blow. n. a slight start.

winch n. a machine for pulling or lifting. v. hoist or haul by means of a winch.

wind n. air that is moving; a gale, storm, hurricane; breath or breathing; the power of breathing freely, especially during exertion; gas formed inside the body making one feel uncomfortable; empty talk, mere words. v. take away the breath by exertion or a blow; rest to recover breath. **wind-break** n. trees or other materials put up to shelter something from the wind. **windcheater** n. a close-fitting garment designed to keep out the wind. **windfall** n. something blown (fruit etc.) from a tree by the wind; an unexpected piece of good luck. **windscreen** n. the sheet of glass which forms the front window of a motor vehicle. **windy** a. accompanied by wind.

wind v. (rhymes with mind) twist and turn; take a bending course; twist or wrap round; coil into a ball or on a spool; adjust (a clock); turn a handle to move weights or wind up springs.

window (win-dow) n. an opening to let in light and air, usually filled by a moveable sheet of glass. **windowdresser** n. a person employed to dress or arrange the goods to be seen in the window of a shop or store. **windowpane** n. a pane of glass used in a window.

wine n. an intoxicating drink made from the fermented juice of the grape; a fermented drink resembling wine but made from fruits, leaves, herbs, flowers etc.

wing n. that organ of a bird, insect or the part of a machine which keeps it in the air when flying; part of a building situated to one side of the central part; that part of an army situated to one side of the centre; one of the two places to the right and left of the stage in a theatre; in football, hockey etc. the person at the far right or left of the forward line; the mudguard of a motor vehicle; a unit in the Royal Air Force consisting of two or more groups. *v.* fly. **winged** *a.* having wings.

vink *v.* close and open the eyes or one eye quickly; give a regular short flash of light; twinkle. *n.* the act of winking; a hint or signal given by winking; an instant. **wink at** pretend not to notice something so as not to have to chide or punish.

winkle (wink-le) *n.* a periwinkle, a small snail used as food.

winter (win-ter) *n.* the coldest season of the year beginning in December and ending in March in the northern hemisphere, and beginning in June and ending in September in the southern. *a.* having to do with winter (wear); sown before winter (wheat) for harvesting in spring or summer. *v.* pass the winter in a place. **wintry** *a.* having to do with winter.

wipe *v.* make clean by rubbing. **wiper** *n.* the device that wipes clean the windscreen of a motor vehicle. **wipe out** *v.* destroy completely.

wire *n.* a piece of flexible metal made into a cord or thread; a length of this used to conduct electricity; a telegram. *v.* fasten with wire; supply electricity to a building by installing wires; send a telegram; put on a wire (beads). **wireless** *n.* radio. **wireworm** *n.* a common garden worm which eats the roots of plants. **wiry** *a.* (of a person) lean with strong muscles.

wise *a.* having the power to know and to judge what is true or right. **wisdom** *n.* being wise; knowledge of what is right and wrong; wise teachings. **wisdom tooth** a back tooth which usually appears after a person is twenty years of age.

wish *v.* want, desire; hope for a person to have good things; greet (good morning etc.). *n.* a desire; a feeling that one wants to have or do certain things; that which is wished or desired. **wishbone** *n.* the forked bone in front of the breastbone of most birds.

wisp *n.* a handful or small bundle (straw etc.); a lock or a few strands (hair).

wistful (wist-ful) *a.* showing longing, desire; regretful, sad.

wit *n.* intelligence, quickness of mind; speech or writing showing this; a person who is noted for wit. **witty** *a.* possessing wit in speech or writing (of a person); having wit (a remark).

witch *n.* a person, usually a woman, who supposedly practises magic. **witchcraft** *n.* the use of magic, the practices of a witch. **witchdoctor** *n.* a person, especially among primitive peoples, supposed to possess magical powers of healing and harming people.

with *prep.* having (blue eyes, long arms etc.); covering (straw, a tablecloth etc.); filled (sand, earth etc.); by means of (a spade etc.); accompanied by (your father; me etc.); against (to fight, be at war); in a certain way (applause, cheers, anger etc.); in the same direction as (the current); from (part with); in the possession of (leave, trust with); in agreement; in some particular relation (sit; side; compare; deal etc.).

withdraw (with-draw) *v.* draw back, move back; take back (a statement, a charge). **withdrawal** *n.* the act of drawing back or taking back. **withdrawn** *a.* shy, modest; deserted, quiet (of a place).

wither (with-er) *v.* fade, decay, become lifeless; lose freshness, shrivel up.

withhold (with-hold) *v.* keep back, hold back, refrain from giving, granting or paying.

within (with-in) *adv.* in or into the interior; inside. *prep.* not going beyond (one's power etc.).

without (with-out) *adv.* not having, lacking (influence, tools etc.); free from (pain). *prep.* not with; lacking.

withstand (with-stand) *v.* stand or hold out against; resist, oppose successfully.

witness (wit-ness) *n.* a person who is present and sees an event and who, because of this, can give evidence in a court of law; one who signs a document to testify that another person's signature is genuine; evidence (bear witness to); *v.* be present and see; give evidence of; act as a witness (of a person's signature etc.).

wizard (wiz-ard) *n.* a person who supposedly practises magic. **wizardry** *n.* sorcery; the art and practice of magic.

wobble (wob-ble) *v.* go or incline to one side and then the other alternately as if not properly balanced; move unsteadily from side to side. *n.* an unsteady movement; a motion from side to side.

woe *n.* an old word meaning great sorrow or distress. **woeful** *a.* full of woe, stricken with grief, unhappy.

wolf *n.* a wild animal related to the dog. **wolf cub** the young of the wolf. **wolfhound** *n.* a cross between the wolf and the domestic dog, originally bred for hunting wolves.

woman (wo-man) *n.* an adult female person. **womanhood** *n.* the state of being a woman; the character or qualities of a woman.

wonder (won-der) *n.* a feeling of awe, admiration or surprise; something strange or surprising; something to be admired or astonished at. *v.* have a feeling of wonder; be curious about something; doubt whether a certain thing is, will be etc.; **wonderful** *a.* causing wonder or admiration; remarkable, extremely good or fine.

wood *n.* the hard part of a tree that is under the bark; used for making useful articles, for burning etc.; firewood; land with trees growing on it (of an area not so large as a forest). **wooden** *a.* consisting of wood, made of wood; dull, stupid. **woodland** *n.* land covered with woods. **woodwork** *n.* objects or parts of objects made of wood; the wooden fittings of a house etc.; the art or craft of working in wood.

wool *n.* the fine, soft, curly hair of sheep, made into yarn, cloth and garments; yarn

of wool for knitting, crocheting etc. material like wool made from other substances (cotton, rayon, glass). **woollen** *a.* made of wool; having to do with wool (manufacture). **woolly** *a.* consisting of wool; soft to the touch like wool; rambling and confused in thought (of persons). **woolsack** *n.* the seat of the Lord Chancellor in the House of Lords, made of a large, square, cloth-covered bag of wool.

word *n.* a sound or a group of sounds standing for a single idea; the sounds of speech represented in printing or writing; news, intelligence, tidings; a promise; something said with authority; a command, an order. **in a word** briefly. **word for word** (of repetition) using the very same words as the original.

work *n.* the use of one's powers of body or mind to do or make something; what one does to make a living; something to be done, not for a living but as a hobby, pastime or for other purposes; something to be worked on; a structure erected by builders, engineers etc.; *v.* do work either for a living or otherwise; get into a certain state (loose etc.) usually through constant use; achieve something by working (way, passage abroad etc.); operate; keep (a person, a horse etc.) at work; move or excite an animal or person (into a frenzy). **worker, workman** *n.* a person who works in an occupation, an employee. **work-out** *n.* a trial at running, boxing, a game or the like, usually before and in preparation for a contest, an exhibition etc. **workshop** *n.* a room or building in which work is done.

world *n.* the earth and all the people and things on it; a particular portion of the world (Old, New etc.); mankind, humanity; one of the three groupings of nature (animal, vegetable, mineral); people connected with special interests (of sport, of fashion, of art etc.); a great deal (of good). **worldwide** *a.* spread through the world (fame, renown etc.).

worm *n.* a small creature without limbs or spine that lives in the ground; a downtrodden, miserable, cowardly or villainous person. *v.* go slowly and patiently through difficulties; creep, crawl carefully through small spaces; get something by continual effort; get to know secrets by continual questioning (with 'out'). **wormcast** *n.* a coil of soil or sand left on the surface of the ground or a lawn by some kinds of worms.

worry (wor-ry) *v.* feel uneasy and anxious; suffer from disturbing thoughts; cause trouble or torment others; seize with the teeth and shake as one animal does with another. *n.* a cause of uneasiness; uneasy, anxious feelings.

worse *a.* the opposite of better; more bad, injurious, dangerous; not so good in quality etc. **worst** *a.* worse than any of the same kind; most unsatisfactory.

worship (wor-ship) *v.* respect and revere God, a god or a sacred person. *n.* reverence and homage paid to God or a god etc.; the title given to certain officers such as mayors and magistrates.

worth *a.* having a value equal to; having property equal to a certain value; good enough for. *n.* excellence of character, value, usefulness; the value of one's property. **worthless** *a.* of no usefulness or value. **worthwhile** *a.* worth the time and trouble. **worthy** *a.* deserving.

wound *n.* an injury to the body of a living being; injury or hurt to a person's pride, feelings etc. *v.* inflict a wound.

wrangle (wran-gle) *v.* (pronounced *rangle*) argue or quarrel noisily. *n.* a noisy dispute or quarrel.

wrap *v.* (pronounced *rap*) enclose, roll up in something; roll or fold in so as to cover or protect; be interested in something. *n.* something to be wrapped about the person, especially a shawl, scarf or mantle. **wrapper** *n.* that in which something is wrapped. **wrapping** *n.* material in which things are wrapped.

wrath *n.* fierce anger; revenge or punishment as a result of anger.

wreath *n.* (pronounced *reeth*) flowers woven into a circle, used as a garland to put on the head or for placing on a grave; a curling line of smoke or mist. **wreathe** *v.* decorate with a wreath; curl round; cover (in smiles etc.).

wreck *n.* (pronounced *reck*) ruin, destruction of a ship or anything; a ship in a disaster on rocks etc. or ruined through the action of the sea or rocks. *v.* cause the wreck of a ship; cause the ruin or destruction of (hopes, dreams, fortune). **wreckage** *n.* the remains or ruins of something that has been wrecked. **wrecker** *n.* some person or thing that wrecks.

wren *n.* (pronounced *ren*) a small brown bird with a short tail and small wings, common in England.

wrench *n.* (pronounced *rench*) a sharp twist or pull; a feeling of pain through separation from a loved one; a tool for gripping, holding and turning. *v.* twist suddenly and violently; injure by twisting suddenly (an ankle).

wrest *v.* (pronounced *rest*) take away quickly by force; twist or turn; pull, jerk or force by a violent twist; achieve (success) by great effort.

wrestle (wres-tle) *n.* (pronounced *restle*) take part in a contest in which two persons try to throw or force each other to the ground; deal with a difficult task. **wrestler** *n.* a person who wrestles others as a professional or an amateur.

wretch *n.* (pronounced *retch*) an unfortunate person; a mean, wicked person. **wretched** *a.* very unfortunate, miserable; poor, sorry, pitiful; wicked, mean.

wriggle (wrig-gle) *v.* (pronounced *riggle*) twist to and fro, squirm; move along by twisting the body as a snake does; make one's way out of trouble; make something wriggle (toes). *n.* a wriggling movement.

wring *v.* (pronounced *ring*) squeeze by twisting; force out moisture from cloth etc., with the hands in this way; clasp the hand of another person. **wringer** *n.* a device with two rollers for taking the water out of anything wet; a mangle.

wrinkle (wrin-kle) *n.* (pronounced *rinkle*) a ridge or furrow on a surface due to contraction, cold etc., often seen on the faces of old people. *v.* form or be formed into wrinkles (of faces, cloth etc.).

wrist *n.* (pronounced *rist*) the joint between the hand and the arm; that part of the sleeve of a garment which goes round the wrist. **wristwatch** *n.* a watch attached to a strap or band and worn round the wrist.

write *v.* (pronounced *rite*) make letters, words or other symbols which give a meaning; express or communicate in writing; produce in words or symbols a message, letter, book, novel, play etc.; a writer, journalist etc. for a living. **writ** *n.* an order issued under the name of a sovereign commanding that certain things should be done or not done. **writer** *n.* one who expresses something in writing; one who writes for a living. **writing** *n.* something written. **write-up** *n.* a written description or account in a newspaper or magazine.

wrong *a.* (pronounced *rong*), not right, not good, unjust; not truthful; not correct; not what is needed (road, way, method, house etc.); not suitable; not in good order. *n.* that which is wrong. *adv.* in a wrong manner, incorrectly, unjustly. *v.* do wrong, treat unfairly or unjustly.

wry *a.* (pronounced *ry*) twisted, the mouth pulled out of shape to show disappointment, displeasure etc.

X

Xerox (xe-rox) *n.* a trademark for a copying process; copies obtained by this process, now widely used.

X-ray *n.* a ray that can penetrate solid substances and make it possible to see into or through them; an examination by the use of X-rays. *v.* use X-rays.

xylophone (xy-lo-phone) *n.* (pro-nounced *zylofone*) a musical instrument consisting of wooden bars of different lengths each of which when struck by a small wooden hammer, produces a different note.

Y

yacht *n.* (rhymes with *dot*) a boat with sails, used for pleasure and racing; a boat driven by an engine or motor. *v.* travel sail or race in a yacht. **yachtsman** *n.* a man who owns or sails a yacht.

yap *v.* give short, sharp barks. *n.* a yelp, a snappish bark.

yard *n.* a space usually enclosed by a wall or fence; a measure equal to 36 inches, 3 feet or 91·4 centimetres. **yardstick** *n.* a stick a yard long, usually marked with feet, inches etc. and used as a measuring-rod. **the Yard** Scotland Yard, the branch of the police engaged in criminal investigation.

yarn *n.* thread which has been specially made for weaving or knitting; a story or tale of adventure; a tale told by a sailor or traveller, often about strange happenings and adventures.

yawn *v.* open the mouth wide, taking in and sending out breath as one does when sleepy; stretch wide open, as a deep space or crater does. *n.* the act of yawning.

year *n.* the time it takes the earth to move once round the sun; 365 days; this period divided into twelve months from January 1st to December 31st; any period of 365 days; the time taken for any planet to make one revolution round the sun. **yearling** *n.* an animal one year old or in the second year of its age. **yearly** *a.* every year, once a year. *adv.* happening once a year. **years** *n.* age, especially of a person; old age; a very long time. **leap year** a year of 366 days, coming once every four years.

yearn *v.* have a very strong desire for; want very much. **yearning** *n.* a strong desire, especially a sad one.

yeast *n.* a yellowish substance used in baking to make dough rise and liquids such as beer and wine ferment.

yell *v.* cry out with a loud, clear sound; scream with pain, fright etc. *n.* a cry uttered in yelling.

yellow (yel-low) *n.* a bright colour like that of butter, lemons and gold. *v.* make or become yellow.

yeoman (yeo-man) *n.* in old England, a farmer who farmed his own land. **yeomanry** *n.* a volunteer cavalry force in Britain, originally made up of yeomen, which later became part of the territorial army. **Yeomen of the Guard** members of the royal bodyguard of the English sovereign.

yes *adv.* a word expressing agreement. *n.* a reply showing agreement.

yesterday (yes-ter-day) *n.* the day before this day. *adv.* on the day before this day.

yet *adv.* at the present time; up to a particular time; still; at some time to come.

yield *v.* produce after having been cultivated; give up to a stronger power; surrender, give in. *n.* the amount produced by cultivation or trade; the action of yielding or producing.

yoga (yo-ga) *n.* a system of meditation and self-control first practised in India. **yogi** *n.* a person who practises yoga.

yoghourt, yoghurt, yogurt (yog-hourt) *n.* (pronounced *yogurt*) a prepared food (sometimes sweetened or flavoured with fruit flavours) made from milk that has been fermented.

yolk *n.* the inner part or yellow of an egg, as compared with the 'white' of the egg that surrounds it.

you *pron.* the person or persons to whom one is speaking. **your** *a.* belonging to you, having to do with you. **yours** *pron.* some-

thing belonging to you. **yourself** *pron.* you. **yourselves** *pron.* you (of more than one).

young *a.* being in the early stages of life, not old; having to do with being young (days, ambitions etc.); near the beginning. *n.* young people, young animals. **youngster** *n.* a child, young person, young animal. **the young** young people.

youth *n.* the state or time of being young; a young man; the appearance, energy etc. of young people or animals. **youthful** *a.* fitting for the young; having the appearance of being young.

yule, yuletide *n.* the Christmas season. **yule log** a large log of wood which in olden times formed the foundation of the fire at Christmas.

Z

zeal *n.* enthusiasm for a cause, an object; eager desire. **zealous** *a.* full of zeal or enthusiasm.

zebra (ze-bra) *n.* a wild animal resembling a horse, which lives in Africa and has black and white stripes on its body. **zebra crossing** a place on a road marked with black and white stripes where people may cross safely.

zenith (zen-ith) *n.* the part of the sky directly overhead; the highest point or state (of popularity, wealth, fortunes etc.).

zephyr (zeph-yr) *n.* a soft, mild breeze.

zero (ze-ro) *n.* the figure or symbol 0 which stands for nothing or nil marked on thermometers and other dials; nothing.

zest *n.* great interest, glad enthusiasm; anything added to give extra flavour or relish.

zigzag (zig-zag) *n.* a line or course in which there are many sudden sharp turns, first to one side and then to the other. *a.* proceeding in such a course. *adv.* with many sharp turns from side to side. *v.* move in a zigzag course.

zinc *n.* a bluish-white metal used in coating iron sheets to protect them against rust. **zinc ointment** an ointment composed of paraffin, white petroleum and zinc oxide.

zip *n.* a device in which metal teeth are made to lock together to unite or to separate two edges. **zip-fasteners** *n.* fasteners consisting of a zip which are put on bags and articles of clothing to take the place of buttons.

zither (zith-er) *n.* a musical instrument consisting of a box with strings stretched over it; when played it is placed on a flat surface and the strings are plucked with the fingertips.

zodiac (zo-di-ac) *n.* an imaginary belt of the heavens in which lie the paths of the sun, the moon and the principal planets. It was divided by ancient people into twelve equal parts known as the signs of the zodiac, each having its own name.

zone *n.* an area set aside for some special purpose (car parking) or under special restrictions (military); one of the five belts into which the earth's surface is divided. *v.* divide into zones or areas for special purposes.

zoo, zoological gardens *n.* a place where the public may go to see animals of all kinds. **zoology** *n.* the science that deals with animals or the animal kingdom.

zoom *n.* a low, deep, humming sound. *v.* go at a high speed making such a sound; rise rapidly (prices); use a special lens in photography so as to make an object appear to come nearer or go farther away from the viewer. **zoom lens** a lens on a camera that can magnify distant objects, making them appear nearer.

Useful Information

234

Foreign Words and Phrases

There are many foreign words and phrases that are commonly used in English. Some of them are particularly convenient as they cannot be translated accurately into our language. Here are some examples (Abbreviations – F: French; G: German; Gk: Greek; I: Italian; L: Latin).

ad hoc (L) For this special object.

ad infinitum (L) For ever; to infinity.

ad nauseam (L) To the point of disgust.

à la carte (F) From the full menu.

à la mode (F) In fashion.

alter ego (L) One's second self.

à propos (F) In reference to.

auf Wiedersehen (G) Goodbye.

au naturel (F) In a natural state; cooked plainly.

au revoir (F) Goodbye till we meet again.

anno Domini (L) In the year of our Lord.

à votre santé (F) Your good health!

bête noir (F) A pet hate.

bon mot (F) A witty saying.

bon voyage (F) Have a good journey.

carte blanche (F) Full powers.

chef d'oeuvre (F) A masterpiece.

compos mentis (L) In full possession of sanity.

corps de ballet (F) The dancers in a ballet.

corps diplomatique (F) Diplomats in a capital city.

de luxe (F) Of especially high quality.

Deo gratias (L) Thanks to God.

Dieu et mon droit (F) God and my right (motto of the British Crown).

en famille (F) In the family.

en passant (F) In passing; by the way.

en rapport (F) In sympathy.

entre nous (F) Between ourselves.

fait accompli (F) An accomplished fact.

faux pas (F) False step; mistake.

fin de siècle (F) End of the century (usually 19th); decadent.

gourmet (F) Lover of good food.

hoi polloi (Gk) The people; the masses.

hors d'oeuvre (F) The first course of a meal.

ich dien (G) I serve.

idée fixe (F) An obsession

in loco parentis (L) In the place of a parent.

in memoriam (L) In memory of.

in perpetuum (L) For ever.

in toto (L) Completely.

lèse-majesté (F) High treason.

magnum opus (L) A great work.

maître d'hôtel (F) Hotel-keeper; head waiter.

nil desperandum (L) Despair of nothing.

nom de plume (F) Assumed name of an author.

non sequitur (L) It does not follow.

nota bene (N.B.) (L) Note well.

nouveau riche (F) Newly rich.

per annum (L) By the year.

per capita (L) By the head.

per centum (per cent) (L) By the hundred.

pièce de résistance (F) Chief dish of meal; main thing.

prima ballerina (I) Principal female dancer in a ballet.

prima donna (I) Principal female singer in an opera.

rendez-vous (F) Meeting place.

résumé (F) Summary.

sang-froid (F) Coolness of behaviour.

status-quo (L) The existing state of affairs.

tempus fugit (L) Time flies.

versus (L) Against.

vice versa (L) The other way round.

vis-à-vis (F) Face to face; opposite.

wagon-lit (F) Railway sleeping car.

People and Language

The Development of the Alphabet

We do not know the point in man's development at which he first made sound which could be described as 'language'. The tracing of the history of written language, however, has been possible to a high degree of accuracy, and the diagram on the following page indicates how most of our present-day letters came to be formed.

Column I shows Egyptian hieroglyphics, or picture-writing, facing to the left. Column II is of later Egyptian writing, in which the picture has become unrecognisable, and the direction has changed to the right. Column III shows the progress made by the time of the Phoenicians and Column IV contains the fairly similar alphabet of early Greek civilisation. Columns V, VI and VII show further development by the Greeks; in Columns VIII, IX and X are the stages through which the Romans progressed, leaving as their legacy most of the present-day alphabet of the Western world.

The English Language

Our own language, English, is a mixture of words drawn from the vocabularies of the various invaders of Britain over a period of some two thousand years. That is why in English there are often several different words meaning roughly the same thing, some having Anglo-Saxon origins and others coming from Latin. Our language is also less 'regular' than French, Italian or Spanish, all of which have direct Latin origins.

Words are placed in categories according to how they are used. These categories are known as parts of speech. The English language has eight parts of speech. They are listed below:

Noun: the name of a person, place or thing. Nouns are of four Genders: Masculine, Feminine, Common and Neuter. These Genders can be illustrated by the following words: man, woman, cousin, hat. Nouns are either Singular or Plural, examples of both being: dog and dogs, penny and pence. Classes of nouns are Proper (the name of a particular person, place or thing, e.g. William, France) and Common (the name common to everything in one group, e.g. house, car).

Right: The illustration shows the development of the alphabet from Egyptian hieroglyphics to the present-day alphabet of the Western world.

	Egyptian			Greek				Latin		
1	🐦	2	△	A	A	ð	ɑ	A	A	aaa
2		5	9	8	B	B	B	B	B	BD
3		Z	7	1	Γ	Γ	ſY	⟨	C	⟨ᴄᴄ̆ɢ8
4			△	△	Δ	Δ̈	δ	D	D	ðdð
5		m			E	℮	Ɛ	℉	E	ee
6					ΥF		F	F	F	Ff
7			‡	‡	I	Z	ƙℇ	‡	Z	z
8		♡		B	H	H	ɦɳ	θ	H	ɦɦ
9			⊕	⊕	⊙	θ		⊕		
10	\\	Y			I	I		I	I	IJ
11					K	K	KK	K	K	K
12			L	✓	∧	⅄	⅄	L	L	⅃⅃
13		3			M	M	MM	M	M	mm
14	∿				N	N	ƳY	N	N	ɳɳ
15			‡	‡	Ξ		Ε,	⊞	+	XX
16			◯	◦	◯	◯	◦	◯		
17	G				Γ	π	πϖ	P	P	P
18		5		N	M		λ	N		
19			φ	φ	φ			8	Q	99
20			9		P	P	℮P	R	R	Rℾ
21						C	ɛσ	⟨	S	ſs
22			+	T	T	T	Τ	T	T	Ƨt

English nouns have three Cases which they take to show their relation to the rest of a sentence. These are Nominative (denoting the person or thing taking action), Objective (the person or thing about which action is taken) and Possessive (that which belongs to a person or thing).

Adjective: a word which describes or qualifies a noun. Adjectives may be divided into three categories: those which express Quality (*bad* company), those expressing Quantity (*ten* boys) and Demonstrative Adjectives (*that* window). There are three degrees of comparison in adjectives—Positive, Comparative and Superlative, examples of which are: good, better, best; young, younger, youngest.

The Articles (Definite: the; Indefinite: a, an) are also adjectives, as are the Numerals (Cardinal: one, two; Ordinal: first, second; Multiplicative: once, twice; Indefinite: many, few).

Pronoun: a word used in place of a noun. Pronouns, like nouns, have Gender, Number and Case. Pronouns may be Personal (I, she, you), Relative (that, who), Demonstrative (this, those), Indefinite (some, one), Interrogative (who? which?), Distributive (either, each) and Reflexive (yourself, themselves).

Verb: a word which states the action of a noun. Verbs are either Transitive or Intransitive. Transitive verbs describe an action which affects an object, e.g. 'I start the car'. Intransitive verbs do not affect an object, e.g. 'The car starts.' 'I start the car' is an example of a verb in Active Voice; in Passive Voice it would be 'The car was started by me.'

Verbs have three Finite Moods: Indicative (I speak); Imperative (Speak!); Subjunctive (I may speak). There is also the Infinitive Mood (to speak).

There are two Participles, used with such verbs as *to be* and *to have:* the Present Participle (speaking) and the Past Participle (spoken). There is also a verbal noun, the Gerund (the *speaking* of English).

The Tense of a verb shows the time of its action (Past, Present, Future). The degrees of completeness of the action are: Simple (I speak, I spoke, I shall speak); Continuous (I am speaking; I was speaking, I shall be speaking); Perfect (I have spoken, I had spoken, I shall have spoken); Perfect Continuous (I have been speaking, I had been speaking, I shall have been speaking).

Adverb: a word which modifies or qualifies a verb, an adjective or another adverb. Adverbs can be divided into the following categories: Time (often, now); Place (here, outside); Quality (well, beautifully); Quantity (enough, almost); Number (once); Cause (therefore, why); Mood (perhaps).

Preposition: a word which shows the relation between words in a sentence. Examples of prepositions are: to, on, by, of, from, for, through, about, after, except, towards.

Conjunction: a word which links words, phrases, clauses or sentences. Examples of conjunctions are: and, but, for, because, also, unless, though, therefore.

Interjection: a word standing alone in a sentence, expressing strong emotion. Examples are: Indeed! Goodness! Bother! Oh! Alas!

Countries of the World

The lists which follow cannot be completely accurate, as not all countries have been fully surveyed and not every area has a census of population, but they are reliable enough for most purposes, based on figures available at the time of going to press.

AFRICA

Country	Population	Capital	Area sq km	Area sq miles
Algeria	22 600 000	Algiers	2 214 400	855 000
Angola	8 960 000	Luanda	1 263 900	488 000
Benin	4 150 000	Porto Novo	121 730	47 000
Botswana	1 130 000	Gaborone	569 800	220 000
Burkina Faso	8 330 000	Ouagadougou	259 000	100 000
Burundi	4 920 000	Bujumbura	27 700	10 700
Cameroon	9 880 000	Yaounde	474 000	183 000
Cape Verde Islands	350 000	Praia	3 900	1 516
Central African Rep.	2 780 000	Bangui	606 000	234 000
Chad	5 240 000	N'djaména	1 263 900	488 000
Comoros	422 500	Moroni	1 862	
Congo	2 180 000	Brazzaville	336 600	129 960
Côte d'Ivoire	10 600 000	Abidjan	328 900	127 000
Djibouti	470 000	Djibouti	23 300	9 000
Egypt	49 280 000	Cairo	997 100	385 000
Equatorial Guinea	384 000	Malabo	28 500	11 000
Ethiopia	46 000 000	Addis Ababa	1 036 000	400 000
Gabon	1 220 000	Libreville	262 600	101 400
The Gambia	698 817	Banjul	10 360	4 000
Ghana	12 210 000	Accra	238 500	92 100
Guinea	6 340 000	Conakry	251 200	97 000
Guinea Bissau	935 000	Bissau	36 260	14 000
Kenya	20 030 000	Nairobi	582 700	225 000
Lesotho	1 630 000	Maseru	30 300	11 700
Liberia	2 500 000	Monrovia	111 400	43 000
Libya	3 960 000	Tripoli	2 097 900	810 000
Madagascar	10 570 000	Antananarivo	590 500	228 000
Malawi	7 100 000	Lilongwe	117 600	45 400
Mali	8 730 000	Bamako	1 204 300	465 000
Mauritania	2 010 000	Nouakchott	1 085 200	419 000
Mauritius	1 041 000	Port Louis	2 090	805
Morocco	23 000 000	Rabat	466 200	180 000
Mozambique	14 540 000	Maputo	771 800	298 000
Niger	6 600 000	Niamey	1 188 800	459 000
Nigeria	105 000 000	Lagos	924 600	357 000
Réunion	564 600	St Denis	2 590	1 000
Rwanda	6 320 000	Kigali	26 340	10 169
St Helena	5 895	Jamestown	122	47
Ascension Is.	1 708	Georgtown	88	34
Tristan da Cunha	325	Edinburgh	98	38
S. Tomé and Príncipe	113 000	Saõ Tomé	963	372
Senegal	6 700 000	Dakar	202 000	78 000
Seychelles	67 000	Victoria	324	125
Sierra Leone	3 600 000	Freetown	72 520	28 000
Somalia	6 110 000	Mogadishu	637 100	246 000
South Africa	23 390 000	Pretoria	1 222 500	472 000

Country	Population	Capital	Area sq km	Area sq miles
S.W. Africa (Namibia)	1 184 000	Windhoek	823 600	318 000
Sudan	25 550 000	Khartoum	2 504 500	967 000
Swaziland	676 049	Mbabane	17 350	6 700
Tanzania	23 200 000	Dodoma	940 200	363 000
Togo	3 160 000	Lomé	54 400	21 000
Tunisia	7 320 000	Tunis	164 200	63 380
Uganda	16 790 000	Kampala	235 700	91 000
Zaire	3 178 000	Kinshasa	2 343 000	905 000
Zambia	7 210 000	Lusaka	753 700	291 000
Zimbabwe	8 640 000	Harare	390 600	150 820

ASIA

Country	Population	Capital	Area sq km	Area sq miles
Afghanistan	9 000 000	Kabul	647 500	250 000
Bahrain	416 275	Manama	600	231
Bangladesh	104 100 000	Dacca	142 780	55 126
Bhutan	1 300 000	Thimphu	46 620	18 000
Brunei	221 900	Bandar Seri Begawan	5 770	2 226
Burma (Myanmar)	37 850 000	Rangoon (Yangon)	678 030	261 789
Cambodia	6 230 000	Phnom Penh	181 300	70 000
China				
Mainland	1 072 200 000	Peking	9 583 000	3 700 000
Taiwan (Formosa)	19 500 000	Taipei	35 980	13 890
CIS (in Asia)				
Armenia	3 400 000	Erevan	30 000	11 500
Azerbaijan	6 800 000	Baku	87 000	33 500
Kazakhstan	16 200 000	Alma Ata	2 717 000	1 048 000
Kirghizia	4 100 000	Frunze	199 000	74 000
Tadzhikistan	4 800 000	Dushanbe	143 000	54 000
Turkmenistan	3 400 000	Ashkahabad	488 000	188 000
Uzbekistan	19 000 000	Tashkent	447 000	172 000
Georgia	5 300 000	Tbilisi	70 000	27 000
Hong Kong	5 590 000		1 050	404
India	748 000 000	Delhi	3 268 600	1 262 000
Indonesia	172 000 000	Jakarta	1 903 600	735 000
Iran	49 860 000	Tehran	1 626 700	628 060
Iraq	17 090 000	Baghdad	445 480	172 000
Israel	4 330 000	Jerusalem	20 720	8 000
Japan	121 670 000	Tokyo	369 720	142 748
Jordan	2 850 000	Amman	97 640	37 700
Korea				
North	20 550 000	Pyongyang	124 320	48 000
South	41 800 000	Seoul	99 720	38 500
Kuwait	1 770 000	Kuwait	19 430	7 500
Laos	3 670 000	Vientiane	233 100	90 000
Lebanon	3 500 000	Beirut	11 140	4 300
Malaysia	16 500 000	Kuala Lumpur	331 520	128 000
Maldive Islands	189 000	Malé	300	115
Mongolia	1 970 000	Ulan Bator	1 567 000	605 022
Nepal	16 630 000	Katmandu	139 860	54 000
Oman	1 200 000	Muscat	310 800	120 000
Pakistan	102 200 000	Islamabad	803 940	310 403
Philippines	57 360 000	Manila	297 850	115 000

ASIA *cont.*

Country	Population	Capital	Area sq km	Area sq miles
Qatar	371863	Doha	10360	4000
Saudi Arabia	11520000	Riyadh	2401000	927000
Singapore	2590000	Singapore	590	226
Sri Lanka	15800000	Colombo	65610	25332
Syria	10960000	Damascus	183890	71000
Thailand	52500000		512820	198000
Turkey (in Asia)	50670000	Ankara	755688	292000
United Arab Emirates	12000000	Abu Dhabi	75150	29010
Vietnam	61950000	Hanoi	334110	129000
Yemen Arab Republic	12000000	San'a	477530	184345

EUROPE AND THE MEDITERRANEAN

Country	Population	Capital	Area sq km	Area sq miles
Albania	3080000	Tirana	27000	10700
Andorra	42712	Andorre-la-Vieille	470	180
Austria	7570000	Vienna	83850	32376
Belgium	9860000	Brussels	30560	11800
Bulgaria	8950000	Sofia	111370	43000
CIS (in Europe)				
Belorussia	10100000	Minsk	208000	80000
Moldavia	4200000	Kishinev	34000	13000
Russia	145300000	Moscow	17075000	6591000
Ukraine	51200000	Kiev	604000	233000
Cyprus	673100	Nicosia	9070	3500
Czechoslovakia **	51500000	Prague	127950	49400
Denmark	5120000	Copenhagen	44030	17000
Estonia	1600000	Tallinn	45000	17000
Finland	4930000	Helsinki	336700	130000
France	55620000	Paris	551670	213000
Germany	80000000	Berlin (admin. Bonn)	357042	137855
Gibraltar	29216	Gibraltar	5	2
Greece	9970000	Athens	132610	51200
Hungary	10620000	Budapest	93240	36000
Iceland	244009	Reykjavik	104900	40500
Irish Republic	3540000	Dublin	68890	26600
Italy	57300000	Rome	339290	131000
Latvia	2600000	Riga	64000	25000
Liechtenstein	27400	Vaduz	168	65
Lithuania	3600000	Vilnius	65000	25000
Luxembourg	369500	Luxembourg	2590	1000
Malta	343334	Valetta	313	121
Monaco	27063	Monaco-ville	2	$\frac{2}{3}$
Netherlands	14620000	Amsterdam	34960	13500
Norway	4200000	Oslo	323750	125000
Poland	37600000	Warsaw	313390	121000
Portugal	10290000	Lisbon	89360	34500
Romania	22700000	Bucharest	237240	91600

**Before separation into Czech and Slovak Republics

Country	Population	Capital	Area sq km	Area sq miles
San Marino	22638	San Marino	60	23
Spain	38900000	Madrid	510230	197000
Sweden	8400000	Stockholm	448070	173000
Switzerland	6500000	Berne	41440	16000
Turkey (in Europe)	*see Asia*	Ankara	23764	9200
United Kingdom	55780000	London	240940	93026
Vatican City	1000	Vatican City	44 hectares	109 acres
Yugoslavia*	23270000	Belgrade	256410	99000

* During Federation

NORTH AND CENTRAL AMERICA; THE WEST INDIES

Country	Population	Capital	Area sq km	Area sq miles
Anguilla	7000	The Valley	155	60
Antigua and Barbuda	81500	St John's	440	170
Bahamas	235000	Nassau	13900	5380
Barbados	253055	Bridgetown	430	166
Belize	171000	Belmopan	23100	8900
Bermuda	57145	Hamilton	54	21
Canada	25400000	Ottawa	9976139	3851787
Cayman Islands	22900	George Town	260	100
Costa Rica	2660000	San José	50900	19653
Cuba	10190000	Havana	114000	44000
Dominica	94191	Roseau	751	290
Dominican Rep.	6600000	Santo Domingo	50000	19300
Grenada	88000	St. George's	344	133
Guadeloupe	335300	Basse-Terre	1780	688
Guatemala	8990000	Guatemala City	108800	42000
Haiti	5300000	Port-au-Prince	27700	10700
Honduras	4300000	Tegucigalpa	111400	43000
Jamaica	2300000	Kingston	11400	4400
Martinique	328500	Fort-de-France	1040	400
Mexico	76000000	Mexico City	1972400	761530
Montserrat	11802	Plymouth	101	39
Netherlands Antilles	183000	Willemstad	1020	394
Nicaragua	3500000	Managua	147600	57000
Panama	2280000	Panama City	77082	29761
Puerto Rico	3196520	San Juan	8810	3400
St Christopher-Nevis	47000	Basseterre	262	101
St Pierre and Miquelon	6300	St Pierre	241	93
St Lucia	143600	Castries	616	238
St Vincent	138000	Kingstown	388	150
El Salvador	5480000	San Salvador	21240	8200
Trinidad and Tobago	1220000	Port-of-Spain	5130	1980
Turks and Caicos Is.	7436	Grand Turk	499	193
United States	238700000	Washington, D.C.	9160400	3536855
Virgin Islands:				
British	12034	Road Town	153	59
US	110800	Charlotte Amalie	344	133

OCEANIA

Country	Population	Capital	Area sq km	Area sq miles
American Samoa	32297	Fagatogo	197	76
Australia	15970000	Canberra	7687000	2968000
New South Wales	5378500	Sydney	800300	309000
Northern Territory	136800	Darwin	1347500	520280
Queensland	2488000	Brisbane	1727500	667000
South Australia	1347000	Adelaide	984200	380000
Tasmania	434700	Hobart	67340	26000
Victoria	4053400	Melbourne	227900	88000
Western Australia	1373700	Perth	2527800	976000
Fiji	714000	Suva	18390	7100
French Polynesia	184600	Papeete	6480	2500
Guam	115756	Agaña	541	269
Kiribati	66250	Tarawa	683	264
Micronesia	123298	Kolonia	893	341
New Caledonia	153500	Nouméa	18650	7200
New Zealand	3300000	Wellington	269400	104000
Cook Islands	17745	Avarua	293	113
Niue	2442	Alofi	258	100
Northern Marianas	19635	Saipan	477	184
Palau	15000	Koror	497	192
Papua New Guinea	3480000	Port Moresby	461700	178260
Solomon Islands	270000	Honiara	29780	11500
Tonga	94535	Nuku'alofa	746	288
Tuvalu	8229	Funajuti	26	10
Vanuatu	141400	Vila	15670	6050
Western Samoa	163000	Apia	2840	1097

SOUTH AMERICA

Country	Population	Capital	Area sq km	Area sq miles
Argentina	31060000	Buenos Aires	2797100	1079965
Bolivia	6250000	Sucre	1074800	415000
Brazil	143100000	Brasilia	8518500	3289000
Chile	12070000	Santiago	751100	290000
Colombia	29500000	Bogotá	1139600	440000
Ecuador	9640000	Quito	585300	226000
Falkland Islands	1916	Stanley	12170	4700
Guiana, French	89000	Cayenne	90650	35000
Guyana	812000	Georgetown	215000	83000
Paraguay	3790000	Asunción	406600	157000
Peru	20200000	Lima	1375300	531000
Pitcairn Island	57	Adamstown	5	2
Suriname	370000	Paramaribo	139900	54000
Uruguay	2950000	Montevideo	186500	72000
Venezuela	17320000	Caracas	916900	354000

FORMER NAMES OF COUNTRIES

Bangladesh	East Pakistan
Belize	British Honduras
Botswana	Bechuanaland
Burkina Faso	Upper Volta
Burundi	Part of (1) German East Africa, (2) Ruanda-Urundi
Central African Republic	Ubangi-Shari
Commonwealth of Independent States	Formed from the Union of Soviet Socialist Republics
Congo (People's Republic)	Middle Congo (French)
Côte d'Ivoire	Ivory Coast
Democratic Kampuchea	Cambodia
Djibouti	Afars & Issas, Tty. of; French Somaliland
Equatorial Guinea	Spanish Guinea
Ethiopia	Abyssinia
Ghana	Gold Coast
Guinea	part of French West Africa
Guinea-Bissau	Portuguese Guinea
Guyana	British Guiana
Iran	Persia
Lesotho	Basutoland
Malawi	Nyasaland
Malaysia	Malaya, Sabah (North Borneo), and Sarawak
Mali	French Sudan
Netherlands Antilles	Dutch East Indies
Pakistan	West Pakistan
Rwanda	Part of (1) German East Africa, (2) Ruanda-Urundi
Somalia	Somaliland (Brit. & Ital.)
Sri Lanka	Ceylon
Suriname	Dutch Guinea
Tanzania	Tanganyika and Zanzibar
Thailand	Siam
Togo	Togoland
United Arab Emirates	Trucial States
Yemen Arab Republic	People's Dem. Rep. of Yemen and Yemen Arab Republic
Zäire	Belgian Congo
Zambia	Northern Rhodesia
Zimbabwe	Rhodesia

246

THE WORLD'S LARGEST COUNTRIES

Country	Area sq km	Area sq miles	Population in millions
1 Russia	17 075 000	6 591 000	145
2 Canada	9 976 139	3 851 787	25
3 China	9 583 000	3 700 000	1 072
4 USA	9 160 400	3 536 855	239
5 Brazil	8 518 500	3 289 000	143
6 Australia	7 687 000	2 968 000	16
7 India	3 268 000	1 262 000	784
8 Argentina	2 797 000	1 079 965	31
9 Sudan	2 504 500	967 000	25
10 Saudi Arabia	2 401 000	927 000	11
11 Zaire	2 343 900	905 000	32
12 Algeria	2 214 000	855 000	22
13 Greenland	2 175 000	839 782	0.049

THE WORLD'S SMALLEST COUNTRIES

Country	Area sq km	Area sq miles	Population
1 Vatican City	0.44	$\frac{1}{6}$	1 000
2 Monaco	2	$\frac{2}{3}$	27 063
3 Pitcairn Island	5	2	57
4 Tuvalu	26	10	8 229
5 San Marino	60	23	22 638
6 Liechtenstein	168	65	27 400
7 Maldives	300	115	189 000
8 Seychelles	324	125	67 000
9 Malta	313	121	343 334
10 Grenada	344	133	88 000

THE WORLD'S LEAST POPULATED COUNTRIES

Country	Population
1 Pitcairn Island	57
2 Vatican City	1 000

	Country	Population
3	Tuvalu	8 229
4	San Marino	22 638
5	Monaco	27 063
6	Liechtenstein	27 400
7	Andorra	42 472
8	Kiribati	66 250
9	Seychelles	67 000
10	Grenada	88 000

THE WORLD'S MOST POPULATED CITIES

	City	Population
1	Mexico City, Mexico	12 932 116
2	Buenos Aires, Argentina	9 927 404
3	Calcutta, India	9 166 000
4	Moscow, Russia	8 967 000
5	Paris, France	8 706 963
6	Tokyo, Japan	8 354 000
7	Bombay, India	8 227 000
8	São Paolo, Brazil	7 033 529
9	Shanghai, China	6 980 000
10	London, England	6 775 200

GREAT OCEANS OF THE WORLD

	Ocean	Area millions of sq km	Area millions of sq miles
1	Pacific	165	64
2	Atlantic	81.5	31.5
3	Indian	73.5	28.35
4	Arctic	14.25	5.5

OCEAN DEEPS

	Position	Name	Depth metres	Depth ft
1	Mariana Trench	Challenger Deep	11 520	37 800
2	Tonga Trench	—	10 630	34 885

Position	Name	Depth metres	Depth ft
3 Philippine Trench	Galathea Deep	10 540	34 580
4 Kuril Trench	Vityaz Deep	10 375	34 045
5 Japanese Trench	Ramapo Deep	10 372	34 035
6 Kermadec Trench	—	9 995	32 788
7 Guam Trench	—	9 632	31 614
8 Puerto Rico Trench	Milwaukee Deep	9 200	30 246
9 New Britain Trench	Planet Deep	9 140	29 987

GREAT SEAS

Name and location	Area sq km	Area sq miles
1 Mediterranean Sea (Southern Europe, Africa, Asia Minor)	2 850 000	1 100 000
2 South China Sea (China, East Indies)	2 486 000	960 000
3 Bering Sea (Alaska, Siberia)	2 274 000	878 000
4 Caribbean Sea (Central America, West Indies)	1 942 000	750 000
5 Gulf of Mexico (USA, Mexico)	1 855 000	716 000
6 Sea of Okhotsk (Siberia)	1 525 000	589 000
7 Hudson Bay (Canada)	1 230 000	475 000
8 Sea of Japan (Japan, Russia, Korea)	1 007 500	389 000
9 North Sea (North-western Europe)	572 400	221 000
10 Red Sea (Africa, Saudi Arabia)	461 000	178 000
11 Caspian Sea (Russia, Iran)	440 300	170 000
12 Black Sea (Russia, Turkey, Eastern Europe)	430 000	166 000
13 Baltic Sea (Scandinavia, Russia)	422 000	163 000
14 Aral Sea (CIS)	67 340	26 000

Local Time Throughout the World

As you travel eastwards from Greenwich, the longitude time is one hour later for every 15 ; to the west it is an hour earlier. But for convenience local clocks don't always show the correct longitude time, otherwise travellers inside even quite a small country would be constantly confused. In Britain, all clocks show Greenwich Mean Time except when Summer Time is in operation. Only in large countries such as Canada, the United States, etc., are time zones necessary.

Summer Time in the United Kingdom is one hour in advance of G.M.T. Many other countries of the world have annual variations from standard time, usually known as Summer Time or Daylight Saving Time. It should be remembered when using the following table, therefore, that there are seasonal variations, and indeed that in the summer local time in Great Britain is 1 p.m. at noon G.M.T.

Here are the local times in various big cities when it is noon (G.M.T.) in London:

City	Time
Adelaide (Australia)	9.30 p.m.
Algiers (Algeria)	1 p.m.
Amsterdam (Netherlands)	1 p.m.
Ankara (Turkey)	2 p.m.
Athens (Greece)	2 p.m.
Berlin (Germany)	1 p.m.
Bombay (India)	5.30 p.m.
Boston (U.S.A.)	7 a.m.
Brussels (Belgium)	1 p.m.
Bucharest (Romania)	2 p.m.
Budapest (Hungary)	1 p.m.
Buenos Aires (Argentina)	9 a.m.
Cairo (Egypt)	2 p.m.
Calcutta (India)	5.30 p.m.
Canton (China)	8 p.m.
Cape Town (South Africa)	2 p.m.
Caracas (Venezuela)	8 a.m.
Chicago (U.S.A.)	6 a.m.
Colombo (Sri Lanka)	5.30 p.m.
Copenhagen (Denmark)	1 p.m.
Djakarta (Indonesia)	8 p.m.
Edinburgh (Scotland)	noon
Gibraltar	1 p.m.

City	Time
Guatemala City (Guatemala)	6 a.m.
Guayaquil (Ecuador)	7 a.m.
Halifax (Canada)	8 a.m.
Havana (Cuba)	7 a.m.
Helsinki (Finland)	2 p.m.
Hobart (Tasmania)	10 p.m.
Hong Kong	8 p.m.
Johannesburg (South Africa)	2 p.m.
Karachi (Pakistan)	5 p.m.
Kingston (Jamaica)	7 a.m.
La Paz (Bolivia)	8 a.m.
Lima (Peru)	7 a.m.
Lisbon (Portugal)	1 p.m.
Madrid (Spain)	1 p.m.
Manila (Philippine Islands)	8 p.m.
Mecca (Saudi Arabia)	3 p.m.
Melbourne (Australia)	10 p.m.
Mexico City (Mexico)	6 a.m.
Montevideo (Uruguay)	9 a.m.
Montreal (Canada)	7 a.m.
Moscow (Russia)	3 p.m.
Nairobi (Kenya)	3 p.m.
New Orleans (U.S.A.)	6 a.m.
New York (U.S.A.)	7 a.m.
Oslo (Norway)	1 p.m.
Panama City (Panama)	7 a.m.
Paris (France)	1 p.m.
Peking (China)	8 p.m.
Perth (Australia)	8 p.m.
Prague (Czech Republic)	1 p.m.
Rangoon (Burma)	6.30 p.m.
Reykjavik (Iceland)	noon
Rio de Janeiro (Brazil)	9 a.m.
Rome (Italy)	1 p.m.
San Francisco (U.S.A.)	4 a.m.
Santiago (Chile)	8 a.m.
Shanghai (China)	8 p.m.
Singapore	7.30 p.m.
Sofia (Bulgaria)	2 p.m.

City	Time
Stockholm (Sweden)	1 p.m.
Sydney (Australia)	10 p.m.
Teheran (Iran)	3.30 p.m.
Tel Aviv (Israel)	2 p.m.
Tokyo (Japan)	9 p.m.
Toronto (Canada)	7 a.m.
Vancouver (Canada)	4 a.m.
Vienna (Austria)	1 p.m.
Warsaw (Poland)	1 p.m.
Wellington (New Zealand)	midnight
Winnipeg (Canada)	6 a.m.
Zürich (Switzerland)	1 p.m.

Useful Tables

Weights. Metric System

10 milligrammes	=	1 centigramme
10 centigrammes	=	1 decigramme
10 decigrammes	=	1 gramme
10 grammes	=	1 decagramme
10 decagrammes	=	1 hectogramme
10 hectogrammes	=	1 kilogramme
10 kilogrammes	=	1 myriagramme
10 myriagrammes	=	1 quintal
10 quintals	=	1 metric tonne

Weight Conversions

Imperial		Metric
1 grain	=	0·0648 grammes
1 dram	=	1·772 grammes
1 ounce	=	28·3495 grammes
1 pound	=	0·4536 kilogrammes
1 stone	=	6.35 kilogrammes
1 quarter	=	12.7 kilogrammes
1 hundredweight	=	50·8 kilogrammes
1 ton	=	1,016 kilogrammes
	=	or 1·016 metric tonnes

Metric		Imperial	
1 milligramme	=	0·015	grains
1 centigramme	=	0·154	grains
1 decigramme	=	1·543	grains
1 gramme	=	15·432	grains
1 decagramme	=	5·644	drams
1 hectogramme	=	3·527	ounces
1 kilogramme	=	2·205	pounds
1 myriagramme	=	22·046	pounds
1 quintal	=	1·968	hundredweight
1 metric tonne	=	0·9842	tons

Linear Measure. Metric System

10 millimetres	=	1 centimetre
10 centimetres	=	1 decimetre
10 decimetres	=	1 metre
10 metres	=	1 decametre
10 decametres	=	1 hectometre
10 hectometres	=	1 kilometre
10 kilometres	=	1 myriametre

Square Measure. Metric System

100 square millimetres	=	1 square centimetre
100 square centimetres	=	1 square decimetre
100 square decimetres	=	1 square metre
100 square metres	=	1 are
100 ares	=	1 hectare
100 hectares	=	1 square kilometre

Linear Measure Conversions

Imperial		Metric	
1 inch	=	2·54	centimetres
1 foot	=	30·48	centimetres
1 yard	=	0·9144	metres
1 rod	=	5·029	metres
1 chain	=	20·117	metres
1 furlong	=	201·168	metres
1 mile	=	1·6093	kilometres

Metric		Imperial
1 millimetre	=	0·03937 inches
1 centimetre	=	0·39370 inches
1 decimetre	=	3·93701 inches
1 metre	=	39·3701 inches
		(1·09361 yards)
1 decametre	=	10·9361 yards
1 hectometre	=	109·361 yards
1 kilometre	=	0·62137 miles

Capacity Measure Conversions

Imperial		Metric	
1 gill	=	1·42	decilitres
1 pint	=	0·568	litres
1 quart	=	1·136	litres
1 gallon	=	4·546	litres
1 bushel	=	36·37	litres
1 quarter	=	2·91	hectolitres

Metric		Imperial	
1 centilitre	=	0·07	gills
1 decilitre	=	0·176	pints
1 litre	=	1·7598	pints
1 decalitre	=	2·2	gallons
1 hectolitre	=	2·75	bushels
		(21·99	gallons)

Nautical Measures

6 feet	=	1 fathom
100 fathoms	=	1 cable
10 cables (6,080 feet)	=	1 nautical mile
		(1,852 metres)
1 knot	=	1 nautical mile *per hour*

Other Measures

1 tablespoon	=	$\frac{1}{2}$ fluid ounce
1 dessertspoon	=	$\frac{1}{4}$ fluid ounce
1 teaspoon	=	$\frac{1}{8}$ fluid ounce

Temperature Conversions

Celsius		Fahrenheit
—40	=	—40
—30	=	—22
—25	=	—13
—20	=	—4
—17·8	=	0
—15	=	5
—10	=	14
—5	=	23
0	=	32
5	=	41
10	=	50
15	=	59
20	=	68
25	=	77
30	=	86
35	=	95
40	=	104
45	=	113
50	=	122
55	=	131
60	=	140
70	=	158
80	=	176
90	=	194
100	=	212

To change Celsius to Fahrenheit, multiply by 9, divide by 5 and add 32.

To change Fahrenheit to Celsius, subtract 32, multiply by 5 and divide by 9.

Normal blood temperature in human beings is 36.9 °C (98.4 °F).